Moreton Morrell Site

The Sports Event Management and Marketing Playbook

The Wiley Event Management Series

SERIES EDITOR: DR. JOE GOLDBLATT, CSEP

The Sports Event Management and Marketing Playbook

Frank Supovitz

WILEY

JOHN WILEY & SONS, INC.

Contents

Foreword

When I am about to leave someone's presence, in person or on the phone, I say "Good-bye." I know this phrase no longer has any literal meaning for me, that I'm not really expressing to others my good wishes when I say them, let alone some contemporary version of "and God be with you." I am simply acknowledging that I am leaving someone's company.

A few years ago, this perfectly good phrase seemed no longer good enough to some, then to most. Wanting to recapture some of the phrase's original meaning, people began saying, "Have a *good* day." Then, hearing their own words, and having them sound suddenly a little stingy—why only a *good* day?—they escalated again: "Have a *great* day." I couldn't handle the "good," let alone the "great." After all, this was a phrase we used a hundred times a day. I didn't know most of the people I said it to, certainly not well enough really to hope that hard for them. I also didn't believe that those who used the phrase meant more with their words than I meant with mine. Further, I resented them for making me feel that I had to say more than I wanted to say in order to be as generous as they were.

It was at about this time that I got to know Frank Supovitz. He was in charge of special events for the National Hockey League, I was president of the Toronto Maple Leafs, and Toronto had been awarded the 2000 NHL All-Star Game. I would be working with Frank. I called him. He wasn't available, and I got his message machine. After the usual words of direction—*After the tone, please*—he told me to "have a spectacular day."

It was not a good start.

But it got better. I came to know the Frank you will get to know in these pages. Someone who is conscientious, thorough, meticulous, who has done hundreds of events, who finds the challenge of events fascinating, and who knows how, step-by-step, to pull them off. More than that, I came to enjoy his approach. An NHL All-Star Game is a complicated event. More than just one game on a single day, it is many activities spread over several days. More than happening in just one arena, it takes place in many different buildings in many different parts of a city. And although there are formula and sameness from year to year and city to city, there is also difference. And it is *that* difference that makes the difference. Frank seeks out that difference in the buildings and restaurants and spaces he chooses, in the activities he organizes. That's where he finds his fun and satisfaction. This, he knows, is where the specialness of the event lies.

He came to Toronto months before the event, and for days he just camped out. He was somewhat familiar with the city from other visits, but he didn't really know it. How does it tick? How does it see itself? What are its points of pride? What place does it hold—in hockey, in Canada, in the world? What are its ambitions? What does it want to be? And with millions of people watching all over North America, what message does it want to deliver? This is what Frank needed to find out. This is what would make one building, one restaurant, one space and activity right and all the others defensibly right, but wrong. In his quest, Frank gets to live other lives—one of his great pleasures, I think. He gets to go to new places, meet new people. He gets to experience through other people's eyes, to listen and to learn. He does this because he knows that the event is not his. It belongs to someone else.

In the pages ahead, you will get all the "how to's" and checklists a book on events demands. But in place of jargon you will get clear prose, and in place of tedium you will get enthusiasm, because that's Frank. He can't help himself. He is a storyteller, and he uses events to tell his stories. He has a practitioner's need to pin down the details, but he has a competitor's need to succeed. He knows his stuff and, what is crucial, he *loves* his stuff.

In my life, I will never (I hope) say, "Have a spectacular day," but because the expression comes from Frank, I understand.

Ken Dryden

Series Editor Foreword

The author of this book uses the phrase "Have a spectacular day!" to send greetings to those who telephone his office. He may or may not know that the term *spectacular* is derived from the Latin term *specere*, which means "to look at." While wishing callers to have a spectacular day he is simultaneously reminding us to examine or look at each day in order to develop greater appreciation and perhaps gain more understanding about ourselves.

This is exactly what this critically important book achieves. Frank Supovitz has distilled his two decades of professional experience into an easy-to-read, useful, and, more important, highly relevant tool to help you manage and market consistently winning sports events. Supovitz has produced hundreds of events all over the globe, and his approach to this book demonstrates his cultural sensitivity, as well as his marketer's savvy, when promoting events to global audiences.

The valuable and useful tables, templates, and models he has supplied will provide the patterns you need to run successful plays every time you enter the field. His highly enthusiastic writing style will inspire and motivate you, just as Vince Lombardi's wise and powerful words led the Green Bay Packers to become world champions. This rare combination of education, motivation, and inspiration makes this book an essential resource for every event professional.

You can greatly benefit from his sage advice, which can come only after someone has contributed to Super Bowl half-time spectaculars, All-Star games, and other major events. Whether you are producing a local soft ball tournament or preparing to organize a major fun run in your city, this book offers you the tips, techniques, and step-by-step plans to ensure that you will succeed. Furthermore, this book also gives you the firsthand experience of dozens of leaders in the sport event industry to help you grow and prosper now and throughout your career.

When I think of the author of this book, I hear the word "champion" ringing loudly. The dictionary defines the word *champion* as one who is in first place or one who wins. The term originates from the Latin word *campus*, which means "field." On the field or off, Frank Supovitz holds first place in terms of his educational contributions in the world of sports event management and marketing. And, yes, this "spectacular" book not only requires that you look but further ensures that you will actually learn the secret plays that will help you become a champion sports event manager.

Dr. Joe Goldblatt, CSEP
Series Editor
Wiley Events Series

Preface

I have the best job in the world. Brian Burke, a veteran NHL general manager, thinks it's the worst and has publicly said so on a number of occasions. To some, balancing the needs and demands of 30 teams and the countless and often conflicting opinions, agendas, and requirements of the NHL's highly competitive internal business units, broadcasters, sponsors, and media at NHL events may seem like navigating through a patch of thorny briars anchored in quicksand. To others, it may seem the most glamorous of occupations. The excitement of the arena, the access to people and places that sports fans can only dream about, and the lure of travel to significant and sometimes historic events, both near and far, are doubtless among the kinds of perquisites that keep delivery services in business as they expedite thousands of resumes between sports event management hopefuls and organizers around the world.

Managing and marketing sports events are all of these and more, but can also be like living in a goldfish bowl. Foul the water, and at least some portion of the world finds out about it pretty quickly. But, so too can the sports events manager enjoy the feedback of applause and the gratifying roar of the crowd, as fleeting as those may sometimes be.

To most of the world, sports events start with the starter's gun, the first pitch, the opening face-off, kickoff, or tip-off. Reporters are frequently amazed when they learn that some events can take two or three years to plan, sometimes even longer. With such extended planning time frames, most organizers also have to work on many sports events at a time. They don't have the luxury of approaching their workload on a linear basis. That is, they cannot start, execute, and finish one event before going on to the next one. To me, that makes most sports event organizers the stress-laden brethren of air traffic controllers, struggling to keep several projects circling overhead in various stages of development and trying to safely land just one at a time. The best organizers keep events from slamming into each other by ensuring sufficient time, applying their expertise, and establishing a methodical framework for planning, managing, and marketing their events. This book provides both first-time planners and seasoned organizers with the expertise and the framework needed for staging top-quality sports events, whether at the community or world-class level. Providing the time is up to you.

I am lucky to enjoy collegial friendships with a great many of the incredibly talented people who make up the professional and amateur sports and entertainment industries. After the release of *Dollars and Events* (John Wiley

& Sons, 1999), the first book I had the honor to coauthor with Dr. Joe Jeff Gold-blatt, a number of them remarked that a companion volume was needed—a step-by-step guide to how sports events are properly built into successful and financially viable properties. Include behind-the-scenes stories that sports insiders, fans, and students of the art of fun and games would enjoy, they said, but most of all tell us how you go about creating the magic of sports events.

I didn't take the challenge lightly. Early in my research, I was surprised by how few books on the subject were authored by full-time practitioners—the people who organized sports events all day, every day. Later I began to understand why. Writing a book is both a great responsibility and incredibly labor-intense. I had to view its preparation as another event all its own, with a number of deadlines to be applied to conceiving its mission, defining its strategies and tactics, devising its structure, and producing the actual book. Because sports events vary from sport to sport, and even within a single organization, it was important that this playbook not merely reflect my own opinions, but also include lessons learned from mentors and colleagues and, through experiences, interviews, and definitive articles from respected authorities in the field.

Now the starter is readying his pistol. Remember that the sports event organizer's run to the finish line is often not over an even track, but is more like racing through an obstacle course. Some obstacles may be avoided completely by leveraging your own experience and the expertise you will gain through reading this book. You will also be able to apply the lessons you learn here to jump, scale, sidestep, or overcome the inevitably unexpected.

Organizing, managing, and marketing sports events is not the easiest job by a long shot. But if you are up to the challenge, it is definitely the world's best.

Acknowledgments

This book is dedicated to a spectacular family—Catherine, Matt, Ethan, and Jacob—who put up with my long days at the NHL office and absences during weeks on the road, only to find me in my office at home, scratching out this book. My heartfelt thanks also go to—

NHL Commissioner Gary Bettman and NHL COO Jon Litner for understanding that there are always new horizons for a restless soul ever looking for the next challenge.

MISL Commissioner Steve Ryan and Vice President of Marketing Steve Flatow, who originally persuaded me to transfer my entertainment event experience into the world of professional sports and, as a result, introduced me to the best job I've ever had.

Barnett Lipton, who during my formative years as an event professional at Radio City Music Hall Productions and later at EVENTURES, was a most eager instructor of the ins and outs of the special events business. Most that I do, and much that I have yet to do, finds its roots in the creativity and ingenuity of this man.

Dr. Joe Jeff Goldblatt, my friend, mentor, coach, and colleague through two decades of the growth of the events industry, who introduced me to the joys of authorship, and to my friends at John Wiley & Sons, JoAnna Turtletaub and Melissa Oliver.

Members of the NHL Events and Entertainment department, from whom I am constantly learning something new about our industry and who make my days truly spectacular: Susan Aglietti, Basak Ayter, Jay Carroll, Ken Chin, Sammy Choi, Jennifer Ciolek, Danny Frank, Kris Loomis, Dean Matsuzaki, Bill Miller, Eileen Murphy, Greta Palmer, Chie Sakuma, and Kristin Stead.

And a host of colleagues whose insights, expertise, and advice can be found throughout this book: Glenn Adamo, Tom Anselmi, Bill Bannon, Pamela Cheriton, James Conrad, Bob Cramer, Ken Dryden, Helene Elliott, Greg Fisher, David Grant, Ethan Green, Tara Green, Paul Hogan, Ed Hula, Mike Humes, Bob Hunter, Lisa Hurley, David Job, Steve Kampf, Stephen Keener, Allan Kreda, T.J. LaMendola, Linda Shetina Logan, Abraham Madkour, Bryant McBride, Devi Mohanty, Barry Monaghan, Sherali Najak, Peter Nawrocki, Tanya Nazarec, Terry Nicklass, Dr. Christie L. Nordhielm, Mike O'Neill, Mike Robichaud, Derek Schiller, Dr. Eric Schwarz, Andre Steel, Gary Stokan, Rick Traer, Michael Westcot, Sheri Wish, Mary Wittenberg, and Richard Zahnd.

An extra, special thanks again to my wonderful wife, Cathy, who took this book into overtime, armed with red pen and Post-its, blowing the whistle on errant commas and coaching the author to his goal.

My thanks to you all,

Frank Supovitz

Introduction

The will to win is important, but the will to prepare is vital.

—Joe Paterno, Penn State football coach and no. 1 winning active college coach

The Power of Sports Event Marketing

To the more than one billion sports fans worldwide who leap out of their seats when the home team scores the go-ahead goal, who sacrifice sleep for the thrills of sudden death overtime, and who read their local daily tabloid from the back cover inward, the grand strategists of sports are the coaches, trainers, and general managers who guide their favorite teams or athletes. The objectives of these leaders are uncompromising and clear—the pursuit of unequaled excellence in the form of a winning score, a championship season, or a record-beating time. They embrace a philosophy, system, and playbook that put them in the best possible competitive position as they seek to identify the talents and player characteristics that will best achieve their objectives. They consider the interpersonal chemistry on the roster, past performance, and in the best cases, take into account the money available to spend against winning. During the game, they act quickly and decisively to capitalize on rapidly unfolding developments and to stave off looming disaster. They change the plan when the plan needs changing, reshuffling the lines, inserting pinch hitters, or pulling the goaltender. And after the crowds have gone home and the locker rooms have cleared, they study the game tapes, uncovering unforeseen weaknesses and learning from the successes of their opponents.

The most successful sports event managers and directors—from professional major league executives to community Little League volunteers—approach their mission in much the same way as the coach and general manager of any successful team. They identify an event's objectives, develop the plan and raise the revenues to achieve them, assemble the best team of dedicated role players, monitor costs, and continually assess the progress they are making. They adjust to changing conditions, reading the field for signs of trouble or triumph. And, finally, when it's all over, they conduct postmortems to determine how to build on their successes and correct their mistakes.

The margin for error in the world of sports events is shrinking just as surely as the influence of the sports event as a marketing tool and entertainment form is expanding. Sports event marketing is big business, by some estimates a $500 billion industry. Reflective of its integral and powerful role in human society, its roots can be seen sprouting in every schoolyard and gymnasium, in parks, on corners, and in cul-de-sacs across the globe. It germinates in countless communities, where kids and coaches, families and friends gather to participate, entertain, and be entertained, and blossoms on the college and professional level, where mega-millions in funding, payroll, and profits are at stake.

What makes sports events the world's most compelling entertainment form is the emotional capital the audience invests in the outcome of the contest. Unlike the outcome of a motion picture, with a more or less formulaic structure, or a concert performance whose repertoire is largely familiar, the ultimate outcome of a sports event is a perfect mystery at the outset and, at its most sublime, even as it unfolds. Sports are the original reality entertainment experiences—unpredictable and involving dramas in which the resolution defies prediction. The consumer invests as much as three hours or more to ride the roller coaster of a sports event's ups and downs until the final score, the day's best, or the winner who will break the finish line first, is revealed at the sound of the final horn.

In today's time-shifting environment, with the proliferation of VCRs, personal digital recorders, and video-on-demand services, sports remains the entertainment vehicle with the highest degree of real-time relevance. Most viewers want to watch an event when it is actually occurring because that is when it is at its most exciting and compelling. Repeat airings and rebroadcasts on regional sports networks and, nationally, across the United States on ESPN Classic, however, are proving that there is a residual audience as well. You don't have to keep the secret of the surprise ending from your friends who will see it later. Everyone discovers how a sports event ends at the very same time—at its official conclusion. Until then, virtually anything can happen.

News and sports web pages and wireless Internet services have exploited this hunger for instant results on the college and professional levels. Sports fans are now able to access scores and real-time game coverage via broadband connection, web-enabled cellular telephones, and handheld e-mail devices when they can neither attend nor view the excitement on television.

The power of sports events is as personal as it is cultural, whether you are emotionally invested in a team of athletes because they are your child's Little League team or because they carry the name of your school or your hometown. It may be because a great athlete swings a golf club the way you wish you could, or can seemingly cover every inch of a tennis court while knowing exactly how to place the ball out of the reach of his or her opponent. It is this emotional investment in sports that attracts not only live audiences, but media, sponsors, and the athletes themselves. The allure of sports in our culture is so pervasive that it occupies multiple pages in every daily general-interest newspaper every day of the week and is featured in its own stand-alone section at least once a week. Those dozens of pages each week and hours of broadcast airtime sell newspapers and magazines, pull in viewers, and sell advertising space to hundreds of companies that know how habit forming sports really are.

It is the mystery of how sports events will conclude that fills arenas for 40 or more home games and stadiums for 8 to more than 80 games per season. The rules are the same from match to match, but the variety and novelty of what will unfold over 60 minutes of clock time provide the uniqueness and excitement that keep people coming back game after game. It is what brings your neighbors out for the big high school football game, and parents and grandparents to your daughter's Peewee Soccer contest. Not only is there a great emotional investment in the game, but there is also an elevated sense of excitement and achievement in victory or exemplary performance. The rush of a win sets high school seniors driving around town with horns blaring, flags waving, and voices raised high. A new world record sends shock waves around the globe, and begins a quest for even greater achievement.

Savvy marketers—from the corner drugstore to giant international companies—know how audiences respond to the action, excitement, grace, and fan interactivity of sports and sports events, and they use this knowledge to great advantage. They appreciate how their potential customers are already categorized and delivered in ready-made, easy-to-classify demographic bundles, because every sport has its distinctive "average fan," every event its target audience. Education, affluence, socioeconomics, computer literacy, geographic distribution, politics, and consumer spending patterns are among the many variables that can be readily identified among the fans or viewers of a particular sport or sports event.

According to a report of the Center for Exhibition Industry Research, *Trends in Event Marketing, 2001–2002* (RCSR18.02), 89 percent of U.S. corporations with annual sales in excess of $500 million utilize event marketing as a component of their overall marketing mix. Nearly the same number, 88 percent, of the marketing executives responding on behalf of these companies indicated an expectation that the future role of event marketing will increase or remain at the same level of importance within their companies, projecting an average increase of 23 percent between 2001 and 2002. Most revealing, perhaps, is the high regard in which event marketing was held among respondents. Almost 47 percent believed that event marketing provided the greatest return on investment relative to other marketing options, as compared with print and broadcast advertising, at 32 percent, and public relations efforts, at 15 percent.

Corporations continue to invest heavily in sports and sports events because their customers, in record numbers, likewise continue to devote their dollars and emotions. Marketers recognize that establishing an association between a consumer's loyalties and passions and a company's product can pay enormous dividends in terms of sales. In addition, the marketplace is unquestionably immense. According to *Sports Business Daily*, the electronic daily journal of the sports industry, more than 462 million people attended organized sports events in 2001 in the United States and Canada alone (see Figure I-1).

Sport	Attendance	% Total
Baseball	123,832,494	26.77
Football	67,542,345	14.60
Basketball	65,228,016	14.10
Hockey	60,634,883	13.11
Auto Racing	35,843,628	7.75
Horse Racing	31,981,569	6.91
Rodeo	22,681,658	4.90
Golf	12,467,031	2.70
Soccer	7,482,702	1.62
Greyhound Racing	5,768,179	1.25
Tennis	3,342,102	0.72
Extreme Sports	3,236,550	0.70
Volleyball	1,998,616	0.43
Lacrosse	1,134,052	0.25
Bowling	520,500	0.11
Figure Skating	483,484	0.10
Curling	370,500	0.08
Other	18,034,581	3.90
TOTALS	462,582,890	100.00

Figure I-1

Organized Sports Event Attendance, 2001.

(Reprinted with permission from the *Sports Business Daily* and *SportsBusiness Journal*. The *Sports Business Daily* and *SportsBusiness Journal* are publications of Street & Smith's Sports Group. Street & Smith's is a registered trademark of America City Business Journals, Inc.)

Add to these encouraging figures the number of North Americans involved as participants and spectators of organized sports competition for youth. More than 2.75 million children are playing Little League baseball, 1.17 million are involved in grassroots ice and in-line hockey, and 360,000 kids are registered in Pop Warner Football. Then consider the friends, family, and businesses that support a community's young athletes by attending and sponsoring their events and the millions more who attend high school sports programs, National Collegiate Athletic Association (NCAA) events, track and field programs, marathons, swim meets, and many more such events. Factor in those who watch sports on television or listen on radio, and the size of the industry and its influence in our daily lives becomes all the more impressive.

Marketers recognize sports as a powerful and influential platform from which to sell their products and services because of both the emotional involvement of the consumer and the great size of the marketplace. The growing collective financial investment they make has become a cornerstone of the event planning and budgeting process and has revolutionized how organizers conceive, prepare, and execute their events.

The Evolution of Sports Event Marketing

Not long ago, captive audiences numbering in the tens of thousands faithfully filled ballparks game after game, leaping to their feet as their hometown's star left fielder went diving for fly balls threatening to drop into the gap. Over the course of a few afternoon hours, fans sat with a full view of dozens of billboards that wallpapered the area above and beside the outfield fence. One of these advertisements might have offered a new suit to the batter lucky enough to hit a bull's-eye with a towering home run. The most common sports marketing activities were stadium advertising, advertising during game broadcasts, and player product endorsements.

Today's more sophisticated sports event marketplace is a rapidly changing environment. Although the sale of advertising and product endorsements remain staples of the industry, the costs of doing business have increased dramatically for all concerned, causing sponsors to demand more and obligating sports event organizers to respond and deliver. Previously unknown economic pressures, changing consumer demographics and spending behavior, time-shifting television viewing habits, increased competition from a host of new entertainment options, and the influence of the Internet, among other factors, have changed the way we consume sports and the way marketers reach us through events. Ticket prices are at all-time highs at the same time that fans experience uncertainty about the state of the economy. A finite universe of television viewers is being diced into ever-diminishing shares of the market as new channels—and new ways of receiving programming—compete for broadcast, cable, and satellite audiences. Fans can interact with their favorite sports, teams, and athletes on a year-round, 24/7 basis, gaining instant up-to-the-second information, and, in some cases, live out-of-town broadcasts over their home computers. Some digital cable services even enable viewers to select their own camera angles as they watch selected sports events.

Changes in the sports event marketplace are particularly evident in the area of event marketing. As the global economy treads new territory daily, corporate partners are increasingly aware of the costs of doing business in the sports arena. They are more vigilant than ever in identifying clear business objectives to guide their participation—and increasingly aggressive about achieving them. Whether they are interested in selling more soda pop, new cell phone services, or business-to-business megaproducts like Internet servers, sponsors measure the success of their sports marketing programs through increases in share of market, the number of people engaged through Nielsen television ratings, or costs per thousand units sold as evaluated against exacting standards.

Much as a batter has to read signals from the dugout as the count advances, so do sports marketers have to read signals from the marketplace to remain in the batter's box. In baseball, the batter only has to look to the dugout for instructions and then pick his pitch. Sports event organizers, however, have to keep a finger on the pulse of the ticket-buying public, evaluate economic pressures on corporate sponsors, and keep abreast of merchandising innovations. They must stay current on television viewing habits and trends, emerging technologies, the day-to-day profit and loss forecasts for associated sports properties or events, the ongoing effectiveness of an event's marketing plan, and a host of other continuously evolving factors that constitute the sports business environment. A sports event organizer must simultaneously be an administrator, a marketer and promoter, a financial planner and prognosticator. (For this reason, the terms "organizer" and "promoter" are often used interchangeably in this book.) He or she must remain creative and cost conscious, freethinking yet focused.

Sports Events Are Something Special

Dr. Joe Goldblatt, CSEP tells the story of how the late Disneyland executive Robert F. Jani developed the Main Street Electric Parade. On opening day, Walt Disney noticed that his guests were leaving his new park in the late afternoon; he turned to Jani, then his director of public relations, to create an attraction to keep people in the park into the night. Jani used the term *special event* to describe his new attraction, and when asked to define this new term of art, he replied: "I guess it is something that is different from a normal day of living."

Applying Jani's definition, every sports competition could be considered a special event. Competitors vary from race to race, opponents change from game to game, and the outcome of any meet, match, or game will remain unpredictable whether the event is 1 of 82 on a schedule or a contest held just once a year. The underlying principles of planning and promotion, management and marketing, budgeting and presentation are similar for organizations that play a full schedule of games and for event organizers introducing a single one-time event. Although this *Sports Event Management and Marketing Playbook* provides insights and proposes the best practices applicable to organizations managing both one-time annual events and season-long schedules, it is devoted to the creation, development, management, marketing, production, and execution of sports events that stand out from the weekly team calendar.

Building a foundation to support and execute unique special events is like building an entirely new company or introducing a new brand. It starts with creating a product (an event) to meet the wants and needs of potential customers (the participants, audience, and sponsors). The costs of designing, fabricating, and bringing the product to market must be identified, the expected revenue projected, and the final financial results forecast. Human resources must be organized and applied to create and sell the product, and modifications to the product must be considered after it is introduced and consumers provide feedback.

Although the management and marketing of sports events require a thorough grounding in traditional business disciplines, they are much more complex than a typical product introduction. To ensure success, event organizers need to build alliances in their host community with local government and businesses, the event facility, sponsors and other business partners, media and broadcasters, and a variety of others with a vested interest in the successful outcome of the event.

Welcome to Your Playbook

Exacting and strategic planning and the effective marketing of sports events are unquestionably integral ingredients for success, but by themselves will not ensure victory or provide a finished product. The flawless execution of these events is equally essential to keep audiences excited, viewers tuned in, and sponsors fulfilled. After all, other than the event's business partners, no one leaves a sports event comparing statistics about how well the marketing plan performed.

Countless hours must be spent attending to the hundreds of management, operations, and production details that are required to execute a seamless event. Although the preparatory process for every sports event is essentially different from that of every other, most of the details on the planning checklist can be applied to a broad range of programs, regardless of size or budget. *The Sports Event Management and Marketing Playbook* helps event organizers to methodically plan, monitor, manage, and evaluate their progress during the entire event planning process. It offers an organic view of sports event planning and, as a result, is the first book to truly combine the disciplines of sports marketing and event management—as defined by their practitioners—into a single, integrated approach.

English poet and essayist Samuel Johnson (1709–1784) once wrote: "Knowledge is of two kinds. We know a subject ourselves, or we know where we can find information upon it." *The Sports Event Management and Marketing Playbook* can serve as a practical reference handbook, as relevant and current for grassroots sports organizers as for professional event managers, marketers, and promoters. Every step of the planning process for developing, planning, managing, and executing flawless sports events is explored and discussed, with checklists, charts, figures, and sample documents to ensure that every detail is considered before the gates open and the score clock begins its inexorable countdown. "Sideline Stories," real-life anecdotes from the field, provide vivid examples of best practices, as well as plays that were proven best to avoid.

Eventually, like a concert pianist's fingers gliding effortlessly across the keyboard at speeds unfathomable and seemingly as reflex, experienced sports event organizers and marketers will come to know much of what it takes to produce spectacular results intuitively. But until you do, keep this book close. It is as important to recognize what the questions are as it is to know where and how to derive the answers.

I selected a playbook theme for this book because of the striking parallels between the activities presented on the playing field and the efforts invested invisibly behind the scenes. Some earn a livelihood by competing in or managing sports events; others are involved for pure enjoyment and the rewarding satisfaction of achieving success for their team or community. The team, whether its members are wearing jerseys or golf shirts and staff credentials, is made up of specialists and role players, each contributing what he or she does best to the overall performance of the event. Athletes and event staff members alike can achieve success by applying the results of their training, as well as a series of predefined plays from their playbooks. Not every play is applicable in every game or in every situation. Proven fail-safe plays are not always executed in the same order or in the same combinations. Their effective use depends on the progress of the event; some make more sense early in the game, others at the end. At the stadium, arena, ball field, track, rink, or velodrome, in parking lots or out on the street, victory is achieved by building the right team. Coaches must provide insightful training, instruction, and even cheerleading, familiarizing the participants with the plays to be run and then turning them loose. Event organizers—those who manage events—and promoters—those who market them—also build and coach a team of planners, managers, and role players, instruct them on the event's objectives, provide guidance on what actions need to be undertaken to achieve them, and then, yes, turn them loose as well. You know you have the right team when the most common trait becomes apparent on the emotional level: Losing is not an option, whether leaving the locker room or managing a budget.

Your Introductory Play— Supovitz's Flying Wedge

More than a century ago an infamous and irresistibly powerful football play called the "flying wedge" made its debut during a second half kickoff return at a historic contest between Harvard and Yale in 1892. With the momentum of a full-speed run, the entire receiving Harvard team rushed from two sides of the field, coalescing to form a tightly packed human spearhead in front of their ball carrier, halfback Charlie Brewer. The speed and sheer force of 11 players pushing each other forward, single-mindedly focusing their energy toward the leading tip of the triangle, ripped through the stunned Yale line before being stopped 20 yards from a touchdown.

It was a play never before seen in football history and one that, for a time, revolutionized on-field football strategy. Early football historian and coach of the 1893 Wisconsin Badgers, Parke Davis, wrote, "Sensation runs through the stands at the novel play, which is the most organized and beautiful one ever seen upon a football field." This crowd-pleasing demonstration of brutal efficiency and focused manpower caused the flying wedge to quickly sweep into coaching playbooks as a fan-favorite opening play.

Ultimately, in those early days of college football, with protective gear virtually unknown, serious and even fatal injuries resulted from the use of the awesome flying wedge. It turned out that the play was too powerful, too efficient for its day, and so it was outlawed within two seasons to protect the health and lives of opposing players. It simply worked too well too much of the time, and at a horrendous human cost.

Coaches' playbooks often include diagrams of successful plays, with X's and O's indicating the field positions and movements of a team's players and their opponents. Figure I-2 illustrates one such play, "Supovitz's Flying Wedge of Sports Event Success," inspired by Harvard's landmark strategy. In this figure, the X's symbolize your event team and all of the partners, sponsors, and stakeholders that will work together with you to achieve success. The O's denote the many obstacles, large and small, that are prepared to stand in the way of your event's progress. The EO between the two wedges on the left, and at the leading edge of the flying wedge on the right, is the event organizer, the individual or group providing the leadership to pull all stakeholders and staff together. The organizer must pilot the wedge from the front, applying the force of his or her expertise and experience to determine whether to meet a particular obstacle head-on or to sweep around its flank.

There is no question that the strength and appeal of a sports event begins on the playing field, with the athletes and participants whom the fans will come to see. But beyond the playing field, the execution of a successful sports event is the result of intelligent planning and well-integrated teamwork. The team is composed of a staff of individuals—professional, volunteer, or a combination of both—working as a single unit, dedicated to the achievement of the event's objectives. Coached by the event director, the leader of the event organization, the staff is joined by a second unit composed of stakeholders, which include the event facility, sponsors, local government and business, broadcasters, and even the media. To achieve greatness for the event, the two units combine to form an irresistible wedge, sweeping obstacles aside or navigating around them.

As illustrated by Figure I-2, the event staff makes up only one side of the flying wedge. It was the coming together of squads from two sides of the field that made Harvard's wedge so surprisingly effective. The event staff members will similarly need to join with a second squad, a combination of outside

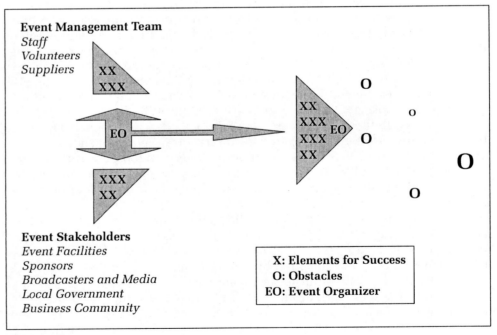

Figure I-2
Supovitz's "Flying Wedge" of Sports Event Success

stakeholders united to create the unstoppable flying wedge. If event organizers can harness and focus the energy of their team of staff and stakeholders to work as one to execute their events, they will surely execute Davis's "most organized and beautiful play ever seen." The glue I use to attract and bind the two halves of the wedge irresistibly together is my own Sports Event Golden Rule: "Understand stakeholders' objectives" (USO).

The Sports Event Golden Rule— "Understand Stakeholders' Objectives (USO)"

As you explore the *Sports Event Management and Marketing Playbook,* you will note a recurrent theme, starting with this introduction. To succeed in the long term in today's sports event marketplace, you must embrace a "USO" philosophy and attitude and truly desire to understand the stakeholders' objectives. In most cases, the days of sports organizers marching into town and dictating how, when, and where a sports event will take place are over, if they ever really existed. With the increased sophistication and pragmatism of event sponsors, broadcasters, facilities, and communities, event organizers are obligated to demonstrate the great advantages of hosting a particular event and the essential contribution their participation will make. A successful sports event is born of a partnership between all of these parties, as well as the athletes who will compete and the fans who will attend. Understanding what each of these entities wants and needs from an event is paramount in building consensus to move this partnership forward, forming a virtually indestructible, diamond-hard point to your flying wedge.

Application of the USO philosophy finds its way into nearly every major play—or chapter—in this book. Although the importance of this golden rule in building partnerships and reinforcing the leading tip of the flying wedge is evident throughout this playbook, the core concept of USO is perhaps most noticeable in the plays devoted to host cities and venues, sponsors, media, broadcasters, and involving the community. Keeping these stakeholders engaged and focused on the success of your event requires regular dialogue and ongoing negotiation. As any good negotiator will tell you, reaching agreement is far easier when each side understands what the other wants from the relationship.

Facilities, such as arenas, stadiums, recreation centers, ice rinks, training centers, racetracks, convention centers, natatoriums, velodromes, marinas, golf courses, hotels, and amusement centers, among others, exist to host events. As you begin planning your program, you will have to recognize that most of these venues look at sports events as means of generating revenues and exposure for themselves. Play 4 will help you to develop an understanding of what sports event facilities want from you and what you can expect from them.

Play 4 will also help you to gain insights into the complex and multidimensional reasons why cities, counties, and states compete fiercely for the honor of hosting sports events. Municipal governments know that sports events generate sales tax dollars, hotel occupancy, expenditures on food and beverages, and income taxes, among many other economic benefits. They also appreciate that advertising, broadcasts of the event, and newspaper and electronic media coverage before and after the fact can generate positive exposure and stimulate the interest of other sports and entertainment properties, as well as business and pleasure travelers. There are a multitude of other reasons why cities spend time, money, and human energy bidding for sports events through their local sports commissions and convention and visitors bureaus. Even small grassroots sports events generate some form of economic and lifestyle impact. Understanding how cities evaluate this impact will help you solicit the support of the community in your efforts to stage the best and most cost-efficient event possible.

Broadcasters are at the same time beneficiaries and risk-taking partners. Unlike corporate sponsors, their investment is not a marketing or brand positioning expense. Their investment, in the form of production expenses and rights fees paid to the sports organization, is generally at risk. Their product is the event broadcast itself, and they have to generate interest at a minimum of two levels. First, they have to sell advertising to offset their rights fees and production costs, and ultimately, to generate profits. A broadcaster also has to promote the event to viewers or listeners, whose very act of consuming the sports event via television or radio will justify the advertising rates it will charge for commercials. If it fails to generate sufficient ratings, the broadcaster may have to "make good" on its promises by offering bonus advertising free or at a reduced cost. Knowing the great benefits they can bring to an event organizer and recognizing that their investments can be so high and their ability to generate profits so risky, broadcasters can be very demanding. Play 13 will help you to better understand their point of view, the issues that inevitably arise during the broadcast planning process, and the best ways to work with these essential partners.

The beneficiaries of sports events that are most frequently overlooked are the athletes, participants, and fans. Events sometimes succeed in generating expected revenues, providing great economic impact to the community, and meeting the needs of corporate sponsors, yet fail to survive in subsequent years because the organizers forgot that the athletes and the audience have to have had a pleasant and rewarding experience during every phase of the event experience. The excitement should begin from the time they first hear of the event and last well after they arrive home upon its conclusion. Losing sight of the needs and expectations of the athletes and fans will endanger the long-term success of your events. Don't forget to identify and deliver what they want and need.

Understand what other sports and entertainment options the contenders and the audience attend, and why. Is your event designed to attract only the sport's loyal, hardcore fan base, those with a vested interest in the outcome of the event? Is there an opportunity to expand the event's appeal to casual fans, or even curious nonfans? Design your marketing plan to communicate how your sports event will deliver value and unforgettable experiences to the audiences you would most like to attract. Remember that sports events are generally at their most exciting when presented before an emotionally charged capacity audience.

A spirit of partnership can provide the wind in the sails of your sports event. You can try rowing against the tide on your own, but it's a lot easier to get things done if you are being propelled by a steady breeze. The fact is you need the goodwill and the hard work of many organizations, both with and without a direct financial interest, to help you make most events successful. This goodwill comes at a price: delivering to your partners what they need to make the relationship worthwhile. The trick is that they may not always tell you what they need. It's helpful to know what these organizations require before you write your first sponsorship proposal or make your first call to city hall. Demonstrate that you understand, or at least want to understand, what makes *their* business go. Be prepared to deliver benefits to the organization, and it will be more inclined to help you make your business go, too.

Current Trends in Sports Event Marketing and Management

Hockey Hall of Fame great Wayne Gretzky explained that his scoring success was not based on where the puck was at any given moment. "I skate to where the puck is going to be," he said. The key to an event's long-term success is dependent on the organizer's ability to understand his or her market and where it is heading. During recent periods of economic uncertainty, sports event organizers have come under increasing pressure to achieve more with less and to provide even greater economic value for their partners. Sponsors continue to seek ways to increase sales and market share while trying to cut costs. Some have cut their sports marketing expenditures, others have redirected where and how their sports marketing budgets are used. Many are exploring how the sports events they support can best use their company's expertise, products, and services, perhaps combined with a smaller amount of cash, to meet their needs. A more detailed exploration of what sponsors want and need from today's sports events partnerships is included in Plays 6 and 7.

Several years ago media partners such as newspapers, radio stations, and television broadcasters participated as sponsors of events by offering advertising space or time in exchange for sponsor benefits. In more challenging advertising environments, media are less willing to offer space for "official sponsor" designations and their associated benefits. In fact, many frequently make their participation contingent on some purchase of advertising space by the event organizer. Some may offer to provide extra space or time to the event, perhaps one or two times as many free ads for every ad purchased. They value the extra space as the "value in kind" that will buy them a sponsorship position. Play 8 will help you to understand the key media wants and needs in today's sports event marketplace. That chapter will also help you to understand what the editorial side of the media world, those who provide reporting coverage before, during, and after an event, need from organizers. It is incumbent upon organizers to understand what journalists need in order to report fairly and comprehensively on an event.

Recognizing current market sensitivities and ensuring that your sports events are being managed and marketed with the application of sound and current business practices are essential to achieving the objectives of your program. The more complex the event, the longer the required time frame for planning. The longer the planning process, the more likely and more often event organizers will have to change planning details midstream—such as ticket prices, participant accommodations, ancillary grassroots events, and facilities—to meet the constantly shifting pressures of the business environment. Anyone who has ever managed any form of budget, at home or in business, knows that it is impossible to determine exactly how much money is going to be spent on precisely every product or service six months, one year, or three years in advance. Yet many large events require two- to four-year planning windows, and almost all events need more than six months. After you have developed your sports event, continuous evaluation and flexibility in planning and financial reforecasting will be needed. This book is peppered with the insights, tips, and options that can help you anticipate areas where such changes might be necessary and how to deal with them.

For example, sports events planned in the United States in the late 1990s for execution after the dawn of the twenty-first century anticipated ever-rising ticket prices and audience demand, increasing sponsor support, and escalating television rights fees based on the then-prevailing trends. However, prudent event organizers working two years ahead budgeted their revenues and expenses to remain flat, as compared with those of previous years. Any increase in revenue potential in the interim would enable them to exceed their financial expectations without the risk of anticipating funds that might never be realized. This philosophy would also enable organizers to cover any increased expenses with increased revenue potential, rather than forcing them to cut other costs to remain on financial target. It turns out that planners who embraced this philosophy of flat-growth budgeting performed very well in the 1990s. They enjoyed greater than anticipated returns or the availability of additional funds with which to expand the scope or scale of their events.

Then, and not without warning, the long-expanding economy slowed and turned downward for a host of historical, political, and cyclical economic reasons. Of course, few unrealistically believed that economic expansion could remain a constant feature of the business environment. In the short term the many organizers who embraced the flat-growth budgeting model were in a far better position to protect their revenues and the health of their events when the economy turned sour. But, obviously, even the best-laid plans can go astray because of unforeseen crises that make moving forward challenging or even inadvisable. In late 2001 a new world, in which security concerns moved rapidly to the forefront, caused many events to be canceled or significantly scaled back in tone and scope. And it's likely that it will be necessary to respond to similar crises in the future. Planning for, dealing with, and responding to conditions beyond your control are discussed in Play 14, which includes a number of particularly valuable Sideline Stories.

The advancement and proliferation of new technologies and software for budgeting, event planning, ticketing, marketing and promotion, event production, and guest management functions, among others, has raised the professionalism of special events and increased the productivity of event personnel. More versatile software is emerging all the time, and as the percentage of offices and households with high-speed Internet access continues to grow, the shift to Internet-compatible systems capable of being manipulated by your fans, event guests, and business partners will accelerate. Advertising, promotion, publicity, ticket purchasing, travel reservations, merchandising, and other ways of touching and interacting with your potential audiences over the Net are already in the mainstream. So is the ability to send video footage and high-resolution graphics, reducing the time it used to take for those of us behind the scenes to effectively promote and bring our events to market.

Sports events with media appeal have also become accessible to fans unable to attend live by allowing them to visit over the Internet, streaming audio and video, or providing a level of live statistical support, extra detail, and even fan participation side by side with conventional television and radio broadcasts. Digital cable, as it becomes more widely available, can also provide a level of extra richness and interactivity to the home-consumed sports event experience. New York's MSG Network, for example, allows digital subscribers to select their own camera angles from which to watch a sports event and offers the ability to call up replays at will.

Although fans will continue to consume sports events live, on television, and via the Internet, it is not farfetched to think that some special events will someday become "cyber-events," accessible only by computer. These special market happenings may not be mainstream, primary events at first, but rather components of larger events. Event-related silent auctions, for example, are already executed over a host of web sites, from E-bay to nhl.com, and other sports sites.

How far can sports events go? Consider the long-term vision of people like Gene Meyers, president of Space Island Group. Steve Cameron of *Sports Business Journal* reported in October 2002 that Meyers's company planned to raise $15 billion to design, build, launch, and orbit large commercial structures in space. Among other things, his vision includes launching massive cylinders that could be used for some yet-to-be-invented zero-gravity sports events for broadcast back to Earth. It seems that even the sky is no longer the limit.

Time to Start Planning

"Dost thou love life? Then do not squander time; for that's the stuff life is made of," said American statesman and philosopher Benjamin Franklin. Time and again, the most common reason I encounter for the cancellation or postponement of a sports event is a lack of sufficient planning time. For the audience, sports events seem to unfold spontaneously, primarily because the nature of sports contests themselves is so spontaneous. But for anyone who has ever tried to organize a sports event, it is no news that these programs—again, depending on their size and complexity—can take as long as six months to four years or more to plan, promote, and execute. (Anyone who has planned his or her own wedding can probably relate—it always seems to take a lot more time to plan than originally anticipated.)

Some events are fixed on the calendar because they are dependent on existing sports schedules, academic calendars, playing seasons, weather, or other factors beyond the control of the organizer. Others are more flexible. In either case, start with the most desirable date for your event and work backward. Read Play 1 to determine what you want your event to achieve, see Plays 2 and 3 to understand the costs and financial benefits, and apply the lessons learned in Play 5 about the event planning process to map out all the details that will have to be considered and how long each will take to complete. It is likely that you will find that no matter how distant the event date, the latest advisable time to start planning is *now*. So let's get going.

PLAY 1

Defining and Developing Objectives, Strategies, and Tactics

All winning teams are goal-oriented. Teams like these win consistently because everyone connected with them concentrates on specific objectives . . . nothing will distract them from achieving their aims.

—Lou Holtz, former Notre Dame football coach

The best place to begin the event management process is at the end. Know what you want the event to do for your organization once the audience has gone home and all the bills have been paid. Decide whether the event is charged with the responsibility of generating a profit, raising funds for a cause-related charity, or promoting a particular lifestyle or sport. Determine the optimal date and time to stage the event that best meets these objectives. Know what you want both the audience and the athletes or participants to experience. Start with a single primary objective, the essential reason for going to all the trouble to organize your sports event, and dedicate all of your planning to achieve—at minimum—this one objective, the one that if met will qualify the event as a success if all else fails.

It would be naive to suggest that any single event should exist for one pure reason. As will be seen shortly, the potential for any sports event can be broadened to achieve a wide range of positive outcomes with a little additional effort. But it is essential to first identify one key objective, the attainment of which is of the highest priority. Ensure that every member of your event team understands the primary objective, and no matter what other bells and whistles you add later, never lose sight of the purest reason beneath. This will help to keep the highest priority in focus for all members of the event organization team and to keep confusion about the purpose of the event to an absolute minimum.

Figure 1-1 illustrates examples of the primary objectives for three fictional sports events: an amateur community baseball event, a not-for-profit participatory athletic event, and a professional sports fan festival. Each of the events' organizers has defined a singular goal that is easy to communicate to their staffs and stakeholders. As will soon become obvious, they can also achieve great secondary benefits for their communities, sports, and organizations.

**Example 1: Community Youth League
All-Star Game**
Primary Objective: To give our town's best youth league players a special end-of-season competition that will recognize them for their great performance during the regular season.
**Example 2: Road Runners Club
Downtown 10K Road Race**
Primary Objective: To promote our sport and healthy lifestyles by giving our city's runners a safe, unobstructed downtown road course, and to reinforce the excitement of recreational running by encouraging the community to cheer them on from the sidewalks.
Example 3: Playoffs Pre-Game Fan Festival
Objective: To reward and excite loyal fans with a street festival preceding the team's first playoff game in three years.

Figure 1-1
Primary Objectives of Three Types of Events

The P-A-P-E-R Test

The primary objective for each of the events in Figure 1-1 is clear, simple, and easily communicated. But if these were the only identified objectives, the organizers would forsake a large number of opportunities that could leverage their events to achieve a wider range of goals. Although some of these opportunities might seem obvious and may automatically surface on their own, a method of more comprehensive analysis is available to ensure that few possible benefits are overlooked. Organizers can maximize their events' value by considering all of the other positive things the events can do for their community and organization, and then putting them on P-A-P-E-R.

The P-A-P-E-R (which stands for *Promotion-Audience-Partnerships-Environment-and-Revenue*) Test is a useful framework within which organizers can create a more comprehensive list of additional, or secondary, objectives. Consider the answers to the questions in Figure 1-2 as you formulate additional aspirations for your event. First, brainstorm strategically about all of the things that your event can do without regard to the tactics you would have to use to achieve these ends. As you let your imagination go wild during this phase of analysis, it doesn't hurt to get others in your organization involved in the P-A-P-E-R Test. The more ideas about what your event can do for you, the better. Don't be concerned if there is some amount of duplication in the answers; duplication only strengthens the validity of the responses.

By considering the answers to these questions, you will quickly see that some outcomes will be more valuable and important to you and your organization than others. Some will also be more complicated and difficult, and others far easier to achieve. Know up front that by expanding your list to include desirable secondary objectives, more time, work, people, and other resources will inevitably be needed to achieve them. Prioritize, selecting the secondary objectives that are most important to your organization, and determine whether it will be more feasible, efficient, and desirable for you to pursue one or two of the more difficult, time-consuming objectives, or a greater number of the easier, less work-intensive goals. Consider your time and financial resources. For example, is long-term growth of an event's profit potential more important than a short-term monetary gain? Go for the goals with the greatest payoffs in whatever time frame is the most relevant, but with the least possible drain on your organization.

To illustrate how this framework can work for you, apply the P-A-P-E-R Test to the three sample events in Figure 1-1. The first is a prototypical grassroots community sports event with little or no budget and a staff composed totally of volunteers. (Throughout this book, *grassroots event* is often used to describe an amateur, not-for-profit community sports program.) Notwithstanding the minimal resources available, the event has the potential to generate excitement and advance the growth and aims of this community organization. Figure 1-3 illustrates by applying the P-A-P-E-R Test to a youth league all-star game.

Promotion
- What essential message or important information do I want to communicate to the public about the event, my sport, or my organization?
- Can I build interest in my sport or organization before, during, or after the event? By what measure can this increased interest be demonstrated?
- How do I want the event to position our sport in the community, and what kind of legacy should it leave?

Audience
- Who is our target audience for the event, the people who are most likely to participate, attend, or purchase a ticket?
- Beyond the most likely target, what audiences with similar interests can be attracted or invited to increase attendance, interest, and relevance for our event and further our organization's overall objectives?
- Is there an opportunity to win entirely new fans or enthusiasts to our sport by encouraging their attendance?

Partnerships
- Can we use the event to develop, maintain, or strengthen relationships with our organization's partners and supporters (e.g., our fans, athletes, members, donors, sponsors, community leaders, local government)?
- What kind of experience do we want to leave our athletes and other partners with? How do we want them to feel before, during, and after the event?

Environment
- Who are our competitors, and what do we want to communicate to differentiate our sports organization from theirs, and our event from the programs they stage?
- Do we need to set ourselves apart from other similar organizations operating in our community or business environment that compete for a share of available dollars, time, or attention?
- What do we need to communicate about the positive attributes of our sports event that sets it apart from other leisure activities similarly competing for the public's, or a potential sponsor's, attention?
- Do we need to address a perceived time or economic inconvenience that attendees, participants, or partners may encounter when deciding to attend?
- Do we need to address a preconceived notion about our sport, or organization, that makes it more difficult to generate attendance or participation?

Revenue
- How much revenue do we need to generate for the event and/or for the organization?
- Do we want or need to generate revenues in excess of expenses? Is this potential profit essential to growing the event in the future?
- How much money can we invest beyond expected revenues to achieve our objectives?
- Is, or should, our event be associated with a community cause or charity? How much money do we need to generate for that cause?

Figure 1-2
The P-A-P-E-R Test

Example 1: Community Youth League All-Star Game
Primary Objective:
To give our town's best youth league players a special end-of-season competition that will recognize them for their great performance during the regular season.
Additional Objectives:
Promotion
1. Encourage the local media to position our youth league as an important component of our community's quality of life, providing our children with a safe, supervised activity that will "keep them off the streets."
2. Generate advance publicity to bring more kids and families to the event to cheer on their friends and relatives.
3. Use the event to get more kids to register to play in the league next season.
Audience
1. Fill the bleachers and standing areas with at least 200 spectators. (The more people who attend, the more importance the All-Stars and the media will place on the game.)
2. Get new kids from the community to the game to encourage registration at the ball field for next season.
3. Get town and civic leaders (e.g., mayor, city manager, councilperson, state senator, chamber of commerce representative) to attend to validate the importance of the game to both the players and the fans. Demonstrate to these leaders the important place our league occupies in our community.
Partnerships
1. Strengthen our ties to the local chamber of commerce and its member businesses to encourage current team sponsors to renew their relationships, and to identify new prospective team sponsors for next season.
2. Use these strengthened ties to local businesses and town government to solicit grants to improve the antiquated dugout area and improve overall field maintenance.
Environment
1. Demonstrate that our league is highly organized, motivated, and dedicated to coaching our kids to improve their skills and to promote good sportsmanship.
2. Demonstrate that our organization is the best alternative to the highly competitive leagues in which winning is more important than having a great time.
Revenue
1. Generate $500 to replace old equipment (e.g., new batting helmets, bases, batting tees) and to help pay for All-Star trophies.
2. Increase player preregistration for next season by 10 percent.

Figure 1-3
Expanded Community Youth League All-Star Game Objectives

DEVELOPING TACTICS

To begin the actual process of planning an event, your objectives have to be supported by the *tactics* you will employ to achieve them. It is against the backdrop of these tactics that you can begin to identify costs and revenue opportunities and, ultimately, formulate a budget. Often, event budgets are developed considering only the cost of staging the competitive event or main program, with insufficient thought and resources devoted to maximizing its marketing and promotional value or, in some cases, even toward attracting and accommodating spectators. Be sure your budget can accommodate the efforts and expenses—the tactics—of addressing your desired objectives.

The volunteer chairman of the youth league in Figure 1-3 realizes that a children's all-star game can do much more for its participants and teams, the community, and its own organization than staging the game simply for competition's sake. As a volunteer with limited time and resources, the chairman knows that the game can exist without any of these additional considerations and achieve its primary objective with a minimum amount of time investment. All he needs is to get a permit for the ball field and to hire an umpire. To achieve even a small number of these added secondary objectives, the chairman will have to appoint a committee or task force to prioritize which objectives should be considered necessary, which would be nice, and which are just not worth the effort. But, as you can see, even the most basic grassroots sports event can achieve a multitude of previously unconsidered aims.

Secondary objectives are frequently interrelated and mutually supportive. Sometimes a seemingly less important, but more easily achieved secondary objective will be pursued to reinforce the success of more pertinent agenda items. In the case of the youth league all-star game, getting community leaders (Audience) to the event will help to impress businesses from the chamber of commerce (Partnerships) and encourage coverage by the local media (Promotion). A full set of bleachers (Audience) will also position future league events as worthy of sponsorship by local businesses and grants sponsored by local politicians (Revenue).

It is also helpful to develop secondary objectives to support the host organization's overall mission and challenges. The event chairman in this hypothetical case wants to keep registration fees as low as possible, but knows that money is going to be required the following season to replace equipment and level a field that tends to flood after even a brief, moderate shower. The all-star game is a perfect opportunity to raise the money required, whether dollar by dollar through the sales of cold sodas or raffle tickets to family members in the bleachers, a few hundred dollars at a time through an expanded group of sponsors, through grants from the county, or all three. Staging the all-star game without engaging in all of the extra work may provide just as wonderful an experience for the children participating. But with some extra forethought, organization, and effort, the game can also provide an outstanding opportunity to improve the experience for the players this year as well as in seasons to come.

The second fictional event presented in Figure 1-1 is staged by a local running club. This organization has a handful of permanent administrative staff members, supplemented by a large body of volunteers, event marshals, and municipal employees assigned by the city. The primary objective for the event is consistent with the overall goals for the organization, but could also pertain to any of the nearly 30 other running events the club stages each year or to any races staged by similar organizations. Figure 1-4 illustrates how the P-A-P-E-R Test can be applied to allow the Downtown 10K Road Race to stand out uniquely from the rest of the club's calendar.

Example 2: Road Runners Club Downtown 10K Road Race
Primary Objective:
To promote our sport and healthy lifestyles by giving our city's runners a safe, unobstructed downtown road course, and to reinforce the excitement of recreational running by encouraging the community to cheer them on from the sidewalks.
Secondary Objectives:
Promotion
1. Demonstrate that our sport is a great lifestyle choice for the entire community, providing health and social benefits to all participants regardless of age or income.
2. Promote our organization as one of the region's top associations of recreational runners.
3. Encourage spectators to gather at the finish line and at designated locations along the route to cheer on the runners.
4. Designate an official radio station in our market that will appeal to our target market, and promote both the registration drive prior to the race and spectator attendance on race day.
Audience
1. Capitalize on advance promotion to increase race registration by 33 percent over last year.
2. Encourage families and friends to try recreational running together for the first time, and reactivate interest among former runners.
3. Convert those trying the event into regular recreational runners.
4. Use advance promotion and the on-site excitement of spectators to increase club membership by 15 percent.
5. Demonstrate the popularity and vitality of running and the benefits of our association to potential sponsors of future races and events.
Partnerships
1. Strengthen our ties to the city's Parks and Recreation, Police, Street, and Sanitation Departments, upon whose active cooperation we depend to run races year-round.
2. Establish a working relationship with the Downtown Business Improvement District, whose objectives include bringing visitors and entertainment seekers to the downtown core during low-traffic weekends and summer evenings.
Environment
1. Demonstrate that as compared with other ways of spending an hour or two, running is fun, healthy, mentally and emotionally refreshing, accessible, and inexpensive.
2. Demonstrate that as compared with other sports, running requires little economic investment and is easy to learn because it has few rules.
Revenue
1. Generate net proceeds of $50,000 to pay for operational expenses.
2. Increase club membership and member revenues by 15 percent.

Figure 1-4
Expanded Downtown 10K Road Race Objectives

The executive director of the Downtown Road Runners Club knows that she can use the scenic attractiveness and excitement of running through the downtown area to revitalize one of the organization's annual 10K races and has set realistic goals to increase membership and race registration. She also recognizes that she can use the event to establish a working relationship with local businesses in the downtown area to achieve mutual objectives—the repositioning of a business district that is exciting in daylight hours five days a week, but sleepy during nonworking hours. Working with the local chamber of commerce, the organizers of the race can create unique opportunities for area business owners and, in turn, present new sponsorship and official supplier opportunities. Area restaurants and retailers can engage in promotions to transform workweek customers into weekend event spectators, and may participate as places for recreational runners to pick up registration materials, application forms, and information. The expansion of the list of secondary objectives also reveals another possible opportunity—the potential for future short-distance road race events in the evening to further promote the vitality of the city after regular business hours.

Amassing and evaluating secondary objectives provides event organizers with a framework within which to develop tactics and strategies to transform an event-for-its-own-sake into a dynamic, multifaceted event marketing tool for its organizers, sponsors, the local community, and a host of other stakeholders. For example, the Road Runners' desire to increase the number of recreational runners in the community may lead them to consider configuring the event to have two starting lines. The second, located near the midpoint of the original route and following in parallel lanes so as not to interfere with competitive runners, might be offered to the public with a reduced registration fee for families with young children so that an upcoming generation of runners can feel the thrill of passing the finish line. The inaugural effort to add a family component to the race could also serve as a market test to determine whether the club might subsequently consider "family" or "junior" membership tiers to increase membership and annual dues revenues.

To strengthen the club's relationship with the city agencies whose participation is integral to the successful execution of the event, organizers might consider offering the police, fire, streets, and sanitation departments a limited number of free race registrations. These agencies can, in turn, donate the free spots to their widows and orphans organizations, Big Brothers/Big Sisters, or another worthy organization, and reap some of the public relations benefits of supporting those in need. The club would be well served by monitoring how these free spots will be used so that it can encourage the media to generate human interest stories about the beneficiaries, further increasing publicity for the event.

As previously mentioned, it is rarely possible to achieve all of the secondary objectives an organization might desire for a particular event. Organizers need to prioritize which are the most valuable, timely, relevant, and cost-effective to achieve with the financial and human resources available.

However, in this fictional case the P-A-P-E-R Test identified several areas of opportunity the organization wishes to pursue, perhaps at future events. To illustrate how multiple objectives can be achieved, we turn from the hypothetical organization illustrated in Figure 1-4 to a real-life analogue, one of the premier running clubs in the world (see the Sideline Story below).

Sideline Story—The New York Road Runners Club

The New York Road Runners Club (NYRRC) is a not-for-profit organization that produces more than 100 events each year, including the world-famous New York City Marathon, the club's Professional Racing Series, weekly races, clinics, and seminars. "Our mission is to support the sports of running and walking for health, recreation, and competition, as well as to give back to our running and local communities," says NYRRC Chief Operating Officer Mary Wittenberg. "Each event is staged to further our primary objectives in line with our mission, but secondary objectives and goals vary by event." The NYRRC divides its 75 race events into several categories with unique appeal to different types of runners, target demographics, and sponsors. These categories include World Class, Premier, Enhanced Classic, Classic, and Traditional levels. Each of the races is defined by the secondary goals it is designed to achieve, as well as by budget and expectations. In this way, the club can work toward achieving the totality of its secondary objectives as viewed over the course of its annual calendar of events.

Two NYRRC races that differ dramatically in size, target audience, and purpose are the Runners World Midnight Run and the Fleet Bank Empire State Run Up. "They both achieve our primary goals, but differ beyond that," says Wittenberg. "The Midnight Run is all about fun. It is a celebration of fitness, exercise, activity, and good humor on one of the most indulgent nights of the year (New Year's Eve). It is not about serious running, it is about having a good time in a healthy way." The event, held in Central Park, is open to all who want to join in, whether as runners or simply as walkers along the route, attracting as many as 8000 participants a year.

The second event, the Empire State Run Up, is as creative, fun, and intriguing as the Midnight Run but, in contrast, is limited to fewer than 100 participants. "It is an invitational race made up of some of the strongest, fittest athletes in the world," Wittenberg continues. One would have to be in world-class condition—the event is a timed run up the steps of New York's Empire State Building—all 1576 of them, from street level to the 86th floor observatory. The annual February contest is no joke to hardy Australian athlete Paul Crake, who won every edition of the 303 m (measured vertically, not horizontally) contest between 1999 and 2003 and is the only athlete ever to break the 10-minute mark. Like the Midnight Run, the event is designed for fun, but with an entirely different set of secondary objectives. "It is largely a promotional activity, drawing amazing press and attention to New York City and the Empire State Building," Wittenberg observes. Doubtlessly so, but both events also further enhance NYRRC's position as a creative, vital, and world-class running organization.

The P-A-P-E-R Test is as useful for event managers and marketers in professional sports organizations as it is in the worlds of community grassroots and world-class amateur events and is perhaps even more essential to their businesses. With budgets and human resources stretched to the limit, it is a matter of survival for sports events to wring every possible benefit from their staging. To fully realize the potential of a multidisciplinary approach to the development of professional sports events, the entire organization, not just the department charged with managing the event, must be mobilized. Because more staff members with divergent skills, contacts, specialties, and reporting relationships are frequently assigned to the management and execution of a professional sports event, it is even more critical to develop clearly defined primary and secondary objectives and priorities.

The third hypothetical sports event in Figure 1-1 is a playoff pregame fan festival to be held on the street outside a team's home arena. There is great demand and excitement in the community because the team has failed to reach the playoffs over the past two seasons, and tickets for the first postseason game have sold out in a single day. Capturing and savoring the buzz in the marketplace can, in itself, be a great reason to stage a fan celebration. But as Figure 1-5 illustrates, the P-A-P-E-R Test can reveal many more possible opportunities.

The organizers of the Fan Festival described in Figure 1-5 have been presented with the kind of opportunity every team dreams of—the ability to take advantage of an appearance in the playoffs to achieve the overall marketing, revenue, and organizational goals of the club. With a program of free festivities presented outside the arena, ticket holders for the game can arrive early and celebrate with their fellow fans. The team and the sponsors of the festival would be happiest if they could fill the plaza in front of their arena with

Example 3: Playoffs Pre-Game Fan Festival
Primary Objective:
To reward loyal fans with a street festival preceding the team's first playoff game in three years.
Secondary Objectives:
Promotion
1. Generate added publicity for the team beyond the sports page and our customary game coverage.
2. Provide the media with attractive, camera-friendly opportunities to capture the excitement of our team's appearance in the playoffs as a lead story or as a lead-in to the local news.
3. Demonstrate how the excitement surrounding the team contributes to the community's quality of life for both residents and local businesses.
Audience
1. Encourage the early arrival of playoff ticket holders to the arena.
2. Bring fans who are not ticket holders to the arena to add to the excitement of game day.
3. Attract casual sports fans to the arena to build their interest in our team and sport.
4. Enable members of the community with limited economic resources to enjoy the playoff celebration to the fullest extent possible.
Partnerships
1. Provide our sponsors with an opportunity to market to, and communicate with, both loyal fans and casual fans at a time of heightened interest in the team.
2. Provide civic leaders with an opportunity to appear before the widest range of their constituents.
3. Provide our radio and television partners with opportunities to enhance the ratings of their pre-game coverage, and attract additional viewers and listeners to the game broadcasts.
Environment
1. Present a celebration at least as highly regarded by the fans, media, and community at large as the one staged by our local baseball franchise before its last appearance in a playoff game three years ago.
2. Demonstrate to those who are unfamiliar with the arena that it is in a safe and easy-to-reach location.
3. Demonstrate to the community that our fans are passionate, loyal, and excited, but also well behaved and good-natured.
Revenue
1. Sell standing-room tickets to the game.
2. Increase season ticket sales and sell multigame plans for next season while excitement for the team is at its zenith.
3. Renew existing and expired season ticket accounts.
4. Generate $200,000+ in sponsor sales to cover expenses.
5. Increase playoff and team merchandise sales by 15 percent over expected in-arena sales.
6. Increase concessions revenues by 10 percent over expected in-arena sales.

Figure 1-5
Expanded Playoffs Pre-Game Fan Festival Objectives

thousands of people, who do not have tickets in addition to those who will be arriving to attend the playoff game, in order to achieve their merchandise and concessions revenue objectives. But they also realize that the resulting traffic and competition for parking could upset their most loyal ticket holders.

If the team has sufficient space, they could create a "season ticket holder only" area with an expanded menu of premium food items, exclusive activities, and meet-and-greet opportunities with former team members, giving their most loyal customers a unique and valuable level of access to the event to compensate for any inconveniences they might otherwise experience. Working with their city to add buses to the mass transportation schedule prior to and after game time could also help to reduce congestion and demonstrate how easy it can be to get to the arena. From the city's point of view, providing extra shuttles would give fans the ability to sample the ease of access the mass transit system can provide.

The team will not want its loyal fans who could not get tickets to the game, but want to enjoy the match on television, to decide not to attend the pregame celebration because they are afraid of missing parts of the broadcast. It makes strategic sense to extend the festivities during the game by installing large video screens on the event site so that the fans can savor every second. The crowds excitedly watching the game outside the arena will also provide outstanding opportunities for incremental sales of merchandise and concessions, as well as compelling news footage and remote broadcast locations for local television and radio outlets not permitted in the building during the game.

The inclusion of civic leaders and elected officials is not a political decision, although to suggest that politics and sports are strangers would be naive. Rather, their presence also demonstrates to a wider audience the importance of the team and the event to the community. These are not the type of guests who shy away from television cameras or radio microphones, so just their presence can help take some coverage of the event off the sports page and place it in the main news section.

Chances are that the team will never have a more exciting opportunity to speak directly to an audience broader than their season ticket holders, unless they go on to win a championship. This is the time to present celebrants with the ability to take advantage of special ticket promotions and thus help sell new season tickets or multigame packages for the following season. Capitalizing on the "got to be there" nature of events of this type, the club could offer purchasers free event-related merchandise with a deposit for a multigame package for the upcoming year.

PROGRESS FROM STRATEGIES TO TACTICS

After the discussion of each of the sample sports events presented in this chapter, a number of strategies and tactics have been described to illustrate how to develop various programs that can meet a wide variety of event objectives. As previously noted, objectives state only what event organizers are hoping to achieve, not how they will set about achieving them. Identifying objectives and developing strategies cost your event budget nothing but time, creativity, and analytical thought. The tactics that are selected and employed are the things that cost and potentially make you money. To illustrate, when you take a road trip, you know where you want to go (objective), and by consulting a road map, you identify what roads you will have to take to get there (strategy). You start spending money once you decide to get in your car and begin paying for gas and tolls to drive there (tactic).

So, before a budget can be drafted, you have to develop your list of objectives and determine the best, most realistic, and most cost-effective strategies that will achieve as many of these goals as possible at the lowest cost of capital and labor. Only then can you design the tactics—the event itself—you will employ that fit your strategies. It is at this stage that you will evaluate whether the tactics you have chosen will be too complex, too expensive, or too labor-intense to achieve. Perhaps even the most simple and inexpensive tactics to achieve a particular objective are still beyond your reach, given your budget, available time, and all else you wish to achieve. At this point you may determine that your event is trying to do too much and that some lower-priority objectives may have to be sacrificed to benefit some of the more important ones. This evaluation process can continue throughout the budgeting process, as the affordability of pursuing a given tactic may not become completely apparent until the numbers start falling into place.

Although there are countless strategies that sports event organizers can consider in their pursuit of identifying the proper tactics to employ, using the P-A-P-E-R Test framework can add direction and focus to the evaluation process. As you review Figure 1-6, a brief checklist of some general questions you can apply to event objectives as identified by the P-A-P-E-R Test, you will note how the answers to many of these questions can serve multiple purposes and achieve multiple aims.

SPORTS EVENTS AS SOLUTIONS

The sample events traced through this chapter are presented as responses to specific challenges or desires on the part of the organizer or promoter. With the growth in popularity of sports event marketing as a powerful addition to the traditional marketing mix for corporations of nearly every size, events are frequently not simply born as a whim or fancy of a sports event organizer, but sometimes also as a response to a business partner company's marketing objectives. Leading sports event managers are often approached by marketers and their agencies to develop a program that achieves the objectives of their partners, such as launching new products, relaunching existing products, increasing sales, and marketing lifestyle programs.

Promotion
☐ What key messages do I want my promotional plans to communicate? How will I encourage the media to help me achieve the outcomes I want before the event (e.g., advance ticket sales, walk-up attendance, increased broadcast tune-in), as well as afterward (e.g., positive press coverage, increased membership, financial contributions)?
☐ How can I use publicity, promotion, and advertising to get my message out to the people whom I want to hear it? In what media—daily, weekly, and monthly newspapers and magazines, radio stations, television stations, Internet web sites—should I try to place stories?
☐ How can I use the event as a publicity and promotional engine for my sports organization before, during, and after the event? What compelling stories can I tell? What can I develop or add to the program to make my event more newsworthy?
☐ Can I work with local school districts to deliver educational programs, school visits, or field trips to students that also promote my message?
☐ What long-term resulting legacies or benefits can the event provide? Is there a possibility of staging the event again in this same marketplace? If there is an opportunity for the growth of the event in future years, how will we achieve it?
☐ How will we clarify, correct, or debunk any misconceptions about my sport or organization?
☐ How will I develop and pursue my promotion strategies? Can I expect to achieve my objectives with existing staff and resources, or do I need to get more help from the outside?

Audience
☐ How can I stage this sports event to keep it fast paced, involving, and exciting for the attendees?
☐ How can I make the event one that is easy to buy tickets to, easy to get to, and comfortable for spectators?
☐ What can I do to add value to the event for our existing fans?
☐ How can I get new people to my event? How can I turn them into fans, boosters, members, or supporters?
☐ What events attract an audience that is similar to the audience of my event, with which I can create cross-promotions to build awareness and attendance?
☐ How can I educate the public about my sport, organization, or event?
☐ How can I bring more people into the event through live or recorded media? Is the event worthy of a live broadcast on television or radio? Alternatively, can a broadcast be packaged into a compressed, tape-delayed, or highlights-only form? How can I present the opportunity to make live radio updates or reports from the event site ("remotes") attractive to a partner station?

Partnerships
☐ How can I use this sports event to strengthen our organization's ties to current sponsors by entertaining their guests and providing them with superior service? Are there opportunities to provide unique access to the event, special hospitality opportunities, exclusive mementos, or other perquisites that go beyond the terms of our contracts and that demonstrate the sponsors' value to our organization?
☐ How can I use this event as a showcase for potential future sponsors? Are there opportunities to provide prospective future partners with one or more of the perquisites of a current sponsor that will demonstrate the value of joining our family?

Figure 1-6
Strategy-to-Tactics Development Checklist

☐ Are there exposure opportunities I can offer a partner through pre- and post-event advertising, on-site signage, participant awards and trophy ceremonies, special entertainment segments and audience promotions, giveaways, sweepstakes, recognition on athlete uniforms and staff attire, or printed materials (e.g., tickets, invitations, flyers, posters, rack brochures, information guides, programs, scorecards)?

Environment

☐ Is there another event or organization with which I am competing for audience, attention, sponsors, or athletes? How can I set my event apart from my competition? Will a cross-promotional partnership with the competitor be in our mutual best interest?

☐ Can the event solve or draw positive attention to a pressing issue in the host community?

☐ How is the local community trying to portray itself, and how can our event support its efforts? How can that portrayal benefit my organization, sport, or event?

☐ What dates and times for the event might fill an entertainment void in the marketplace?

Revenue

☐ Can or should I sell admission tickets? How many and for how much? If we are interested in having children attend, should there be a reduced children's price? A family package price? Discounted prices available only through sponsor promotions? A special price for friends and family of staff and athletes?

☐ Can I sell merchandise? How much? Will I be selling existing inventory and/or event-specific merchandise? What kind of merchandise—low price points for kids, high price points for premium adult merchandise? Is there a market for high-priced collectibles and memorabilia?

☐ Can I sell food and/or beverages? What kind and how much? Hot foods and drinks for open, cold-weather venues; cold foods and drinks for open, hot-weather events? Are there special regional foods that should be among the offerings? Is it appropriate to serve beer at the event?

☐ Can I sell sponsorships? How many, for how much, and to whom? Can I package such sponsorships with similar opportunities at upcoming events? Should I make low-cost packages available for new sponsors who want to test their association with my event or organization? Can I offer multi-event, or multi-year sponsorship packages? Do I need outside help to design and sell these packages?

☐ Can I create a printed commemorative program and sell it, or sell advertisements and give it away for free? Who will sell the ads and to whom will they be sold?

☐ How can I use the event to encourage sales of tickets to other upcoming events? Can I sell those tickets at the event? Should I distribute discount coupons for these or other events?

Figure 1-6
(Continued)

Sideline Story—The Labatt/NHL Pick-Up Hockey Marathon

The 2000 National Hockey League All-Star Weekend, an event that concluded with the playing of the fiftieth NHL All-Star Game, was held in Toronto, the site of the first NHL All-Star Game in 1947. The Labatt Brewing Company, a Toronto-based sponsor, requested that event organizers create an event surrounding the weekend that would capture the attention of the national public and would embrace two key attributes of their Labatt Blue brand of beer: genuineness and being "uniquely Canadian." In response, the NHL created the Labatt Blue/NHL All-Star Pick-Up Hockey Marathon. Labatt and the NHL solicited the heartiest amateur adult hockey players throughout Canada to play on one of two teams that would compete on a frozen rink in front of Toronto City Hall continuously, 24 hours a day, until one side no longer had the ability to put a sufficient number of players on the ice. The puck dropped on Monday at 8:00 A.M., and play continued through four days and three nights until approximately 7:30 A.M. on Thursday morning, attracting thousands of curiosity seekers, generating hours of national television and radio coverage, and earning a place in the *Guinness Book of World Records* (2001). Though the event clearly met many objectives for the NHL, this memorable program would never have been developed without the inspiration, challenge, and support of the Labatt Brewing Company. (See another Sideline Story in Play 6 for more details on the Labatt Blue/NHL All-Star Pick-Up Hockey Marathon.)

The Sideline Story above demonstrates that a sports event organizer can apply the needs of a sponsor, as well as those of its own organization, to the creation of a completely new and compelling event concept. It is even more important to apply the P-A-P-E-R Test to these events to expand the relevance and impact of the program beyond the primary objective of positioning the sponsor's product. The development of additional secondary objectives ensures that the event can be used to achieve multiple benefits for the sponsor, the sports organization, and other stakeholders.

Post-Play Analysis

To realize the full potential of a sports event, it is essential for organizers to develop a comprehensive list of event objectives before creating a budget and devising a business plan. Identify the primary objective first—the goal the organization believes is essential, above all else, to reach. Use the P-A-P-E-R Test (Promotion-Audience-Partnerships-Environment-Revenue) as a framework to develop the host of secondary objectives that will offer additional benefits for the organizer, sponsors, and other stakeholders.

Defining your objectives sets up the targets you want to hit. Developing strategies defines how you will achieve your objectives (e.g., "I will hit the target with my bow and arrow"). Identifying tactics helps you to define in detail how those strategies will be actualized (e.g., "I will buy a quality bow and the right kind of arrows, learn how to use them, practice my marksmanship, and fire from a reasonable distance"). Developing the skills you will need to accurately hit a bull's-eye is the focus of the rest of this book.

Coach's Clipboard

1. Your school's football team is in the top third in the standings. As a result, the campus may host a regional championship game in three weeks. Use the P-A-P-E-R Test to outline what the game can achieve for the school, the athletic department, and the team. Prioritize these objectives based on their importance to these three entities and how feasible they are to achieve, given the time remaining before a possible event. What are the implications if the event must be canceled the week before it is to be staged because the team does not make the playoffs?

2. You are the brand manager of a line of lifestyle clothing with a modest budget for sports marketing. How can you use the P-A-P-E-R Test to identify the best sports events to fit the marketing aims for your product?

3. What tactics can you employ to make the 10K road race in Figure 1-4 more attractive to a potential business-to-business sponsor (i.e., a company whose customers are primarily other companies, instead of individual consumers)?

4. An energy bar sponsor approaches a minor league sports organization, seeking a new event or promotion that will help to fight the perception that the product is candy, rather than a viable and nutritionally balanced meal replacement bar. The sponsor wants the event to portray an active lifestyle and to be something it can "own" (i.e., to be instantly and ever recognized as a program associated with its product). Design an event that achieves the sponsor's aims and expand this primary objective to serve the needs of the league.

PLAY 2

Identifying Costs

Lack of money is the root of all evil.
—George Bernard Shaw, Irish dramatist (1856–1950)

Now that you know what you are trying to achieve, and have a reasonable concept of the kind of event you would like to stage as your plan to get there, it is time to begin constructing an event budget. Your budget will identify areas of revenue opportunity and expenses. Although revenue generally appears first on most budgets, I usually start developing my budget from the expense side first, so I know how much revenue I will need to generate to support my event and fulfill my objectives. If there are not enough obvious revenue opportunities to cover these expenses, I try to develop new ones. If there is still insufficient funding, it's time to go back to my objectives, tactics, and expenses to determine which expense categories I can reduce or live without.

Fledgling sports events most frequently fail to take wing for the same reasons new businesses so often fail—undercapitalization and an underestimation of expenses, the root of Mr. Shaw's evil. Simply put, it will take money to plan, develop, manage, and execute an event, and a fair amount of it will have to be spent before the very first ticket, T-shirt, or sponsorship is sold. Therefore, some investment is almost always required to get a project moving, and the larger the event, the greater the initial cash outlay that will likely be needed.

A thorough examination of all of the expected and potential costs will be required to ensure that your event's budget is realistic and that your revenue goals will meet or exceed the costs of doing business. You will find that there are a limitless number of ways to spend your money when planning an event, and it is essential to know exactly on what, and have some idea of how much, you will have to spend before the invoices start piling up. Use the widely available Microsoft Excel or Lotus 1-2-3 spreadsheet program to chart your expenses, and make it a point to use the formula functions that instantly add columns and perform other mathematical functions so you can automatically calculate the effect on the bottom line as you adjust individual budget categories.

A worksheet of typical event budget expenses appears in Appendix 1. It provides a comprehensive list of major expense categories suitable for many sports events, though it is by no means complete. Use this table as a guide in preparing the expense budget for your event, but be sure to think of all of the equipment and other peculiarities of your sport and event to ensure that all of your anticipated costs are considered.

The definition of many of the expenses in Appendix 1 will be obvious and familiar to the reader. The rest of this chapter provides you with more details, as well as some vagaries, peculiarities, tricks of the trade, hints, and warning signs for expenses that are more particular to sports events.

Expenses fall into two broad categories—fixed costs and variable costs. Fixed costs, as the name implies, remain immutable regardless of how successful the event is in attracting spectators or selling sponsorships. Examples of fixed costs include player and equipment costs and operational expenses, marketing costs, and flat-rate facility rentals. Variable costs, however, increase as attendance or sales grow. Examples of variable costs include facility rentals based on a percentage of ticket sales, sales taxes, commissions paid on sponsorship sales, and, to some extent, expenses for facility staff and security (i.e., more ushers and security personnel are required as attendance grows).

Facility Costs

Because a significant portion of a sports event's funds may be spent on leasing and preparing a site to host the event, it is wise to begin constructing your budget by selecting the venues most suitable and affordable for holding your event. If you are restricted to a particular city or community, your choices will likely be limited to one or, at best, a few event-appropriate facilities. Yet, if you have some flexibility as to the community that can host your event, you will, of course, have more venues to choose from and your bargaining power during the selection process can save you thousands of dollars in venue costs. Play 4 provides more details on how to apply the economic benefits of an event to drive down venue and host city expenses for an organizer who can make their program available to competitive bidders.

RENT

In most cases, the facility you will use to host your sports event is in the business of making money, or must at least cover its operating costs. That you may have to pay some form of rent or permit fee is probably obvious, but if you have never leased an arena, stadium, convention center, or similar facility, you will be amazed at the unexpected additional costs that can burden a budget. Request a pro forma copy of the lease agreement for any facility you are thinking of using while you prepare your expense budget. A pro forma is essentially a "fill in the blanks" standard lease form that outlines the major points of an organizer's relationship with a facility. The facility may request some amount of information about the event to help it prepare the most appropriate first-draft lease. The agreement should also contain the rules and regulations pertaining to hosting events at the venue, the rates for additional charges such as labor, equipment rentals, and value-added event services provided by the facility. The more potentially profitable your event is for a prospective host venue, the more its management may be willing to negotiate with respect to adjusting the terms and prices in the lease agreement.

The biggest, most prestigious events can provide sufficient noncash incentives for a city or building owner to consider hosting an event at a reduced rate or, in some cases, on a rent-free basis. The incentives that often tip the scale toward reduced-rate rentals include an unusually large number of hotel room-nights that the event may generate for the city, unusually strong promotional benefits for a local team or favorable publicity for the host city, and national or international television exposure, among others.

Most sports events fall into the realm of potentially profitable prospects for an arena, stadium, or other public venue, but the rental rate formula is frequently negotiable. It may be paid as a flat sum, a percentage of gross ticket sales, or some combination of a reduced flat fee plus a percentage of sales. If you are relatively confident in your organization's ability to sell tickets or your ticket prices are premium priced, your budget will go further if you can secure the lowest possible flat rate. If, however, your ticket prices are low or you are less confident in your ticket-selling prospects, either because of the event's past history or as a result of external factors such as the economy or political instability, consider negotiating a variable rental fee that is more heavily weighted toward a percentage of sales. This strategy can also help you better manage a tight budget, inasmuch as the effective rental rate will rise only as the success of your event increases. In most cases, you will probably have to pay a minimum guarantee if the rent will be calculated, in some measure, on a percentage of sales. Remember that facility managers are smart and experienced businesspeople, and they will be vigilant and conscientious about finding ways to maximize their revenue while you are attempting to reduce your event's financial exposure. Work honestly and candidly with the facility during negotiations. Your mutual interests are best served when both sides have realistic expectations and benefit from each other's success.

The rental rate, as well as other facility costs, will be covered in the lease agreement for the venue. The lease should be negotiated early in the budgeting process, because building costs can make up a sizable portion of your event budget. When you receive your first copy of the lease agreement, expect that most terms will be written to benefit and protect the facility. Work with an experienced attorney to review all terms of the agreement before signing.

TICKET SALES DEDUCTIONS—TAXES AND FACILITY USAGE FEES

Although the deductions from ticket sales revenues are technically costs, they are not listed on my sports event budget worksheet under "Expenses." I prefer to classify them as "negative revenues," because that money is never really received from the box office or ticket sellers. Every dollar of each ticket sold may carry with it payment obligations in the form of taxes, levies, usage charges, or commissions, to name a few. Thus, although these costs are discussed here, they will appear on the revenue side of the budget worksheet. They are, nonetheless, costs of doing business that have to be accounted for when constructing your financial model for the event.

Make sure your lease agreement covers all expected areas in which the event will incur facility costs. For example, be sure that all deductions from ticket revenues are unambiguously defined in your contract. Many facilities charge a small per-ticket fee variously known as a "capital replacement fee" or "facility usage fee." This deduction usually ranges from $1.00 to $2.00 per ticket and may represent an obligation the building must collect on behalf of the local government to cover the financing costs on the facility's construction. As a result, these fees are often nonnegotiable. Be sure to determine whether this fee is traditionally charged to the organizer or whether it is most often passed along to the ticket buyer as a cost added to the face ticket price. The total impact of this expense on the overall budget will, as a variable cost, increase or decrease with the tickets actually sold. Events are not charged a usage fee for seats that go unsold, and such a fee may or may not be payable on tickets that are issued on a complimentary basis, depending on the facility.

There are several other costs that will vary with ticket sales. In most cases, payment will be the responsibility of the event organizer, and the costs are not usually added to the consumer's ticket price. As they are variable costs and not payable before a ticket is sold, these charges are usually deducted from your ticket revenues by the venue before you receive them. The most common deductions, sales and amusement taxes, are commonly levied by local, state, or provincial governments. Being set by acts of legislation, the rates are normally not negotiable. They will differ widely between municipalities, so analyze the effect of local taxes on your bottom line before you award an event to a host city or facility. A table of sample applicable tax rates, as effective in 2003, appears in Figure 2-1.

Host Site	Ticket Tax Rate
Atlanta, Georgia	7.00%
Columbus, Ohio	0.00%
Fort Lauderdale, Forida	6.00%
Los Angeles, California	3.50%
Saint Paul, Minnesota	6.542%
Toronto, Ontario	17.00%
Vancouver, British Columbia	7.00%

Figure 2-1
Sample Ticket Tax Rates (Tax rates are as of 2003)

It is not safe to simply assume that the prevailing local sales tax rate will be the ultimate rate you will be charged on ticket sales. In some cases, the rates may be higher because of an added "amusement" or "entertainment" tax levy, or lower because a separate amusement tax will apply, but the sales tax will not. Be sure to check with the finance managers of your selected event venue to determine the actual rate for which you will be liable on ticket sales in that locality. In Columbus, Ohio, for example, the sales tax rate is 5.75 percent, but no tax is applied to the sale of sports event tickets.

Sideline Story—A Major League Tax Waiver

There have been instances in which state or local legislators agree to pass a bill that waives tax liabilities for specific sports events. Such a waiver was granted to Major League Baseball (MLB) in the State of Florida specifically excluding MLB All-Star Games from having to pay taxes on ticket sales. This waiver extended only to baseball for the purpose of providing additional incentive for the league to stage All-Star Games in the state and was applicable only for those specific events. While potentially beneficial, such considerations can also become politically sensitive and matters of public debate and have potential to result in serious public relations fallout for both the host city and the event organizer.

In many states, provinces, and cities, sales and/or admissions taxes may be payable on the value of at least some tickets that are issued on a complimentary basis. Generally, if the tickets are exchanged for some form of valuable consideration, they are subject to taxation. For example, an organizer may be required to provide complimentary tickets as a benefit to companies that provide an event either with cash or with products and services, gratis, as part of their sponsorship agreements. Even if tickets make up only a small portion of what the sponsor is entitled to as part of the deal, the value of those tickets may be taxable as though you accepted cash for their face value. In most instances, where complimentary tickets are issued as a courtesy to VIP guests, player families, charities, and the general fan population as a gesture of goodwill, for which no recompense in any form is received or expected, they are usually free of tax obligations. Event organizers should seek professional local advice on whether, and how, sales or amusement taxes may apply to complimentary tickets issued in the locality where an event is to be held. If the host venue has been the site of a number of similar events, its chief financial officer can usually provide this information.

TICKET SALES DEDUCTIONS—COMMISSIONS

There are a number of other deductions from ticket sales revenues that usually apply, which are often overlooked during the budgeting process by first-time sports event organizers. Credit card commissions, for example, can erode ticket revenues by as much as 3 percent. When tickets are purchased by credit card, it is the responsibility of the event organizer to pay a fixed percentage of the transaction to the credit card company. If you are working with an established sports or entertainment venue, you will probably be asked to pay commissions to that venue at a blended rate, that is, a flat fixed percentage of the transaction. This amount is deducted from ticket revenues by the box office to cover the commissions the facility must pay to the card issuer plus a nominal handling fee for the facility. It is usually best to utilize an existing box office and its relationship with the credit card companies to save you the inconvenience of installing data lines, establishing an account, and employing your own ticket sellers.

Not all of your tickets will be paid for with a credit card, such as those paid by check on behalf of groups and corporations. If you expect to be accepting credit cards and you forecast that at least some sizable portion of ticket buyers will be using that method of payment, it is recommended that your budget presume that *all* patrons will take advantage of this option. This will protect your budget with a small, hidden contingency fund should other expenses rise beyond expectations.

Many larger sports events, particularly those held in existing sports and entertainment facilities, make use of a computerized ticketing system such as Ticketmaster or Tickets.com, among others. Using a centralized, automated system provides fans with more convenient ways to purchase tickets, whether over the phone, via the Internet, or at remote box offices in other locations throughout the community. Anyone who has ever purchased an event ticket knows that the ticket service will collect some "per-ticket" and "per-order" service fee. What many novice sports event organizers may not realize is that they too may be liable for certain transaction fees as well.

The contracts between event venues and their automated ticket sales provider will vary, but in many cases you will not be liable for any appreciable fees for tickets sold through the system by the "home box office," that is, at the stadium, arena, or other facility in which the event will occur. You may have to pay a small charge of $0.25 a ticket or less, or nothing at all, depending on the venue's agreement. Tickets sold over the phone, via the Internet, and at remote box offices, however, may have a service charge attached that is payable by the organizer, even though the consumer has also paid a fee for the service. Usually, you will get the best deal by being included under the venue's existing contract. If your event is very large or if you are not staging your event in a facility with existing computerized ticket options, and you wish to avail yourself of the additional sales opportunities a ticket service can provide, you will have to negotiate your own best deal with the ticket service.

Many stadiums and arenas maintain a database of tour groups, bus companies, youth organizations, booster clubs, and other avid ticket buyers that make purchases in block quantities, through either an in-house group sales department or an outside agency. Group sales can be a very effective supplemental means to fill your event venue, but the old maxim "There is no such thing as a free lunch" applies here too. You will have to pay the group sales agency, and any in-house group sales function provided by the arena, a pre-agreed commission rate in the form of discounted prices (the agency charges the group the full price and retains the balance), a service fee per ticket, and/or a flat fee for handling and processing. In today's E-mail environment, however, getting group sales information into the hands of likely buyers is quicker and more cost-efficient than ever. Because of the large multiples of tickets that can be sold through group sales efforts, this is, in most cases, a cost-effective option for event organizers that is generally worth the expense of commissions.

FACILITY LABOR

It takes dozens, and sometimes hundreds, of facility employees to staff a sports event, and you can expect to have to pay for all of them. The most obvious are the front-of-house staff—the ushers, ticket takers, security officers, and box office personnel the public most often encounters, along with their supervisors and managers. These facility employees are usually paid by the hour, with a minimum call of four hours per day, plus an overtime differential before and after certain times of the day (e.g., after midnight or before 7:00 A.M.), on certain days (e.g., Sundays and holidays), or after a specified number of working hours per day. The facility will most often charge you an hourly rate that is marked up from the employee's actual pay rate, "plus benefits" (e.g., the cost of health insurance premiums and/or vacation accruals). You may also be charged an "administrative fee," which is the facility's way of offsetting the costs of scheduling employees, keeping track of their hours, and servicing its payroll. Once you have provided the facility with enough detail to give it a good understanding of your event, its management can provide you with an estimate of what to expect in the way of front-of-house labor costs. Make sure the estimate includes all administrative, payroll, and benefits charges as well.

Your labor costs will surely also include some "back-of-house" building staff, including electricians, carpenters, riggers, and presentation staff such as stage-hands, stage managers, spotlight operators, audio technicians, video crews to provide images for the scoreboard screen, matrix board operators, cleaners, and others. Many facilities are bound by labor agreements with union locals for at least some of these jobs, which will further obligate any lessee to honor such agreements. The venue will gladly provide you with the hourly rates for each of these labor categories, from which you can calculate costs based on your load-in (installation), rehearsal, event, and load-out (dismantle) schedule.

The event organizer's obligation to pay for back-of-house staff may also include a "conversion" charge. The facility may have to reconfigure itself from the form or condition it was in the day before loading-in your event, and then back again after your event has vacated. For example, if an arena is being leased to present a martial arts competition following an ice hockey game, a number of operations personnel will be required for the conversion. For the area to be in a condition conducive to host the martial arts event, the boards and glass around the rink will have to be removed and the ice covered with homosote, a paper-based insulating board, and/or plywood. Additional floor seating may be added, and the center scoreboard lifted to a higher position. In such cases, the cost of the labor required to convert to and from the ice hockey configuration is charged to the event organizer.

Facility costs are not limited only to those described here, and are dependent on both the nature of the event and the type of venue in which it is held. The expenses for some items are charged to the organizer by the facility; other items are purchased or rented directly by the event organizer to prepare the venue to properly host the event. The checklist in Figure 2-2 can assist you in the process of identifying these types of costs.

Player- and Game-Related Expenses

There are few instances in the sports event world in which the participants or players are not recognized in some fashion. In grassroots and amateur athletics, this recognition may take the simple form of medals or trophies. In pro-

---

☐ Rent
☐ Building labor
☐ Front-of-house staff (ushers, ticket takers, security)*
☐ Electricians
☐ Carpenters
☐ Scoreboard and matrix board operators
☐ Cleaners
☐ Conversion crew
☐ Credit card commissions*
☐ Group sales and other sales commissions*
☐ Crowd control equipment (e.g., barricades, ropes and stanchions)
☐ Chair and table rentals
☐ Pipe and drape dividers

*Variable costs

Figure 2-2
Typical Sports Event Facility Costs

fessional sports, trophies, if awarded at all, are increasingly supplemented with more valuable consideration, including expensive championship rings, cars, and other gifts, as well as cash awards, which may be in the form of appearance fees, cash prizes for outstanding performances, bonuses for achieving certain benchmarks, and a winner's prize pool, among others.

In addition to setting aside funds for prizes, appearance fees, and winner pools, consider whether you will require the services of athletes beyond the actual competition and whether you can include incremental appearances in the compensation or recognition structure for professional or semiprofessional players. Including a meet-and-greet opportunity with athletes for fans, or for a sponsor's guests, can go a long way toward generating new ticket buyers and corporate partners, so it is strongly recommended that event organizers either seek to include an appearance or two within an athlete's understanding of his or her obligations, or put some cash aside to pay for some number of appearances. (This is not something to be offered in most amateur and grassroots sports organizations, where payment in cash, products, or services may violate league or collegiate rules or those of another governing body.)

Some organizations combine the participation of star athletes with amateur competitors to add star power to an event and pique spectator interest. The New York Road Runners Club, for instance, invites a roster of elite runners who are paid appearance fees to participate in the New York City Marathon, running side by side—at least for the first mile or so—with accountants, lawyers, clerks,

Appearance fees	$100,000
Winner's prize pool	$100,000
MVP award	$10,000
Supplementary appearance fees	<u>$15,000</u>
Total player prize pool	$225,000

Figure 2-3
Sample Prize Pool

businesspeople, and other purely recreational runners. Many Pro-Am golf tournaments use a similar approach, allowing weekend amateurs to play the sport they love alongside the greats of the links.

For organizers who must offer cash incentives to participating athletes, there is no one right way to design a compensation package. Figure 2-3 illustrates how a prize pool can be constructed for a two-team sports event that ensures that every player has an incentive to participate and compete. In this example, the event organizer has budgeted for a $225,000 prize pool. The organizer can decide to award the entire sum to the winning team or to split the funds available to see that everyone goes home rewarded, at least to some degree.

For the purposes of this example, assume that there are 15 players on each of two teams, for a total of 30 players. The organizer wants to reward each player with a guaranteed minimum fee for participating. Dividing the $100,000 appearance fee pool by all 30 participants provides a $3,333.33 guarantee for every player. In this compensation scheme, a player can triple his or her award to $10,000 by playing on the winning squad. This figure is derived by dividing the winner's prize pool of an additional $100,000 by the 15 winning players, adding $6,666.67 to the guaranteed appearance fee. The event's Most Valuable Player (MVP) is awarded an additional prize of $10,000. Presuming the MVP is on the winning team, that player would be paid a grand total of $20,000. Exclusive of additional fees available for supplementary appearances, the total player prize pool has been divided into $3,333 for players on the losing team, $10,000 for players on the winning team, and $20,000 for the MVP (if on the winning squad, and $13,333 if on the losing side).

The prize pool includes funds for supplementary appearance fees, allowing opportunities for the players to meet and greet sponsors, guests, or fans. For illustrative purposes, assume there are 20 such opportunities during this event, each representing one hour of time beyond participating in the competition itself. Players can earn $750 for each hour they agree to participate and may increase their earnings by appearing for more than a single hour. A player on the losing team can then increase his or her earnings to more than $4000 with one supplemental appearance.

☐ Accommodations
☐ Appearance fees
☐ Equipment
☐ Equipment managers and trainers
☐ Locker room supplies
☐ Meals and per diems
☐ Medical staff, EMTs, ambulance
☐ Officiating fees and expenses
☐ Player guest expenses
☐ Playing surface preparation and mainte-
nance
☐ Prize money and recognition
☐ Timing equipment and score clocks
☐ Trainers' fees and equipment
☐ Transportation, inbound/outbound (to/
from home airport, airfares)
☐ Transportation, local (to/from airport, ho-
tels, and event sites)
☐ Uniforms, including numbering and
lettering

Figure 2-4
Typical Game- and Player-Related Costs

If you are organizing a tournament, determine how you will recognize the winners. Consider how many age and gender brackets your players will be divided among and to what level in each bracket (e.g., first place only, first through third place, etc.) you will recognize players with trophies, medals, or other prizes. Determine those to whom you expect to award the trophies or medals—the coach, the captain, all the players? Identify all of these expenses and capture them in your game- and player-related expense budget. See Figure 2-4 for a checklist of game- and player-related line items to include in your budget, if applicable.

Event Operations

The event operations expenses category contains all the costs classified as "overhead," the items that are essential to run the event but have little direct visible impact on the experiences of the audience or the athletes. They would include the costs for staff hired specifically for the event and all of the support equipment, systems, and supplies required by the staff members to execute their responsibilities. See Figure 2-5 to help you account for the most common event operations expenses.

☐ Accounting services
☐ Computers and printers
☐ Copiers
☐ Credentials or ID cards
☐ Facsimile machines
☐ Gratuities
☐ Insurance
☐ Legal services
☐ Mobile communications equipment (e.g., walkie-talkies, cell phones)
☐ Office space, hotel meeting rooms, and/or office trailers
☐ Office supplies
☐ Payroll services
☐ Postage
☐ Power and generators
☐ Power distribution (the labor required to bring power where it is needed)
☐ Shipping, trucking, and overnight couriers
☐ Software (existing applications and custom programming)
☐ Staff and volunteer expenses (meals or per diems, transportation, parking)
☐ Staff attire
☐ Storage and warehousing
☐ Telephone and high-speed data lines (installation and usage)
☐ Temporary staff, including event specialists, freelancers, and interns
☐ Volunteer program expenses (e.g., recognition, food and beverage, parking)

Figure 2-5
Typical Sports Event Operations Expenses

Most of the expenses listed in Figure 2-5 are relatively straightforward and may be estimated by simply contacting prospective vendors and requesting quotations. The area of most financial exposure and business concern, however, is insurance. How much and what kinds of insurance should be purchased varies with the type of event you are staging, where you are holding it, and the kinds of athletes participating (e.g., amateur or professional, their age and training). In today's litigious society and world political climate, the recommended coverage and the cost of insurance are climbing at an alarming, almost unsustainable, rate. You cannot afford not to have adequate insurance coverage for your sports event and its organizing entities, and it is essential to the financial well-being of your program to get preliminary quotes before you complete the budgeting process. At minimum, some form of liability coverage is required to protect the event, its parent organization, and its executives, employees, and sponsors. Proof of liability insurance coverage of at least US$2 million, and sometimes as much as $5 million, per occurrence is a requirement that appears in the leases of most event facilities. Organizers should consult with their legal counsel and insurance brokers to determine the additional insurance coverage that would be advisable, particularly in regard to audience and athlete safety and the potential for injury.

Outdoor events may also consider acquiring "weather insurance," coverage that will pay benefits to the organizer if the program must be canceled because of adverse weather conditions. Premiums for this type of coverage are often expensive, and the conditions that are required to trigger the payment of benefits are often extreme. An organizer should carefully weigh the financial exposure of an uninsured weather cancellation or postponement against the expense of purchasing insurance. The greater the potential loss to the organizer, the more attractive weather cancellation insurance may become. Unless an organizer is able to self-finance unrecoverable expenses and refunds to sponsors and ticket holders, coverage merits serious consideration.

An extremely expensive consideration in regard to cancellation insurance has recently emerged—terrorism insurance. This type of policy protects organizers from the financial calamity that might be faced as a result of terrorist activity directed at the event or a similar action occurring within a prescribed geographic radius that makes holding the event inadvisable. In these uncertain times, insurance companies are charging premiums for this type of coverage that are, unfortunately, out of reach for most event organizers. A more comprehensive discussion of this and other types of insurance coverage, as well as risk management issues, can be found in Play 14.

Marketing and Promotion

You may be planning the best and most compelling sports event ever staged, but unless you have a plan that will get the word out to both participants and the potential audience, you could be faced with a sparsely populated tournament or empty bleachers. You may not have designed a complete marketing plan at this point, but you will need to earmark funds for advertising, publicity, and promotions, as well as for the entities that will help you create and manage these marketing vehicles. Pre-event publicity will help generate public awareness and ticket sales, but a well-conceived advertising plan is strongly recommended to supplement such efforts.

The marketing of your event does not end once the program is under way. Post-event coverage is particularly useful in demonstrating the vitality and relevance of your event to community leaders, potential sponsors, and future ticket buyers. If your event is particularly newsworthy, you may have to provide press facilities that will enable the media to cover your event. Relevant items of importance include a comfortable and unobstructed vantage point from which to view the event, as well as media working space with access to power and phone lines for both credit card calls and the electronic filing of stories directly from the event site. In addition, a press conference area for interviewing athletes, coaches, and other key officials is often prepared for major events. Members of the media are accustomed to the periodic receipt of official statistics during an event and, in the case of televised sports events,

---

☐ Advertising agency expenses (copying, postage, faxes, phone calls, press kits)
☐ Advertising agency fees (hourly charges for staff time and creative charges)
☐ Internet web site development
☐ Kickoff or announcing press conference or event
☐ Logo development
☐ Media accreditation
☐ Media center expenses (rental of furnishings, draping, phone, copier, fax, television monitors, and meals, refreshments, and snacks)
☐ Media hospitality
☐ Outdoor advertising (creative, production, and rental of billboards and street banners)
☐ Pre-event promotional giveaway items
☐ Press conference area
☐ Print advertising creative
☐ Print advertising space
☐ Public relations agency expenses (see "advertising agency expenses")
☐ Public relations agency fees (see "advertising agency fees")
☐ Radio advertising production (i.e., costs of creating a commercial)
☐ Radio advertising time
☐ Staff photographer and videographer
☐ Statistician(s)
☐ Television advertising production
☐ Television advertising time
☐ Telephone information center or recorded 800 number

Figure 2-6
Typical Sports Event Marketing and Promotion Expenses

television monitors that allow them to view replays and live broadcast coverage. Many organizers also provide media personnel access to complimentary food or snacks appropriate to the time of day, along with soft drinks, water, and coffee. Draw applicable expense categories from Figure 2-6 as you develop your marketing budget, and refer to Play 9 for more details on how to work with and service the media.

Sponsor Fulfillment

Sponsors expect, and are entitled to, a host of contractual benefits and, in many cases, noncontractual perquisites attendant to their support of your event. Expenses undertaken to service sponsor needs, whether dictated by contract or provided as added bonuses by the organizer, are called *fulfillment expenses.*

Almost every event sponsorship agreement includes a minimum number of site-specific signage positions that display the sponsor's logo, company name, or product identification to the public. Unless otherwise defined by the sponsor's contract, the expense of designing, fabricating, installing, and dismantling this signage is a cost to the event budget. Event organizers are usually obligated to provide a specified number of complimentary tickets, the cost of which (i.e., the lost revenue represented by these complimentary tickets) should also be accounted for in the budget.

Because the content of sponsor packages varies so widely across the industry, there is no rule of thumb governing what percentage of an organizer's sponsor revenues should be set aside to cover fulfillment costs. The revenue-to-expense ratio will differ even among the family of sponsors for a single event. Any expense that results from an obligation to a sponsor, which would not have been incurred if that sponsor was not involved, should be included in this budget line. Extra perquisites that you intend to bestow that are not contractually required should also be included. Such expenses may include hosting private VIP receptions, advertisements acknowledging a sponsor's support, special gifts, premiums and presentations, supplemental athlete appearances, custom-made staff wardrobe displaying the sponsor's logo, labor for product sampling—the list and variety of these costs are endless.

By budgeting for sponsor fulfillment costs before a package of benefits is offered to potential sponsors, event organizers can avoid one of the most basic mistakes in event marketing—offering a sponsor package that will cost more to fulfill than the revenue it will generate. Creating sponsorship packages of value to both the organizer and the business partner is discussed more fully in Plays 6 and 7.

Guest Management and Hospitality

Sports events have become major hospitality opportunities, not only for the sponsors that support them, but also for the organizations that stage them. From tournaments to touring events, championship matches to all-star games, and fan festivals to player drafts and skills exhibitions, organizers take advantage of the cachet generated by their programs to invite, excite, and attract VIP guests, sponsors, potential future business partners, celebrities, and other influential individuals to their events. Determine early in the planning process how many guests you will be able to accommodate on a complimentary basis and to what degree you will entertain and service them. Although Play 11 explores this area in greater detail, organizers can use the checklist in Figure 2-7 to identify the most common guest management and hospitality expenses.

☐ Custom ticket printing
☐ Directional signage
☐ Gifts
☐ Guest transportation (e.g., airport pickups, shuttle transportation to event)
☐ Hospitality suites
☐ Hotel accommodations
☐ Hotel attrition and cancellation penalties
☐ Information kiosks and printed information guides
☐ Invitation design, printing, and postage
☐ Parties and receptions
☐ RSVP tracking software and web applications
☐ Welcome baskets and room amenity drops

Figure 2-7
Typical Sports Event Guest Management and Hospitality Expenses

Event Presentation

Many sports events include opening ceremonies, pregame festivities, player introductions, and intermission or halftime entertainment programs—ranging from the most simple to the visually spectacular—that require some level of creative, technical, and production support. Stadium organs have been providing entertainment value during stoppages in play for decades. Today, the playback of recorded music is programmed for specific game situations (and in sports such as figure skating, is essential to the competition itself), and video scoreboards entertain and inform fans with computer-generated animations, player head shots and statistics, features, blooper reels, and highlight packages. Special lighting and effects are frequently used to excite the crowd and to celebrate game-turning plays, goals, and home runs. Live talent may perform during pregame periods, deliver anthems, and entertain during halftimes and intermissions. Some sports events are pure entertainment, celebrating a sport with live performances, pageantry, and noncompetitive athlete appearances, such as at an opening ceremony, awards dinner, or fan festival. All of the traditional elements of entertainment event production may be applied to sports events, including those enumerated in the checklist in Figure 2-8 and discussed in more detail in Play 12.

Depending on the nature and scale of the sports event, a team of production specialists may be required to properly plan and stage the entertainment portions of the program, including event producers, stage managers, technical directors, lighting designers, and script writers, to name a few. The right team of experts and the right presentation tools can elevate a simple sports contest to become a sports entertainment vehicle that makes a lasting and positive impression on the fan, the viewer, and the public at large.

☐ Anthem performer (usually travel expenses only)
☐ Costumes
☐ Electricians and technical staff
☐ Flags, banners, and bunting
☐ Lighting (e.g., follow spots, computerized lighting, television lighting)
☐ Music and voice recording
☐ Pre-game and intermission performer(s)
☐ Production staff (as required, see text for more details)
☐ Props
☐ Public address announcer
☐ Riggers
☐ Set Design and construction
☐ Sound (e.g., playback equipment, public address system, microphones, mixer)
☐ Special effects (e.g., pyrotechnics, lasers, flame effects, confetti cannons, etc.)
☐ Stagehands
☐ Staging and risers
☐ Video production
☐ Video screens, matrix board, camera package, and playback equipment

Figure 2-8
Typical Sports Event Presentation Expenses

Capital Investment and Amortization

Your sports event budget may require the acquisition of physical assets that are included in many of the aforementioned expense categories, which can be stored and reused in future years or applied to other events your organization stages during the same year. These assets may include equipment for the field of play, signage and display hardware, timing equipment, reusable banners, props, costumes, video and sound equipment, television monitors, computer equipment, tools, road cases, and more. If you purchase these items for an event you expect to stage annually, or for a series of events during a single year, the expense may be amortized, or spread, for bookkeeping purposes, over the course of their expected useful lives.

It is usually my preference to rent what is needed when possible, because capital assets that are not used all the time can create additional annual expenses such as the leasing of storage space, trucking, and refurbishment. But some custom-designed and custom-built elements may still be required for a particular event. If you have the storage space and are certain these assets can be used again, you can amortize their costs. Of course, all the cash will have to be spent now. But the event expenses charged against the first year can be reduced as long as you are prepared to carry that same amortized expense forward until the full cost has been completely accounted for. For example, suppose you have to acquire 25 television monitors at $400 and 4 VCRs at $100 each and you have plenty of storage space available to accommodate them after the purchase. Although you have to spend the entire sum of $10,000 immediately to take possession of these assets, you expect to use these television sets and videocassette players for three years before they will have to be replaced. By dividing the total expense by the number of years you will use these assets, you can charge only one-third, or $3333, to this year's budget. However, you must remember that you will have also "already spent" the same sum in the budgets that will be created for the event for the next two years.

There is nothing to say that you cannot amortize your assets over a series of events during the same year or that you have to charge the same percentage to each. Let's say you have to build three interactive information kiosks that cost $5,000 each. You will use all three kiosks at your biggest annual event, and only one at three smaller events. Although you will have to spend $15,000 in cash right now, you can charge each of your event budgets a smaller figure. Figure 2-9 illustrates the calculations for this hypothetical case.

There will be occasions when assets, the costs of which you have already amortized, do not reach their projected useful life because of accidental damage, wear and tear, or simple malfunction. If an asset must be replaced, you will need to liquidate, or "write off," the balance of its value, that is, the portion not yet used by future events. In the preceding example, for instance, if a kiosk becomes unusable after two years (two-thirds of its useful life), the value charged to events in the third year (the remaining third of the total value, or $5,000) may be reallocated among the budgets of the events at which the asset has already provided a benefit. If the kiosk is replaced, the ability to amortize that new individual asset over a new three-year period begins again. Similarly, if an event is canceled or the use of a particular asset in future events is no longer required, the remaining value will have to be liquidated

---

Total Expense to Build Kiosks: $15,000
Annual Championships: 3 units used × 1 time per year × 3 years useful life = 9 usages
Fund Raising Events: 1 unit used × 3 times per year × 3 years useful life = 9 usages
Total Usages = 18
    Amortized Value Per Kiosk Per Use = $833.33
Charge to Each Annual Championship = $833.33 × 3 kiosks = $2500.00
    Charge to Each Fund Raising Event = $833.33 × 1 kiosk = $833.33

Figure 2-9
Sample Capital Amortization Calculation

by reallocating the remaining value over one or more of the budgets for events at which the asset was utilized.

Obviously, if you are acquiring assets for a sports event that is a program that will likely occur once and only once, and those assets will have no further use at any future events, you will not be able to enjoy the financial advantages of capital amortization. Renting assets is the most advisable and cost-effective approach for such one-time sports events. There may, however, still be a need for unique capital items that cannot be rented but must be designed, built, or acquired. The total cost of such assets should be charged to the event budget, even if you have a plan to later sell or otherwise derive some value from salvaging the items. Any value received on the post-event sale of an asset can later be counted as miscellaneous revenue.

Miscellaneous Expenses and Contingency Allowances

Wise drivers always fasten their seat belts before leaving the driveway because they know that an accident can happen without warning—in front of a person's home or miles away. They also know that there is an 80 percent or greater chance that they will survive a mishap simply by taking this precaution before leaving the driveway. The unforeseen can also befall a sports event organizer from the moment the budget is drafted, throughout the planning process, and even after an event is long concluded. For this reason, a wise organizer includes a contingency allowance line for unexpected expenses. By buckling this financial seatbelt before work on an event begins, the organizer will vastly improve the budget's—and the event's—probability of survival.

The contingency line in your budget should not be confused or commingled with a line for "miscellaneous" expenses. The miscellaneous expense line is where individual expenditures that are too small to warrant their own budget categories, or odds and ends that do not easily fit a specific budgeted expense line, should be charged. A contingency line exists as an additional safety net, in fervent hope that it will not be needed in large part, or at all. It is there to be used in an emergency, to cover cost overruns, or, if all goes according to plan, to contribute to net profits if it ultimately goes unused.

If possible, set aside a contingency allowance representing 10 percent of the total event budget. A 10 percent contingency is often impractical because of already-known expense demands and constraints on the availability of capital. Contingencies of 10 percent, or as much as 15 percent, are most important for sports events with relatively modest expense budgets of less than $50,000 to ensure that sufficient funds are set aside in case of emergency. For larger budgets ($50,000–$250,000 in expenses) it may be safe to lower the contingency to

7.5 percent if it helps to close a budget gap. It is recommended that for the largest budgets ($250,000 or more), the safety belt not be permitted to slip below 5 percent, but set higher if possible.

A miscellaneous event expense line, as discussed earlier, is a catchall for anticipated small-cost items, but is not for the payment of unforeseen expenses—that is what the contingency allowance is for. The miscellaneous amount is comparatively small, as individual large expenses deserve their own budget lines. A large allotment for miscellaneous expenses in a sports event budget is often viewed by management with suspicion, a warning signal that the organizer may not have a clear and firm understanding of the expenses the event will ultimately encounter.

Reforecasts

Experienced sports event organizers periodically reforecast their expense estimates after the budget has been finalized, throughout the planning, production, and execution phases leading to event day, and even up until the books close months after the event. The worksheet in Appendix 1 provides a partial illustration of the form for a simple sports event reforecast. The original budget spreadsheet is extended to include several additional columns of figures. Immediately beside the approved budget is a column of forecast expenses, the final amount the organizer expects on each budget line at the end of the event. Once finalized, the numbers in the "Budget" column are never adjusted. It is in the forecast column where expectations on the final disposition of each budget line will be periodically updated. Next is the column for actual expenses, those costs for which invoices have been received or contracts have been signed. The actual expense column will help validate the accuracy of the forecast column to its left, showing the money already spent and, by extension, indicating the amount remaining. Finally, a variance column shows the difference between the original budget and the forecast, line by line.

The reforecasting process enables the organizer to reallocate budgeted funds originally overestimated in one area to another budget line that may be suffering from cost overages. Throughout the planning and production process, the combined value of forecasted expense budget overestimates must be matched or exceeded by the subtotal of underestimates for the budget to balance. If it does not, the event organizer must go through the painful process of cutting expenses. To be effective, forecasting, like the budgeting process itself, must be grounded in realistic expectations. Make sure that when you reduce a budget line to make up for a cost overrun in another area, you will be able to reduce the expense in fact, and not simply on paper.

Post-Play Analysis

Sports event expenses may be many and varied. The major categories of expenses include facilities costs, game- and player-related expenses, the costs of event operations, marketing and promotion, sponsor fulfillment, guest management and hospitality, and event presentation, as well as miscellaneous expenses and contingency allowances. Certain costs for the acquisition of assets that may be used over several events and/or several years may be written off over the useful life of those items, allowing event organizers to spread the cost of an asset over several event budgets. Throughout the planning and execution process, event organizers reforecast the financial performance of their budgets to better manage costs and apply cost savings in some areas to offset cost overruns in others.

Coach's Clipboard

1. Create an expense budget for a new college tournament in the sport of your choice, featuring teams from five universities in your region and five from outside the area.

2. A children's hospital asks you to manage a Pro-Am golf tournament (foursomes composed of both professionals and amateurs) to raise awareness of, and generate revenues for, its facility. What is the amount you will advise the hospital it must invest in order to stage the tournament before the start of any revenue flow? How can this initial investment be covered if the hospital is unable to contribute any capital in advance?

3. An annual street hockey tournament for amateur adult teams requires the acquisition of two portable rink board and flooring systems costing $15,000 each. If the rinks have a useful life of three years, what amount should be allocated to each year's event? If you can use the rink systems more often by organizing similar annual tournaments in two nearby communities, what amount should be allocated to each event per year?

PLAY 3

Identifying Revenue Streams

Never spend your money before you have it.
—THOMAS JEFFERSON, THIRD PRESIDENT OF THE UNITED STATES (1743–1826)

Few sports events can exist without some form of funding. Successful sports event organizers are not in the habit of investing capital without great confidence that they will be able to recoup it by the time an event has concluded. But expenses begin to accumulate the moment an event budget is approved, if not before. Be sure you have developed revenue streams that start as early as the bills begin to arrive, to ensure that you will have cash on hand to satisfy your financial obligations.

Naturally, the larger and more complex an event is, the greater the costs will be and the more urgent the need for revenues to offset expenses. By defining your event's objectives in detail, you already have an idea of how you want your bottom line to turn out, that is, whether you aim to make money, break even, or spend a predetermined sum as a promotional or fan development investment. You next compiled a detailed analysis of the resources that will be required to stage your event and projected the level of expenses you expect to encounter. Then, by comparing your desired bottom line against anticipated expenses, you know how much total revenue you need to generate. The question now is how to go about generating it.

The revenue streams available to a sports event organizer depend on the type of event, the venue in which it will be held, and its net income objectives

☐ Admissions (i.e., ticket sales)
☐ Broadcasting rights fees
☐ Grants and donations
☐ Merchandise sales
☐ Parking
☐ Programs and journals
☐ Sponsorship and advertising
☐ Tournament registration or participation fees
☐ VIP hospitality packages

Figure 3-1
Typical Sports Event Revenue Streams

(i.e., the amount of profit or loss). Is the event the beneficiary of a charitable endeavor, a break-even not-for-profit effort, or a profit-generating enterprise? Unfortunately, there are far more ways of spending money than making it. Although revenue streams vary from event to event, Figure 3-1 provides a list of the most common from which to choose when creating your event budget.

Ticket Sales

Admission tickets are probably the oldest and most common income generator for sports events. Today they remain the lifeblood of most top amateur and professional sports events, commanding prices that range from just a few dollars to several hundred. Although ticket revenue can account for 50 percent or more of total revenues for a sports event, the financial value provided by the ticket holder goes far deeper. A full stadium, arena, or stand of bleachers adds value to sponsorships and to an organizer's other business relationships by exposing an event's corporate partners' products and promotional messages to the eyes of more potential customers. For televised programs, a standing-room-only (SRO) crowd adds prestige and excitement to an event for the viewing audience and demonstrates that there is a market for your event large enough to fill the stadium or arena and, by extension, beyond, into the viewers' living rooms.

There is, of course, a more practical, immediate reason why struggling to fill your inventory of seats or spectator space is of paramount importance. The more people at your event, the more revenue you can generate beyond ticket sales from the sales of merchandise, food and beverages, and, for those who operate their own facilities, parking.

There are, of course, many sports events where it is either impractical or even undesirable to sell tickets to spectators. Running events such as 5Ks, 10Ks, and mini-marathons, for example, derive much of their revenue from registration fees and sponsorships. A finish line seating or standing area might be created to accommodate financial contributors, city officials, and partner corporations, but access to such areas is usually a benefit of some form of association with the event, such as sponsorship, or provided as a form of VIP hospitality and is not usually sold to a ticket-buying public. (However, it is important to the perception of an event's success to ensure that these areas are filled.) Grassroots sports events, such as those staged by community youth leagues and other not-for-profit organizations, also generally do not charge for tickets. In their world, it is frequently more important to draw the greatest number of family members and spectators possible and to cover their expenses by selling merchandise, refreshments, journal advertising, and low-cost sponsorships.

CALCULATING THE GROSS POTENTIAL

For events that rely on admission income, the first step in projecting ticket revenues is to assess your inventory. If your sports event is being held in a stadium or arena, chances are good that there is a seating plan for a similar program held previously, with a section-by-section accounting of the precise number of seats available. As the playing surface configurations of various sports differ in shape and size, a facility's seating plan may vary widely by sport. New York's Madison Square Garden, for example, will seat 18,200 for hockey, 19,763 for basketball, and even more for boxing. The seating plans for most permanent sports and entertainment facilities feature natural and obvious divisions of desirability, most often defined by the relative height of the seating levels and the distance and orientation radiating from the center of the playing action (e.g., red line, 50-yard line, home plate, behind the basket). These divisions, also known as price breaks, provide a convenient way to offer the ticket-buying audience with different economic options. Generally, the closer a seat is to the action, the higher the price you can charge for a ticket.

If you have to provide a seating area where none normally exists—for example, in a convention center, on a field, in a parking lot, or on a city street—you should contact a reputable bleacher or seat rental company during the budgeting process. The rental company can measure the proposed site to determine the number of seating locations that can be installed so that your audience can enjoy the event in safety and comfort. If you must install temporary seating for which tickets will be sold, it is essential that a reliable seating plan be created before sales begin. As it is not usually practical to wait until the bleachers or chairs have been physically installed to first begin selling tickets, the organizer must depend on the expertise of the vendor, or his or her own experienced resources, to accurately define the seating plan. This is absolutely essential if tickets are sold on a reserved seat basis, as opposed to general admission. Reserved seat tickets entitle each purchaser to a specific location defined by a seat number. General admission ticket plans, sometimes also known as festival seating, allow the purchaser to sit in any location on a first-come, first-served basis.

Temporary seating areas can also be designed to have natural price breaks. Whether in permanent or temporary locations, it is always a good idea to ensure that price breaks are separated by some obvious landmark or barrier—different levels, sections separated by aisles, or rows separated by a concourse or transverse aisle. Otherwise, ticket buyers at the outer edge of a price break may be upset that someone sitting just a few feet immediately behind, or next to them, paid less for those tickets than they did.

Before entering a sum in the budget for ticket revenue, an organizer must first calculate the event's gross potential. To derive the gross potential, multiply the number of tickets within each price break by the price you wish to set for each. Figure 3-2 depicts a fictional event with 2350 seats broken into six price breaks. In this case, because the promoter believes that front-row seats will sell well at a premium price, he has created a special category for just this small number of seats. Promoters who embrace this philosophy should ensure that front-row seats—even without a visible break—actually offer a prestigious, unobstructed view of the event. The sidelines between the audience and the playing surface in some sports, such as football, can be crammed with officials, trainers, television cameramen, photographers, and unengaged players, so unless the seating in the front row is elevated above the shoulders of those individuals, patrons purchasing front-row seats are actually enjoying less of the event than those farther distant. In many cases, however, front-row seating for a live sports event can be so exciting that a price premium of 50 to 100 percent, or more, can be commanded.

Unless your event is a proven property that enjoys a consistent track record of selling out year after year, it is not recommended that the gross potential be the final number included in the budget as ticket revenue. Project the percentage of your inventory that you can expect to sell with a great de-

Seating Area	Inventory	Ticket Price	Potential
Front row	150	$50.00	$7,500
Lower seating, mid-arena	750	$35.00	$26,250
Lower seating, end zone	500	$25.00	$12,500
Upper level, mid-arena	500	$25.00	$12,500
Upper level, end zone	350	$17.50	$6,125
Standing room	100	$10.00	$1,000
Gross Potential	**2,350**		**$65,875**

Figure 3-2
Calculation of Gross Revenue Potential

gree of confidence. A good rule of thumb is 75 to 85 percent. If you are uncertain of selling at least 75 percent of your gross potential, you may have selected a facility that is too large for your event's audience. If you think that you can safely sell 80 percent of the gross potential, use that number on the ticket revenue line of your event budget. Referring to Figure 3-2, this would mean selling a minimum of 1,880 tickets (2,350 × 0.80) for a projected $52,700 ($65,875 × 0.80). Do not forget to deduct any applicable sales and amusement taxes and facilities use fees from the gross potential. As the organizer will never see any of those revenues, they are best deducted here. (There are no taxes or fees payable in this example.)

You will likely issue complimentary tickets to special guests, sponsors, and other business partners. If desired, you may also deduct "comps" from your ticket revenue line. I prefer to categorize complimentary tickets as expenses, so I deduct them like any other expense on the opposite side of the income statement. My philosophy is that issuing of comps is a cost of doing business, as opposed to a missed revenue opportunity. A comp seat is really sold, but instead of accepting cash, the event is deriving some other benefit. Comp tickets are usually provided to sponsors as a benefit of their association, and the event has accepted a sponsor's cash, product, or service somewhere else in the budget. Part of the cost in fulfilling a sponsorship agreement is providing the ticket, and therefore it is categorized as an expense. Other comps, for special guests, may lend an event more prestige, legitimacy, or even increased cooperation from local businesses, suppliers, and municipalities. They may also help to develop new business opportunities or future fans. Therefore, you will find "Complimentary Tickets" listed as an expense item in my event budgets, as opposed to having their value deducted from the "Ticket Revenue" line.

SETTING TICKET PRICES

Figure 3-2 also suggests that seats located in the middle, or along the long axis, of the arena are more desirable than those in the end zone for this event. As a result, there is a price break between mid-arena and end zone seating. This price break is also reflected in the upper level of the arena, where upper end zone seats are the second lowest priced. The promoter of this fictional event believes that the lower end zone and the upper mid-arena tickets are of similar desirability and has priced these sections equally so fans can select a mid-priced ticket in either section, according to their own preferences. Finally, the facility, with permission from the local fire marshal, has determined that a small number of patrons can be safely accommodated in standing-room locations. The promoter has scaled these tickets at the lowest possible price to encourage the attendance of die-hard fans who cannot otherwise afford tickets or who purchase tickets after all seating sections are sold out. As a general rule, event organizers should not offer standing room options unless approved by the facility and/or local fire marshal.

Sideline Story—Is Ticket Scaling Ancient History?

Historians tell us that admission to one of the oldest and most famous icons of sports facilities—the Roman Colosseum—was totally free. The emperor staged all manner of sporting events, including those infamous gladiator death matches, for free to maintain the support of the citizenry. Where you sat, however, was a function of class or office, with the commoners occupying the highest, most distant locations and government officials and visiting dignitaries enjoying the best views. As many as 50,000 spectators could attend each day of competition at the Colosseum courtesy of the Caesars. Perhaps the original multiuse arena, the Roman Colosseum remained a dominant sports and entertainment venue for more than 400 years.

The next step is to determine how much should you charge for tickets. Setting ticket prices can be very tricky, and mistakes can prove disastrous. If you set prices too high, it may prove difficult to sell your entire inventory of tickets. If you charge too little, you may have insufficient funds with which to pay your expenses or you may generate a smaller than otherwise possible net profit. The checklist in Figure 3-3 provides some useful questions, tips, and philosophies to be considered when pondering how much to charge for tickets.

PRICING FOR MULTIDAY EVENTS

If your event spans the course of more than a single day, your revenue opportunities and expense liabilities will increase accordingly. Many events, particularly tournaments, begin with "preliminaries," or early round matches, or may, in some cases, include events that are in some way subsidiary to the main event. Events that run for several days, resulting in quarterfinals, semifinals, and final matches, frequently increase their ticket prices with each succeeding round, presuming that the latter rounds are more exciting and attractive to the audience. The premium, as competition progresses, can range from 10 to 100 percent of the prices for the initial, preliminary rounds. Event organizers frequently sell tickets as a package deal that includes all rounds, also known as a "strip," or "subscription," before individual tickets go on sale to the general public. With this arrangement, the best seats are made available to the best customers, those who will attend the most matches. As a side benefit, it also creates a sense of urgency in the market among those interested in only one or two rounds. It is not unusual for a number of friends to decide to purchase a package together and then split the individual tickets to ensure they get the best seats before the opportunity is opened to single-date ticket

☐ Is this the first year for your event in this market? If it is not an annual event, how long ago was it last held? How well have tickets sold in prior years? If they have sold well and sold quickly, a modest increase in prices may be considered.

☐ How unique and prestigious is your event? Will fans pay a premium price to see or experience what you have to offer?

☐ What do similar events in your marketplace charge for admission? Do their tickets sell well at the prices they set? Realistically, will your event be perceived as more, or less, prestigious than those similar events?

☐ Are those similar events well established? Do their ticket buyers attend annually, thus sustaining a tradition of the price levels they have set? Unless your event is significantly more prestigious (i.e., includes more and better activities, features more marquee athletes, is a championship event, etc.), it is unlikely you will be able to charge more than the established prices. If your event is just breaking into the market, you may want to encourage sales by setting prices a little lower until your program becomes better known. (However, setting prices too low, as compared with those of similar programs, can also create the impression that the event is a vastly inferior experience.)

☐ Do you think the local economy and your most likely ticket buyers will support the event at the ticket prices you propose to set? Will your target audience react positively or negatively to the prices you propose?

☐ What time of year will you hold your event? How do people spend their time and money during that time of year in that market? Will you be competing with other events for attendance and revenues?

☐ Are there star athletes or performers scheduled to participate who will help you command a premium price for your ticket prices?

☐ Is your event venue sufficiently small to create a perceived demand for tickets? The larger the venue you have chosen, the greater the perception that buying tickets will be easy and that an immediate or timely purchase is not a matter of urgency. Go for a sellout in the early years of your event by selecting a venue that offers fewer seats than will be in demand. If you are able, let the perception build over the course of two or three years that those who wait until the day of the event to try to purchase tickets may be out of luck. Then, in subsequent years, you can either select a venue of greater size to accommodate more people or increase prices while demand is still outpacing supply. There is a secondary reason to limit the number of seats available. It may be preferable for your event to appear to be sold out at 5000 seats in a smaller venue, than appear to be two-thirds full with 6000 seats in a 9000-seat venue (assuming you can afford to look the other way in regard to the revenue that can be derived from the extra 1000 seats). Of course, if you can fill the larger venue, by all means go for it.

☐ Will the prices you select help the event meet its revenue requirements? You may have to adjust your thinking on prices—or expenses—after plugging all your numbers into your budget.

Figure 3-3
Sports Event Ticket Pricing: A Checklist for Decision Making

buyers. Usually, there is no discount for buying a strip of tickets. To the ticket buyer, the benefit derived is often simply receiving the best possible seating locations. But if your event is new, and you want to sell tickets more quickly, you can certainly consider a discounted package price just to get rid of inventory.

Packaging tickets also helps to sell tickets to the "weaker" events, those that may be perceived as less desirable to the public because of any number of factors, such as the day of the week (weekends naturally sell better than weekdays), time of day, location, familiarity of the event in the local market, marquee value of the athletes involved, relevance of a particular match or event, and so forth.

Sideline Story— Packaging NHL All-Star Weekend

NHL All-Star Weekend always includes at least two major arena events—NHL All-Star Saturday and the NHL All-Star Game. The first event is composed of the NHL YoungStars Game, a fast-moving exhibition match between emerging NHL talents and the NHL Super-Skills competition, a series of contests for the all-star players, including Fastest Skater, Hardest Shot, Accuracy Shooting, Puck Control, and two events designed to feature goaltending skills. Consumer research has shown that those who attend NHL All-Star Weekend consider Saturday's events to be as much, if not more, entertaining than the marquee game on the following day, but approximately two-thirds of the arena audience is composed of local ticket holders who are not so familiar with the program. For that reason, NHL All-Star Saturday and the NHL All-Star Game are sold as a two-event package; there is generally no option to purchase a ticket to only one of the two main events. The NHL All-Star Game sells out in every market in which it is played, and by packaging NHL All-Star Saturday with it, the latter, less well known event is ensured to sell out.

Not every arena event during NHL All-Star Weekend is packaged with All-Star Game tickets, however. In selected markets, an "open practice" featuring the all-star players is staged at a low (less than US$20) ticket price to raise money for charity and to provide access to the stars for fans who cannot purchase an All-Star Weekend package because of the unavailability of tickets or personal finances. This event is not included in the package in order to enable an entirely new group of up to 18,000 fans to enjoy an NHL All-Star event.

As discussed in Play 2, do not forget to consider the costs of local, state, and federal taxes, facilities fees, credit card commissions, group sales commissions, and electronic box office services when determining your ticket prices. The higher your ticket prices, the greater the expenses you will encounter in many of these variable cost categories.

Sponsorship and Advertising

Sponsorship has become a pervasive, persuasive, and necessary source of funding for sports events at all levels. If organizers had to rely only on ticket sales and the other revenue sources discussed in this chapter, the cost of most event tickets, already rising alarmingly fast, would have to be astronomical to cover the rapidly increasing costs of staging sports events. The support of sponsors, and the overt, sometimes obtrusive, manifestations of their participation, is generally accepted by ticket buyers as a natural component of today's event experience. Sidelines, scoreboards, and time clocks the world over are covered with sponsors' advertising messages. In North American professional sports, games are halted after whistles to stop the action for extended periods, long enough to allow broadcasters to air commercials. Ticket backs include promotional coupons or a sponsor advertisement. Even Little League baseball uniforms are emblazoned with the name of the team's primary sponsor. Plays 6 and 7 explore in detail how sports event organizers can join with sponsors to stage better events to their mutual benefit. In any case, the event organizer has to assess the degree of relevance and interest of the program to the corporate community and the dollars the event may generate. Sponsors evaluate sports events against their own sets of objectives and criteria, and the sponsorship revenue potential for each event will vary, depending on factors such as its size, scope, audience demographics, visibility, and cultural relevance. From grassroots handshake deals involving a few hundred dollars to the multimillion-dollar contracts negotiated with the Olympic Games and professional major league sports, the guiding principle is generally the same—the event must deliver certain benefits for a sponsor: sales opportunities both onsite and at its regular retail locations, exposure at the event and in the media, and goodwill, among others.

So how much should your budget project for sponsorship revenue? Corporate support for mature sports events can be the single most lucrative source of revenue for event organizers, but also the most elusive and potentially the most labor-intensive to capture. Success usually lies in a combination of the personal business contacts of the event promoter or agency, past event history, and the ability to design, communicate, and deliver clear, obvious, risk-free opportunities for the companies writing the checks. Set reasonable expectations and attainable revenue goals for your event, and get out into the sponsorship marketplace as early as possible, long before you have gone to market with ticket sales (because, among other reasons, top-level sponsors will want recognition on either the face or the back of the ticket).

Many first-time sports events overestimate their appeal and price their sponsorship packages beyond the amount a sensible company would spend. Because sponsorship revenues can provide the major source of funding for event planning and operations, overpricing can cause the entire program to fail even before the first ticket is sold. It is also far less risky to have the option of altering the size and budget of your event after it is determined that sponsorship revenue appears to fall short of expectations, before advertising has begun and tickets have been sold. Generally, if you have other sources of revenue, try not to weight your event budget to be significantly dependent on corporate support for a first-year sports event. If your objective is to generate a net profit, it is safest to plan to have sponsorship support provide all or most of the profit margin, assuming you are confident that ticket sales and other revenue streams can get you to at least a breakeven position. As your event becomes better established and its sponsorship track record becomes more predictable, you can start thinking about using more sponsor money to pay for expenses. Established events, especially those with multiyear sponsorship deals, however, can rely on past history to project sponsorship income. It is a good idea for event organizers with multiyear sponsors to keep a close eye on when the deals expire and take these expirations into account when preparing their revenue projections.

In many cases sports events require some amount of sponsorship capital to provide the cash for expenses that will be incurred before any other revenues are received. As you prepare the expense side of your budget, identify the costs you will encounter early in the planning process before tickets are sold. Unless you have other sources of capital to invest in planning and staging the event, the total of those costs may form your minimum sponsorship revenue requirement. (*Caution*: Keep in mind that using ticket revenues to pay for all of your pre-event expenses is also inherently risky, as the cancellation or postponement of an event may require you to have cash on hand to issue immediate refunds to ticket holders and, eventually, to sponsors. Event cancellation insurance can protect against some part of this risk; however, payment will not be immediate enough to satisfy ticket holders. See Play 14 for a more complete discussion of event insurance.)

Remember to include a line in your expense budget for "sponsorship fulfillment" whenever you expect to generate sponsor revenues. You should not expect simply to cash a check without providing service or value to your sponsor, and it will surely take some amount of money to do so. You may have accounted for some of your costs in your "complimentary tickets" line, but there will certainly be more expenses to consider, such as the costs of banners and signage, gifts, and advertising, among many others.

BUDGETING VALUE-IN-KIND (BARTER)

Sponsors and other business partners are increasingly asking sports event organizers to accept their products and services in lieu of, or in addition to, cash. This makes good sense to sponsors because it costs them far less to compensate your organization with their products or services, even when calculated at a wholesale value, than to pay you in cash. It can also move excess inventory out of their warehouses, and in cases where the products are used in view of the public, provide them with additional promotional value. This practice is variously known as accepting "value in kind" (VIK), barter, or contra, which, in tight economic times, becomes an increasingly attractive option for business partners.

Accepting VIK is most attractive to sports event organizers when it offsets an anticipated expense that would otherwise have been paid in cash. The partner company provides the required product in partial or total payment for receiving sponsor benefits, and the event organizer accepts these necessary items without expending cash. VIK can also be attractive when the products or services add value to an event without adding expenses to the budget.

Although no cash changes hands in pure VIK deals, it is wise to account for them as though cash was accepted and the cash was then used to purchase the products. In other words, if you estimate that your event will encounter $10,000 in gasoline expenses, and a sponsor oil company offers to provide you with $10,000 VIK, forecast the same $10,000 in gasoline expenses and $10,000 in sponsor revenue. In cases where a VIK deal adds value to an event without offsetting costs, you will ultimately "gross up" your budget, adding the retail cost of the product as a new, unbudgeted expense on one side of the ledger, and an unanticipated extra source of revenue on the other side. Even though these "value added" deals may improve the event experience or deliver better operational solutions to the organizer, they do not help you reduce anticipated expenses, nor do they help you reach your revenue goals.

Finally, be selective about agreeing to accept VIK deals. If a potential VIK deal would provide you with products or services that neither offset cash expenses nor add value to the event experience, it is probably not a worthwhile deal. To encourage companies seeking VIK deals to spend a little cash along with providing their products, you can create a sponsor category for purely VIK partners with fewer or reduced benefits, such as an "official supplier" designation, and offer full benefits and "sponsor" designation in return for an added amount of cash.

Prospective sponsors also occasionally offer "activation only" deals in lieu of providing cash or product. As further explored in Plays 6 and 7, activation can be loosely defined as those activities a partner company undertakes to support its sponsorship beyond the fees and expenses spent directly with the organizer. A pure activation deal may offer attractive advertising and promotional benefits to the event without payment of cash or VIK. A soft drink distributor, for example, might create a bottle cap promotion, or a quick-service restaurant a tray liner offer, each with a corresponding advertising campaign that would add significant exposure benefits to build attendance or ticket sales for the event. To some extent, these activities could reduce the amount of money originally set aside by the organizer for advertising and may be incredibly attractive from a promotional point of view. However, organizers must weigh these benefits against the fulfillment costs that will still be incurred, recognizing that an activation-only deal does not generally reduce the revenues required to meet the sponsorship goal in any way. (Although ideally, the savings realized by reducing forecast advertising expenses can cover these costs.) Such a deal will also prohibit the organizer from making a cash or VIK deal with any competitor of the activation partner. Cash will still be required for most events to remain viable, so an activation-only deal should represent only a portion of the value provided by the event's family of sponsors.

ADVERTISING

Although advertising and on-site marketing rights are usually a perquisite of sports event sponsorship deals, smaller sports events may offer limited advertising benefits that do not require the larger investments that define more comprehensive sponsor relationships. The ability to sell a limited amount of advertising that does not conflict with the rights of existing event sponsors can provide sports event organizers with an added revenue stream from the corporate community. Assuming you will reserve the best signage positions for sponsors who are paying top dollar, additional scoreboard and venue signage, video scoreboard commercials, entrance/exit sampling areas, and other venue-dependent advertising positions may be offered on a limited basis to corporate advertisers.

Before committing to specific advertising benefits, be sure to consult your facility lease. Your agreement with the event venue may preclude certain forms of added advertising or charge you a fee for its display. In most cases, existing advertising sold by the facility may not be covered or obstructed by event-specific signage, so organizers may have to create new positions for advertising, again with the advance approval of the venue.

Event organizers should also take care not to offer advertising benefits to a company in an industry category in which a relationship with a potential sponsor may later be available. Closing a sponsorship deal with a soft drink company after selling an advertising package to its competitor would be difficult to impossible. For this reason, most organizers sell nonsponsor advertising packages only late in the process, after it appears that sponsorship prospects have largely dried up.

Merchandise

The process of budgeting revenue for merchandise sales at sports events must blend realistic expectations, a familiarity with the audience, and your gut instincts. Merchandise first must be designed and purchased by the event organizer, incurring costs to create inventory, and then (it is hoped) resold to consumers with sufficient profit margin to cover all other expenses that may be involved in the transaction (e.g., shipping, labor/commissions, taxes, credit card fees, etc.). Thus, the net revenues projected for merchandise sales will subtract the "cost of goods sold" from the gross revenues the event organizer expects to realize.

Most professional sports stadium and arena facilities either provide in-house retail merchandising services or have entered into an exclusive partnership with a retail merchandise concessionaire to provide this capability. The terms of what the in-house retailer will be paid to sell your merchandise must be negotiated at the same time as the facility lease. Most often, the facility retailer will expect to sell event merchandise on a "consignment" basis, that is, it will sell your items without purchasing them from you first. At the end of the event the retailer will return the unsold inventory to you, along with payment for the items it sold according to a previously negotiated price schedule (e.g., 65 percent of the retail price), less agreed-upon deductions (e.g., taxes and credit card commissions). Facilities insist on this type of arrangement because it presents the least amount of risk to them. Creating event-related merchandise is risky for the same reason it is attractive to the ultimate purchaser, the fan—it is a souvenir of a specific time, place, and event, and once the event is over, its value drops precipitously. Therefore, not having to purchase event-related merchandise in advance is usually essential to third-party retailers.

If a sports event is well established, with a proven track record of high merchandise sales results, the organizer has more leverage in negotiating a better deal with the retailer, or one that shifts more of the risk to the merchandiser. In such cases, the organizer can designate "licensees," or exclusive suppliers, from whom the retailer can purchase approved event merchandise, and receive royalties on sales from the licensee, the merchandiser, or, to some degree, both. Organizers of proven, major events with a history of high merchandise sales volume may be able to negotiate a 10 to 15 percent share of sales in cases in which the in-house retailer purchases event-specific merchandise directly from a licensee, usually net of taxes and credit card commissions. Event organizers prefer this arrangement because now they incur no risk of unsold inventory remaining after the audience has departed.

Local amateur grassroots sports events in community sports facilities usually have the luxury of assigning their own volunteers and boosters to sell merchandise themselves, accepting only cash, and offering some combination of event-specific and organization-generic items. To minimize the likelihood of being stuck with excess, unsalable merchandise, volunteer organizers are well-advised to limit their acquisition of event-specific items (e.g., 2004 Long Island Hockey Association All-Star Game T-shirts), and weight their inventory toward organization-generic merchandise (e.g., Long Island Hockey Association caps). To reduce or eliminate any possibility of financial risk, grassroots organizations may want to consider attempting to have their merchandise donated by a local supplier in return for name or logo recognition on the item, or sponsored in part by a local business for similar recognition.

Regardless of how items are acquired or sold, the most common method of deriving a budget number for merchandise revenue is based on a per capita estimate of sales (also known as a "per cap"). The per cap is the amount of money the event organizer expects to realize in merchandise sales, on average, from each person at the event site. For professional sports events, the number of audience members is generally used, whereas grassroots events may include both audience members and the participating athletes who would also be likely to buy remembrances of the day. The projected per cap for the event will depend on the product mix being offered and the price ranges, as well as a judgment on the part of the organizer as to how desirable the merchandise will be to the attendees. Remember, it is not generally realistic to expect that every spectator will purchase an item, so organizers are advised to think conservatively when projecting the per cap for their events. To derive a merchandise revenue number for your event budget, simply multiply the per cap by the number of spectators and/or participants expected to attend. Figure 3-4 illustrates an example of how to derive a merchandise revenue projection utilizing a per cap estimation.

The example in Figure 3-4 shows a very conservative per cap. Established sports events can enjoy merchandise per caps in the range of $4.00 to $10.00

A. Per cap estimation	$ 0.75
B. Number of spectators expected	2,500
C. Projected gross revenue (A × B)	$1,875.00
D. Cost of merchandise sold	$950.00
E. Budgeted net merchandise revenue (C−D)	$925.00

Figure 3-4
Sample Sports Event Merchandise Revenue Calculation

and even more. As previously mentioned, per caps are also dependent on the product mix and the price points of the various items for sale. For such a determination, you must have an understanding of your audience. Will you have an upscale audience that will pay $50.00 to $70.00 for a sweatshirt, or is it composed of families who are more likely to buy a $20.00 T-shirt, a $15.00 cap, or an $8.00 ball? Alternatively, does the audience include a significant number of kids, whose parents will send them off to the merchandise stand by themselves with a $10.00 bill for souvenirs? Consider who is likely to be in the stands before determining what kind of merchandise you will offer, how much you need to acquire, and how large a per cap you want to work toward. Think, too, about whether the merchandiser can accept credit cards. Will attendees be expecting to purchase high-priced items and have brought enough cash?

Event programs or journals are special merchandise items from which you may derive revenue from more than one source. Most printed programs include advertising, the revenues from which should, ideally, offset or exceed the cost of their design and printing. If the organizer can completely cover the cost of the program or journal with advertising revenues, he or she may distribute the program free to all attendees without any further financial risk, providing very attractive exposure for advertisers. Alternatively, the item may be sold to produce an additional revenue stream, presuming the quality and content are attractive enough to potential purchasers.

Here are some more tips that can help to increase your merchandise sales potential. Consider negotiating a deal with one or more local retailers to help promote your event by selling your products on consignment (they will pay you only for what they sell and then return the rest of the items for full credit), or on another basis, in advance of game day. If your event will be staged in a public space where no retail merchandiser has exclusive rights, you may be able to keep costs down by recruiting a body of volunteers or using your own hourly staff to sell your merchandise. For a more professional presentation without the headaches of managing inventory and labor, you may consider contracting the merchandiser of the local arena or stadium or a large reputable sporting goods store. These vendors may have an interest in servicing your event on a mutually agreeable fee schedule and may also be able to provide point-of-sales kiosks, stands, tables, chairs, and other fixtures if they are not being used by their home facility or store during the same time period.

Concessions

Concession revenues comprise the net income from food and beverage items sold to spectators on the event site. As in the case of merchandise sales, most professional sports stadium and arena facilities either provide concession services or have entered into an exclusive partnership with a food and beverage concessionaire to provide this capability. In these venues, it is most common that event organizers will not be able to negotiate to receive any share of food and beverage sales, nor will they be able to vend any of their own products.

If you are fortunate enough to be hosting your event in a facility or public space where no such exclusivities exist, you may be able to engage a volunteer staff and provide your own products for sale. For grassroots, not-for-profit, and charitable organizations this may present an even greater opportunity to generate significant revenues by vending products donated by a retailer, distributor, or manufacturer. Event organizers can also negotiate deals with food vendors just as festivals and carnivals do, in which an event is guaranteed either a flat fee for each vendor authorized to be at the site or some mutually agreeable negotiated share of sales. Try to negotiate a 20 to 40 percent share of sales after expenses (such as labor and provisions), keeping in mind that the higher your percentage, the more expensive the food items will be for the fans. Think carefully about whether you will achieve greater net sales by taking a 20 percent share on a $4.00 hamburger or a 40 percent share on the same item at $6.00, but selling fewer of them.

If your event is in the position to either vend or arrange for others to vend food and beverage products, the same evaluation process used for merchandise, with respect to product mix, price points, and per caps, applies. Know your audience, and provide the kinds of refreshments they would enjoy, appropriate to the time of day, the time of year, and the age groups expected to be present. Sports events that promote healthy lifestyles should ensure that healthful refreshment options are also available and should always offer a selection of beverages.

Broadcasting

A small percentage of sports events are desirable enough to broadcasting programmers that they will devote time to covering them on radio or television, and an even smaller percentage so attractive that a broadcaster will agree to pay for the right to cover them. With the recent explosive growth of niche cable and digital programming services, there are more options for event organizers than ever on regional sports networks, local cable affiliates, and public access channels. Here is the simple challenge: It costs broadcasters a significant amount of money in labor, equipment, talent, and airtime to cover an event, so they have to be confident that they will be able to sell sufficient advertising, or resell the program to another broadcasting entity, for far more money than it will cost them to cover it. The value of their programming time is also a consideration. In other words, can they spend less and make more money by airing alternative programming? And that's before they start thinking about paying any fees to the organizer for broadcasting rights.

Even though relatively few sports events out of the thousands being staged generate broadcast opportunities, not to mention rights fees, the budget line for broadcasting rights is mentioned here so that you do not forget to include it if your event is fortunate enough to realize such potential. As in considering sponsor revenues, be sure to check your broadcasting agreement to determine what expenses, if any, you are expected to cover out of your part of the fee. Check your facility lease as well, to identify any costs, such as "broadcast origination fees" and labor expenses that may be payable to the venue, and determine whether the event or the broadcaster will be responsible for either.

There is one other option available to sports event organizers seeking to get their program on the air, most commonly known as a time-buy. Time-buys are generally risky for organizers who undertake them without having corporate sponsors ready to pay the bill. In a time-buy arrangement, an event organizer obtains an agreement with a broadcaster to actually purchase the time required to cover the event on its channel or network, generally costing in the range of tens, or even hundreds, of thousands of dollars. The event organizer is then responsible to sell the advertising time to generate the revenues that will cover the cost of the time-buy. The organizer is also likely to be responsible for the costs of actually producing the television program. If you pursue a time-buy, be sure to identify all of the expenses you will be expected to cover, and all of the advertising revenues you will require to cover these costs, before finalizing an agreement. More details on time-buys and other broadcasting issues are found in Play 13.

Tournament Fees

Grassroots tournaments most often do not charge admission for spectators, but may derive their income from registration or entry fees on a per-player or per-team basis. The process of fixing a fee for tournament participants is similar to determining ticket prices for a spectator event. Consider what similar tournaments charge participants, the prestige or rewards attached to your tournament as compared with others, and how many and what other tournaments you are competing against in the marketplace; there may be other relevant factors as well. Adapt the ticket-pricing checklist in this chapter to help structure your thinking. Tournaments also have an inventory limit. Organizers will need to structure their tournament brackets in advance of finalizing a revenue budget to determine how many teams or participants may be accommodated, given the time and facilities available, and therefore, their gross potential for registration or entry fees.

Most organized amateur competitors are familiar with the concept of paying fees to participate in tournaments. They know that it takes money to rent facilities, provide trophies and recognition, and manage a tournament. Tournament fees can vary from just a few dollars for individuals to hundreds of dollars for teams, and the organizer should survey the pricing structure of similar meets to be sure to include similar features. For example, do other tournaments in which the same athletes compete offer dormitory housing, meals or refreshments, merchandise, ground transportation, and other considerations, included in the registration fee? Can you provide features of the same value—or even greater?

Grants and Donations

Sports events staged by a not-for-profit organization or that aim to provide a community with significant "quality of life" benefits can further pursue their objectives by applying for and receiving grants in the form of cash or services from governmental, quasi-public, or corporate foundations or other charitable entities. Many state, county, and city sports foundations and commissions maintain budgets to assist events that bring economic or other benefits to a community, its local businesses, or its citizens. Generally, a lengthy application and review process is required, during which the grantor evaluates the event and its organizer according to formalized criteria, and after which the foundation determines whether the event will qualify. If an event does indeed meet these criteria, the grantor can determine how much funding it is willing to offer and specifically how the funds may be used to benefit the program. If you have sufficient lead time, as much as a year or more, investigate your area to discover organizations whose missions involve supporting and promoting events such as the one you are planning. Don't overlook charitable foundations managed by major corporations. They can make funds available to qualifying events from budgets that are totally separate from the sponsorships that are managed by the company's marketing department.

For events that travel or tour from year to year, it is best to apply for grants before awarding the event to a particular community. Most sports commissions and foundations are charged with the responsibility of attracting events to their areas and occasionally offer grants to compete more favorably against other candidate communities.

Tickets to some sports events are sold in the form of a donation. That is, the proceeds of ticket sales are used to fund a not-for-profit group's operations or to generate income for an important humanitarian cause. Invitations or direct mail pieces are often used to sell tickets to a qualified list of people whom the organizer believes are most likely to support the cause. Organizers of events of this type can increase the bottom line, with respect to charitable donations, by including a line on the response card that enables recipients who cannot attend to send a donation in lieu of a ticket purchase (e.g., "No, I cannot attend. Please accept my donation of $____ to help support programs for para-athletes.")

Miscellaneous Revenues

In addition to the most common and important sources of revenue for sports events already described, the additional possible opportunities available are as diverse as the types of events organizers can develop and where they may be staged. Areas of potential revenue may include site-specific opportunities such as parking and valet services, coat and bag checking, the sale of passes to VIP hospitality receptions, purchased admissions to postgame parties or other exclusive-access events, on-site fund-raising activities, and raffles and lotteries, to name just a few.

Sideline Story—The Party of the Year

The NHL All-Star Reception, held on the Saturday evening before the All-Star Game, is the hockey world's most prestigious party. Because of space and budget constraints, only a limited number of guests can be invited, who primarily include league sponsors, licensees, broadcasters, media personnel, alumni, and guests of NHL clubs. The event is the largest social event on the league's calendar and is considered the ultimate networking opportunity for businesses and executives who work in or market in cooperation with the sport of hockey. Corporate business partners are each allotted a specific number of tickets, as defined by their respective sponsor, broadcasting, and other agreements.

The popularity of the event has grown over the years to the extent that partners regularly desire significantly more tickets than they are allotted. Although tickets to this exclusive event are not sold publicly, a per-person price for additional party tickets has been derived *for partners only* to accommodate this demand and enable the organizer to cover the additional food and beverage costs, table and chair rentals, and décor expenses involved in expanding the invitation list, while remaining on-budget for the party.

Balancing the Books

Total your projected revenues and subtract your estimated expenses (including the ever-important contingency allowance line). Have you met your net income goal? If the first pass at constructing the event's budget falls short of your expectations, welcome to a very large, very nonexclusive club. It is now time to go back to your expense budget and adjust the numbers so the bottom line meets the event's financial goals. Or reexamine your ticket prices and other revenue assumptions. Have you been too conservative in projecting revenue or too liberal in projecting expenses? Sharpen your pencil and take another pass at balancing the budget.

Although we are now in the early years of the twenty-first century and able to enjoy the many advantages of user-friendly software and technologies, a source of constant amazement is the number of people who cannot navigate their way around an electronic spreadsheet. For sports event budgeting, a working knowledge of Microsoft Excel or a similar spreadsheet program is absolutely essential. Remember to set up your spreadsheet with formulas that automatically recalculate totals and subtotals as you make adjustments to the budget so that you can see the immediate effect of any single decision on the bottom line.

Figure 3-5 illustrates a small portion of an event budget, specifically the event ticket revenue section, prepared on a Microsoft Excel spreadsheet. The "Budget" column includes a formula that automatically multiplies the num-

---

XYZ Sports Event
Projected Ticket Revenues
(Preliminary draft—subject to change)

Ticket Revenue	#	Price	Budget
Front row	150	$50.00	$7,500.00
Lower seating, mid arena	750	$35.00	$26,250.00
Lower seating, end zone	500	$25.00	$12,500.00
Upper level, mid arena	500	$25.00	$12,500.00
Upper level, end zone	350	$17.50	$6,125.00
Standing room	100	$10.00	$1,000.00
Subtotals	2,350		$65,875.00
Ticket Revenue Deductions			
Sales tax (3%)			($1,976.25)
Facilities use fee ($1/ticket)			($2,350.00)
Net Ticket Revenues			$61,548.75

Figure 3-5
Sports Event Budget Worksheet Sample: Ticket Revenues

ber of tickets in the section by the price per ticket. The subtotal row includes a formula that automatically adds the columns containing the number of tickets per section, and the budget lines for the ticket sections, respectively. The number in the sales tax cell is a formula that multiplies the budget subtotal by 0.03 (representing 3 percent sales tax), and the number on the facilities usage fee line is derived from a formula multiplying the sum of the ticket inventory lines by $1.00 for each ticket.

Figure 3-6 shows the same spreadsheet segment with three adjustments subsequently made by the organizer. In this example, 25 lower seating section locations have been eliminated from inventory (commonly known as "killed" seats) because of obstructed views. The upper-level end zone was increased in price to $19.50, and 10 additional standing room ticket locations have been approved by the facility. The only changes made by the organizer to the spreadsheet are noted in the three shaded cells. The formulas inserted into each of the cells, as noted in the description of Figure 3-5, have automatically adjusted each cell, line, and column affected by these three revisions, eliminating the necessity of manually changing each line in the budget and reducing the inherent possibility of arithmetic errors by the organizer. It is also a good idea to include a footnote with the date and time of each revision, which can also be automatically stamped by the Microsoft Excel program.

The process of revising the budget must be accompanied by the greatest forethought and most realistic expectations. Increasing or decreasing budget

XYZ Sports Event
Projected Ticket Revenues
(Revised—January 6, 2004, 8:30 A.M.)

Ticket Revenue	#	Price	Budget
Front row	150	$50.00	$7,500.00
Lower seating, mid arena	725	$35.00	$25,375.00
Lower seating, end zone	500	$25.00	$12,500.00
Upper level, mid arena	500	$25.00	$12,500.00
Upper level, end zone	350	$19.50	$6,825.00
Standing room	110	$10.00	$1,100.00
Subtotals	2,335		$65,800.00
Ticket Revenue Deductions			
Sales tax (3%)			($1,974.00)
Facilities use fee ($1/ticket)			($2,335.00)
Net Ticket Revenues			$61,491.00

Figure 3-6
Sample Event Budget Worksheet Sample: Revised Ticket Revenues

lines or forecasts does not necessarily cause the actual expenses you will incur to go up or down. Make sure that revising the budget is not simply a case of moving numbers around to make the budget look better to you, as tempting as that may be. Make sure that you will actually be able to reduce or avoid costs that you remove from early drafts of the budget, and that you will really be able to generate the additional revenues you will need, before you finalize your spreadsheet. Once you set these numbers in stone, you will have to live with them.

Reforecasts

Once the budget has been finalized, new information will invariably show your budget to be less than a totally accurate prediction of actual revenues and expenses. As discussed in Play 2, you will discover that some budget lines are inadequate to cover both the actual expenses already incurred plus those still expected, others may suggest lower-than-expected revenues, and still others may point to probable areas of cost avoidance or extra cash. You will be better able to manage the finances of your event by reforecasting each budget line regularly. Rather than altering your finalized budget during this process, extend your electronic spreadsheet to include more columns, as illustrated in Figure 3-7.

In this depiction of a partial budget spreadsheet, the organizer has inserted an "Actual" column next to the finalized budget figures, showing the total of invoices received so far that are applicable to these expense lines. This will help her estimate the values in the next column, the "Forecast" for each line. The organizer believes that most areas appear to be on target, but sees that $985, almost all of her original estimate of $1000 in staff travel expenses, has already been paid. Knowing that she still has a few weeks until the event, she can safely assume that she will be over budget on this line and has forecast an overage of 50 percent, or $500. She similarly sees several areas of potential savings, in staff meals and site surveys, where less money than expected has been spent to date. She can see this immediately because she has set up her expense budget worksheet electronically, whereby the values in the "Variance" column are automatically calculated based on the difference between the budget and the forecast.

Her biggest problem area is in Location Office Equipment, where a significant overage is predicted. To make her post-event analysis easier, she has inserted a note as to why there was such a large difference between budgeted and forecasted expenses. Her automatic subtotals tell her exactly where she is—$1500 short of expectations. To stay on track financially, she will have to enact cost-savings measures that must reduce her forecast in other areas.

Expenses	Budget	Actual	Forecast	Variance	Notes
Event Operations					
Temporary staff	15,000	7,500	15,000	0	
Temporary staff expenses	4,500	2,238	4,500	0	
Volunteer staff expenses	3,500	0	3,500	0	
Staff travel expenses	1,000	985	1,500	(500)	
Staff meals or per diem	2,000	540	1,500	500	
Staff wardrobe/uniforms	2,500	1,200	2,500	0	
Site surveys/planning trips	1,500	450	1,000	500	
Pre-event planning meetings	500	200	500	0	
Event location office rent	5,000	2,500	5,000	0	
Event location office equipment	1,000	1,400	3,000	(2,000)	Higher copier costs
Event location office supplies	750	500	750	0	
Subtotal	**37,250**	**17,513**	**38,750**	**(1,500)**	

Figure 3-7
Sample Budget Reforecast

Again, it is important that she does not simply adjust the numbers, but instead take actions that will result in the numbers as adjusted.

The use of an electronic spreadsheet provides event organizers with maximum flexibility in designing a form that works best for their projects. Because many of the events I produce are held annually, I place some additional columns between the budget item descriptions and the current budget that show final line item figures from one or more of the previous years' events. By doing so, I can compare exactly what I spent in each budget line the year before, and the year before that. This is a very useful tool for events that take place in a different city each year, allowing me to predict expense increases or decreases from city to city, where such items as taxes, labor rates, hotel room rates, airfares, and many others can be expected to vary widely. For example, I am able to predict intuitively that hotel room rates for an event in Florida in January, at the height of the winter tourist season, will be significantly higher than those of an event held at about the same time a year before in St. Louis.

Use a budget form with column headings that work best for you and your event. But, at minimum, reforecast your budget and analyze your variances as regularly and frequently as you can. Expect surprises, but manage their effects by staying on top of your budget at all times and taking the actions necessary to stay on track.

Post-Play Analysis

Although there are many ways to generate the revenue needed to fund a sports event, there are many more ways to spend it. Examine your objectives to determine what you must target for your bottom line (a cost of doing business, an investment, break-even results, or profit), and find ways to maximize your revenue to get there. Major revenue streams include ticket sales, sponsorship, and merchandise and concessions, among others. Grassroots tournaments frequently charge a registration or entry fee instead of selling tickets to generate revenues. Broadcasting fees are generally available only to events of major importance to the viewing public, or to organizers who are willing and able to take on the financial exposure and labor-intensive effort of buying airtime and selling the advertising themselves.

Compare your projected revenues with expenses on an electronic spreadsheet, such as Microsoft Excel. Design a spreadsheet that works for your event, and be sure to include automatic formulas that maximize accuracy and efficiency. Above all, monitor all costs and revenues and reforecast the financial performance of your events on the most regular and frequent basis possible.

Coach's Clipboard

1. You are organizing an adult recreational softball tournament for employees of businesses in your area. You want to generate at least $1,000 for a local children's hospital. What revenue streams can you create to meet this objective? What kinds of expenses will reduce your net revenues? Set up a budget for this event on a Microsoft Excel or similar spreadsheet.

2. The alumni team from your local hockey club has reserved a rink containing 1500 seats and standing room for another 500 spectators. Create a financial model for an event that will maximize the revenue streams to cover event costs and generate a profit for the team's alumni association.

3. You have been asked to organize a youth football skills competition and have been given $2,500 in starting capital to develop the event and recruit participants. How will you use your seed money to generate enough revenue for an event you estimate will ultimately cost $10,000?

Soliciting and Selecting Host Cities and Venues

If you don't try to win you might as well hold the Olympics in somebody's backyard.

—JESSE OWENS, AMERICAN OLYMPIAN, 1913–1980

Winning sports events begin their path to glory by selecting hosts that will actively support and promote your program. An excited, enthusiastic host community and a cooperative, engaged host facility can dramatically increase a sports event's chances for success. In June 1995, the NHL Entry Draft was to be held in Winnipeg, Manitoba. Approximately seven weeks before the event was to be staged, the host team, the Winnipeg Jets, announced its intention to move its franchise to another city, and suddenly the event needed a new home—and fast. Within days, the city of Edmonton, Alberta, its storied Edmonton Oilers, and the Northlands Coliseum offered to serve as last-minute substitute hosts. With little more than 45 days to plan and promote an event that normally requires a year of preparation, the city, team, and arena mobilized to fill the stands with 12,000 enthusiastic fans. Working with motivated hosts can indeed produce winning results.

Sports event managers who take their properties to different cities, either annually or as part of a multi-stop seasonal tour, know well that organizing successful events is in large part dependent on developing, cultivating, and maintaining a series of strategic and functional partnerships in each market they visit. To forge an effective partnership, the parties involved—both hosts and organizers—must acquire an intimate understanding of the wants, needs, and interests of each other. When savvy sports event organizers set out to find a home for an event, they are careful to evaluate the extent to which they can count on the active support of the local government and various segments of the indigenous business community. Regional business groups essential to the success of sports events commonly include the hotel and restaurant industries, area newspapers, radio and television stations, and the membership of local chambers of commerce. Experienced organizers know that except for having to acquire necessary permits and observing community ordinances, managing an event without the active participation of local businesses and city government is far from impossible. There is no question, however, that one is virtually assured better results by engaging top regional officials and obtaining at least their philosophical investment in the event's success. Soliciting and obtaining their more active involvement can help to achieve even greater success.

Generally, every city that is in the market for hosting sports events will sing its own praises and offer glowing platitudes on how uniquely successful an event will be if awarded to its community. It is essential that event organizers get a clear and true sense ahead of time of how a community will embrace a program once the event has been awarded. All too often, ambivalence, a diminished sense of the event's importance, and even laziness begin to emerge after the deal is finalized. Some sports commissions, for example, are charged only with the responsibility of promoting and selling a city to event organizers. There are, of course, exceptions to the rule, but the service provided by many sports commissions disappear once the event is awarded. As their mission is fulfilled, they are already applying their limited resources to promoting their destinations to other potential business prospects. Sports commissions that remain involved to help identify and mobilize local resources are of great value to visiting event organizers and the business community, as their assistance can result in an even greater share of the budget being spent locally.

Although there is no way to guarantee how a community will eventually respond, the best way to engage its leaders' interest and support is to understand what *they* want to gain by hosting a sports event and then to demonstrate a sensitivity to their needs. Ask community leaders what they envision the event will achieve for their city, and respond with a plan that addresses what the event can reasonably deliver and how. Open a dialogue to determine how the community defines success and to provide it with insights on how you do too. If you want the community to invest in the success of your event, demonstrate your organization's commitment to invest in the success of the community.

What Host Cities Really Want from Sports Events

Sports events may be exciting, involving programs that improve a city's quality of life, but just like most event organizers, the local governments, business communities, and facilities that host events are most interested in generating revenue. Cities often undertake financial responsibility for many hidden costs when hosting events, including paying for the extra police, fire, and sanitation department members that may be assigned to provide for traffic flow, public safety, and the protection and maintenance of community assets. The local government may have helped to finance the community's sports facilities and may be paying interest on the debt it incurred in construction or renovation of its arena, stadium, or convention center.

Visiting sports events can help the local government offset these costs in both direct and indirect ways. Events that increase hotel occupancies generate revenue in sales taxes and, in many cities, special hotel taxes. These special taxes are usually the result of local legislation, earmarking the revenue generated by visiting guests for specific purposes, such as paying the debt service on airport improvements, a convention center, or other public buildings that attract business to a city or region. In addition, any event that brings visitors to area hotels also generates sales taxes on the meals they will consume in restaurants, on rental cars and taxis, and on significant direct spending in the local market by the organizer. The more hotel rooms your event can fill with athletes, staff, guests, and visitors—whether the event budget is paying for them or the guests are reaching into their own pockets is immaterial—the more a city will love you and the event you are organizing.

To gauge the interest of a potential host community, the first group to contact is the city's convention and visitors bureau (CVB), an organization dedicated to attracting business meetings, sports and entertainment events, and tourists to its hotel, resort, convention, meeting, and event facilities. The CVB often shares office space with the executive director of a sports commission or has an account representative on staff that specializes in attracting sports events. These individuals will be able to guide you to the best facilities, hotels, and hospitality sites to accommodate your sports event's needs.

The two factors that most frequently determine the degree to which a city will strive to attract an event, although there are others, are economic impact and its close cousin, hotel room occupancy generated by inbound visitors.

CVBs use the "room-night" as their unit of measure for hotel occupancy, defined as one room occupied for one night.

ECONOMIC IMPACT

As is its mandate, the CVB or sports commission will analyze the potential economic impact an event can be expected to generate based on information from the organizer, the results of which will determine how aggressively it will pursue and invest in a sports property. Economic impact is a measure of the dollars that will flow into, or out of, a region solely and specifically because of the presence of a particular event, be it a sports event, a convention, a political action, an act of legislation, or virtually any activity that generates new revenues or losses for the local economy.

Economic impact figures provided by event organizers have come under increasing media scrutiny in recent years, owing to their seemingly fantastic numbers. Georgia State University estimated the impact of Super Bowl XXXIV on Atlanta in 2000 at approximately $292 million, and in an economically challenged year, *Business Week* noted with disappointment that Super Bowl XXXVI in 2002 generated only an approximate $250 million for the city of New Orleans. The Bay Area Sports Organizing Committee (BASOC), the task force that had overseen the San Francisco Bay Area's bid for the 2012 Olympics, estimated in 2003 that the region would have enjoyed a total economic impact of $7.5 billion had it been awarded the summer games.

Although some quotes of economic impact may seem difficult to conceive, it is inarguable that the positive effect of sports events on a local economy can be impressive. Published estimates for Major League Baseball's All-Star Game have been pegged at approximately $60 million. The 2003 NBA All-Star Game brought an estimated $25 million to Atlanta, and the 2003 NHL All-Star Game $18 million for Broward County, Florida. But you don't have to be one of the "Big Four" professional North American sports leagues to provide the kind of value and economic impact to a city that makes a sports event a highly prized and hotly contested property. The Nashville Sports Council estimated the impact of the 1998 AAU Girls 12 and Under Basketball Tournament Championship at $800,000, and the 2002 Southeastern Conference (SEC) Women's Basketball Championships at $6 million. A 1995 study commissioned by Pittsburgh's Three Rivers Regatta estimated the event's impact at a whopping $59 million.

The cumulative effect of a concerted and continued effort to attract sports events to a region is even more impressive. Atlanta Sports Council and Chick-Fil-A Peach Bowl president Gary Stokan estimated that the city enjoyed a positive economic impact of almost $2 billion flowing from 71 major sports events between 1993 to 2002, *excluding* the 1996 Olympic Games. Stokan further asserted in an October 2003 presentation at the International Conference on Sports and Entertainment Business that $1.65 billion in additional economic impact was expected from the 51 events already planned between 2004 and 2012, with more on the way.

The Canadian Sports Tourism Alliance (CSTA), recognizing the value of being able to evaluate a credible and reliable measure of an event's economic impact, has developed a Sport Tourism Economic Assessment Model (STEAM). The on-line model is accessible to CSTA members by visiting its home page and clicking on the appropriate link at *www.canadiansporttourism.com*. By entering estimated values in a series of pull-down questionnaires, local and provincial governments can calculate and compare the impacts of various potential events on their regions based on a consistent set of criteria, including gross domestic product (the net value added by industries), wages, employment, taxes (e.g., income, sales, payroll, etc.), and arrive at a total gross economic impact figure. All events analyzed by the STEAM model generate results according to uniform guidelines, enabling member sports commissions and CVBs to make sound business decisions on the comparative desirability of hosting specific sports events in their communities.

Similarly estimating your event's economic impact can make it more salable and attractive to a city actively seeking to host sports events. Your organization may be best served by retaining an independent consultant, such as those who advertise regularly in trade publications like the *Sports Business Journal* and *Event Marketer* magazine, particularly if the objectivity and reliability of your figures is of particular political importance. If the limited resources of your organization require devising a more do-it-yourself estimate of economic impact, you can prepare one using the formula in Figure 4.1 and the instructions that follow.

A. Direct spending by organizer in market		_____
B. Participant/audience hotel room-nights	_____	
C. Participant/audience hotel room rate	_____	
D. Participant/audience hotel spending (B × C)		_____
E. # Participants/audience	_____	
F. # Days in market	_____	
G. Per diem spending estimate per participant/audience	_____	
H. Participant/audience per diem spending (E × F × G)		_____
I. Direct spending by sponsors/partners in market		_____
J. Other estimated spending		_____
K. Subtotal (A+D+H+I+J)		_____
L. Economic multiplier		2.25
M. Total Estimated Economic Impact (K × L)		_____

Figure 4-1
Preparation of an Economic Impact Analysis for a Sports Event

Examine the event's expense budget and determine, line by line, what portion of each category might be spent in the local market. Exclude expenses that are paid to vendors outside the region where the event will be held, as well as any overhead costs and payroll for event offices and staff that are not located in the community hosting the event. If your organization will spend additional funds in the community that are accounted for outside of event budget, or by other departments within your organization, be sure to include an estimate of their spending as well and enter the sum of all such expenses on line A.

Then calculate the number of hotel rooms that will be occupied by event participants or spectators but are not already accounted for on line A (i.e., those not paid for by the event budget). Multiply the number of rooms by the average number of nights they will be in use to determine the number of room-nights your event will generate. Enter this sum on line B. Rooms not paid for by the organizer should include estimates for inbound athletes, spectators, fans, sponsors, vendors, and others whose presence in the community is directly attributable to the event. The local sports commission or CVB will be most interested in the number of room-nights generated by the event, whether paid for by the event budget or by other visitors arriving specifically to attend or participate in the event. Enter the average hotel room rate per night, plus occupancy and sales taxes, gratuities, and any other fees, on line C. Multiply line B by line C and enter the result on line D.

Estimate the number of participants and spectators coming from outside the community, and enter this figure on line E. As this number refers to individuals, rather than traveling parties, it should be greater than the number of hotel rooms you expect the event to fill. Spectators from within the community are excluded from this number because they do not represent a flow of new money into the marketplace, and therefore they generate no additional economic impact. Estimate the average number of days, and fractions thereof, that you expect visitors to be in town for the event, and enter this on line F.

Next, enter an estimated "per diem" number on line G. A per diem is the amount of money you expect the participants and spectators to spend in the area on meals, refreshments, entertainment, and personal items such as laundry and other services. This amount can vary widely according to the demographics of your participating athletes, target audience, and the cost of living in the city in which the event is held. To get an idea of reasonable per diem rates in various communities in the United States and beyond, several government web sites maintain information used for recompensing their employees and vendors, including the General Services Administration at *www. gsa.gov*, for domestic rates, and the U.S. State Department at *www.state.gov*, for rates in cities outside the United States. Although these figures should be considered minimums if your guests are paying for all of their meals and expenses, the actual per diem rates for participants may be lower if the event provides a number of meals or receptions that have already been included in line A. You may also add to or subtract from the per diem rate if you think it does not adequately reflect the actual expenses you expect your inbound participants or spectators to encounter (e.g., a more upscale audience is very likely to spend more than an average federal employee on meals and entertainment). Multiply lines E, F, and G and enter the result on line H.

An event's sponsors, licensees, merchandisers, broadcast rights holders, vendors, and other stakeholders may host meals or receptions, purchase gifts, or stage events for their own guests during your event. Even though the event organizer does not manage these events or purchases, they are a direct result of the event's being staged in that market and therefore may be included in the economic impact analysis. Estimate the direct spending within the community of your various partners in each expense area, including staff they may need to house, the additional guests they may attract to hotels, and the direct spending on the ancillary events they may host, and enter your best judgment on line I.

There may be any number of other spending categories specific to your audience, the marketplace, or the event. Sports events held in resort or vacation destinations, for example, often result in extended stays by attendees, resort and/or greens fees, skiing and other recreational expenses, attraction admission fees, and non-event-specific souvenir purchases. These, plus other estimated expenses for participants and spectators, such as for local ground transportation (e.g., taxi and mass transportation, car rentals, gasoline, tolls, parking), local retail purchases, and any other reasonably imaginable spending, should be inserted on line J.

Add the expenses estimated on lines A, D, H, I, and J, and enter the sum on line K. This subtotal is the direct economic impact generated by your event. Many economists, however, consider the overall economic impact of an event to be greater than this direct spending sum. It is believed that every dollar spent, as previously described, stimulates the local economy and causes each new dollar to be spent again within the community, and more than once, so the final impact can actually be 2.25 to 2.50 times greater than the direct spending total. Applying the more conservative number, multiply the subtotal on line K by 2.25 and enter on line M. This quantity is the gross economic impact of your program, a key figure sought by host cities when considering whether to host a sports event.

ROOM-NIGHTS AND OTHER FACTORS

The importance of the hotel room-nights generated by sports events has been discussed as a component of the event's overall economic impact. For CVBs, it is often a key determinant, as room-nights are the lifeblood of their most influential and vocal constituents, members of the hotel industry. In the accommodations business, the quantity of room-nights generated by an event is like a fossil record left behind by an organizer. Past host hotels and CVBs share intelligence with potential future event hosts, so the truthfulness of an organizer's estimates will affect how the community will judge the reliability of every assertion that follows. Event organizers should therefore be candid—and careful—with the numbers they throw around during the bidding process.

Potential host cities may also combine their thirst for room-nights and economic impact with other business, political, quality-of-life, and/or promotional motivations in pursuing certain sports events. An event's time frame may fit what convention and visitors bureaus call an "opportunity period," a time of the year when hotel occupancy is otherwise low. A city may also wish to demonstrate to organizers of larger events its ability to host and handle smaller, but relevant, visible, and well-regarded sports events. City leaders may believe that media coverage of an event will help promote their city as a tourist destination or may invest in the event with extra city services to attract future corporate meetings, incentives, and conventions held by companies associated with the program. Or a particular sport may be very strong on the grassroots level in their region, and its ubiquity in the marketplace perceived as a portent for an event's likely success (thus generating a greater economic impact and publicity for the region).

Every community evaluates its interest in bidding on an event based on different criteria and the needs of the marketplace. According to Tara Green of the Dallas (Texas) Convention and Visitors Bureau, her city targets at least one "major" sports event per year and attempts to fill the rest of the calendar with as many "head and bed" events (high room-night generators) as possible. "A major event is one that brings national or international media exposure to the city as well as significant economic impact," says Green. "The 'head and bed' events are your amateur youth events. They fill up the hotels but don't bring any kind of media exposure. Those have as much importance to the hotel community as the major ones. They become a city's 'bread and butter,' so to speak," she adds.

Linda Shetina Logan, the executive director of the Greater Columbus (Ohio) Sports Commission, analyzes more than just an event's projected economic impact, hotel occupancy potential, exposure opportunities, and contributions to the region's quality of life. She researches the history of an event with past hosts, analyzes the availability of appropriate event facilities in the market, and tries to match the grassroots interest of the community with events up for bid. "The Ohio Valley Region of USA Volleyball has the largest membership in the country, thus we pursue many volleyball events," says Logan. "Not only to 'grow the game,' but to provide Ohio Valley members more opportunities to participate in marquee events, and for bragging rights. Because of our strong membership, we can host a first-class event." Columbus also favors hosting fencing events because of the strong leadership of Ohio State University's fencing coach Vladimir Nazlymov. "Athletes are moving to Columbus to train with him," says Logan. "U.S. Fencing is considering moving their training center to Columbus, so we are hosting more fencing events."

If U.S. Fencing does ultimately locate training facilities in Columbus, the community will enjoy significant, new long-term economic impact and full-time employment opportunities.

The USO Principle (see page 11) is hard at work uniting event organizers and host cities. Organizers are best served when they understand what a host city wants and expects from its involvement in a sports event. Do not be shy about trading a demonstrated willingness to assist a community in achieving their objectives in return for the city's understanding and support of your own. Ask the sports commission, the convention and visitors bureau, the office of the mayor, and other government officials what they would want your event to do for their community and constituents. Talk to local chambers of commerce and business associations to learn what the area's leaders of industry might hope to gain from the event. And consult with one or more public relations agencies on which past events have proved successful and why. Gain insights on why others may have gone wrong. By hearing the community's side of the story, you will at minimum make its members feel invested, listened to, and as though they are event insiders. At best, you will be able to design the event and its supporting promotions to help them achieve objectives they would be less likely to accomplish without your coming to town, thus gaining their support in return.

Figure 4-2 summarizes some of the most common reasons communities seek to host sports events, many of which have already been discussed. As may be seen, there are many motivations, ranging from the altruistic to the political, and their relative importance may differ from city to city based on local priorities. Keep in mind that any number of motives may be operating at the same time.

☐ To generate hotel room occupancy
☐ To stimulate the local economy (i.e., generate economic impact)
☐ To generate tax revenues
☐ To showcase new sports or athletic facilities to the community, media, and potential corporate sponsors
☐ To attract larger, or more newsworthy, events to their facilities or to the community
☐ To showcase the community or region to potential future visitors
☐ To attract professional teams and athletes to their premier facilities
☐ To position themselves as leaders among neighboring (sometimes rival) communities
☐ To revitalize an economically disadvantaged or newly developed part of the community
☐ To present a positive quality-of-life program to the community
☐ To present a high-profile event in a critical election year
☐ To demonstrate the need for improved sports facilities

Figure 4-2
Common Reasons Why Communities Host Sports Events

What Sports Events Really Want from Host Cities

Successful sports event organizers know that achieving their objectives is far easier with the support of local government and its constituent businesses, trade organizations, and citizens than without them. It is neither impossible, nor, unfortunately, unheard of, to stage an event in an ambivalent or even antagonistic marketplace, although doing so raises the possibility of great tribulations and rough roads ahead. For this reason, it is strongly suggested that event organizers get a clear understanding of the degree and nature of a community's support and, if at all feasible, to have as many relationships formalized in writing with letters of agreement and contracts as possible during the romance period, before an event is awarded. Although it is usually counterproductive and detrimental to an organizer's reputation to pursue legal remedies should a city government or business group renege on promises made during early discussions, it is less likely that such organizations will back away from promises, knowing that their assertions are in writing and their own reputations are on the line. Having these assurances in writing greatly reduces the potential for later misunderstandings.

Naturally, event organizers attempt to manage their budgets by avoiding whatever costs they can. Sometimes, the community can provide services, equipment, or other forms of support, on either a governmental or business level, that will help organizers spend their budget money more efficiently and enable them to expand and improve an event without encountering otherwise avoidable drains on expenses.

Sideline Story—Hometown Hosts— World-Class Event

The partnership between host cities and sports events can be so strong that it is hard to conceive of the events ever moving elsewhere. The city of Williamsport, Pennsylvania (30,706 population, 2000 census), is the birthplace of Little League Baseball and arguably the most popular grassroots sports event in the United States. What started as a statewide tournament in 1947 has grown to the 16-team Little League World Series, drawing more than 300,000 live spectators as well as millions of viewers on ABC and ESPN. Tickets to the event are free.

Spectators eight times outnumber the combined local population of Williamsport and the neighboring host borough of South

Williamsport. "Both communities roll out the red carpet for the Little League World Series," says Little League Baseball president Stephen Keener. "We are very fortunate to conduct a premier sports championship event in a small town atmosphere. It really is what gives this event its charm." The entire region mobilizes in preparation for event day. Fire, police, security, and medical emergency personnel of both communities assist with the operation of the event. The Chamber of Commerce's Tourism Department assists with housing, transportation, and the other needs of inbound visitors and hosts a hospitality day for corporate partners at the Williamsport Country Club. In the case of the Little League Baseball World Series, the hometown values of the organizer and the community are truly as one—their objectives are simply demonstrating a well-deserved pride and providing service to America's youth.

SOLICITING BIDS WITH A REQUEST FOR PROPOSAL

Sports event organizers owe it to both themselves and prospective hosts to clearly identify their needs and expectations from the start. This allows organizers to eliminate less serious contenders and permits the most interested communities to make the best impression. If a community knows how an organizer will make his or her decisions, it can communicate the salient benefits of awarding the event to its city and incorporate relevant commitments in their expressions of interest. The most effective way for organizers to begin the process of identifying the ideal host for a sports event is to generate a thoughtful and comprehensive bid document, or "Request for Proposal" (RFP). RFPs are also frequently used to qualify vendors who wish to bid on supplying or contributing products or services.

An effective RFP is not just an outline of the organizer's expectations. It is also a sales tool. Through this important document, the event organizer is formally asking the prospective host community to participate in ensuring the success of the program. The preparation of a winning bid will require a significant investment of time and energy by the community, so it is wise to present an event in the most exciting and enthusiastic, but genuine, terms. To illustrate, a sample RFP for a fictional event entitled the "Big Street Sports Tournament" may be found in Appendix 2. The components of this hypothetical RFP are based on the generalized format illustrated in Figure 4-3, and further described in the following paragraphs.

The RFP for an event should begin with an introduction that describes the event in general terms and communicates some of the advantages of hosting the event to the interested community. In the case of the Big Street Sports Tournament, the organizer points out that the event will attract fans and a family

> I. Introduction
> II. Event Description (including history and impacts)
> III. Event Schedule
> IV. Role of the Event Organizer
> V. Role of the Host City
> VI. Definition of the Ideal Event Site
> VII. Benefits to the Host City
> VIII. Sponsors and Marketing Rights
> IX. Response Format

Figure 4-3
Sports Event "Request for Proposal"
Components

audience from the surrounding region, as well as athletes who will travel to the area from across North America. The RFP further describes the most exciting elements of the event and notes that the program has been completely updated to capitalize on the growth of extreme sports.

The next section, "Event Description," should describe the event in more detail, providing estimates for the number of inbound athletes, guests, and fans, based on historical performance, if available. State whether the event will be ticketed or free and open to the public. In the case of this fictional event, the fact that the event is free to all was included in the first section because the organizer thought that it was a sufficiently significant sales point to be worthy of particular emphasis. If the event has a history of being held in other communities, their identities should be disclosed. The prospective host will almost certainly want to research the experiences of, and the event's impact on, host cities in the past. This research can be conducted via the Internet, newspaper accounts, and other third parties without several prospective cities inundating a single contact individual from a previous host with requests for information. It is best to provide individual contacts for past references only upon request for two reasons—first, so that only serious contenders, those who take time to call you to seek this information, will disturb your past contacts, and second, so that you know which cities are doing their due diligence and will most likely submit a bid. Resist the urge to overdramatize, embellish, or exaggerate past history in your RFP, as cities commonly share intelligence on events and you will want to protect the reputation of your organization, as well as your own, by providing truthful, candid, and accurate information. Include a paragraph at the end of the "Event Description" section that describes how the prospective host should respond, provides a deadline for submissions, and identifies a personal contact at your organization to whom questions may be directed.

The "Event Schedule" section that follows may contain as many details as the organizer is comfortable in providing, but at minimum should state a target date for the event and dates on which athletes, guests, and fans can be expected to arrive in and depart from the community. Operating hours, ancillary social and hospitality events (parties, receptions, fan events), and other details, if available, should also be included in this section.

The next section, the "Role of the Event Organizer," should list all of the responsibilities, both operational and financial, of the organization requesting proposals. Try to be as comprehensive as possible, as inadvertent omissions may be perceived as areas of responsibility that will fall to the community. It is also a good idea to provide background information and the qualifications of the event organizer in this section to reinforce the legitimacy of the program and the experience and reliability of its management.

If the event is supported by sponsors who have already secured exclusive rights to the program, it is essential that the organizer provide their identities in the RFP. This will let the prospective host city know that these sponsor categories are already occupied and may not be offered to competitors in the marketplace. As sponsors are added, you may list these in a separate attachment to the RFP that can be updated periodically.

Host communities should play a prominent and significant role in ensuring the success of sports events. The section entitled "Role of the Host City" should provide the details that those preparing proposals will need in order to determine their community's ability to accommodate and successfully compete for the event. It is likely that the individual or group formally applying for the event will know their community far better than the event organizer. Their familiarity with facilities, history of similar events, city ordinances, and other market-specific data allows them to provide the essential information that will make the selection process faster, more efficient, and less expensive for everyone involved.

As this is the section that will outline the minimum requirements for a successful bid, the organizer should provide and request as much detailed information as possible. Although the response to an RFP can take any form, I find it helpful to include a questionnaire at the end of the document that can be used by the reviewer as a uniform executive summary to make it easier to compare the first round of submissions. The majority of the bid requirements will often be found in the "Host City" section and may include requests for detailed information, including event site recommendations, venue floor plans and seating diagrams, hotel and local office space recommendations, proposed newspaper, radio, and television promotional partners, signage requirements, equipment and services available from the host city, sources of volunteer staffing, and other items of interest.

It is not uncommon for sports event organizers to request letters of support from various government officials, such as the mayor, governor, senators, congresspersons, or county commissioners, as well as representatives of the local sports commission, convention and visitors bureau, chamber of commerce, and other essential city partners. These letters will ensure that the highest offices in the region are aware of their constituents' interest and are committed to a successful event in their jurisdiction.

Because the availability of an appropriate event site is one of the most important factors in evaluating a bid submission, it is recommended that a section entitled "Definition of the Ideal Event Site" be included in the RFP. This section should define the minimum requirements and dimensions of the event site, seating configurations, locker room and other support areas, and the dates required by the organizer for loading in, setting up, conducting the event, and loading out. Any other requirement, definition, or disclosure specific to the event site, such as requests for information regarding signage restrictions, sponsor exclusivities, merchandise sales, or maximum rental fees, should also be included here.

Now that you have outlined what the community must do for you, it is time to let the community know what you can do for it in the "Benefits to the Host City" section. Your ability to deliver benefits to the city in exchange for its interest and participation in hosting your event is the city's indication that you will approach your relationship in a spirit of partnership. Outline all of the rights the community will enjoy as your partner, including the use of event logos, pre-event promotional exposure, on-site exposure, and special, exclusive opportunities, events, and marketing rights available only to the host city. If the host has the ability to sell local sponsorships, all of the specifics, including categories available for sale, pricing (if available), and the formula for revenue sharing between the organizer and the city, should be outlined in this section. Finally, describe precisely how you would like to receive the information you require in the section entitled "Response Format."

DISTRIBUTING YOUR RFP

One copy of the RFP should be sent to the senior decision maker in each community under consideration, most often the top official at the local convention and visitors bureau, or sports commission. Copies may also be sent to other stakeholders in the community upon the decision maker's request. If information for your event is best disseminated to a wide range of communities in the United States, contact the National Association of Sports Commissions (NASC), an outstanding resource of target organizations in more than 225 cities across the United States. The NASC website, at *www.sportscommissions.org*, offers a comprehensive roster of member organizations and key contacts. An organizer who wishes to make events available to NASC members on a bid selection basis may become a "Rights Holder" member for about US$100 per calendar year. Rights Holder members are entitled to post detailed information about their events on the NASC web site and may include brief electronic RFPs. Members are also entitled to receive the NASC newsletter containing valuable intelligence on the North American marketplace, as well as member-only rates on the organization's popular Sports Event

Symposium held each April, among other networking and professional development benefits. The National Association of Sports Commissions may be contacted via its web site, or at 2368 Victory Parkway, Suite 401, Cincinnati, OH 45206 (Tel: 513-281-3888; Fax: 513-281-1765).

Another excellent resource for intelligence on potential host cities, as well as for posting information on events seeking proposals, is *SportsTravel* magazine (*www.sportstravelnet.com*). This publication also hosts an annual networking, conference, and expo event called Travel, Events, and Management in Sports (TEAMS). *SportsTravel* magazine is available from Schneider Publishing Company, Inc., 11835 West Olympic Boulevard, 12th Floor, Los Angeles, CA 90064 (Tel: 310-577-3700; Fax: 310-577-3715).

Every RFP should contain realistic deadline dates for the submission and acceptance of proposals. Depending on the amount of information requested by the organizer, giving interested cities 60 to 90 days after receipt of an RFP is generally reasonable. The more work required of a prospective city (e.g., soliciting and holding hotel rooms and event venues and confirming points of agreement that may require acts of legislation), the more time should be allowed for its response. Seeking the right home for your event is like finding the right home for your family. It is a process best not rushed. Permit sufficient time for the community preparing the bid, as well as for analysis and evaluation after submission. Be sure to be as specific as possible in your request for all of the information you will require so that you are able to make the best decision for your event.

EVALUATING RESPONSES TO RFPs

Once the deadline has passed, it is time to begin evaluating and comparing the proposals you have received. Read and analyze each submission carefully and list salient points of comparison, the pros and cons offered by each city. You can set up another Microsoft Excel spreadsheet to compare responses to the questionnaire at a glance (see example in Appendix 3). Contrast the opportunities of the various markets, such as the size of the population, the size of the business base (the most likely universe of sponsors), and the degree of interest in your sport that might be expected of residents in the local community. Compare the event facilities that are available and the costs of doing business in each market. Consider the convenience and accessibility of each city to the athletes or participants who will travel to compete there. Review the letter of commitment included in each response, and evaluate the depth of support that each community will apply to your event in the form of facilities, services, labor, and equipment. If your event will be located outdoors, examine weather records for the targeted event dates in each region. If you are selling tickets, compare household income levels, amusement and sales tax rates, and other factors that might detract from gross revenues. Remember that the prices of tickets that would be deemed reasonable may vary greatly among the bidding cities. Analyze the gross potential in each city based on the venue being proposed, the expected ticket sales, and the ticket prices likely to be set market by market. Don't forget to deduct applicable taxes and payable facility usage fees.

The most important item to be included on your RFP response form is whether the applying city agrees to meet all of the specifications and requirements contained in the RFP. If the answer is "Yes," you can generally bank on an interested city following through. If the answer is "No," be sure to ask respondents to provide a complete list of any exceptions they wish to make to the bid specifications. Sometimes these exceptions are minor, or legally required by local ordinances, and may be worth overlooking if the rest of the bid is particularly strong. In other cases, they may be so significant that no further consideration of the bid is required and the city may be eliminated from contention. Agreeing to bid specifications, presuming they are reasonable, is certainly a major factor in a positive response to a host city proposal, but it is by no means the sole determinant. Figure 4-4 lists some of the most common reasons why cities are chosen by organizers to host sports events, the relative importance of each being dependent on the event's objectives and business model.

Some RFPs issued by event organizers require a bid fee that must accompany the submission of a proposal, or payment of a host fee upon being awarded the event. Bid fees are relatively rare and more commonly required for large, prestigious, and high-exposure events. They are sometimes necessary to offset the organizer's costs of having one or more of his or her event managers travel to the market to survey the proposed event sites and meet with prospective hosts, officials, and sponsors. Bid fees are not recommended for smaller, less well known events, as sports commissions and CVBs are less willing to invest their money chasing after an unknown quantity or a program that does not generate significant impact or exposure. Few events are awarded without a physical inspection of event facilities and other important resources such as hotels, convention centers, and other city infrastructure. If your event has not required a bid fee, select

☐ Availability of best facilities to stage an event
☐ Favorable rates on facility rentals, labor, and services in the local market
☐ Active support of the organizer's objectives by local government, businesses, and media
☐ Services and support beyond the minimum requirements of the RFP
☐ Demonstrable community experience in hosting successful sports events of similar size, scope, and structure
☐ Financial incentives or cost savings offered by local government, the facility, and local businesses beyond those required by the RFP
☐ No, or affordable, taxes on event revenues
☐ A natural local affinity, or fan base, for the sport

Figure 4-4
Common Reasons Why Communities Are Chosen to Host Sports Events

only the top two or three most attractive proposals and visit only those communities for a full evaluation. It is not unusual, nor unseemly, to request that the host city cover the cost of hotels and ground transportation during the site visit. Chances are that the CVB will be able to secure complimentary accommodations on behalf of the city to defray the costs of your survey.

If you represent an event with a successful track record or a totally new event that offers exceptionally good value for a prospective host city, you may encounter two or more responses that meet your minimum bid specifications exactly and are equally attractive in every other respect. All other things being equal, it is both acceptable and common practice to reapproach the two "finalists" with the response that their proposals are being viewed favorably and that there is an opportunity for them to offer additional incentives that further strengthen their bids. Rather than being forced to make an arbitrary

Sideline Story—Winning by Going Beyond the RFP

The bidding process for the 2004 National Hockey League All-Star Weekend involved as many as nine interested cities in the first round. After extensive analysis, pro forma budgeting, site visits, and meetings with city officials, two finalist cities emerged with almost identically attractive proposals. Each agreed to meet at least the minimum requirements of the RFP without exception, offered letters of support from highly placed government leaders, and possessed similar infrastructure characteristics with respect to air access, hotel quality and availability, and arena facilities. Both cities were informed of their status as finalists and encouraged to consider submitting additional information or further incentives to the organizer within 30 days. The City of Saint Paul, Minnesota, responded with a comprehensive plan to incorporate the NHL All-Star Weekend into the theme and promotional efforts of the Saint Paul Winter Carnival, the oldest and largest winter festival in the United States. In addition, the festival committed to moving its finale weekend to the same dates as the All-Star festivities to offer local fans, as well as arriving NHL guests, an unparalleled copromoted celebration of winter and the quintessential winter sport. Although this opportunity did not offer additional direct revenue potential to either party, it presented both the organizer and the community with outstanding possibilities to create unique, memorable impressions on all who would attend, as well as great potential for generating intriguing national news and business stories. As a result, the City of Saint Paul was selected as the host of the 2004 NHL All-Star Weekend.

decision between two or more equally competitive cities, the organizer can encourage prospective hosts to contribute more benefits to the event as a demonstration of their interest and commitment, so as to find a point of differentiation between them.

Despite the best of intentions on the part of prospective event sites, only one is typically selected to play host to an event. Cities and venues failing to be chosen have every right to inquire as to where their proposals fell short. Figure 4-5 lists some of the most common factors contributing to a city's elimination from the bidding process. Surprisingly, the most often encountered factor is an inability or unwillingness to meet the minimum requirements of the RFP. This does not mean that cities must adhere with blind obedience to the minimum requirements. Some RFPs may be more demanding than their prestige, economic impact, exposure potential, or other attendant benefits may warrant. Host cities should certainly evaluate the bid specifications of an RFP before simply agreeing to everything an event organizer requests. Prestigious, high-profile events can demand and receive more from a bidding city, and prospective hosts risk losing the opportunity to win the award by falling short of the minimum requirements. Developing and less prestigious events or event organizations may issue RFPs that are perfectly reasonable and well scaled for the benefits they offer prospective hosts, but reasonableness is always in the eyes of the beholder. Organizers may simply be testing the marketplace to see what cities will offer the best deal, even if the "minimum" requirements are not met by any who ultimately submit responses. Prospective host cities submitting proposals that do not meet the minimum specifications may still be considered by event organizers, particularly if no other community offers a superior deal. But cities that do not submit proposals at all can be assured that they will be passed over. As hockey great Wayne Gretzky once said, "You will miss 100 percent of the shots you never take."

☐ Failure to meet the minimum requirements of the RFP when other cities' competing bids agree to them
☐ Superior incentives offered by competing cities beyond the minimum requirements of the RFP
☐ Inadequate or poorly located event facilities
☐ Inadequate, inappropriate, or high-priced accommodations
☐ Excessive facility rental fees
☐ Comparatively high tax rates on ticket sales
☐ Comparatively high costs of doing business (e.g., hotel room rates, labor rates, etc.)
☐ Restrictions placed on the organizer regarding event sponsor recognition

---

Figure 4-5
Most Common Reasons Why Communities Are Eliminated from the Bidding Process

My advice to prospective host cities: Take your best shot, and offer the deal that best fits both the economic reality of your community and the importance of the event to your civic objectives. If the opportunity to stage a highly desirable event presents itself, and the bid specifications are commensurate to its attractiveness (and will therefore be equally attractive to other cities), by all means submit your best effort. However, if an event of lesser importance to the community comes knocking with unreasonable expectations, but still offers great opportunities (and does not charge a bid fee), you lose nothing but time by putting your best foot forward, even if it means falling a little short of the minimum bid specifications.

Once a host city has been selected, there may be great interest on the part of both parties to announce the award. It is wise to resist the temptation to circulate this information to the media and the public until some form of agreement is reached between the organizer and the host entity, as well as with any essential stakeholder whose participation is considered vital. Such stakeholders may include the actual event facility, hotels, or other local resources without which the deal would fall apart. A letter agreement or contract, as detailed as possible, should be drafted to confirm what the host has agreed to provide, as well as any important deadline dates pertaining to the disposition of any areas not yet confirmed. Failure to meet certain deadline dates may force unfavorable or unacceptable changes to the program or risk its viability in that market. Therefore, the organizer should include a stipulation allowing cancellation or postponement if the host parties fail to meet their obligations as outlined in the agreement. Frequently, the initial letter agreement with the host entity is relatively brief and attaches the RFP and proposal response form as appendixes. In these cases, the letter usually states that each requirement of the RFP is material to the agreement unless modified by the contract. Any additional points not addressed by the RFP, but agreed to between the parties during the evaluation process, should also be included. Without completing this important extra step, entities that were essential to the success of the bid can subsequently back away from promises they may have made before the announcement, and any leverage the organizer once had will vaporize as soon as the award becomes a matter of public record.

What Event Facilities Really Want from Sports Events

Like event organizers and the cities that pursue them, event facilities are most frequently interested in generating revenue. How they generate revenue, and how much they must generate, varies from one venue to the next and is also dependent on the ownership and management of the facility.

Event venues are of two general types—those that are privately owned and those that are public facilities. Privately owned event sites are generally in the business of making money. They aggressively pursue sports events that can contribute to their profitability and try to fill every available date on their schedules. The busier the facility, the more potentially lucrative to the event site an organizer must be to schedule an event's dates there. However, event facilities lose money every day they are empty, so sometimes an event with low profit potential looks better to a facility manager than no event at all (although facilities are likely to confirm dates for less profitable events late in the process, when it appears that nothing more profitable is likely to be scheduled).

Some recreation facilities that operate for public participation allocate time and space to special events for additional revenues and promotional exposure. Greg Fisher, event coordinator at Mount Snow Ski Resort in West Dover, Vermont, notes: "If someone comes to our department proposing holding an event at the mountain, the first thing we do is crunch the numbers. Will we make a profit, break even, or lose money?" How an event will affect other regularly scheduled facility operations is another key consideration. "We never want to disrupt or take away a highly used area, or an area that would disturb lodging guests and on-hill skiers or riders," adds Fisher.

A special subset of privately owned sports facilities are those run by colleges and universities. Some of these venues forgo the opportunity to host outside events completely to comply with the stipulations of their charters or the directives of their boards. Others may have criteria other than financial gain that they use in considering whether to host outside events. Although generating revenues is often mentioned as a reason why collegiate facilities consider hosting outside sports events, Paul Hogan, director of athletics, men's basketball coach, and professor of sports management at New Hampshire Technical Institute in Concord, New Hampshire, cites "exposure . . . getting . . . people on our campus and having a chance to converse about our facilities, programs, departments, and majors" as another key incentive. Steve Kampf, director of recreational services at State University of New York at Brockport, agrees that hosting certain sports events on campus can help promote recruitment efforts.

Public event facilities operate in a totally different and frequently more flexible marketplace. These venues may include convention centers, fairgrounds, municipal arenas and stadiums, outdoor playing fields, armories, parking lots, streets, and any other event site that is owned by the local community, state, or provincial authority. In some cases, and particularly commonplace in the arena or stadium business, a facility is owned by a local government entity and a management company is charged with the responsibility to rent space, sell event tickets, and manage its overall business. The facility's contract with the government may charge the management company with the responsibility of generating a minimum amount of revenue or profit. Its own corporate profitability is often tied to achieving or exceeding this minimum.

Facility management companies can be wonderful partners who enthusiastically embrace the philosophy of keeping their facilities utilized and filled with spectators, realizing revenues on some combination of rent, ticket sales participation, concessions, merchandise, and parking. They are not obligated to accept a deal with an event organizer that does not meet their corporate objectives, although the government/owner may occasionally exert some pressure to accept an event that may serve the community better than the management company's balance sheet, with a slightly less attractive financial deal. Although event facility managers are not generally in the business of sponsoring the programs staged in their buildings, their contracts may obligate them to accept a fixed number of "civic" events per year at the government's direction at no, or a reduced, rental cost.

Public facilities without an outside management entity may also be motivated by the need to generate revenue to pay down the debt of their construction or to fund day-to-day operations. Alternatively, the mission of a public facility may simply be to serve its community and may be satisfied with a nominal fee for the usage of space. Others, as is often the case with many convention centers, may be operated by the local CVB, and exist primarily to attract the booking of events that generate those "heads in beds." These facilities will trade hotel room-night guarantees in the local market against a reduced, or even a waived, rental fee. Still others, including nontraditional event sites such as streets, parking lots, abandoned runways, and other unorthodox venues, may be made available by the host city at no cost simply to contribute to the success of the event and the enjoyment of the community.

NEGOTIATING WITH SPORTS EVENT FACILITIES

If you are a sports event organizer, maintain a realistic image of the prestige your event carries as you negotiate with potential host facilities. A facility's history of hosting previous high-prestige events can have a significant impact on its ability to attract future events of equal or greater impact and magnitude. Therefore, the more prestigious an event, the more negotiating power accrues to the benefit of the organizer. Remember that the number of events that facilities may consider high-profile or high-prestige lessees is but a small fraction of the marketplace that such venues serve. As Dallas's Tara Green reminds us, there are countless other tournaments, meets, matches, and other contests and exhibitions that have great earning potential but are not globally significant events. There are many more events whose earning potential is questionable, speculative, or risky, and against which facilities managers must remain ever vigilant.

It will come as no surprise to facilities managers that sports event organizers want to get as much as they can for as little as they can spend. They will always seek the best possible rental rates, the highest possible percentage of the gross potential, and the greatest freedom in hiring third-party vendors and labor. Of course, event facilities are best served when they seek precisely the opposite—the highest possible rental rates, the highest percentage of the gross potential for themselves, and the ability to charge for as many additional items and services and as much labor as they are equipped to provide or arrange.

With the objectives of event organizers and those of the facilities in which they hold events at such polar extremes, negotiations for mutually agreeable terms can be long and arduous. The more prestigious, attractive, and potentially profitable an event appears, the more likely a facility will concede some portion of the rent or share of ticket revenues in favor of concluding a deal with the event organizer. The more speculative the event or the less familiar the promoter is to the venue, the more likely the facility will demand substantial guarantees against ticket sales and/or other revenues.

James Conrad, the chief legal officer for Orca Bay Sports and Entertainment, the managing entity of General Motors Place, an 18,000-seat arena in Vancouver, British Columbia, knows that the performance of an event organizer reflects directly on his facility. "We are more concerned because the public has invested through the prepurchase of tickets, and has an expectation of a professional production," says Conrad. "Most dates are taken by the big name international promotion companies, all of whom are familiar to us and with whom we have long-standing relationships." But less familiar, sometimes less sophisticated promoters, who may be local businesspeople with no sports event experience but with a vested interest in a particular event, often approach General Motors Place for dates. "The process of booking the building to these [kinds of] promoters tends to be a lengthy one. There is an opportunity to get to know the promoter and assess his capabilities and resources," says Conrad. "We follow up [with] references and do credit checks. If we determine to go forward with the date, the posting of nonrefundable deposits helps us establish bona fides. In some cases we might also ask for letters of credit or other forms of security." The nonrefundable deposit may represent 50 percent of the rental fee, plus 50 percent of the additional estimated costs for labor, equipment, and other in-house charges. Payment of these obligations in advance provides some degree of proof to the facility that the promoter is sufficiently capitalized and will not run out of money before event day. "Our License Agreement allows us to control the box office," Conrad adds. "The money on deposit through ticket sales serves as security for the facility against expenses."

Aside from cash deposits, another key determinant that event facilities use to evaluate the bona fides of an unfamiliar event promoter is the latter's ability to secure an acceptable liability insurance policy. Proof of insurance is also proof of insurability. That is, the facility can enjoy some sense of confidence if an event promoter is sufficiently capitalized to be able to purchase coverage for $2 million to $5 million in liability protection, under which the venue will be named as an additional insured. To facility managers, sports event organizers who are able to secure underwriters confident enough to write sizable liability policies may be sufficiently good risks with whom to enter into a lease.

What Sports Event Organizers Want from Event Facilities

Just as facilities seek to host profitable events managed by reputable, reliable organizers, so most organizers search for venues that will be interested, involved, and service-oriented partners in achieving success. Promoters want to work with facilities that actively participate in ensuring that their clients' events achieve their objectives and reach their attendance and profitability goals. "Arena management and staff know their building, its possibilities and limitations, and especially how to deal with real-time problems as they occur," says Major Indoor Soccer League vice president of marketing Steven Flatow. "Their support, or lack thereof, will literally make or break the event. It is hard to imagine having a successful event without a good working relationship with the venue."

Smart facilities managers know that an established event organizer will stage more events in the future and will want that organizer to consider their venues in subsequent years or for other programs. A building whose staff is pleasant, professional, competent, helpful, and involved will earn the loyalty of event organizers and establish a reputation within their circle of influence and opinion. For example, event directors want to know what to expect with respect to a facility's billable costs with a reasonable degree of accuracy. Hidden or undisclosed charges don't remain hidden for long after an event has concluded and frequently become subjects of contention during the settlement process.

Presuming the physical characteristics and costs are equal between two facilities, event organizers will look for flexibility in their ability to fulfill sponsorships and in the hiring of vendors and labor. In the facilities business, being forced to work with vendors and labor providers that have exclusive contracts with the venue generally means higher costs to the promoter. Facing no significant competition, there is little incentive for contractors enjoying exclusive rights in a facility to negotiate with organizers over rates or prices. Organizers will also look at what labor and equipment is included in the rental rate, as well as the costs they will have to incur to procure the people and equipment that are not included in the overall deal. They will also favor venues that can help them promote an event through E-mail, blast fax, and "snail mail" customer databases, in a facility's advertising programs, exterior signage, and marquees, and through publicity channels. These services may be provided by the venue at a cost, but being able to reach a prequalified group of potential ticket buyers is of great value to sports event promoters.

EVALUATING SPORTS EVENT FACILITIES

Many factors contribute to an organizer's final decision in facility selection. Some sports events—competitive diving, for instance—enjoy few options with respect to the types of facilities that can host a particular event. Venues with a diving pool are the only feasible choices. Other sports event organizers need only file for a permit with a community's parks and recreation department to reserve a pool, ball field, rink, or court. Those in search of a professionally operated events facility, whether a stadium, arena, exhibition hall, hotel ballroom, theater, or gymnasium, are advised to prepare a Facility Selection Survey Form such as the one in Appendix 4. This document can help you to organize your most pertinent requirements before examining facilities, ensure that you neglect no important detail during your inspection, and assist in the subsequent comparison of venues. Event facilities and how they do business may differ greatly from city to city or even within the same municipality. Once completed, the form will allow you to compare venues along uniform guidelines. The following paragraphs describe the process of completing the survey form in detail.

Every event will have some time requirement for loading in (the process of delivering, installing, and setting up the things you need to conduct the event) and loading out (the process of dismantling and removing your property and rented equipment from the facility). Load-ins range from a few hours to set up tables, chairs, and decorations for a simple sports awards dinner, to a week or more to build sets and tents, install playing surfaces, and decorate an event site for a major fan festival. Even a community ball field hosting a schedule of Little League games needs some "turnaround time" to remove the banners and equipment belonging to the previous team (load-out) and to install the banners, bats, and bases for the next one (load-in). You will need some understanding of what your event will require in terms of setup and dismantle times when checking on available dates with a potential host facility to ensure that sufficient time will be available. This is also important because your rental terms may increase as you hold a building for more load-in or load-out time than necessary. It is not uncommon, however, for the rental rates on these nonevent days to be offered at a cheaper per-day cost.

Determine whether your load-in and load-out can be accomplished during normal working hours to avoid overtime labor costs. Or will it be more cost-effective to pay for one day less in rent and absorb the overtime to move in and set up overnight? Regardless of cost, an organizer can ill afford to have too little time to set up an event and risk not being ready on event day. Nor can the organizer delay the next event moving in by booking too little time or labor to vacate the premises as scheduled in the lease. It is therefore essential that these requirements be evaluated before booking a venue.

Next, it is important to consider the number of tickets that may be sold at various levels of the facility. If the seating plan will define a single price for every ticket or a general admission policy (i.e., nonreserved seats offered on a first-to-arrive, first-to-enjoy basis), your planning will be made easy; your gross potential is calculated simply by multiplying the ticket price by the number of available tickets. Event facilities, however, usually offer the ability to create "price breaks" based on a particular section's distance from the playing surface or height off the event floor. Although it is not necessary to finalize a ticket price in each price break during the initial site selection survey, the facility director can provide you with sample price breaks, and the number of available seats per break, for your budget planning purposes. The Facility Selection Survey Form provides a place to record the name of the section (e.g., lower end zone, lower sidelines, mezzanine end zone, mezzanine sidelines, etc.) and the number of tickets available for sale in each area. It also offers planners an area to record whether the facility has any "build out" capability, that is, whether there are standing room areas for which tickets may be sold or other normally unutilized spaces that can be converted to safe, temporary seating, thus increasing the available inventory—and profit potential—beyond the standard seating manifest. Knowing this in advance can help organizers plan for the eventuality of selling out and then expanding the seating to accommodate more potential ticket buyers.

In addition to a rental rate paid to the facility, there may be additional charges against ticket sales, as discussed in Play 2. This information should also be recorded on the survey form, along with information on the merchandising and catering contacts, each of which may be managed by a facility's own staff or by an exclusive concessionaire hired to manage these businesses on behalf of the building. The terms quoted by these entities may be noted here. Any capability offered by the facility to assist in the promotion of ticket sales may be recorded as well.

From city to city, and even from venue to venue within a single community, the cost of labor can vary widely. If not analyzed and adequately planned for, facility labor can add a considerable burden to an event budget. Organizers of large, complex events should consider hiring or identifying an event operations specialist who can estimate the number of man-hours that will be required from each type of laborer, as listed in the Facility Selection Survey Form. Organizers without this capability can have the host facility provide an estimate of what will be required if it is given sufficient detail. Regardless, it will be easy to compare the hourly rates, fees, and markups of the various venues by completing this section. Even small differences in hourly labor rates can prove significant when the total number of man-hours to load-in, stage, and load-out an event are tabulated.

Before budgeting estimates for labor, it is important to confirm whether the facility has entered into exclusive relationships with a labor provider. In dealing with any vendor whose exclusivity is guaranteed by the facility, the organizer's ability to negotiate what are likely to be inflated rates and fees is severely limited. (As unpleasant as inflated rates can be, we have to understand this stakeholder's objective as well. An exclusive vendor must often pay a percentage of its sales to the facility and must therefore charge these higher rates to make a profit.)

Higher labor costs and restrictive work rules do not always indicate that these resources are unionized, however. Union labor is frequently more skilled and experienced in trade professions and may actually be preferable to nonunion workers with respect to familiarity with the facility and the appropriate safety procedures. Riggers and electricians, presuming the minimum crews and work rules required by the union local are not unreasonable (e.g., such as when time-and-a-half and double overtime rates take effect, break times, meal allowances, minimum number of workers per crew, minimum number of hours per call, etc.), can fall into this category. But, whether union or nonunion, event organizers need to know all of the charges associated with labor, including the hourly rate, benefit payments (e.g., accruals for health benefits, insurance, vacation, retirement, etc.) charged to the promoter, and any administrative markups imposed by the venue for managing the labor pool. Organizers of large events staged in a right-to-work state (i.e., a state in which an event can hire anyone it wants to perform work in certain capacities), or who have the potential to employ many union members to work a significant number of hours preparing for and executing an event, may be able to negotiate a more favorable rate with the business manager of the union local.

Many facilities, particularly those with exclusive labor contracts, charge more per man-hour than is received by the worker, wages and benefits combined. The venue may be charging an "administrative fee," a percentage of the labor costs booked through its management, which also represents some degree of profit margin. This practice provides a common revenue stream for the facility and is sometimes negotiable (depending on the overall profit potential of the event in other areas).

There are many sound reasons for a facility to enter into exclusive agreements with merchandisers and concessionaires and, to a lesser extent, with labor. The venue usually receives a percentage of merchandise, food, and beverages sold by these external entities. In addition, it takes no risk on the costs of inventory, equipment, or human resources. This is one reason why the costs for food and merchandise is significantly higher inside the facility than outside. (This is only a contributing factor, of course. Having a monopoly on sales also makes captive consumers of people inside the venue.)

The next two sections of the Facility Selection Survey Form provide organizers with space to record observations about some of the physical characteristics of the building, as well as the equipment that may be available either as part of the lease rate or at some additional cost. Are there sufficient locker and dressing room facilities of the size required, and are they in good repair? Are the marshaling areas (back-of-house staging areas that are hidden from public view and used to hold sets, props, equipment, and people before they are needed) sufficiently large, safely lit, and accessible to the playing sur-

Sideline Story—The Costs of Exclusivity

Exclusive vendor agreements do not just pose enormous challenges for event organizers, they can also create ill will toward vendors who have exclusive contracts in one facility and are nonexclusive in others. The NHL All-Star FANtasy, a large indoor fan festival, was introduced in Boston at the 1996 NHL All-Star Weekend at a convention facility that required the use of an exclusive third-party provider for all hourly labor. The rates quoted by the exclusive labor provider were in some cases 50 percent higher than the standard rate in other local venues where competitors vie for the ability to serve as contractor. Overtime rates were billed at an even more astronomical rate. The difference in labor costs between those in the original expense budget based on standard rates available throughout the city, and the costs of using the exclusive provider, exceeded six figures. With no other venue available for the dates required, the league and its event producer pursued fruitless negotiations with the labor provider to significantly reduce the costs of hourly labor at the facility. The provider also maintained offices throughout North America to service events on a nonexclusive basis as well.

There were two key results to this painful and costly exercise. First, sites with exclusive third-party labor providers would no longer be considered by the organization for future events. Second, the national labor provider that refused to lower its rates to more competitive levels has not since been considered for subsequent activities in any other location.

face? Are they filled with storage items belonging to the facility, and, if so, will they be cleared by building management without the event incurring additional labor, shipping, or storage costs? Are there lockable and unlocked storage areas in the facility that may be used by the organizer, and how far in advance of the event may they be used? Are there score clocks, timing equipment, and other equipment required for competition (e.g., nets, boards, baskets, etc.) in the facility's possession that may be used or modified for the event without additional charge, or will the organizer have to purchase or rent and then install these items? Are there existing facilities for the media expected to attend, such as a press box, media seating areas, press conference facilities, workrooms, darkrooms, and/or a press lounge? How much parking is located within reasonably close proximity to the facility, and how many complimentary spaces for staff can be included in the rental deal?

Does the facility possess a quantity of tables, chairs, and staging risers that may be used by the organizer, and will they add cost to the budget? How many phone lines can the organizer rent from the building, and what is the cost to install the phones and data lines for Internet access? (These costs vary wildly and can be considerable.) Does the building have a forklift or other equipment for material handling that may be used by the organizer's paid hourly labor during load-in and load-out, or will the use of such equipment incur additional costs? If marshaling or storage areas must be temporarily divided to create additional operational or hospitality facilities, does the building have pipe-and-drape units to lend or rent, and in what condition are they? Are there crowd control barriers available for the organizer's use, or must they be rented? Many other venue-related questions should be answered in these sections, including those that are specific to the particular sport or event that will be utilizing the facility.

The presence or absence of sponsor exclusivities may figure prominently in evaluating the best venue for a sports event. Most every sports facility now has rules as to what kinds of event sponsor signage will be permitted and precisely where such signage may be exhibited. In most venues, the brand of beverages served (or "poured") is governed by an existing building sponsorship deal and, in the case of products containing alcohol, by the local liquor authority. The issues relating to sponsorship, which are many and varied, are discussed in detail in Play 6 and 7. For purposes of the site selection process, Figure 4-6 provides a checklist of some of the sponsor-related questions that should be asked.

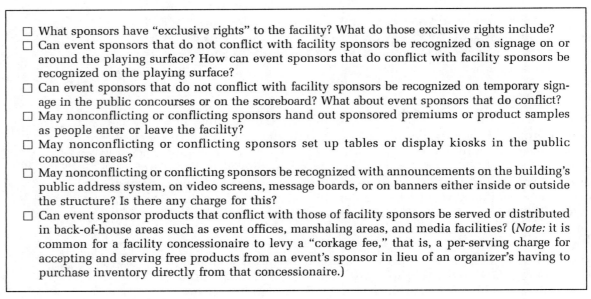

□ What sponsors have "exclusive rights" to the facility? What do those exclusive rights include?
□ Can event sponsors that do not conflict with facility sponsors be recognized on signage on or around the playing surface? How can event sponsors that do conflict with facility sponsors be recognized on the playing surface?
□ Can event sponsors that do not conflict with facility sponsors be recognized on temporary signage in the public concourses or on the scoreboard? What about event sponsors that do conflict?
□ May nonconflicting or conflicting sponsors hand out sponsored premiums or product samples as people enter or leave the facility?
□ May nonconflicting or conflicting sponsors set up tables or display kiosks in the public concourse areas?
□ May nonconflicting or conflicting sponsors be recognized with announcements on the building's public address system, on video screens, message boards, or on banners either inside or outside the structure? Is there any charge for this?
□ Can event sponsor products that conflict with those of facility sponsors be served or distributed in back-of-house areas such as event offices, marshaling areas, and media facilities? (*Note:* it is common for a facility concessionaire to levy a "corkage fee," that is, a per-serving charge for accepting and serving free products from an event's sponsor in lieu of an organizer's having to purchase inventory directly from that concessionaire.)

Figure 4-6
Sponsor Exclusivity Checklist

Finally, examine the facility for areas in which hospitality functions may be staged to entertain VIP guests, athletes, sponsors, and others. Are there restaurants, cafeterias, cafes, or lounges that can be sectioned off for private use while the venue is open to the public? Are there meeting rooms, conference rooms, or boardrooms easily accessible to audience areas that can hold smaller functions? Can part of the exterior grounds be reserved for tented functions? (*Caution:* Installing tents can be a very expensive option.) Is the provision of catering in these areas exclusive to the building concessionaire?

Obviously, the needs of every event and organizer will differ greatly. The Facility Selection Survey Form can be modified to include additional sections for any information pertinent to the specific project being planned to ensure that the same questions are asked of every venue under consideration. The answers can then be compared and analyzed fairly and with relative ease.

Selecting a Facility

Usually, awarding a sports event to a city is coincident with the confirmation of a facility in which to hold it. Event organizers will weigh multiple factors in reaching a decision, including the costs of operating the event in each building surveyed, whether the capacity of the facility is appropriate to the event, the reputation and geographic desirability of the venue (e.g., is the facility one that local ticket buyers would associate with a sports event?), and each party's flexibility with respect to protecting each other's sponsor relationships. Once a tentative decision has been reached, the event organizer is forwarded a lease, or license agreement, that lists all of the agreed-to terms of the relationship. Because facility license agreements are considerably detailed, it is not unusual for a host of new issues to emerge that had not been discussed during initial negotiations. This is typically only a minor inconvenience, and it is better for such issues to surface and be settled during the negotiating process rather than at a time closer to the event. It is almost certain that significant "boiler plate" language, that is, legal requirements for insurance, indemnifications, force majeure conditions (cancellations due to various unforeseen disasters or conditions that would make moving forward with an event impossible), and other protections for the venue will not previously have been discussed in detail. It is essential for event promoters to have qualified legal counsel review and propose redrafts of these points to ensure that they are as well and justly protected as the facility. Although the nature of the facility license agreement differs from venue to venue, as well as from event to event, a generalized sample facility license agreement is presented in Appendix 5.

Once the facility agreement has been signed and agreements are substantially in progress with other stakeholders without whom the event cannot be staged (e.g., the local convention bureau and hoteliers), it is usually safe to announce the dates and the host of the event. Depending on the economic, political, and cultural significance of the event to local community, the parties involved may stage a press conference or simply distribute an announcement press release to inform members of the media, and through them, the public. Now it is time to begin the production planning process and building the team required to stage the newly awarded event.

Post-Play Analysis

A spirit of partnership between host cities, facilities, and event organizers is essential to success for all involved. It is incumbent upon all parties to develop an understanding of each other's wants and needs to achieve this level of cooperation. Host cities for events that travel or tour are most interested in the economic impact sports events offer, including how much in tax revenues and how many hotel room-nights they will generate. They also pursue events for political, cultural, and emotional reasons peculiar to each respective market. Event promoters communicate their wants and needs through the development and dissemination of Requests for Proposal, documents that identify the minimum requirements for a community's or facility's bid to host an event to achieve success. Event facilities are generally interested in generating revenue, whereas event organizers are searching for the best and most cost-effective site to stage an event. A Facility Selection Survey Form is an effective tool for organizing, comparing, and analyzing information derived from surveys of each interested venue.

Coach's Clipboard

1. You are the organizer of a regional high school track-and-field event for which there are limited facilities in your home city. Assuming the costs of staging the event in your local arena are too great and that the winter season during which it is held makes holding an outdoor event inadvisable, what venues in your city that are not traditionally associated with track-and-field events might be investigated and approached to host the event?

2. Create an RFP for a statewide college ice hockey tournament that will attract teams from 16 universities to a single city yet to be selected. Include requirements for a sports memorabilia collector's show envisioned to run concurrently during the tournament. Develop an economic impact estimate for the tournament and show.

3. The best facility available for your minor league all-star game is sponsored by a soft drink company that directly competes with one of your most important sponsors. Both your organization and the management of the facility want to stage the event there, but also want to protect their respective sponsors' rights. How do the two parties work to resolve the conflict? (Consider this exercise again after reading Plays 6 and 7.)

PLAY 5

Starting the Clock on the Sports Event Planning Process

Winning can be defined as the science of being totally prepared.

—GEORGE ALLEN, NFL HALL OF FAME COACH

Professional and college sports teams prepare themselves for the pursuit of a championship season by opening training camps and conducting exhibition games to both identify and fortify areas of competitive weakness and take best advantage of their on-field strengths. Of course, the process of drafting the blueprint for the construction of a winning team does not begin the moment the first player reports to the training facility. The coaching staff spends the off-season evaluating the players on the team roster and reviewing scouting reports to identify positions that should be filled or reinforced, as well as prospective rookies to invite to camp. Scouts must have attended a variety of games during the previous season to assess the abilities and potential of players on other teams and in lower-level leagues. Scouts also attend the games of a team's upcoming opponents throughout the season to identify their rivals' strengths and weaknesses and help the coach prepare the system of plays that will best position the team for victory. Careful planning and adequate time are required to prepare a team for an important game, within a strategic framework of interlocking deadlines and milestone dates. For coaches and players, far more time is spent preparing for a game than actually playing it.

As a sports event manager, you too will spend vastly more time planning than actually executing your events. By this time, you have defined what you want your event to accomplish and what it will cost to achieve your objectives. You have set a strategy for how you intend to finance the event and determined the optimal place to stage it. Now, it's time to begin the planning in earnest and putting the right organization together that will make it all happen. Sports event organizers must proceed down both paths at once, because detailing the event management process will inevitably reveal how much and what kind of help you will require and when you will need it. Although this chapter explores these efforts independently, the functions of planning and building a team to execute the chosen strategies and tactics are inextricably linked.

An excellent resource worth consulting in regard to the planning process applies many of the techniques of industrial project management to the world of corporate events. *Corporate Event Project Management*, by William O'Toole and Phyllis Mikolaitis (John Wiley & Sons, 2002), also proposes that many systems and decisions made in the planning process are interwoven and must be broken down into tasks and subtasks. These authors offer detailed insights into the "Project Management Process," which parallels many of the concepts covered in the early chapters of this *Playbook*. Their technique separates the planning process into three key phases: (1) definition of the project, (2) the scope of work, and (3) a work breakdown structure, further subdivided into budgeting, scheduling, and risk analysis. The first half of this chapter explores the methodology of identifying management tasks, analyzing those tasks to discover all of the decisions and activities that must precede them, and setting a system of deadlines that will keep the project on schedule.

Compile a Critical Dates Calendar

Many sports event managers begin the sports event management process by compiling all of the major component parts required to stage an event and assigning deadline dates to each task's completion. A critical dates calendar, or production schedule, is an efficient means of organizing all of these functions in a chronological order that begins to define the many paths of work required and checks the validity of each deadline against a structure of internal logic. In other words, by listing all of the primary tasks that must be completed, the event director can assign deadline dates that logically fit together, consistent with all the deadline dates of other activities that must precede or follow them.

This process, which I call *critical task analysis*, will ultimately help you determine the optimal dates by which to complete specific aspects of the event planning process. When complete, the calendar will include myriad details and deadlines and may appear so comprehensive as to seem daunting. The more detail devoted to assigning the completion of tasks and subtasks to meet realistic deadlines, however, the more effective the organizer will be in keeping the event planning process on schedule. Constructing the calendar starts with dividing each operational goal into its component subtasks that must first be completed, through the application of critical task analysis. Start with the end point of each process and when that work must be concluded. Then work your way back through all of the many steps and decisions (subtasks) that must be taken or made to complete the task.

Consider the seemingly simple, elementary task of inviting VIP guests to attend a sports event. Intuitively, we know that we will have to send invitations and receive responses. However, as Figure 5-1 illustrates, there are more than 20 other decisions that must be made, actions that must be taken, and procedures that must be determined before the first invitation can be mailed. Every indented passage in the figure denotes a subtask or activity that must be considered and completed before plans for the preceding task can be finalized.

LIST ELEMENTARY TASKS

The best method of creating a comprehensive critical dates calendar is to begin by developing a list of elementary tasks. In Figure 5-1, the elementary task is "Invite VIP guests to the event." The process of identifying the elementary tasks required to manage an event should start with a thorough examination of the tactics to be applied to meeting the program's objectives, as described in Play 1. Inviting VIP guests, noted in the preceding example, may fulfill a tactic devised to realize the strategic objective of raising the profile of the event, or it may be the event director's preferred way of thanking the influential individuals who contributed in some way to the execution of the event. Examine all of the event's strategies and tactics to ensure that a structure of elementary tasks to achieve them is in place. Then apply the process of critical task analysis to "explode" them (take them apart) to expose all of the details required to make them work and succeed.

Elementary tasks are broken into "key activities," in this case, "Design," "Print," and "Send" invitations. The successful execution of these key activities is then dependent on the "supportive tasks" and "decision points" that must precede each of them, and which may be further subdivided to reveal additional required supportive tasks and decision points.

Let's go back to the fictional playoff pre-game fan festival to which we applied the P-A-P-E-R Test in Figure 1-5 and develop some elementary tasks. The primary objective of the event was to reward loyal fans with a street festival

Elementary Task: *Invite VIP guests to the event*
Process: Invitations sent to VIPs, and RSVPs received

- Design invitations (key activity)
  - Allocate printing and postage budget
  - Finalize logo to include in design
  - Identify the events and activities to which the VIPs are being invited
  - Determine RSVP deadline date
    - Determine when seating assignments must be made
    - Determine when unclaimed VIP tickets must be released to the public
  - Identify the RSVP mechanism (e.g., phone, E-mail, mail, Internet)
    - Determine how and where responding guests will pick up their tickets
  - Determine the information that must be included with the invitations (e.g., hotel, transportation)
    - Finalize hotel/vendor contracts and booking procedures
  - Determine how many VIPs can be accommodated
    - Allocate complimentary seating for VIPs and remove tickets from public sale
    - Make sure that the lost revenue from comp seating can be accommodated by the budget
  - Determine by what date invitations must be printed
- Print invitations
  - Identify number of invitations required
    - Generate and finalize the mailing list
      - Determine which VIPs should be invited (e.g., city officials, local businesses, celebrities, athlete families, media)
  - Determine time required for design, typesetting, proofs, production, delivery
  - Determine by what date by invitations must be sent
- Send invitations
  - Determine date by which invitees must receive invitations
    - Provide sufficient time for invited guests to clear personal calendars and respond
    - Determine the time that will be required to assign seating
    - Provide sufficient time for follow-up event information to be returned to the responding guest (e.g., confirmation, schedule of events, ticket pickup information)
      - Create event information package for responding guests
        - Create VIP guest itinerary

Figure 5-1
Critical Task Analysis

preceding the team's first playoff game in 3 years, with the desired secondary objectives of exploiting the program for promotional and revenue-generating purposes (see page 27 for a complete description of the event's objectives). Figure 5-2 lists the elementary tasks, in rough sequential order, that will form the nucleus of a critical dates calendar for this event.

- Develop an event budget
- Create a schedule of events
- Develop attractions and activities
- Sell sponsorships
- Create a merchandise area
- Create a ticket sales area for next season
- Identify food and beverage offerings
- Book entertainment
- Create a floor plan
- Invite dignitaries, VIP guests, sponsors, business owners
- Invite media to cover the event
- Advertise and promote the event to fans and nonfans
- Set up and install the event
- Operate the event
- Document the event for future sponsorship sales efforts
- Evaluate the event

Figure 5-2
Elementary Tasks

ASSIGN DEADLINES TO ELEMENTARY TASKS

It is often helpful to assign preliminary deadlines or end dates before you begin to break the list apart to identify the many supportive tasks and decision points that will ultimately form the bulk of the planning calendar. Put the elementary tasks in the most logical sequence, starting with the first that will have to be completed and ending with the tasks whose completion will come last. The tasks listed in Figure 5-2 are already presented in rough chronological order. Now add deadline dates, that is, the date by which each task must be completed, as illustrated in Figure 5-3. The most helpful method for assigning deadline dates is to start from the end, with those tasks that are completed closest to event day, and work your way backward.

Tasks that are to be completed after the event has ended, such as "document" and "evaluate the event" have been excluded from the rest of this process. It should be noted, however, that some subtasks may require scheduling before event day for their completion. To properly document the event, for example, a photographer or videographer would have to be hired in advance.

Although the list of elementary tasks in Figure 5-3 is in logical chronological order, the deadlines were assigned by starting with "operate the event."

Elementary Task	End Date
Develop an event budget	04/01/05
Create a schedule of events	05/01/05
Develop attractions and activities	05/10/05
Sell sponsorships	05/12/05
Create a merchandise area	05/14/05
Create ticket sales area for next season	05/14/05
Identify food and beverage offerings	05/14/05
Book entertainment	05/14/05
Create a floor plan	05/20/05
Invite dignitaries, VIP guests, sponsors, business owners	05/23/05
Invite media to cover the event	05/23/05
Advertise and promote the event to fans and nonfans	05/25/05
Set up and install the event	05/29/05
Operate the event	05/30/05

Figure 5-3
Elementary Tasks with Deadline Dates

The organizer then worked backward through the list of tasks to "develop an event budget," estimating the time that must be allowed to complete each before the next on the list may be conquered.

ADD START DATES

Most teams in competitive leagues, both amateur and professional, do not clinch a playoff position until very close to the end of the regular season. In our example, let's suppose the team is doing well enough to reasonably expect to reach the playoffs but is not yet assured of postseason play. The team will want to set deadlines that are as late as possible so the event may be canceled with the least embarrassment possible and with minimal or no financial exposure. In Figure 5-3, deadlines are set very close to event day to avoid having to pay for most requirements until their playoff participation is confirmed. It is suggested for most events, when and where possible, that deadlines should be set earlier than in this example, with extra time built in for the inevitable fulfillment of tasks that take longer than expected.

Just because end dates are set late does not mean that planning should also start late. Work on all of these tasks should begin as early as possible, even before the probability of the team's playoff appearance increases to even odds. For this reason, it is strongly suggested that critical dates calendars include start dates as well. Figure 5-4 expands the calendar for our fictional fan festival to include start dates for each elementary task.

Elementary Task	Start Date	End Date
Develop an event budget	02/01/05	04/01/05
Create schedule of events	02/01/05	05/01/05
Develop attractions and activities	02/01/05	05/10/05
Sell sponsorships	03/01/05	05/12/05
Create merchandise area	03/15/05	05/14/05
Create ticket sales area for next season	03/15/05	05/14/05
Identify food and beverage offerings	04/15/05	05/14/05
Book entertainment	04/15/05	05/14/05
Create floor plan	05/01/05	05/20/05
Invite dignitaries, VIP guests, sponsors, business owners	05/01/05	05/23/05
Invite media to cover the event	05/01/05	05/23/05
Advertise and promote the event to fans and nonfans	04/15/05	05/25/05
Setup and install the event	05/28/05	05/29/05
Operate the event	05/30/05	

Figure 5-4
Elementary Tasks with Start and End Dates

Note that in the expanded list of elementary tasks, some action areas that have the same deadline date will take longer to plan and execute than others. Including start dates to the critical dates calendar allows event organizers to prioritize the order in which tasks with similar end dates should be initiated. Thus, planners will not run out of time to manage an elementary task that was not initiated with sufficient lead time. By maintaining the critical dates calendar on a Microsoft Excel or similar spreadsheet program, organizers can sort their tasks by either start date or end date—or maintain two calendars, one organized in chronological order by start dates, and the other by end dates, if desired.

EXPLODE CALENDAR WITH SUPPORTIVE TASKS AND DECISION POINTS

Now it is time to expand the critical dates calendar by exploding each elementary task into its component parts through critical task analysis, as previously seen in the example provided in Figure 5-1. Once you do this, you are likely to discover that many of your original dates are not early enough in the overall process to accommodate all of the activity and decisions that will be required between the start and end dates. You will also discover that certain supplemental tasks or decision points for one elementary task will have to be completed before the supplemental tasks of one or more other elementary tasks. It is perfectly natural for even the most experienced sports event managers to have to make these adjustments as the calendar is developed.

Let's take a look at three elementary tasks from the current series of examples: "develop an event budget," "develop attractions and activities," and "sell sponsorships." Work on planning all three of these key elementary tasks must start early, and they are developed concurrently. Figure 5-5 partially explodes each task into its component parts to illustrate.

These three elementary tasks were chosen for illustration because they are closely interrelated. To sell sponsorships, you have to create a package of benefits for the sponsor to buy. To create the benefits package, you will need to know what inventory, or the slate of attractions and activities, you will have to sell. To know what attractions you will have to sell, you will have to know what they are expected to cost. To know what they will cost, you will need to conceptualize what you want, contact potential suppliers, and solicit estimates. To sell attractions to a sponsor at the right price, you will have to know what they cost, what overhead costs will also have to be covered, how much your organization is willing to invest, and how much income you are trying to achieve overall. Later, you will have to order signage to acknowledge and promote your sponsors. To have the signage ready in time, you will have to

Elementary Task	Start Date	End Date
Develop an event budget	02/01/05	04/01/05
Identify net income/loss goal		
Estimate total expenses		
Estimate total revenues		
Determine sponsor revenue needs		
First draft budget		
Budget finalized		
Develop attractions and activities	02/01/05	05/10/05
Identify attraction areas		
Request and receive cost estimates		
Confirm roster of attractions		
Order signage		
Sell sponsorships	03/01/05	05/12/05
Create sponsorship tiers and packages		
Create sponsorship presentations		
Solicit potential sponsor companies		
Finalize sponsors		
Order sponsor signage		
Order other sponsor fulfillment elements		

Figure 5-5
Exploding Elementary Tasks

have a deadline by which all of your sponsors will be finalized. (In real life, however, few sports event organizers will turn down a late-arriving sponsor, and most will do everything in their power to accommodate them, even if it means incurring higher expenses and a last-minute effort to get the deal done.)

After exploding each elementary task, begin filling in start and end dates for each of its supporting tasks and decision points, as illustrated in Figure 5-6. This is the step during which the event organizer must be particularly vigilant to ensure the calendar is internally consistent. In other words, all of the tasks that require other tasks to occur, as either pre- or corequisites, have start and end dates that are consistent and not contradictory. As a result, it is not unusual for some dates to slide to an earlier or later position during this stage of the process to accommodate the need for consistency. In this example, the task of ordering signage must slide to a slightly later date than originally anticipated in the list of elementary tasks because of the event organizer's need to delay activities that will incur costs, just in case the team falls out of play-off contention. Moreover, the later date will also allow the organizer to accept new sponsors later in the planning process. The experienced sports event planner in this example has not simply assumed, of course, that his vendor can meet these later, just-in-time ordering and delivery dates. The vendor was made aware, and was accepting, of the delayed time frame.

Several additional examples of internal consistency may be noticed in Figure 5-6. The organizer must have a pretty good idea of his sponsor revenue

Task	Start Date	End Date
~~Develop an event budget~~	~~02/01/05~~	~~04/01/05~~
Identify net income/loss goal	02/01/05	02/08/05
Budget total expenses	02/01/05	03/01/05
Budget total revenues	02/08/05	03/22/05
Determine sponsor revenue needs	02/08/05	03/22/05
First draft budget	02/15/05	03/08/05
Budget finalized	03/08/05	04/01/05
~~Develop attractions and activities~~	~~02/01/05~~	~~05/10/05~~
Identify attraction areas	02/01/05	03/01/05
Request and receive cost estimates	02/15/05	03/08/05
Confirm roster of attractions	03/08/05	04/01/05
Order and receive signage	05/17/05	05/25/05
~~Sell sponsorships~~	~~03/01/05~~	~~05/12/05~~
Create sponsorship tiers and packages	03/01/05	03/15/05
Create sponsorship presentations	03/01/05	04/01/05
Solicit potential sponsor companies	04/01/05	05/08/05
Finalize sponsors	04/15/05	05/17/05

Figure 5-6
Exploded Critical Dates Calendar (partial)

needs before marketing the event to potential sponsors and will not be able to confirm the pricing of sponsorship packages until the budget is in some complete, if not final, form. Because of the short time available to bring the event to the attention of sponsors, the organizer is prepared to begin creating the packages to be offered to the sponsors as soon as the first draft budget is completed. The creation of a physical presentation to sponsors is under way as soon as the first draft expense budget is nearing completion. While the organizer waits for the development of the business end of the presentation (e.g., creating and pricing the package of benefits to be offered to sponsors), work may begin on the portions of the proposal that will build excitement and anticipation (e.g., introduction, graphics, background information). The presentations are therefore ready to go to market as soon as the budget and the business terms of the sponsorship package are finalized.

To get to this point, the roster of attractions must be confirmed. This, too, depends on completing at least the first draft of the budget. To ensure that the budget contains all of the pertinent information relating to each of the attraction areas, vendors must be contacted to begin developing cost estimates. The roster of attractions and the budget are finalized simultaneously and, not coincidentally, at the same time that sponsors are first approached by the organizer.

Note that the original elementary tasks may now be removed from the calendar of critical dates. With all of the new detail added to the calendar, the elementary entries are now too broad to be very useful to the planning process and are struck through in the figure for the purpose of illustration. Because of the fine level of detail in a truly functional critical dates calendar, the number of entries is often very large. The 3 sample elementary tasks selected from the 14 listed in Figure 5-4 generated 14 entries on their own, which are abridged for the purpose of simplifying the illustration. Critical date calendars can contain lists of a hundred or more tasks for even the simplest sports event. It is therefore wise to add one more column to the spreadsheet to assist the event director in managing the planning process, as well as the various paid and/or volunteer staff members who will be recruited to execute it—the assignment of staff to each area of responsibility.

ADD RESPONSIBILITIES

Most sports event organizers must delegate responsibilities to a group of area managers, supervisors, helpers, and workers, whether paid professionals, volunteers, vendor companies, or employees of other partners. In Figure 5-7 a column has been added to complete the critical dates calendar, noting the individual responsible to complete each task within the time frame noted.

Note that the entries in Figure 5-7 have been resorted into chronological order, first by start date, next by end date. This is another strong reason for deleting the list of elementary tasks, as now the entire flow of work is inte-

Task	Start Date	End Date	Responsibility
Identify net income/loss goal	02/01/05	02/08/05	George
Budget total expenses	02/01/05	03/01/05	Ed
Identify attraction areas	02/01/05	03/01/05	Helene
Budget total revenues	02/08/05	03/22/05	George
Determine sponsor revenue needs	02/08/05	03/22/05	George
First draft budget	02/15/05	03/08/05	Ed
Request and receive cost estimates	02/15/05	03/08/05	Helene
Create sponsorship tiers and packages	03/01/05	03/15/05	Tom
Create sponsorship presentations	03/01/05	04/01/05	Francine
Budget finalized	03/08/05	04/01/05	George
Confirm roster of attractions	03/08/05	04/01/05	George
Solicit potential sponsor companies	04/01/05	05/08/05	Tom
Finalize sponsors	04/15/05	05/17/05	Tom
Order and receive signage	05/17/05	05/25/05	Kelly

Figure 5-7
Calendar of Critical Dates (partial)

grated into a single organized chart in chronological order for use by all involved in the production, regardless of what process each task belongs. The power of spreadsheet software such as Microsoft Excel for event organizers has probably been particularly apparent throughout this chapter as we sort the calendar by start and end dates. In addition, Excel may be used to generate separate charts of responsibility for each individual listed in the calendar. This provides the sports event organizer and the managers responsible for each functional area with a ready and useful tool to ensure that the workload is properly and equitably distributed, as well as access to information on exactly who is supposed to be doing what and when. For added flexibility in the creation, management, and maintenance of the critical dates calendar, explore the features of Microsoft Office Project. This project management software application can track the status of individual tasks and milestones with even more detail and can generate flowcharts and other graphic tools for presentation purposes.

Remember not to neglect those activities that occur *after* an event has been completed. Functions such as dismantling an event, vacating and restoring the event site, finalizing the budget settlement, scheduling postmortem event evaluations, documenting the event for sponsors, and releasing temporary seasonal employees are just some of the activities that happen post-event, which should also be included in the calendar.

DISTRIBUTION OF CRITICAL DATES CALENDARS

Critical dates calendars are most useful when they are distributed to as wide an audience as is practical, feasible, or desirable. Confidential or organizationally sensitive information, if any, should be deleted from these more widely distributed copies. At minimum, everyone listed in the Responsibility column should receive a copy of the calendar. Staff in other areas of the organization who need to know may be sent copies to assist them in demystifying what often looks like chaos to those outside the event team. The information provided can allow them to direct their questions, comments, and feedback to the individual overseeing a particular function, rather than solely to the event director. The question now is: "Who are the people doing all this work, and where are they coming from?"

Build a Support Organization

Whether you plan to use some combination of volunteers and part-time or full-time paid staff, or an event planning or production firm to staff your sports event, a structure must be put in place that will define areas of responsibility and accountability for each contributing individual. Many sports organizations exist explicitly to stage special events and are geared up 365 days a year to function as their own special events companies. Others are highly seasonal, in which a small core staff is retained on a permanent, full-time basis, periodically outnumbered by a more considerable temporary, in-season workforce. Still others (perhaps most) retain help from outside organizations, applying some combination of internal staff with resources such as vendors, consultants, temporaries, interns, freelancers, and volunteers. Because the structure of the event team should be defined by the workload ahead, event organizers frequently build their critical dates calendars early in the planning process to determine the human resources, skill sets, and talents that will be required and when they must be applied. They can then create an organization plan that employs both internal and external resources, retaining those resources only for the period required to execute their responsibilities. Before beginning to look at areas of responsibility, however, it is important for the event organization to define levels of authority and determine how decisions, both short-term and long-term, will be made.

DEFINE THE DECISION-MAKING PROCESS

In 1974, as a freshman reporter for WQMC-AM radio at Queens College, City University of New York, I was assigned to cover a planned demonstration protesting our financially troubled city's decision to begin charging tuition at what was until then an institution totally supported by taxpayers. On the way to City Hall, I interviewed a student from campus I had come to know who seemed to represent—or at least belong to—a group called the Revolutionary Student Brigade (RSB). I cannot honestly remember whether the RSB members considered themselves Trotskyites, Marxists, Leninists, or some other kind of "ists," but I do remember being stunned by the answer to the first question I asked: "Who is in charge of the RSB and what do they hope to accomplish at today's protest?" "No one is in charge," he replied. "We are all in charge. Each and every one of our opinions is equal and valid."

Although we embrace the notion of equality among all men and women, I knew then as I know now that *someone* has to be in charge in order to keep things focused, progressing, and responsive to any number of lurking challenges. The decision maker may be an individual, a task force, or a committee, but there must be a structure in place that assigns the right amount of responsibility at each level of the organization, as well as knowledge, recognition, and acceptance of that structure by all who operate within it. The genesis of every sports event organization starts with the ultimate decision makers—the individual or body of individuals who have the authority to set objectives, determine strategies, and approve the spending of money to pursue and achieve them.

Frequently, a committee, task force, board of directors, or senior officer of a client organization occupies the top rung of the event team. It is helpful to define the role of this individual or group, particularly with respect to what decisions must be brought to them for discussion and resolution. Defining these jurisdictions and limitations in the earliest stages will help the senior individual who reports to the group, in this case the event director, fully understand the responsibilities and authority he or she may exercise autonomously. Although *autonomy* suggests areas of total control over clearly defined areas, it does not obviate the complete accountability the event director has to the overarching group. It is essential, however, to move most of the day-to-day decision making to a level below the committee, board, or client organization to provide the event team the freedom to quickly respond to the myriad challenges, changes, and opportunities that will inevitably present themselves suddenly and often during the event planning process. Figure 5-8 is a chart of typical authorities and responsibilities for an event's board of directors (which may take the form of an organization's Chief Executive Officer, an event committee, task force, or client organization) and the top individual charged with managing the event (in this case, the event director). This chart is for illustrative purposes only, as authorities and responsibilities may shift from one category to another, depending on the needs of a specific event or the reporting structures of existing sports event organizations.

In Figure 5-8 a system of checks and balances is in place to empower the event director to make the day-to-day decisions required to manage the event without having to run every question, challenge, or issue past the board. In

Management Entity	Authorities and Responsibilities
Board of Directors	Definition of event objectives
	Approval of strategies and tactics
	Approval of event budget
	Approval of host city and venue selection
	Approval of sponsor, supplier or broadcast deals with terms of more than one year
	Hiring and firing of event director
Event Director	Budget development and management
	Strategy and tactic development
	Approval of expenses
	Supplier selection, negotiations, and contract approval
	Sponsor solicitation, negotiations, and contract approval
	Broadcast solicitation, negotiation, and contract approval
	Hiring and firing of event staff

Figure 5-8
Decision-Making Authorities and Responsibilities

this example, the event director has the broad authority to make operational decisions that will keep the event, or the business, running efficiently. The event director is totally responsible to the governing authority, which in this case is a board of directors. As the individual is held accountable for both triumphs and failures, the director may be removed by the board at any time for failure to meet the demands and expectations of the position.

The board is in place to define the objectives for the event. The director is, in turn, responsible to develop the strategies, tactics, and budget required by the event to meet these objectives, although all three of these areas require presentation to, and approval by, the board. The event director in this example can approve expenses autonomously but is responsible to inform the board if the budget is expected to experience any significant overall variance.

This illustration also limits the event director's authority to approving sponsor, supplier, or broadcast deals of only a single year's duration or less. This frees the director to manage the business of the most immediate event, enabling him or her to make a short-term deal without the approval of the higher authority. Having a free hand allows the director to make deals that may help an organization respond quickly and authoritatively to emerging challenges, such as unexpected budget overruns, supplier or sponsor defaults, unfruitful sponsor contract negotiations, or other previously unanticipated revenue shortfalls. Sometimes a "fire sale" sponsorship at below market rate, or a last-minute value-in-kind deal, must be effected in order to reduce losses or cover shortfalls. Frequently, these deals are consummated late in the plan-

ning process and require the kind of rapid decision making that board inter-
cession would render unfeasible.

Although such deals may be justifiable and appropriate in the short term,
they may not be in the best interest of the event promoter, client, or organization, over the long term. In the example offered in Figure 5-8, deals with
terms exceeding one year must be approved by the higher authority to ensure
that they fit into the overall business objectives and strategies of the organization. As the event director serves at the pleasure of the board of directors,
agreements made by this senior manager should not be able to long outlive
him or her, in case that person's career proves to require abbreviation.

CREATE AN ORGANIZATION CHART

The substance of an organization chart will differ dramatically from event to
event; the chart in Figure 5-9 illustrates a generalized presentation of a fictional sports event provided for the purpose of discussion. The boxes that
make up the most common form of organization charts most often represent
the names and titles of individuals, but may just as easily describe specific
functional areas. The latter format is useful for large events, where the simplicity of listing functional areas rather than names of individual staff members can make the portrayal of the organization easier to understand to those
on the outside. The position of each job on the chart, and how it is joined to
those above and below, symbolize the structure of the reporting relationships.

There are many different ways to graphically portray an organization's
structure, and several software tools are available in the market to assist in the
preparation of professional-appearing charts. One such tool with a long and
proven history of serving this need and available for less than $100 is OrgPlus
by Human Concepts of Mill Valley, California (*www.orgplus.com*). Other packages available in the market include SmartDraw from San Diego, California-
based SmartDraw.com (*www.smartdraw.com*), which includes a wide range of
additional drawing capabilities for layouts and time lines, and OrgTraks by
EntraSpan, Inc., of Encinitas, California (*www.entraspan.com*). The Microsoft
Windows XP Professional Software Suite can also generate basic organization
charts.

There are three key reasons for taking time to construct an organization
chart for your sports event. The first is to define areas of responsibility and
accountability. This will let everyone know what his or her job is and how
each relates to other areas of responsibility in the organization. The second is
to streamline decision making. Construct an organization chart with several
management tiers so that not each and every issue need be presented to the
event director for evaluation and definitive resolution. By limiting the number of staff members reporting only to the event director ("direct reports"),
as well as those who report to each of the top managers in charge of each
functional area (e.g., operations, guest services, marketing, presentation, etc.),

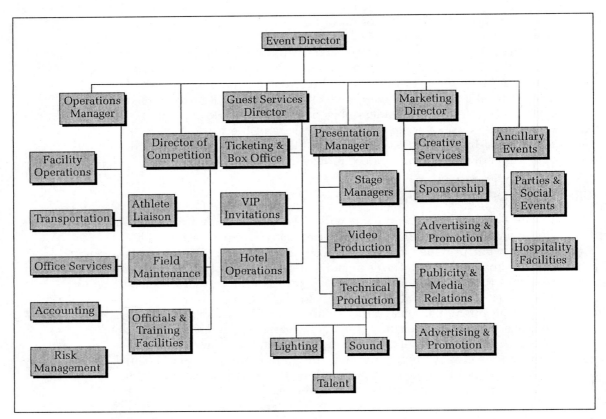

Figure 5-9
Sample Sports Event Organization Chart

top-level managers can delegate responsibility along clearly defined paths to those one level below. The third reason for institutionalizing an organization chart is to clearly communicate, both within the organization and outside, how each functional area fits into the event's overall management structure. Distributing the chart to all those who work within the organization, as well as to key outside contacts, ensures that questions about, and issues arising from, the event will be directed to the individuals who can best handle them.

The fictional sports event organization in Figure 5-9 divides the management team into six key functional groups: operations, competition, guest services, marketing, presentation, and ancillary events. Although the structure of every event team will vary with the nature and needs of the program being managed, it is preferable to limit to as few as possible the number of functional areas reporting directly to a particular position. Although all members

Operations
  Facility Management
    Space Allocation Management
    Load-in, Installation, Dismantle, Load-out
    Labor
      Ticket Takers, Ushers, and Front of House (FOH) Staff
      Security
      First Aid/EMTs
    Lockers and Dressing Rooms
  Staff and Vendor Accreditation
  Transportation
    Competitor Transportation
    Shipping and Receiving
  Office Services
  Staff Uniforms and Attire
Competition
  Tournament/Competition Scheduling
  Athlete Scheduling and Communication
  Playing Field Preparation and Maintenance
  Competitive Equipment Acquisition and Maintenance
  Officiating and Judging
  Training Facilities, Equipment, and Personnel
  Athlete Medical Services
Guest Services
  Ticketing
  VIP Invitation Process and Seating
  VIP Gifts
  VIP Hospitality
  Information Guides
  Hotel Rooms and Function Space Management
Marketing
  Sponsorship
    Business Development and Sponsor Sales
    Account Service and Fulfillment (Account Executives)
  Creative Services
    Logo Development
    Style Manual
    Printed Materials
    Marketing Artwork
    Sponsor Signage
  Advertising
    Newspaper
    Radio

Figure 5-10
Typical Functional Areas for Sports Events Organizations

Television
Outdoor
Billboards
Street Banners
Posters, Window Cards, and Handbills
Promotions
Sponsor Cross-Promotions
Retail Promotions
Publicity
Pre-Event
Media Relations and Accreditation
Media Center Operations
Merchandise and Programs
Presentation
Creative
Rundowns
Scripting
Music
Costumes and Wardrobe
Production Management
Talent Booking
Announcers
Entertainers
Rehearsal Scheduling
Stage Management
Scoreboard Operations
Video Production
Technical Production
Staging and Set Construction
Lighting
Sound
Special Effects
Lasers
Pyrotechnics
Other Common Functional Areas
Hospitality and Social Events
Receptions
Parties
Spouse Programs
Fan Festivals and Activities
Broadcasting
Television
Radio

Figure 5-10
(Continued)

```
      Internet
   Business Affairs
      Accounts Payable
      Accounts Receivable
      Purchasing
      Legal
         Contract Negotiations
         Risk Management and Insurance
```

Figure 5-10
(Continued)

of the event team are ultimately responsible to the event director, this top manager has only six "direct reports," managers who are responsible solely to the director. Functions are grouped beneath each of these managers so that each of them, in turn, has fewer than six key areas for which he or she is responsible.

Regardless of the vast differences between sports organizations, events apply staff to the management of many common functions. Figure 5-10 lists some of the most common functions, along with key activities frequently undertaken by each. To meet an event's specific needs, some may be combined in a single area of responsibility, and others more finely subdivided, depending on the size, organization, and objectives of the event.

Once you have identified the functional areas that are required for your sports event and they have coalesced into an organization chart, it is time to begin assigning staff to these various functions, or to search for, identify and retain resources from the outside world to handle the workload.

Find the Right People

One of the wonderful things about sports events is there is usually no shortage of people who want to help staff them. Grassroots organizations enlist parents, siblings, and friends of the participants to create the workforce they need to stage their events. Professional sports teams and their respective leagues are besieged by resumes—not just of those already working in the field, but also of sports and event management program graduates, career shifters, and job seekers willing to start as low-paid interns just for the work experience and credits on their resumes. The thousands of lesser-connected event organizers in between look to these same pools of experience, talent, and energy, and throw their nets even wider to meet their human resources needs.

Established organizations frequently draft full-time employees from other areas of the company temporarily to assist in the management and execution of key annual or one-time sports event programs. This is the most common practice for the staging of a first-time event in an established organization. Borrowing internal staff helps the company test the event, allowing it to evaluate the desirability of holding the program again in the future without having to staff it with permanent employees the first time around. To keep costs down, organizations often supplement their on-loan event staff from other departments with temporary "seasonal" employees, individuals hired with predetermined start and end dates for their employment. Seasonal staff may be retained part-time (less than 35 hours per week) or full-time (35+ hours), and may be paid either hourly or weekly.

VOLUNTEERS

In sheer numbers, there are easily more than enough men, women, boys, and girls volunteering to help staff and support sports events in venues ranging from the community ball field and the town rink to the campus gymnasium and the downtown arena. Volunteerism is what makes most sports events go, often providing the glue that keeps an event together. Given the passion many feel for their favorite sport, school, community, or team, it is not hard to understand why. The practice of strategically employing well-briefed volunteers is not restricted to small-community grassroots events. Events staged by large amateur sports organizations and professional sports businesses also require the participation of motivated volunteers to provide short-term and event-day staff for their programs. For example, more than 1,200 volunteers join the NHL event team during the average NHL All-Star Weekend, and 12,000 for the New York City Marathon. In the summer of 1996, more than 60,000 assisted the Atlanta Committee for the Olympic Games (ACOG).

Staffs for community-oriented grassroots events are often 100 percent composed of volunteers. The people recruited to fill positions, ranging from those of great authority to those of more limited contribution, are usually made up of friends, neighbors, and family members. Some participatory organizations, like running and skating clubs, have hundreds or even thousands of members, some of whom often assist in running the schedule of events as volunteers. Although volunteers are, by definition, unpaid, it is recommended that their responsibilities be as well defined as if they were paid staff, to eliminate confusion and ensure that important tasks are not overlooked.

When a combination of paid and volunteer staff members work together, volunteers are best suited for positions that require intelligence and people skills, but little training beyond an orientation session or two. Professional event organizers must recognize that to the attendee, volunteers can be indistinguishable from paid staff. As ambassadors for the event organizer and often the first point of contact for participants, guests, and/or the audience, volunteers must be selected judiciously and provided with all the information and materials they need to do their jobs. But first they must understand what their jobs are. Create a brief bullet-point job description for each volunteer position, as illustrated in Figure 5-11. Consider the personality traits and knowledge they must possess to fulfill these positions, and then identify the right resources in your market that can provide the body of volunteers most motivated to do a great job on your behalf.

As may be seen in the examples in Figure 5-11, volunteer jobs are not usually the most glamorous, and as such may seem as though they would be difficult to fill. But don't underestimate the excitement that sports events generate. Most potential volunteers understand that they will not be running the show. They know they are providing the muscle and connective tissue that keeps everything together, but not necessarily the brain.

Position: Airport Greeter
Description:
- Meet incoming athletes and VIP guests at the airport and direct them to the ground transportation provided for their convenience.
- Assist with the recovery of luggage and equipment from baggage claim and with its transfer to the guests' transportation.
- Offer to answer guests' questions about the event schedule and the dining and entertainment options in the city.
Reports to: Event Transportation Dispatcher
Dates Required: At least two days between Thursday, January 25, and Monday, January 29

Position: Media Host
Description:
- Duplicate and distribute press releases, statistics, and other information to the working press.
- Escort athletes to and from the press conference area.
- Assist the public relations team in the Media Center during the event, as assigned.
Reports to: Media Relations Manager
Dates Required: All days between Friday, January 26, and Sunday, January 28

Position: Operations Center Representative
Description:
- Answer phones, direct calls, and take messages for event staff, athletes, and VIP guests.
- Assist staff with copying, faxing, overnight packages, messenger services, and other office support functions.
- Other office functions, as assigned.
Reports to: Office Manager
Skills Required: PC-literate
Dates Required: At least two days between Wednesday, January 24, and Sunday, January 28

Figure 5-11
Sample Sports Event Volunteer Job Descriptions

Beyond the event staff's circle of friends, where do sports events find these masses of excited and devoted enthusiasts? That depends on the kinds of functions that are needed to be filled by volunteers. Many local convention and visitors bureaus and sports commissions maintain databases of local residents who enjoy volunteering for special events and are experienced in dealing with the public, such as airport greeters (see Figure 5-11) and other individuals who will meet and provide information to incoming visitors. In some cities, the office of the mayor or the department of parks and recreation may maintain similar databases of potential volunteers.

If your city is blessed with sports teams, whether recreational, amateur, or professional, a highly motivated resource may already exist. Contact the recreational enthusiasts of your sport for the most enthusiastic pool of volunteers. In addition, many amateur and professional teams have boosters or fan clubs that enjoy supporting sports events. Consider approaching their membership even if they are not specifically fans of the sport featured at your event. Many members just enjoy being around a variety of sporting events. Do not overlook the power of "swag," the exclusive event merchandise most organizers use as uniform wardrobe for paid and volunteer staff. An event golf shirt or a T-shirt and cap can go a long way as an additional motivation to volunteer.

Is there a university with a sports or event management program in the host community on either the undergraduate or graduate level? There are no more motivated prospects for volunteers than those who are looking to make contacts in the sports business and students training for future careers in this exciting but hard-to-break-into industry. Contact the dean of the school offering these programs to investigate whether an entire class or individual students can volunteer as part of a field experience. Many schools see great value in providing their students an opportunity to participate in a sports event as staff members.

These sources are the most promising and best proven for finding volunteers. Being targeted toward those most driven to serve, they usually bear the most fruit, but sometimes more effort is required to fill the ranks. Consider distributing a press release to the local media announcing the need for volunteers. Be sure to include information on how to apply. Post notices on your organization's web site and advertise for volunteers through your print, radio, and television media partners. You may even be able to get media partners to provide these spots as public service announcements (PSAs), for which there is usually no charge.

There are many instances in which volunteer staff alone will not meet the human resources requirements of an event. Professional expertise not available within the existing organization may be required to help plan, manage, and execute a successful program, and some talented temporary staff members may have to be retained to achieve the desired result. A brief discussion of the temporary paid staff options available to event organizers follows.

Sideline Stories—The Power of Volunteerism

The National Hockey League uses as many as 1200 volunteers to staff the NHL All-Star Weekend and its associated fan festival, NHL All-Star FANtasy. The event's volunteer program, under the direction of freelance producer Pamela Cheriton, has supplemented its annual drive for local assistance with a successful following of academic programs and individuals who return to the volunteer staff year after year, regardless of the location of the host city. Eric Schwarz of Daniel Webster College in Nashua, New Hampshire, has included participation in the volunteer program for NHL All-Star Weekend as part of the academic calendar for his undergraduate sports business students since 2001. His classes have traveled to California, Florida, and Minnesota to work on, and learn about, the inner workings of this sports event firsthand. "Working at events such as those produced by the NHL has given the students an opportunity to apply the theory they have learned in the classroom in real-world settings," says Dr. Schwarz. "It provides the opportunity to try out different aspects of sports event management, which in turn can help students determine what aspects of the career they might wish to follow, and which they would like to avoid."

Some hockey fans actually plan their vacations around volunteering for the NHL mid-season classic—some 75 people, at last count, representing all ages, and professions, including students, workers, retirees, and families hailing from coast-to-coast. "The simple answer may be that these folks have found an activity that allows them to make the most out of their love of the game, the adventure of exploring a new city and the chance to make some new friends," explains Cheriton. "FANtasy is like the Love Boat . . . we provide planned activities throughout the day, a fun group of fellow travelers, many interesting ports of call . . . and most importantly, a volunteer program that is geared to providing them with the time of their lives."

One of the most intriguing stories about the power of volunteerism comes from British Columbia. The backbone of staff required for the now defunct Greater Vancouver Open (GVO) golf tournament was drawn from a pool of 1700 highly motivated volunteers. "Each and every one of them paid $125.00 for the privilege of participating. Perks and benefits weren't directly linked to having paid the cash, although everyone was aware of what you could get if you were a volunteer," recalls James Conrad, General Counsel for Orca

Bay Sports and Entertainment, one of the founding organizers of the tournament and among the volunteers who paid to help out. What volunteers got was a uniform consisting of a cap, a windbreaker, and two golf shirts, a light meal for most shifts, and a big volunteer party at the end of the tournament. "I would have to say, however, that membership in the group, the satisfaction of contributing to the success of one of the best run tournaments on the PGA Tour, and the fact that the tournament was pumping significant money and support into charity objectives were more incentive for volunteering than the uniform and parties," suggests Conrad, "and having paid the volunteer fee, they had a stake in seeing that their tournament was a success in every possible way." The GVO is inactive because of rising costs of PGA Tour prize purses and the unfavorable exchange rates of the late 1990s for the Canadian dollar, not because the event charged a fee for the honor of volunteering. To the contrary, as the fee to volunteer helped bring more money to the charity's bottom line, it is likely the number of civic-minded volunteers would still be quite high if the event were still active, according to Conrad.

FREELANCERS: EMPLOYEES AND INDEPENDENT CONTRACTORS

Freelance event staff may be retained as either temporary employees or independent contractors. If they are hired and compensated as employees, the event director may dictate work hours, set the policies and procedures to be followed, and supervise the freelancers as though they were regular full-time employees. Freelancers hired as temporary employees may also be entitled to all of the rights and protections offered to other employees, such as health insurance benefits and overtime pay, except, of course, that their last date of employment is known by both parties at the outset. Executing an employment contract with a freelance employee is not necessary, although having both parties sign a letter agreement defining compensation, basic work rules, and the date of termination is strongly recommended.

Independent contractors, however, function as one-person vendors. A contract is typically negotiated, containing many of the same terms as the letter agreement used for temporary employees, but because the contractor is generally paid a rate for his or her completion of the project upon presentation of an invoice, a payment schedule is usually included. The event director does not directly supervise the work of an independent contractor, and unless stipulated by the contract has no control over what hours the contractor must invest at the event office. Contractors are free to work for more than one client over the course of their terms and have the right to hire and fire additional employees at their own expense to assist them in completing an assignment.

Independent contractors are particularly useful for very specialized functions in which the type of expertise needed differs from, and its level exceeds that of the event's senior staff. Such specialized contractors may include transportation system consultants, presentation directors, tournament competition organizers, construction or production managers, technical directors, and party planners, among others. It is preferable, however, to put event team members on the payroll as temporary employees when the positions call for the execution of plans set by supervising managers or the event director. This by no means suggests that temporary event employees are any less skilled or professional than independent contractors. If supervisors hire wisely, they will always search for freelancers that add more talent and skills to the event team. If the culture of the event requires direct and constant interaction with management, however, retaining a freelancer as a temporary employee is usually preferable. There are a number of additional procedural and legal differences between the retention of freelancers as temporary employees or as contractors. A more thorough exploration of these distinctions may be found in *Dollars and Events: How to Succeed in the Business of Special Events* by Joe Jeff Goldblatt and Frank Supovitz (John Wiley & Sons, 1999).

If it is determined that temporary event employees are required, it is strongly suggested that a staff job description be created for each position. The job description should provide greater detail than the version used for volunteers (see Figure 5-11), providing both management and the employee with a clear understanding of the position's responsibilities, work rules, and limits of authority.

AGENCIES

Some organizations consider staging sports events even though their main line of business may be only marginally or tangentially related to such activities as a sponsor or promotional partner. It may simply make good business sense for the company to own, develop, manage, and execute a sports event itself to further its corporate objectives or to market a particular product. Event marketing agencies exist for the purpose of assisting such companies. There are advantages to using agencies because you can apply an entire outside organization's resources toward your event marketing objectives without having to staff internally for what could be a costly and labor-intensive endeavor. The client company is strongly advised to exercise the greatest discretion and thorough due diligence in selecting an event marketing agency, checking references and pursuing independent research on the company's experience, achievements, and financial health before agreeing to any relationship. Most agencies will work on a fee-plus-expenses basis, and it is the client company's right to request an explanation of how the schedule of payments will be derived.

It is also not unusual for sports event organizations to retain specialist agencies to assume the management responsibilities of defined functional areas, such as sponsor sales, advertising, public relations, and group ticket sales, among others. Agencies that assume cost center functions (i.e., those areas that are represented by expenses in the budget) generally work on a fee-plus-expenses basis. Those that are charged with developing profit centers (i.e., those areas represented by revenues in the budget) usually work on some form of commission basis and are compensated according to the amount of revenue they generate for the event.

Managing Your Support Organization

The acts of planning an event and building an event staff are very similar to those employed in launching an entirely new company, brand, or product. An event requires defined objectives, strategies, and tactics, a source of capital, and a staff to manage and execute it. The key difference between creating a sports event organization (with permanent, temporary, and volunteer staff) and staffing a start-up company is that event teams are designed to be built up until they can meet an event's objectives and are then deconstructed, at least until the next event, when the building process begins anew.

The analogy of an event organization as a start-up company is reinforced by the working environment of long hours and workweeks, entrepreneurial multitasking employees who fill more than one function, guarded finances—and, for those of us who love this business—tremendous excitement. But start-ups can be confusing environments without clearly communicated goals and procedures and without constant communication between staff members. Event teams can operate in similarly confusing environments and, with a firm, climactic end to their existence set for the day of the event or soon thereafter, with great anxiety if not properly managed.

CREATE AN EVENT STAFF MANUAL

Articulate and circulate a statement of your primary and secondary event objectives to your key event staff and, if you are not revealing confidential information unnecessarily, the results of your P-A-P-E-R Test (see Play 1). Your key managers will not know how to hit the target if they don't know what or where the target is and how you expect them to reach it. This information can make up the first section of an event staff manual. Keep the event manual in a looseleaf binder so that sections can be periodically updated and corrected. The manual will serve as the definitive information source to which the event director and staff will constantly refer throughout the planning process, as well as during the event itself.

Add sections to the event staff manual that include the information you think will be most useful to the team's planning and execution of the event. Most manuals include contact lists of staff members, with phone numbers and extensions, addresses, fax numbers, and E-mail addresses. For ease of use, divide the contact list into four subsections: internal (members of the event team organization), facility, vendors, and external (nonvendors, such as city services contacts). Figure 5-12 provides a list of essential sections in a sequence that is common to most event staff manuals. The figure also lists several optional sections that may be included if applicable to your event or appropriate to the level of employee receiving the binder.

Note that the list of essential sections for the manual includes an area for "policies and procedures." This section is particularly important for event teams that come together on a temporary basis, although it will be of value to even permanent event teams. In this area, it is wise to include specific information on how purchases are to be authorized and made and how expenses incurred by event staff should be approved and filed for reimbursement. Include blank forms used for these procedures, such as purchase orders and expense report blanks that may be photocopied for use, along with instructions on how they should be completed. If employees will be required to travel, include policies governing reimbursable travel expenses (e.g., preapproval procedures, class of service for air travel, hotel limits, food and beverage per

---

Essential Sections
   I.   Event Mission and Objectives
  II.   Contact List
 III.   Calendar of Critical Dates
  IV.   Emergency Procedures
   V.   Event Time Line or Schedule
  VI.   Organization Chart
 VII.   Maps and Floor Plans
VIII.   Policies and Procedures

Optional Sections
   1.   Financial Information
   2.   Contracts
   3.   Event Rundowns and Scripts
   4.   Facility Information
   5.   Sponsorship (list of sponsors and summary of benefits)
   6.   Transportation Plan
   7.   Travel and Hotel Information

Figure 5-12
Event Staff Manual Sections

diems, etc.). Minimum workdays and hours, codes of conduct, guidelines on attire, equal opportunity employment statements, and other administrative information should also be included. In the long run, taking time to include these explanations in the event staff manual will avoid costly misunderstandings for both the staff and the sports event organization.

A more concise variant of the event staff manual should also be created for volunteer staff. If volunteer staff members are fulfilling functions of assistance rather than management, the policies and procedure section should be changed to include only those areas applicable to their positions. More background information may be included, as well as a compendium of frequently asked questions (FAQs) and answers.

SCHEDULE REGULAR EVENT STAFF MEETINGS

It may seem obvious that the scheduling of staff meetings is the best way to keep event personnel current and updated on the constant changes occurring throughout the life of an event. Schedule meetings at regular intervals and include them in the critical dates calendar. If possible, set and circulate an agenda a few days before a meeting, with a request for staff members to review it and provide recommendations for additions at least 24 hours in advance. You will discover that these meetings tend to become less efficient as the number of attendees increases. Therefore, it is best to keep staff meetings compartmentalized for mid- to large-size events. One meeting unit should include the event director and the directors, managers, or heads of functional areas to share pertinent updates, announce tactical and scheduling changes, set policies, discuss challenges faced by the event, and propose solutions. Each functional head should, in turn, conduct meetings with his or her own direct reports.

Another important meeting should be included on the critical dates calendar—the "tie-down" meeting. Usually held just once, one to three weeks ahead of the event, the tie-down meeting includes all event staff, as well as representatives of important stakeholders such as key vendors and freelancers, agencies, facility representatives, and broadcasters, among others. The tie-down is best organized as a communications tool to impart information and procedures and to identify the remaining tasks ahead. With a potentially large assemblage of many dozens of event personnel, it is best not envisioned as a problem-solving session. Nevertheless, it is inevitable that some issues will be identified during the tie-down meeting as all pertinent functional areas report on how they will operate during the event. That is why holding this important session at least a week ahead of the event is so important. The time remaining until event day will be used by the staff to solve these late-emerging problems. It is therefore recommended that the larger the event, the earlier the tie-down should be held to provide adequate time to solve the greater number of issues that are bound to surface.

Now the event director has a road map and a timetable for all of the many tasks and activities that must be executed in order to successfully manage and execute the event. Based on this more clearly defined workload, he or she has built an organization to undertake the challenge of producing a well-managed, flawlessly executed sports event. It is time to take the event to market and start to develop a roster of active, engaged sponsors to meet the event's revenue goals and to activate the program's promotional plans.

Post-Play Analysis

The framework of the event planning process is assembled by compiling a production schedule, or calendar of critical dates. This schedule lists the myriad essential tasks required to manage and execute the event and includes start dates, end dates, and the individual responsible for each entry. The best way to begin creating the schedule is to break up the tactics and strategies defined by the P-A-P-E-R Test into their component "elementary tasks." These elementary tasks are exploded into all of the supportive tasks and decision points required to meet them and then sorted into chronological order.

The process of building an event organization begins once the scope of the work is clarified by the critical dates calendar. Define the decision-making process and create an organization chart to begin adding muscle to the framework. Regardless of whether the organization will be composed of volunteers, existing staff, temporary staff, freelancers, or some combination thereof, create a job description for each position. Be sure to communicate essential information to all staff members through the creation of an event staff manual and by holding regularly scheduled staff meetings.

Coach's Clipboard

1. Compile a calendar of critical dates for the community all-star game discussed in Play 1. Create an organization chart and job descriptions for the all-volunteer team you will assemble to manage and execute this event.
2. What kind of organization will you need to assemble in order to manage and execute the 10K event discussed in Play 1? How many event-day volunteers do you think you will require? Assuming the event is being held in your community, what specific resources will you employ to fulfill your requirements?
3. What kinds of information would you include in the volunteer staff manual for the positions discussed in Figure 5-11?

Understanding the Sports Event–Sponsor Relationship

Business is a combination of war and sport.
—ANDRÉ MAUROIS, FRENCH AUTHOR (1885–1967)

In a free market economy, businesses, brands, and products devote significant resources to keeping their customers satisfied and wresting new ones from the grasp of their competitors. The stakes are as high as the life and death of the company, and the battle is joined on a multitude of fronts—in retail locations and with wholesale distributors, in advertising media and at trade events. Perhaps the most visible and intriguing battlefield of all is at sports events, where brand marketers spend millions on the attempt to transfer even a fraction of the avidity, excitement, and emotional involvement of a sport's loyal audience to the consumption of their products.

There is probably no more zealously sought-after, hard-fought, essential—and delicate—partnership in the business of event marketing than that which is forged between a corporate sponsor and a sports event. For participating companies, event marketing has matured into a discipline all its own, an exciting, high-impact addition to the more traditional implements in the marketing mix tool shed—advertising, publicity, promotion, and direct sales. All of these common and conventional marketing elements have been part of the sports scene for more than a century. It is nearly impossible to remember a time when teams did not offer advertising signage in the outfield or ads in the team yearbook, promote "bat day" giveaways for weaker, tough-to-sell matchups, or stage wacky fan-friendly promotions to drive more fans into seats.

The Roots of Sports Event Sponsorship

The benefits of advertising a company's product at sports events have long been recognized because of the simplicity of their measurement and verification. The sports marketer can guarantee exposure to a number of fans in a facility based on the number of games played, or events staged, over the life of an ad. The relative attractiveness and cost of an ad may vary according to its position. That is, how visible is the ad to how many fans, and how often is it in their field of view?

Television exposure, whether part of dedicated coverage or a result of news reporting, is also measurable, based on ratings, the position of a particular sign, and the frequency of its appearance on the screen. These measures are still in use today as key yardsticks for determining the value of signage at a sports event. It is similarly simple to value an ad in an event program based on the number of copies printed and purchased and the position of the advertisement within the book. Marketers, both the advertiser and the event promoter, commonly use a "cost per thousand" (CPM) calculation to determine the value of an ad. Simply, the CPM represents the amount of money spent for every thousand consumers who view the advertisement. In general, advertisers look for the lowest, most cost-efficient CPM when evaluating the attractiveness of purchasing a particular exposure opportunity.

Although the extent of an advertisement's exposure can be objectively measured by its CPM, it is more difficult to quantify its "stickiness," or how well a fan will remember the ad and how effective it will be in motivating someone to buy the product, visit the store, or employ the service being promoted. Because the excitement and emotional involvement generated by a sports event can add considerable glue to the stickiness of an advertising sign, banner, or commercial, some event organizers limit the ability to advertise at their events solely and exclusively to sponsors, those companies that are willing to support the event beyond simply buying an on-site advertisement to further their marketing objectives. In the simplest terms, the ideal sponsor relationship is defined as one in which a business partner, through its association with an event, realizes marketing benefits in excess of its investment and offers an event value beyond its financial participation.

To make sense from the sponsor's perspective, a sports event must offer the company more business opportunity than could be purchased for the same dollar through other means. From the organizer's point of view, the sponsorship must provide benefits well beyond the costs that will be incurred to fulfill them. Therefore, both parties—the sponsor and the sports event organizer—are investing in each other, and both should expect returns that far outperform a simple cash-for-product (e.g., advertising) transaction.

Thus, although advertising continues to be an important—and sometimes the central—component in the package of benefits enjoyed by a sponsor, the corporate partner can receive outstanding additional value and more ways to achieve improved "stickiness" for its message through an increased association and investment in an event. These benefits may include the ability to engage in pre-event promotions that increase the sales of both the sponsor's product and the event's tickets, participation in the event presentation itself, exclusive access to VIP tickets, receptions, parties, and associated events, and more.

To justify this increased investment, event organizers must design and construct packages of highly attractive and tangible benefits that are available exclusively to sponsors. It is also a quid pro quo for a sponsor's increased investment that it should enjoy some measure of exclusivity that bars their competitors from participating and promoting their products or message in any way associated with the event. The sponsor's ability to promote its product's superior and unique attributes without any interference from its competition is a valuable and essential ingredient in most sponsorship packages.

As companies have different marketing needs, event organizers must demonstrate some degree of flexibility in designing benefit packages that are individually tailored to their understanding of a particular sponsor's business objectives. A sponsor that markets a snack food to consumers may place more value on advertising, sampling, and direct sales opportunities. In contrast, a partner that sells high-priced technology solutions to other businesses may place greater value on exclusive access to the best tickets in the house, meet-and-greet opportunities with the athletes, and VIP hospitality opportunities such as insider parties and receptions, and place less emphasis on advertising.

What Sports Event Organizers Really Want from Sponsors

Before approaching a potential business partner with a program designed to meet what they believe are the company's objectives, sports event organizers should have a clear understanding of what they themselves want out of the relationship. Although it may seem obvious that sports events are in the sponsorship business to meet revenue goals, the organizer must recognize that in today's ultracompetitive sports event marketplace, more sponsors are

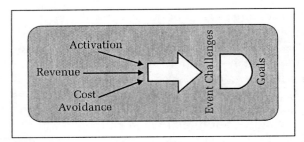

Figure 6-1
What Sports Event Organizers Need
from Sponsors

demanding greater results for their money. Consequently, sports event organizers have to work harder to provide more value for the sponsor. Savvy organizers know that there is more to what a sponsor can bring to an event than just cash. So what do sports event organizers really want—and need—from their sponsors? The three key things that organizers look for a sponsor to provide are *revenue, cost avoidance* and *activation* (how a sponsor will promote its relationship with an event). Forging a sponsor relationship that offers a measure of all three can offer an organizer solutions to his or her event marketing challenges with greater effect than can any one alone (Figure 6-1).

REVENUE

The vast majority of sports events that include corporate sponsorship as part of their business model do so to generate revenue. Generally, the fewer or more modest the revenue streams (particularly ticket revenue and participation fees), the more an event will rely on some form of support from sponsors. An event that is free to participants and attendees—for example—will require a sizable portion of its revenue budget to be generated from corporate sponsorships.

It is very tempting for sports event organizers to view sponsorship as "spackle for budgets," the great gap closer that will cover any shortfall on the balance sheet. A common approach of event promoters in determining how high to set a sponsorship revenue goal is to first estimate expenses, then set a reasonable and salable ticket price or participation fee, and, finally, decide to cover almost all of the difference and profit, if any, with sponsor dollars. Although that is not a bad approach to start developing a sponsorship revenue goal, it can be a dangerous way to finish.

The amount of sponsorship revenue a sports event can generate is not a function of how much of the budget an organizer needs to cover, but rather the event's intrinsic attractiveness to a sponsor and its potential effectiveness in achieving the sponsor's business objectives. The sponsor will compare the demographics of an event's audience with its own customers to determine the whether various characteristics such as age, gender, income, education, and other consumer determinants complement each other. If they match well, the sponsor will then evaluate how effectively the rights and benefits offered by the event will deliver its message or sell its products to this common target audience. Organizers will need to make a candid and realistic assessment of how much interest an event will generate among the field of potential sponsors. Specifically, they will have to estimate how much money these companies are likely to spend to communicate with an event's ticket buyers, viewers, or participants, and what the event will have to deliver to its sponsors before finalizing their sponsorship revenue goals.

COST AVOIDANCE

Sponsors are increasingly attracted to the option of providing products and services in lieu of, or in addition to, cash in payment of some portion of their event sponsorship fees, particularly in a challenging economic environment. This practice is known variously as "barter," "contra," or accepting "value in kind" (VIK). VIK sponsors provide products or services to an event and value them at the retail price an organizer would expect to pay if he or she had to expend cash to procure them. For the sponsor, this practice has multiple benefits. Obviously, it reduces the cash the company will need to spend in exchange for sponsorship rights. To sponsors, cash represents money that has already been earned on past sales. Providing VIK, however, moves product inventory out of their warehouses, so sponsors are actually paying for their sponsorship with what amounts to new, *incremental* sales. VIK sponsors realize added efficiencies when using their products instead of cash. The real cost a sponsor incurred in manufacturing the product may be only 50 percent or less of the retail value provided to the event organizer.

Event organizers should, by all means, avail themselves of VIK possibilities that truly provide a level of cost avoidance equal to, or exceeding, the value of a cash sponsorship. In other words, make sure that the bartered products or services will really reduce your event expenses by at least an amount that equals your income goal had you been paid cash. Avoid deals that do not truly decrease budgeted expenses. Also avoid bartered products and services that add a level of operational inconvenience to the event. Ideally, they should be the actual products you would require and purchase if the VIK offer was not available. If the products or services are inferior to those that would otherwise have been selected, or are provided in excess of what is required or usable, a VIK deal can be more harmful than helpful.

To illustrate, imagine that a VIK deal is desired by an office equipment supplier, offering copiers and fax machines in place of cash in exchange for its designation as an event sponsor. The top-of-the-line copy machine offered by the sponsor can copy 30 sheets per minute and collate 10 sets at a time. The event's media center, however, routinely copies large numbers of press releases, newspaper clippings, and statistics, requiring a high-speed copier that can handle at least 50 sets at a time and at speeds of at least twice the speed at which the sponsor's copy machines can process them. If the proposed sponsorship deal depends on a VIK deal, the organizer must determine whether the lost productivity and greatly reduced speed so negatively affects the media center's ability to service the press that it would reflect poorly on the event. If it does, the event organizer would be wise to insist that the VIK deal exclude the provision of copy machines for the media center. Perhaps these reduced-speed copiers can instead be used in lower quantity and in other functional areas. Because they would now provide less real value to the event, the pure VIK arrangement may have to be reconfigured as a combination of cash and VIK or simply a sponsorship at a lower level.

If quality, quantity, and utility match up with operational and budget requirements, then accepting barter avoids costs, and that can be as good as cash. During economically challenging times, the ability to incorporate VIK partners into the portfolio of sponsorships can mean the difference between closing a deal and watching one slip away. VIK is not just becoming a popular alternative to pure cash transactions in small and moderate-size deals. Its prominence is increasing in larger sponsor relationships as well. *Around the Rings* (*www.aroundtherings.com*), an independent newsletter covering the business and politics of the international Olympic movement, reported that Olympic Airways, the national airline of Greece, agreed to sponsor the 2004 Olympic Games in Athens at a $10 million level, an amount paid entirely in credits for airline tickets.

ACTIVATION

Activation is an industry buzzword that embodies a concept not easily described by a simple synonym. Best put, organizers need sponsors that will invest dollars beyond their sponsorship fee to promote their relationship with a sports event to build awareness of the event, drive ticket sales, and promote the purchase of merchandise, among other benefits (thus, their "activation"). The sponsor can use the event to drive more customers to its brands or business through the placement of event-themed advertising in newspapers and on radio, television, and the Internet, through outdoor (billboard) advertising, in-store displays, and sales promotions. The organizer, as a result, can enjoy the benefits of significant additional exposure through this associated advertising.

In today's sports marketplace, sponsor activation is an essential component of what makes the event-sponsor partnership work because of how effective it is in achieving the objectives of both parties. According to IEG, a Chicago-based authority on event sponsorship and the publisher of the *IEG Sponsorship Report*, sponsors generally allocate between $1.20 and $1.70 in activation spending for every dollar spent on sponsorship fees. Some sponsors offer organizers "activation-only" associations, guaranteeing an event valuable advertising and promotion not otherwise available or affordable to the organizer. For the sponsor, this strategy can be an effective way of financing its partnership by incorporating activation plans into existing advertising budgets at no incremental cost. Before an event organizer agrees to an activation-only deal, even if it provides outstanding media value, that organizer should evaluate whether he or she will still be able to meet the event's cash revenue goals in other ways.

It should be noted that the ultimate objective of a sponsor's event activation strategies is to realize its own marketing objectives—winning new customers and selling more product. From the partner's perspective, "sponsorships are effective or ineffective based on one thing and one thing only—how they are activated," agrees David Grant, principal and cofounder of Velocity Sports and Entertainment. "Sponsors who are not getting full value either have selected the wrong sponsorship, or have developed the wrong marketing plans," he continues. Although a sponsor's activation strategies are geared primarily to fulfilling their own marketing objectives, working cooperatively to provide effective platforms for promotional activity can benefit both the event and its corporate partners. Some of the many ways a sponsor can activate its association with a sports event property to achieve these objectives are explored in the sections that follow.

COMMITMENT TO, OR PROSPECTS FOR, CONTINUED ASSOCIATION

It may seem self-serving, and perhaps patently obvious, to suggest that some form of continuing commitment to future events is important to organizers in a sponsor relationship, but any list of event organizer's desires would be incomplete without mentioning it. Although not as essential as cash or activation campaigns in the short term, it is almost always in the best interest of a sports event organizer to sell the rights to more than a single year's edition as part of a sponsor's package of benefits. A multiyear deal reduces the expense and effort involved in selling each and every sponsorship annually and provides the organizer with a degree of certainty as to achieving at least a portion of his or her revenue goals for one or more succeeding years. From the sponsor's perspective, a multiyear deal can provide the attractive benefit of price protection. The organizer of a successful event would be unable to increase the price of a sponsorship package beyond the terms of the contract for the years covered by an agreement. Nor would an event organizer have the opportunity to open the event for bidding to a sponsor's competitors, possibly replacing an incumbent that invested heavily in making an event a success with a newcomer promising additional activation, cash, products, or other benefits.

The continuity of a sponsor's involvement in an event from year to year builds a strong and valuable association between the partners in the minds of the consumers. Nevertheless, sponsors are frequently reticent to commit financial resources to events or event organizations that are not so singular or prestigious that protecting their investment over a period of years is an essential part of their corporate business plan. To encourage multiyear support, sponsors can be offered various escape clauses in their agreements. Such provisions may include a "right of first refusal," whereby a sponsor must formally turn down renewal before a deal may be finalized with any other company. Alternatives include a "right of first negotiation," whereby a potential renewal must be negotiated with the sponsor before any other company is approached, and a "right to terminate," permitting the sponsor or organizer to end the deal after the first event based on predetermined circumstances or measures (e.g., failure of the organizer to reach a defined attendance plateau, or the sponsor to achieve certain sales levels). These inclusions provide both parties with an explicit statement of intent indicating that a sponsor will consider extending its association if it does not wish to firmly commit itself for a number of years (see Figure 6-2 for a summary of the benefits that organizers seek from sponsors).

The sports event business often seems as though it is rapidly approaching the point of saturation, a time when the clutter of too many sponsors in too many places at a single event interferes with making an efficient and effective impact on the audience. For this reason, sponsors have become justifiably more discerning and more demanding about the value of benefits offered by sports event organizers. Although they continue to accept the traditional and valuable features of advertising, signage, and tickets, many express the desire to receive an increased sense of "ownership" at a sports event. When sponsors refer to ownership, they are expressing a need to develop public perception of the company as the most dominant sponsor of the entire program, or of specific event elements that can make a uniquely strong and memorable impact on the consumer.

- Revenue
- Cost avoidance (value in kind)
- Activation
  - Advertising
  - Promotions
  - Publicity
- Commitment to, or prospect for, a continued association

Figure 6-2
What Sports Event Organizers Really Want
from Sponsors

What Sponsors Really Want from Sports Events

Although sponsors have differing motivations for their participation in a sports event and vary as to the value they place on the specific benefits of involvement, what they do share is confidence in the strength of sponsorship as a powerful marketing tool. According to an IEG/Performance Research survey released in March 2003, of particular note because it was conducted at a time when the American economy was in a substantially weakened position, 40 percent of the corporate sponsorship decision makers surveyed stated an intention to increase their sponsorship budgets in that year, whereas only 18 percent said they were planning on spending less than they spent during the preceding year. The 2003 MPI/George P. Johnson Event Trends Study, published in part in the June/July 2003 issue of *Event Marketer* magazine, supports these results. This study revealed that 47 percent of senior corporate executives surveyed placed greater importance on events than in the year past, and 33 percent expected to increase their event budgets for the coming year.

Sports event sponsorships are not immune to economic, social, and political pressures, but they remain powerful, effective, and compelling marketing tools because they are complex, multidisciplinary, multisensory, involving, and, when properly activated, motivational. To attendees and guests, a sports event may be enjoyed as a competitive contest, an entertainment event, a television or radio broadcast, a social activity, or a meeting place to strengthen business ties. To a sponsor, they can be all of these, plus targeted, opportunistic, and high-impact advertising vehicles, promotional platforms, product demonstration and sampling opportunities, sales generators, forums for customer interactivity, and even fund-raisers for a company's charitable endeavors.

Figure 6-3 lists some of the most often mentioned sponsor benefits that partner companies seek from sports events. They are presented in no particular order of significance, because the relative importance of these features will vary widely even among sponsors of the same event. The first four—exposure, customer hospitality, sales opportunities, and fund-raising for corporate causes—are sponsor benefits derived directly from an event. The organizer should carefully consider, during the negotiating process, how a prospective partner will value each type of benefit in order to design a sponsorship package that will achieve optimal success and return on investment (see Play 7).

Three of the associative benefits listed in the figure—exclusivity, ownership, and prestige/reputation—are properties that may be associated with a sponsorship, but which will provide little in the way of easily measured results without formal studies being conducted, such as through the use of focus groups, intercept surveys, or the distribution and collection of audience questionnaires. These associative benefits reinforce the effectiveness of the

Direct Sponsor Benefits
- Exposure
  - In-event advertising
  - Off-facility advertising
  - Product placement
  - Promotions
  - Publicity (media coverage)
- Customer hospitality
  - Event tickets
  - Reception/party invitations
- Sales opportunities
  - Direct sales
  - Product demonstrations
  - Sampling opportunities
- Fund-raising for corporate causes

Associative Benefits
- Exclusivity
- Ownership (de facto or perceived)
- Prestige and reputation
- Pass-through rights

Figure 6-3
What Sponsors Really Want from
Sports Events

more direct benefits and can add considerable intangible value to the relationship between sponsor and event. As will be further described in this chapter, the associative benefit of pass-through rights can offer sponsors tangible cost savings as well as the perception of a strong relationship to an event in the minds of their customers.

EXPOSURE—ADVERTISING AND PROMOTION

For new and emerging products and companies, exposure is frequently one of the most valuable components of the event sponsorship experience, although most established companies also recognize the value that can be realized by exposing their brands at sports events. Exposure opportunities at sports events abound and are most often manifest in advertising, promotion, and publicity programs, all basic and familiar pillars of the traditional marketing mix.

As previously mentioned, advertising opportunities are among the oldest forms of purchased exposure at sports events. It is widely accepted that repetition of advertising aids in viewer, listener, or reader recall, suggesting repeated placement of ads in order for them to have their intended effect. However, some singular advertising opportunities at sports events can make more lasting impressions because, in effect, they are repetitive. Advertising signage within the audience's field of view may be seen repeatedly and over prolonged periods of time, requiring some modification in how value is normally measured for more traditional television, radio, or print advertising. In these more conventional forms, once an ad has aired or the page has been turned, most of its impact dissipates. Advertising opportunities during an event, however, can deliver impressions continuously and with varying impact throughout the two or three hours spectators are in the venue. On television, a single advertising location in the event venue, comes into and out of view repeatedly throughout the program. Sponsors and their agencies have been measuring this effect in regard to television broadcasts for many years. Simply, the number of signage impressions can be multiplied by the number of seconds the ad is visible on television. This philosophy can be extended, to some degree, to a live audience as well. The most valuable advertising location will be in the place where spectators will be looking most often.

Another dynamic that greatly enhances the value of advertising signage at sports events is the degree to which its exposure is reinforced by other forms of a sponsor's advertising, promotions, and messages during the program. Public address announcements that recognize a partner's company or product, accompanied by logos displayed on the video scoreboard, provide additional repetition and may aid in spectators' recall of the advertising. With so many larger venues now providing video playback capabilities on the scoreboard, the judicious airing of commercial spots for the live audience can provide bonus impressions and further reinforce the impact of static display signage. With the audience already familiar, prepared, and receptive to a sponsor's message, on-field or in-stand promotions can be all the more effective.

The different forms of advertising messages during the course of a sports event may actually aid in consumer recall beyond the effects of simple repetition. The Nordhielm/Dual Process Model of Advertising Repetition Effects, developed by Christie L. Nordhielm of the J.L. Kellogg Graduate School of Management at Northwestern University, proposes that the positive effect of repetition for some advertisements may actually begin to decline after three to ten appearances, an effect known as "wearout." At first, Nordhielm explains, repetition generates "familiarity and positive affect, but subsequent exposures eventually lead to wearout." Nordhielm's study ascertained that the practice of developing different forms and executions of an advertising message, with some number of common features such as the logo and brand name, but varying other components of the advertising vehicle, can greatly delay the onset of consumer wearout. It can be argued, then, that an advertising execution such as signage at an event can be reinforced and its effect on the audience enhanced with various complementary activities such as promotions, public address announcements, and direct sales activities such as sampling and product demonstrations, taking advantage of the benefits of repetition, and reducing or avoiding the effects of wearout.

Valuable advertising exposure may also be incorporated on the competitive field of play, on score clocks and timing devices, bordering the playing surface, at start and finish lines, and behind goals, player benches, dugouts, and penalty boxes. The relative value of each of these positions is, again, determined by the frequency with which the signage is in the spectators' or television viewers' active field of vision. During competitive downtime, such as intermissions, and between heats, innings, or matches, special video features and promotions and on-field fan activities may be "presented by" a sponsor who is both visually and verbally recognized.

A sponsor's exposure benefits can also extend well before and beyond event day, both in advertising purchased by the organizer and in space arranged by the sponsors themselves in fulfillment of their activation strategies. Event advertising placed by the organizer may list just a primary, title, or presenting sponsor (see "Exposure—Publicity" on page 153), or may include a rotating list of other participating companies. Event promotions that at once help to sell tickets and offer dollars-off incentives with the purchase of sponsor products can provide both exposure and sales opportunities as direct benefits of sponsorship.

EXPOSURE—PRODUCT PLACEMENT

One of the most valuable, sought-after, and closely protected advantages of sponsorship is the benefit of product placement. Sponsors attach great importance to the notion that their products, to the exclusion of any competitors, are those that will be used by the sports event organizer or are available to the public at, or through, the event. Food, beverage, and beer sponsors will insist that their brands be vended at the event. Apparel manufacturers will likewise demand that their lines of merchandise be those affixed with the event's logo and sold at the event site. A cap manufacturer will want to see its logo on the side of the event caps worn by athletes during press conferences. Any product category that can be imagined to be useful in preparing for and executing an event is likely to have product placement provisions tied into the sponsorship deal—from airlines, car rentals, and hotels to telecommunications services, computers, and office equipment. In a returned spirit of partnership, of course, the event organizer can negotiate for preferred pricing on these products and services or accept some portion of an event's requirements as part of a VIK arrangement. Product placement requirements may also involve other manifestations unique to the product category. Examples include soft drink sponsor names on beverage cups and squeeze bottles, the use of sponsor vehicles in and around the event venue, and staff wardrobe sporting logos integrating the event and the manufacturer.

Sponsors often provide their products or services for consumer sweepstakes, promotions, and even awards for the athletes, to create excitement and exposure at the event and in the publicity generated immediately following.

A lucky fan may win an all-expenses-paid trip to a future event provided by an airline and hotel sponsor, or the free use of a cellular telephone with service for a year. The top-scoring hitter in Major League Baseball's Home Run Derby wins a house worth $250,000 from Century 21 Realty for a sweepstakes contestant drawn at random. The "Most Valuable Player" at the NHL All-Star Game wins a Ram truck from Dodge, the event's automotive partner. (*Caution:* There are strict guidelines governing gifts, prizes, and awards to athletes, particularly amateurs and students, which can affect their future competitive status. Event organizers must be fully informed of any restrictions on a participant's acceptance of a sponsor gift or award.) These benefits provide sponsors with exposure benefits that are even more powerful than those of advertising, in the form of an endorsement demonstrating the event's strong preference for using a particular sponsor's product.

EXPOSURE—PUBLICITY

Sponsors spend millions of dollars each year to generate publicity for their products because they know that media coverage is generally perceived by the public as more objective and credible, and holds the public's attention for a longer period of time than a typical advertisement. The most effective way for a company to consistently capitalize on the publicity generated by a sports event is to literally appear within its name, as a *title* or *presenting* sponsor. Title sponsors are companies or brands whose names appear before or within the name of a sports event, such as the McDonald's Open, the Dodge/NHL SuperSkills Tour, and the Molson Indy. Presenting sponsors, companies with identities linked to the end of an event name, such as the NHL All-Star Weekend presented by Nextel, also hope to increase their public exposure through a close association with the name of the event. Companies that invest heavily in title and presenting sponsorships recognize the publicity value offered by their elevated association, appreciating the likelihood that their brand will be routinely mentioned in news reports and sports articles during the normal coverage of an event. Title and presenting sponsorships command premium sponsorship fees for the organizer because of all of the extra public recognition the partner receives. These top-tier sponsors benefit from the inclusion of their identities within the event logo and/or word marks, in advertising, on tickets, in information sent to participants and guests, and on virtually any printed material generated by the organizer.

Title and presenting sponsorships supported by supplemental activation budgets tend to reach deepest into the public consciousness. However, this is not the only way companies develop opportunities for enhanced publicity through their event partnerships. Sponsors often participate in intriguing and involving fan promotions that can capture the imagination and active interest of both the media and the public. Watching an average spectator attempt a difficult athletic feat for an impressive cash prize, for example, has become a popular feature of major televised sports events in recent years. These "Million Dollar Shots," sponsored promotions in which a finalist qualifies for a chance to win an astronomical cash prize, can generate considerable interest in the media, and measurable impressions in advance and post-event coverage. The payoffs for these promotions are frequently designed as "insurance prizes" to keep the sponsor's costs within reason. That is, because the odds of someone winning the prize are low, but not zero, the sponsor can purchase an insurance policy to protect against the possibility of having to pay the enormous sum. Several agencies specialize in offering sponsors and organizers insurance prize policies, with premiums ranging from 10 to 50 percent of the prize value, depending on the difficulty of the contest. Obviously, the insurance agency will require involvement in the setting of contest rules to ensure that there is a very good probability that the contestant will fail. Alternatively, the sponsor can self-insure the prize by setting aside the full amount in advance if it desires to better the odds that a contestant will succeed.

Significant donations made to a worthy cause as a result of a sports event sponsorship can also generate significant media interest if properly promoted. Funds may be raised as a donated percentage of ticket sales, through silent auctions, via contributions made by fans or viewers and matched by the sponsor, or as a percentage of sponsor product sales during a specified period of time. Charitable promotions, which can firmly and favorably position both the sponsor and the event in the public's perception, are explored further on page 157.

CUSTOMER HOSPITALITY

Companies have long regarded sports events as excellent opportunities to extend hospitality and demonstrate appreciation to customers and important clients, dealers, distributors, franchisees, agents, and top salespeople. The 2003 MPI/George P. Johnson study further noted that events help sponsors close business deals faster, with sports marketing cited as a major "lead maturation" opportunity (i.e., effective venues to help convert business prospects into customers). For this reason, sponsors who most value sports events as customer hospitality vehicles expect access to what are perceived as "the best seats in the house" for the purpose of entertaining important guests and prospects. Customer hospitality is of particular importance to companies that transact most of their business with other businesses (commonly known as "B-to-B" companies). The average monetary value of a B-to-B sale can be significantly greater than that of a sale from a business to a consumer. Therefore, the marketing effort and dollars B-to-B companies apply to developing each new customer, and servicing existing ones, are often much greater than those of consumer companies. The experiential aspects of event sponsorship, that is, the ability to host prospects and reward current customers, are of increased importance and often represent a greater percentage of sponsorship spending for B-to-B companies. Treating special guests with tickets for preferred seating locations, passes to private receptions or invitation-only hospitality suites, the ability to meet the athletes, and other exclusive and unique considerations can put B-to-B sponsors at a great advantage over their competition.

Figure 6-4 describes the sports event marketing strategies employed by one major U.S.-based company that services both consumers and the B-to-B

Nextel Communications, Inc.'s director of Sports and Event Marketing, Michael Robichaud, explains how sports events can provide the company with direct connections to its customers through its "Top 5 Strategies."

1. **Brand Exposure**

"Our category is very competitive and we have large competitors with significantly larger budgets to compete with. Sponsorships offer us windows of opportunity to reach our very targeted customer segments in a unique and impactful way."

2. **Customer/Prospect Interaction**

"Fortunately for us, we have a competitive advantage through product differentiation. Nextel's unique Direct Connect (two-way walkie-talkie radio) feature is unlike anything else in the wireless industry. While this is certainly an advantage, we also must work hard to present this to prospects so they can fully understand the feature. Through our various sponsorships, we have been able to create activities at major events to expose people to this service in a fun and interactive way. There is no substitute for experiencing our product, and sports sponsorships put us at events where we can directly meet our target prospects."

3. **Support Media**

"Nextel has traditionally purchased media during sports programming prior to initiating a sponsorship. By adding sponsorship components to these media buys we are able to increase the exposure, block our competitors, and put our brand alongside other well-thought-of brands."

4. **Increase Purchase Consideration**

"While Nextel has been successful exposing the brand to its target market, it is important to encourage people to increase their consideration to purchase, and ultimately close a sale. We hope to accomplish this by a combination of the first three elements."

5. **Customer Hospitality**

"Since Nextel has such a business-to-business focus, sponsored events can be great places to host customers. While Nextel does this in many of the traditional ways, we also look for unique opportunities that only a major event sponsor can offer, such as special access to limited events or opportunities to meet with athletes."

Figure 6-4
Nextel's Sports Event Sponsorship Strategies

market, Nextel Communications, Inc. The company's confidence in its product is evident in its emphasis on using sports events to showcase its unique technology by putting it in close proximity with corporate executives who can make purchasing decisions for their organizations.

SALES OPPORTUNITIES

Sponsors that have invested significantly in the success of a sports event expect that organizers will, in the spirit of good partnership, afford them opportunities to offset some of their costs with direct sales or the development of potential future sales. Most often these objectives are achieved by engaging in on-site activities such as product demonstrations, sampling, couponing, or premium giveaways. Organizers who actively help a sponsor sell more of its products at an event are actually helping themselves. The more business a sponsor can develop at an event, whether manifest by direct sales or as leads for subsequent sales, the more likely it will deem the investment a success and want to return as a partner for future programs.

For some companies, a sports events venue offers an attractive marketplace for direct sales of their products, the most common being marketers of food, beverages, apparel, and collectibles. Other products and services also offer special event-day sales promotions and subscription incentives. MBNA, for example, a financial services company specializing in "affinity" credit cards, payment instruments that display the applicant's choice of sports team or other association on the face of a card, frequently offers free and exclusive event merchandise to attendees who apply for a card at the event. Recognizing the highly motivated viewing habits of sports fans, cable and satellite television operators often offer special sports packages on a trial basis to those who apply at an event for their services. A cellular telephone company that offers web-enabled phones can similarly promote the fan's ability to use its product to access scores of games in progress.

Many organizers offer sponsors areas for product demonstrations and sampling on the event facility's public concourses, in kiosks sprinkled through the event site, or in special tents or booths. The Bolder Boulder 10K road race held each May in Boulder, Colorado, for example, opens an entire athletic field filled with tents offering free samples of healthy lifestyle products and purchasable items for the 45,000 runners and the 100,000 spectators who cheer them on. Philips Arena, in Atlanta, Georgia, features an interactive, high-tech Philips/Magnavox consumer electronics product fair, open to fans attending every event. Many sports fan festivals include memorabilia areas for collectors, sponsored by trading card companies such as Topps and Upper Deck, which may offer a special card or set available only at the event. Or a local restaurant may provide coupons and samples of appetizers to event attendees, designed to drive traffic to its business location.

Marketers discover that sports events are effective places to reach their customers, because attendee demographics are generally predictable and fans are in a highly excited, and therefore receptive, state of mind. The more a sponsor can associate its product or offer with the event itself, such as with MBNA's affinity cards, the better it can leverage that excitement and receptivity to influence sales.

FUND-RAISING FOR CORPORATE CAUSES

Some socially conscious companies combine their commercial involvement in a sports event with an effort to raise awareness and revenue for important causes and quality-of-life social programs. Whether the sponsor views the fund-raising component of its participation as simply a public relations gesture or as part of its corporate philanthropic philosophy, sports events offer outstanding opportunities for doing good beyond the stadium gates.

Many sports event organizations are themselves not-for-profit associations that exist to promote a particular sport, lifestyle, or quality-of-life benefit. The International Special Olympics, the New York Road Runners Club (organizers of the New York City Marathon, among many other events), the many national Olympic committees and national governing bodies, Little League, and hundreds of other not-for-profit sports associations are also organizers that stage sports events to promote their sports and movements. Although sponsor dollars are required to stage their events, most of their business models include raising needed revenues to fund operations, awareness programs, research and development, and other cause-related activities. Some events, like the AIDS Run for a Cure, are activities staged exclusively to achieve philanthropic and social missions, the sports event providing a compelling backdrop for the worthy cause.

Sponsors understand the enormous public relations benefits of funding cause-related activities, and many reinforce their marketing investments with additional grants from their philanthropic budgets to ensure a sizable return for a charity. In addition to maintaining their good intentions, many corporate supporters still want to take advantage of the rightfully attendant sponsor benefits that are due them through their association with an event regardless of from which budget the money originates.

The benefits of being associated with a not-for-profit cause or movement are well understood by event organizers as well. It is often the charitable aspect of an event that spurs ticket buyers into action and can attenuate one of the key components of a ticket buyer's hesitation—price sensitivity. As long as the cost of admission remains within a range that is not completely unreasonable, members of the ticket-buying public will respond more favorably to an event whose proceeds benefit a charity with which they feel some affinity, than to a similar program without a not-for-profit beneficiary. Charitable

Sideline Story—NHL All-Star Celebrity Challenge presented by Microsoft Windows XP

Among its many philanthropic efforts, Microsoft Corporation stages celebrity sports events benefiting children's hospitals across North America to generate money for constructing lounges and activity centers for their young patients. For the National Hockey League, the 2002 NHL All-Star Weekend in Los Angeles provided an outstanding platform upon which to organize and promote a celebrity hockey game. Microsoft perceived the NHL All-Star festivities as a perfect opportunity to generate publicity and funds for its children's hospital project in Los Angeles while building public awareness for its new Microsoft Windows XP computer operating system.

The company committed to funding the NHL All-Star Celebrity Challenge presented by Microsoft Windows XP guaranteeing the purchase of more than 2,000 tickets at $25 each, which they used for customer hospitality and promotional purposes. The sponsor further activated its association by committing to additional spending to cover sponsor fulfillment costs such as print advertising, arena signage, gifts to the players, and consumer marketing demonstrations in the arena concourse. The alluring combination of skating on the All-Star ice with the donation of significant funds to a worthy cause attracted producers Jerry Bruckheimer and David E. Kelley to serve as team captains, leading players that included Cuba Gooding Jr., Tim Robbins, Rachel Blanchard, Chris Jericho, Alan Thicke, Bobby Farrelly (producer, goaltender, and game MVP), and dozens more. More than 12,000 Los Angeles fans purchased tickets to watch a high-profile recreational hockey game at the Staples Center that generated charitable revenues for the hospital and awareness of the sponsor's new product.

objectives are especially helpful in generating ticket buyers—as well as athletes—for events that, without this association, may otherwise be of marginal interest to the public at large.

ASSOCIATIVE BENEFITS—EXCLUSIVITY

With some few exceptions, business partners expect that their financial participation in an event will buy them some level of exclusivity—the ability to promote their company or brand without the interfering presence of their competition. This is not a universal truth, as demonstrated by events such as auto racing, in which the participants themselves are individually sponsored, supported by companies that often conflict with the supporters of the overall event. It is, however, true that although exclusivity is not a characteristic that can be ascribed a measurable financial value, its presence can constitute a significant portion of the sponsorship price tag. Sponsors understand that this premium is a necessary component of their fee. They know that once they enter into an agreement with a sports event, the organizer is no longer able to accept revenues from any other company or brand within their defined and protected category.

When a business partner enters into an agreement with an event organizer, the contract should define the exact corporate identity being granted sponsorship rights. For example, is it the company being recognized as an official sponsor (e.g., Anheuser-Busch), or is it a specific brand (e.g., Bud Light beer)? Because many companies market multiple brands and product lines, the agreement should also note the categories of exclusivity being protected by the sponsorship. For instance, the corporate parent of an event's soft drink sponsor may also distribute snack foods and own chains of fast-food or quick-service restaurants (QSRs). Sponsors often wish to prohibit the event organizer from entering into relationships with companies that compete with their other brands or lines of business, even though they are not represented at the event. Organizers often respond by seeking to negotiate a higher sponsorship fee as recompense for the lost revenue opportunity forced by excluding these other business categories from a possible event partnership.

The exclusivity sponsor's demand goes far beyond the walls of the event venue. A sponsor's exclusive rights must be protected in sales promotions, advertising, and other activities that take place before the event or outside of the facility. Organizers must pursue the perpetrators of "guerilla marketing" activities, efforts undertaken by nonsponsor companies to give the public an impression of their being associated with an event. Common guerilla marketing activities are characterized by the unauthorized use of the event name, logos, and images, or terminology and artwork simply suggestive of an association with the event. Illicit techniques include the use of event tickets for promotional purposes, the creation and sale of unauthorized merchandise, and advertising that implies a relationship with an event without using any of the organizer's trademarks.

One of the most bedeviling developments facing event organizers today is the increasing frequency with which event sponsors and the partners of the host facility are direct competitors. Conflicts between facility signage advertisers and competitive event sponsors are not new. The more recent and economically necessary practice of facilities renaming themselves after a major sponsor, however, has created many more, and more noticeable, conflicts than those that have existed between the sponsors of a facility and an event sponsor.

The economic realities of both the sports and facilities businesses have manifested themselves in the increasingly common practice of selling title sponsorship of new and existing sports facilities to a corporate partner. This partnership is highly valuable to both the owner of the venue and the sponsor that buys the right to name it. The sponsor may contribute millions of dollars over the term of its contract to help finance construction or reduce some of the debt incurred during development of the facility. In return, the sponsor knows that thousands of newspaper articles, sports reports, and game broadcasts will make regular and frequent reference to the name of the facility without any additional purchase of advertising in those media. Millions of ticket buyers who enter the building will also be bombarded with the name and logo of the presenting sponsor on exterior signage, ticket faces, scoreboards, even highway signs directing drivers to its parking lots. There is probably no better or more positive way for a sponsor to become a household byword than by lending its name to one of a community's most exciting places of gathering.

How does this level of ubiquitous corporate identification affect a sports event organizer's ability to protect their own sponsor's rights? While it can be challenging, it is an increasingly common phenomenon, as illustrated by the next two Sideline Stories.

The enormous investment made by a facility's naming sponsor may well stretch its marketing budget to the point that additional sponsor opportunities may no longer be affordable to it. Because the namesake sponsor of a sports event facility will enjoy thousands of incidental references in the media, it correctly presumes that this recognition will provide additional exposure benefits de facto before the fans of visiting events. A naming sponsor's overarching presence can also effectively discourage competitor companies from entering into agreements with event organizers leasing the facility, further protecting its exclusivity. Naming sponsors, therefore, may not believe there is any need to participate as sponsors of teams or events inside their facilities. As illustrated in the Sideline Story on page 162, this is not always a sound, foregone conclusion.

Presuming that the competitive issues between an event's sponsor and a host facility's namesake can be overcome, organizers are well advised to determine what restrictions a facility's manager will place on an event's corporate supporters before confirming the host venue. Beyond prohibiting the obscuration or obstruction of existing sponsor signage and displays, and insisting on pouring official beverages from their concessions (specifically soft drinks and beer), most facilities in today's marketplace will put few restrictions on event organizers. The sponsor that has purchased the naming rights to its building understands that it is in the venue's best interest to encourage organizers to book events there, even those with competing sponsors. Whether an existing sponsor will want to participate in an event facility named for a competing sponsor is a matter of corporate culture and strategy. Some relish the sweet irony and will expend even greater effort to generate publicity about be-

Sideline Story—A Coca-Cola-Sponsored Event at Pepsi Center

It was not the first time the NHL All-Star Weekend was awarded to an arena bearing the name of a company competitive with one of the league's major sponsors. Vancouver's General Motors Place hosted the event in 1998, despite Dodge's status as the NHL's automobile sponsor. But when the Pepsi Center in Denver, Colorado, was awarded the 2001 NHL All-Star festivities, a program sponsored by Coca-Cola, it captured the attention of a number of leading business writers. "Remember when magician David Copperfield made the Statue of Liberty disappear?" mused the *Denver Post*'s Dick Kreck. "That's nothing compared to making the entire Pepsi Center vanish. But, the year-old building will become "invisible" during the National Hockey League All-Star Weekend Feb. 3 and 4. That's because the NHL's soft drink is Coca-Cola and, obviously, the pop giant is in no hurry to share the spotlight with archrival Pepsi. . . . First, there will be no mention of the words "Pepsi Center" on the game tickets or on the air. It will be "the arena" or "the home of the Colorado Avalanche."

Mr. Kreck was absolutely right. Out of respect for Coca-Cola, the "P" word did not appear in any NHL press release or advertisement, on any ticket, promotional piece, or on any signage inside the arena seating areas. Although Pepsi had the exclusive right to be the sole provider of soft drinks in the arena, the NHL replaced all of the concessionaire's Pepsi Center drink cups with special commemorative cups sporting the All-Star event logo and excluding the name of the arena. "Given the state of sports sponsorships (everything that can be named, will be named), such conflicts are inevitable," Kreck observed. Thus, the sponsors of sports facilities will not prohibit a competitor from staging events in their namesake buildings. It is up to the organizers to work double time to protect the interests of their own sponsors in such facilities.

ing in "enemy territory," while others will want to avoid being near a "competitor's building" completely.

ASSOCIATIVE BENEFITS—OWNERSHIP

Sponsors are not vigilant solely about ensuring the absence of their competitors at a sports event. They also consider the degree to which other, noncompetitor business partners are present and recognized. As may be expected, the

Sideline Story—Southwest Airlines and the Phoenix Suns

Although this story does not portray a specific sports event, important and applicable lessons may be learned from the sponsorship agreement reached between the NBA's Phoenix Suns, who play at America West Arena, and America West's competitor, Southwest Airlines. As the title sponsor of the arena in which the team plays, America West enjoys considerable exclusivity in the airline category, prohibiting signage and all other recognition of any competitor within the building's walls. Conventional wisdom suggests that, armed with the automatic public recognition and on-site category exclusivity that comes with title sponsorship of the arena, America West would have no incentive to sponsor the team. The Suns, however, successfully reached an agreement with Southwest Airlines in June 2003 that provided the building sponsor's competitor with significant exposure opportunities on game broadcasts, in outdoor advertising, and in promotions and activities outside the arena, as well as on the team's web site. In this case, the team was able to avoid violating the in-arena exclusivity owned by America West by offering Southwest Airlines sponsor benefits in a host of other areas, an industry category that might have otherwise been closed to it. Can your event benefit from such innovative thinking?

greater a sponsor's financial commitment, the more protective it will be about how its company or product will be perceived as compared with all others who are associated with the event. Sponsors will expect the organizers to protect them from excessive "clutter," a condition in which there are so many sponsors that the impact of their event identification is greatly diminished. To rise above the clutter of their fellow event partners, experienced sponsors strive to develop unique and innovative promotions or to pursue an association with specific event elements they can "own" exclusively. Such elements may include being identified as the presenting sponsor of a championship trophy, an MVP ("most valuable player") award, or some other form of participant recognition. Intermission or halftime entertainment, pregame shows, individual heats, races, or competitions, or in-venue promotions that benefit one or more fans are other components commonly offered to corporate partners that seek to rise above the sponsor clutter, even if only for a few minutes during the program.

Some companies in nonsports industries have taken event ownership to its purest form by developing, owning, and, in some cases, managing sports events themselves. Ethan Green, former vice president North America for international sponsorship consultants Redmandarin, predicted that the number of these proprietary sponsorships, events that are owned outright by the sponsoring corporation, would experience growth in the coming years. "Property ownership allows companies to control everything—branding, audience composition, number and type of associate sponsors—and maintain control over the budget at the same time," Green wrote on *www.redmandarin.com,* the company's web site. His further prognostications included a trend toward sponsors involving more than one of their brands in a single event, allowing corporations to spread their rights fees over multiple products and services, appealing to multiple demographics with distinct messages that could be directed toward each target market.

Whether managing and executing an event with its own employees or retaining the services of a professional event management firm, owning an event outright offers a corporation total control over the number and types of other brands that will be permitted to participate in the event, and at what price. The company can customize sponsorship programs for its own business partners that can maximize sales opportunities for both. A soft drink company that owns its own sports event, for instance, might offer an opportunity for participation to a QSR to whom that company itself is a supplier. In this example, promoting the restaurants can have the secondary effect of increasing consumption of the company's own products at those locations. The corporate sports event owner can also define precisely how partners will enjoy exposure at the event and ensure that its own company or brand message dominates above its colleague organizations. As owner of the event, the company can limit consumer-directed activities to promotions that most effectively market its sports property, best enhance its sales, and control the clutter of too many advertising messages competing for the audience's attention.

Some of the most commonly encountered sports event "owners" can be found within the publishing industry, particularly the segments dedicated to both general- and special-interest sports.

Primedia is one of the world's leading publishers of special-interest magazines, with 250 titles, including *SG: Surf, Snow, Skate Girl.* The relaunch of the magazine in 2003 was supported by the first annual "SG Queen of the Mountain" professional and amateur snowboarding event held at Mountain High Resort in Wrightwood, California. The publisher planned to introduce an "SG Queen of the Beach" pro surfing event later the same year to reenergize and expand its appeal. The magazine's costs of staging the events were reported to be approximately $20,000 each, offset in part by advertising in Primedia publications provided on a VIK basis to the host resorts.

The advantages of corporate event ownership are clear. By controlling every aspect of the program, the corporate owner can ensure its dominance and avoid the effects of multiple-sponsor messages and clutter. Smaller-scale, precisely targeted niche events like the *SG* programs are prime candidates for corporate ownership because of their manageable cost and the relatively straightforward ability to measure the effectiveness of the program through increased sales (in this case, subscriptions). Grassroots and community programs involving local amateur athletes offer similarly attractive opportunities for corporate ownership by small local businesses for the same reasons—low costs easily compensated by incremental sales.

Corporate ownership of large-scale, high-budget events has not become as prevalent for a host of reasons. The financial risks are usually too great for a single company to assume. This is why sports event organizers must develop opportunities to attract multiple sponsors from a wide range of industries. In the professional and semiprofessional sports world, an athlete's personal endorsement contracts can prove another obstacle to a sponsor corporation's owning a sports event. Contracts signed with competitive companies can prevent a top-drawer athlete or team from appearing at a corporate-owned event. In today's sports event marketplace, genuine, strategic, and effective partnerships between event organizers and corporate sponsors remain the business model standard because of the potential to realize at least a portion of the partners' corporate objectives without their assuming the financial risks of staging the entire program.

ASSOCIATIVE BENEFITS—PRESTIGE AND REPUTATION

Another intangible benefit sought by sponsors is simply being associated with an event considered highly attractive by their most valued customers. The prestige and reputation of an event, its participating athletes, and, in some cases, its organizing entity can add significantly to its attractiveness to sponsors. The greater the public's interest in an event, the greater the hunger will be for tickets. The greater the demand for tickets, the more desirable the event will be for sponsors as an opportunity to entertain their important business guests. Prestige also adds to the effectiveness of consumer promotions and efforts that increase the likelihood of media coverage, which can reinforce the association between a business partner and the event it sponsors.

PASS-THROUGH RIGHTS

Some sponsors whose businesses depend on the advertising or promotional efforts of other companies to bring their products to the consumer, such as retailers, media outlets, credit card brands, and software developers, among others, favor securing pass-through rights to help make their event partnerships more efficient. *Pass-through rights* refer to the transference, by a sponsor, of some of its event benefits to its suppliers, distributors, retailers, advertisers, or other business partners. Such rights can, however, lead to serious misunderstandings if their limits and restrictions are not defined before a sponsor enters into a final sponsorship agreement.

When a sponsor requests the inclusion of pass-through rights, what it really wants is to offer a portion of its contracted entitlements to a third party. In so doing, the sponsor hopes to offset its financial obligations to the event or extend its reach to the consumer through copromotions with its existing business partners. An electronics manufacturer, for example, may desire to offer pass-through rights to an electronics retail chain in return for that retailer providing advertising, in-store sales, and point-of-purchase displays featuring the manufacturer's products and their joint association with the sports event. Similarly, a software developer may want to reduce its cash costs by sharing a portion of the sponsorship fee with a manufacturer that bundles its software into the purchase of every new computer.

Media partners are particularly aggressive in pursuing pass-through rights. Being able to offer existing advertisers some limited benefit flowing from their association with an event often helps media sponsors offset their sponsorship fees, whether they are paid in cash or with the value of free advertising space or time. (See Play 8 for a closer look at media relationships.)

To Fox Sports Net Florida's director of marketing, Peter Nawrocki, the ability to exploit pass-through rights can be a win-win for his cable network and the events it sponsors. The network likes to offer pass-through rights to its advertisers and to other business partners "that can make our presence at the event even bigger, thus giving the impression to consumers-at-large that you have more 'ownership' of the event," he says. Nawrocki involves Fox Sports Net's advertisers by using event benefits as sales or promotional incentives, which helps him to offset his organization's investment as an event sponsor. Yet the benefits of offering a sports event's media partner pass-through rights are not completely weighted on the side of the sponsor. In Nawrocki's view, the more flexibility he is permitted to spread benefits among his advertisers, the more promotional muscle and advertising time he can offer an event.

Conferring pass-through rights to sponsors, if they are offered at all, is something that event organizers should consider both judiciously and selectively. When a third party agrees to an association with an event through a sponsor that passes rights to it, it is effectively removed from the universe of potential sponsors that can be solicited for revenues directly by the organizer. After all, why would a company make the large investment to be a sponsor if it can pick and choose only the benefits it absolutely needs, passed through by an existing sponsor at potentially a far lower cost? Perhaps more significant, this practice could remove an entire category of sponsors from the organizer's list of potential targets. If a quick-service restaurant enjoys an association with an event via pass-through rights from a sponsor (a soft drink company, for example), the event organizer would have a very difficult time selling a sponsorship to any other QSR. In addition, the event organizer must protect his or her current sponsors by guarding against the possibility of pass-through rights being offered to an existing partner's competitors. An organizer's vigilance against competitors, regardless of how they may come to associate with an event, is an essential component of what a sponsor pays for.

Pass-through rights, on the other hand, can be very advantageous to an event organizer if they provide the potential for ticket sales, promotions, or exposure opportunities far beyond those otherwise available in the market. In the example discussed earlier, it may be that no QSR will make the commitment to support the event in cash. Working through the soft drink sponsor, however, the restaurant may agree to undertake promotions involving significant exposure through tray liners, in-store posters, and on-bag advertising. If the demographics of the event and the restaurant complement each other and there is a low probability of attracting a sponsor in the QSR category, there may be very good reason to accept a pass-through provision in the soft drink company's sponsorship deal. The limits to which a sponsor will be permitted the right to pass through specific benefits should be clearly defined in its sponsorship agreement. It is recommended that every proposed third-party relationship be reviewed by the event organizer, and that none be permitted unless specifically approved in advance by the organizer in writing.

Know Your Sponsors

Armed with a familiarity of what sponsors generally seek from its sports event partnerships, it is now time to combine the organizer's revenue objectives with an analysis of what a specific prospective sponsor will want, need, and expect from its investment. Many event organizers begin by creating standardized packages of benefits for prospective sponsors at a number of different investment levels, assigning the quantity and quality of included features that correspond to the size of the proposed fee. Although presenting a package of consistent, predetermined benefits is often a good place to start the sales planning process, customizing a benefits package based on intelligence about a prospective sponsor's objectives is often a much more effective way to increase that sponsor's interest and accelerate the closing of a deal.

Customizing a sponsorship package that includes the right features in the right quantities requires an understanding of a prospective partner's business objectives, its target market, and the marketing strategies it employs to communicate with and sell to its customers. Figure 6-5 provides a useful checklist of questions, the answers to which can help sports event organizers better understand the businesses of their prospective sponsor partners and the customers they serve.

Once in possession of the answers to as many of these questions as possible, the organizer can evaluate the prospect company as to whether it is a

□ Who are the company's customers?
- Do they transact most of their business with individual consumers or with corporate clients?
- If they sell to both businesses and consumers, to whom do they want to direct their event marketing efforts?
- What are the demographics (i.e., the objective statistical characteristics) of the customers they most want to speak to?
  - Are they young, middle-aged, or senior citizens?
  - Are they married, have children living in their household, or "empty nesters" (i.e., married with grown children living elsewhere)?
  - Is their disposable income modest, average, or appreciable?
  - What is their average level of education?
  - Do they rent an apartment or own a home?
  - In what parts of the country, state, or community do they live?
- What are the psychographics, or behavioral characteristics, of the company's target customers?
  - What kinds of sports do they enjoy participating in?
  - What kinds of sports do they enjoy watching? How often?
  - Are they the kinds of people who try or purchase new products and emerging technologies soon after they are introduced ("innovators"), or after most others have adopted and proven the worth of such innovations ("late majority")?
  - Do they enjoy an active lifestyle or do they pursue largely sedentary leisure endeavors?
  - What do they watch on television?
  - What kind of music do they enjoy?

□ What are the marketing and communications strategies the company applies to appeal to its target customers?

□ Is the company's brand well established or new to the public? Is it declining or increasing in popularity?

□ Does the prospective sponsor have a corporate culture or reputation for innovation and creativity?

□ What other sports events does the prospect sponsor?
- How does it use these events to achieve its objectives?
- What promotional benefits associated with these events does the company find work successfully for it?

□ What does the prospective sponsor want to gain from a sports event relationship in general, and from this relationship in particular, presuming the event provides opportunities that match its needs?

□ With what events are its competitors associated? How successful have their competitors been in their event marketing efforts?

□ How will the company evaluate the success of its association?

Figure 6-5
Getting to Know Your Prospective Sponsor and Its Customers

likely candidate for a sponsorship. Presuming the event presents a good opportunity for the prospect to reach its customers, the organizer is now better prepared to design a program that meets the sponsor's needs and provides the benefits of the greatest and most relevant value. What kinds of features can the event organizer offer, and in what quantity can they be made available to help the sponsor realize its goals? Would its sales efforts be better served by loading the deal with more premium-location tickets, trade or consumer advertising, sales promotions or event promotions with publicity potential?

After considering all existing opportunities, it may become apparent that the company's objectives would be best served by adding an entirely new and previously unplanned feature to the event. The Sideline Story on page 170 describes the development and evolution of an event program designed to precisely fit the needs of a sponsor, but which was an added feature to the program already in place. Although the sponsor received a standard package of tickets, advertising, and promotional benefits, the event organizer proposed this higher-priced inclusion in recognition of the sponsor's desire to stand above its competitors as a creative and innovative marketer and to position its brand as genuine and exciting.

The specific needs of prospective sponsors and the event elements they will judge as best meeting their business objectives will vary widely from company to company. Although there are fundamental differences between the marketing practices most often employed by consumer-oriented businesses and those of B-to-B companies, some generalizations may be made regarding the types of sponsor benefits they seek from their event relationships. Contrast the overall characteristics of the consumer company sponsor package described in Figure 6-6 with the comparable features of a typical B-to-B sponsor package illustrated in Figure 6-7. Keep in mind that the relative importance of each type of benefit may differ between any two sponsors even within the same major business category, depending on those companies' individual marketing strategies.

- Event tickets
- Limited exclusive-access opportunities
- Consumer advertising
- Discount and premium sales promotions
- Direct sales opportunities
- Product sampling opportunities
- Commercial time (for events covered on television and/or radio)

Figure 6-6
Typical Sponsor Benefit Features for
Consumer Products Companies

- Premium event tickets
- Broad exclusive access opportunities
- Business, trade, or specialty advertising and publicity
- High-value promotions
- Product demonstration opportunities
- Client hospitality opportunities
  - Hosted by the event organizer
  - Staged directly by the sponsor

Figure 6-7
Sample Sponsor Benefit Features
for B-to-B Companies

CONSUMER PRODUCTS COMPANY SPONSOR BENEFITS

Consumer products companies are those whose end users are individual customers, marketing products they manufacture or sell at retail, with costs ranging from just a few cents to thousands of dollars—such as producers of candy bars or beer, long-distance telephone carriers, makers of kitchen appliances, real estate agencies, and automobile manufacturers. These types of companies commonly use event tickets to entertain their distributors, agents, wholesalers, retailers, and key executives, as well as for prizes in consumer sweepstakes and promotions. Their needs for exclusive access opportunities, such as "meet and greet" encounters with athletes and celebrities, visits backstage, and passes to receptions and media events, are usually limited in quantity as pleasing additional features for consumer sweepstakes promotions.

As marketers of products or services to the public, consumer-oriented companies usually find advertising opportunities to be the most beneficial. These advertising benefits may include print advertising in the event program, public address and scoreboard announcements, commercials aired on the facility's video screen, and display signage near the playing surface or elsewhere in the host venue. Acknowledgments and sponsor logos placed by the organizer in consumer publications to promote the event, as well as on the Internet and in broadcast media, are also highly desirable elements for companies marketing primarily to a consumer audience. The use of time for airing sponsor commercials during television or radio coverage of sports events is usually a key component of major consumer company sponsorship deals.

The exclusive right to engage in promotional activities directed toward ticket buyers and other consumers, whether managed by the sponsor or presented by the event organizer under the sponsor's name, is highly attractive to these types of companies. Consumer-oriented promotions may include event merchandise or premium giveaways, ticket and/or travel sweepstakes, and

Sideline Story— Labatt Blue/NHL All-Star Pick-Up Hockey Marathon (Revisited)

One of the most memorable Canadian television commercials in the late 1990s was for Labatt Blue beer, in which a carelessly discarded aluminum can inspires a spontaneous game of street hockey among passersby en route to work. Shortly after the ad's premiere, the 50th NHL All-Star Game returned to Toronto, Ontario. The league sought to create a series of special events to celebrate this golden anniversary in a way that would capture the hearts and minds of the knowledgeable and passionate hockey fans of Toronto, as well as the Canadian media. Recognizing Labatt's innovative reputation, as demonstrated by this popular commercial, the City of Toronto was approached about creating a reenactment on a grand scale—closing a four-block-long stretch of Bay Street for a lunchtime street hockey game featuring thousands of area workers. Perhaps, it was reasoned, Labatt would even be inspired to use some of the images from the day as the basis of its next commercial. Visualizing an ambitious restaging of a very familiar commercial, it took the city less than a minute to agree to stopping midday traffic in the heart of the city's busy financial district.

The Labatt Brewing Company was presented with a detailed plan preapproved by the Toronto Police Department and other required city agencies. Although members of the sponsor's marketing staff politely allowed that the event might have some merit as a media opportunity, they felt that the event was too exaggerated with its giant goal nets and thousands of players. As such, it did not embrace one of their product's key brand attributes—genuineness—and was not sufficiently true to the sport they so actively supported.

The organizers went back to the drawing board to develop an event that was more genuine to the game of hockey, the Canadian hockey experience, and of course, Labatt Blue. The Labatt Blue/NHL All-Star Pick-Up Hockey Marathon was born and embraced by the sponsor. A rustic set of rink boards and benches would be constructed around an existing outdoor ice surface in front of Toronto City Hall. The puck would be dropped for a game between two teams of adult amateur players at 8:00 A.M. on Monday, and play would continue 24 hours a day until it was no longer possible to ice a full squad of players. The game proceeded on schedule until Thursday at 7:30 A.M., four days later, when the bench of 90 players per side could no longer continue. The Labatt Blue/NHL All-Star Pick-Up Marathon captured national media attention for almost 72 hours and stayed true to Labatt's desire to portray the genuine passion for hockey felt by their loyal customers.

event admission or merchandise discounts with a sponsor's proofs-of-purchase or coupons. They may also feature opportunities to offer fans unique participatory activities, ranging from trivia and skills contests to an honorary ceremonial role in the event (e.g., honorary bat boy, honorary trainer, dropping of the first puck).

Realizing that they provide outstanding opportunities for reaching fans directly, consumer products companies frequently take advantage of sports events as direct sales and sampling opportunities, passing out full- or trial-sized samples or coupons for discounts at an associated retail location. Consumer product sponsors also often distribute premium items such as event posters, visors, or other souvenir items prominently sporting their company or brand logo. "Tabling," the ability to set up a table or kiosk for product sampling, direct sales, or demonstrations, is another form of direct interaction with the fan often considered appealing by consumer product companies. The Pepsi-Cola Company has used this opportunity with great success for many years, staging its familiar "Pepsi Challenges," during which consumers at events are offered a chance to participate in a blind taste test of the sponsor's product against its competitor's. MBNA, the affinity credit card distributor, uses tabling to enroll new card members at events, adding the element of immediacy by offering free, exclusive event merchandise to all who apply during the event.

BUSINESS-TO-BUSINESS COMPANY SPONSOR BENEFITS

Companies that market their products or services to other businesses (B-to-B companies) may find attractive many of the same benefits as consumer products companies, but frequently with differing perspectives on their relative importance. The units of sale for B-to-B marketers may be significantly higher in price, and the average purchasing decision maker is often a more highly educated, highly compensated individual—someone who could have afforded to reach into his or her own wallet to purchase a ticket to the event. Therefore, the key attribute that contributes to providing a positive, exciting experience for such decision makers is exclusive access, something they could not have purchased for themselves. This access begins with event tickets, and for many B-to-B companies, only the very best available will suffice. Those in the B-to-B sponsor's target market must be entertained in seats they would have had difficulty procuring had they called the box office themselves.

The kinds of exclusive access opportunities for a sponsor's VIP guests that are of greater importance to B-to-B companies go far beyond premium seat locations. Meet-and-greet receptions—exclusive opportunities for a sponsor's guests to interact with athletes or celebrities and other VIPs—backstage access, attendance at media events, and other behind-the-scenes inclusions provide great value to business marketers. These are the kinds of exciting experiences a company's prospective customers could not obtain without a prestigious invitation from the B-to-B sponsor, and as such are sometimes considered "must include" components of the deal.

B-to-B companies may consider the inclusion of consumer advertising benefits extremely attractive, especially those businesses that also market directly to consumers. Few will turn down an opportunity for in-event signage or public address and video scoreboard acknowledgments, if only to reinforce their integral association for the benefit of their own guests in the stands. Most B-to-B companies, however, will ascribe great benefit to any advertising placed by event organizers in business or trade publications directed toward the industries and decision makers they most often market to. In a multiple newspaper market, they prefer placement of event advertising that contains recognition of their sponsorship in publications that more closely match the reading habits of the purchasers of their high-priced products (e.g., the *New York Times*, the *Globe and Mail*). They are less concerned about whether these periodicals are also the best for communicating with the event's most typical ticket buyers.

Some B-to-B promotions may differ from those offered by consumer marketers in the average value of premiums, prizes, or awards. The sponsor may offer incentive awards, such as all-expense-paid trips to the event, to authorized dealers who reach a new, exemplary plateau of sales. Premier-quality merchandise, such as leather event jackets, may be offered as premiums to top-performing sales representatives who achieve significant percentages above their quotas or to retailers who have outperformed expectations. This is not to suggest that more modest promotions are not encountered in the B-to-B market. Event tickets and promotional premiums of lesser value may be offered to new clients and those with existing business relationships. Promotions of reduced value can also provide incentives to clients while respecting the ethical compliance regulations that guard against conflicts of interest in many corporations.

Product sampling opportunities often take the form of more sophisticated, personal, and comprehensive product demonstrations in a B-to-B sponsorship. Rather than marketing to the entire event audience, these sponsors target their own guest list and other qualified attendees (such as purchasers of premium-priced tickets) for limited product or service demonstrations and even direct personal sales. Microsoft Corporation, for example, installed Internet kiosks in Staples Center hospitality suites that accommodated invited guests during the NHL All-Star Celebrity Challenge to demonstrate its new software to selected potential buyers.

There is probably no more attractive opportunity to a B-to-B sponsor than the availability of exclusive client hospitality options. Receptions, parties, golf outings, luncheons, dinners, and walk-in hospitality suites provide sponsors with direct and personal occasions to interact with clients and future business prospects. As casual entertainment experiences that surround sports events, these more insulated environments provide exclusive sales opportunities away from the clutter of other sponsors' messages more prevalent at the main event. Invitations to VIP events and activities hosted by the event organizer will be expected in quantity for client hospitality, although many sponsors also host their own exclusive events for their guests, either at the event site or at another nearby location.

Armed with an understanding of how corporate partnerships can work to the advantage of both the sports event and its sponsors, and recognizing the differing and highly individualized needs of consumer and B-to-B marketers, the organizer can begin to formulate a program of benefits that will convert prospects into sponsors. Effective marketing to prospective sponsors starts by identifying these wants and needs and determining how the power of a sports event can deliver measurable results to satisfy a company's sales objectives and exceed its business expectations.

Post-Play Analysis

As in any good partnership, all parties benefit from a well-conceived and well-constructed event sponsorship. Organizers seek relationships with companies that can provide their events with a source of revenue and opportunities for cost avoidance. To stretch an event's promotional budget, organizers seek companies that will reinforce their association with a program of advertising, promotions, and publicity at spending levels beyond their sponsorship fee, also known as activation. They also hope to create alliances with companies that demonstrate a commitment, or at least an intention, to continue their association with the event in future years.

Sponsors can derive a wide range of exposure opportunities from their event partnership, such as advertising at and beyond the event site, product placement, promotions, and media coverage. Sports events offer companies outstanding opportunities for customer hospitality through the provision of event tickets, VIP receptions, parties, and other exclusive access. An event can also be a marketplace for direct sales efforts, product demonstrations, and sampling opportunities. Sponsor companies also employ events as fund-raising vehicles for corporate philanthropic efforts. Some of the attractive intangible properties of sports events sponsorships include category exclusivity, perceived ownership of event elements, an association with an event of prestigious reputation, and the ability to offer pass-through rights to other business partners.

Although the relative importance each company places on the various elements in a sponsor package varies widely, prospective companies may be divided into two key groups, each with generally similar business strategies—consumer products companies and business-to-business marketers. Event organizers begin the process of designing a sponsor package by understanding how a prospective partner markets its products or services to its customers and what a company wants or needs from the relationship in order to achieve these marketing objectives.

Coach's Clipboard

1. You are organizing a tournament of regional police department baseball teams with the objective of raising money for their Widows and Orphans Funds. What kinds of companies would be most likely to be attracted to the event? With a projected admissions and donations revenue of $15,000 and operating expenses of $20,000, how can sponsor sales generate $20,000 net for the charity? Consider both cash and VIK sponsorship opportunities.

2. You are the marketing director for a consumer products company that supports esteem-building programs for physically disadvantaged children. Identify an existing sports event or create a new one, and explore how the company can help generate needed capital and exposure for the cause. Discuss how this effort can meet your company's marketing needs while supporting this worthy endeavor.

3. A marketer representing a major B-to-B corporation approaches an event organizer seeking a large block of premium seating, exclusive access, and hospitality opportunities for its upscale clients. The event already has a presenting sponsor under contract that paid more than the B-to-B company is willing to spend, and is receiving less in return than is sought by the marketer. How can the event organizer increase the value of the relationship for the existing sponsor or increase the consideration offered by the B-to-B company to ensure that all partners are satisfied and treated fairly?

PLAY 7

Teaming with Sponsors

Every day is a new opportunity. You can build on yes-
terday's success or put its failures behind and start
over again. That's the way life is, with a new game
every day, and that's the way baseball is.
—Bob Feller, Cleveland Indians Hall of Fame pitcher from 1936 to 1956

Once a sports event organizer has gathered all of the intelligence possible to
gain an understanding of his or her prospective partner's business, the next
step is to apply this knowledge to the development of a sponsor program that
will meet their respective needs. The right program must not only provide
demonstrable value and unique business opportunities to the sponsor, but
must also help generate the net revenues required by the event organizer's
budget.

Scaling and Pricing Sponsorship Packages

What benefits, and in what quantity, should an event organizer include in a
prospective sponsor's package? How many tickets and of what value? What
kind of recognition should the sponsor receive in pre-event advertising? How
many scoreboard mentions, playing field signs, public address announcements, and in-event logo placements should it be given?

To sports event organizers, sponsor benefits may be divided into two basic varieties—those that will generate expenses against the event budget, and those that, although offering value to the sponsor, can be provided without the organizer's encountering any out-of-pocket expense. Before finalizing the sponsorship package, it is essential that organizers consider the actual costs of providing the benefits to sponsors that will impact the event's bottom line, also known as "fulfillment costs."

DEVELOPMENT AND FULFILLMENT COSTS

Among the most overlooked calculations by event organizers during the budgeting process are the costs of selling and fulfilling the package of benefits to which sponsors are entitled. The packaged goods and retail industries are quite familiar with the concept of ensuring that their prices reflect a "cost of goods sold" plus a margin of profit, as do most event organizers who sell merchandise as part of their business plans. Before fixing a price for a product, a manufacturer must estimate the cost of materials, labor, tools, and equipment required for its fabrication, as well as the packaging, shipping, advertising, promotion, sales commissions, and other expenses encountered in bringing it to market. An allocation of overhead costs, such as for office staff and equipment, research and development, supplies, utilities, furnishings, and other expenses not directly associated with the manufacturing process must also be applied to truly reflect the cost of creating and selling a product for more than it cost the company to produce.

Retailers and sports event organizers understand this concept when they apply a price to the merchandise they sell. They consider the cost of acquiring the product, paying the sales staff and cashiers, acquiring the fixtures required for display and storage, allocating a sufficient percentage to cover overhead, and then add a profit margin before attaching a price tag. Sports events seeking corporate relationships to help fund their operations must plan in a similar manner. All of the various expenses expected to be incurred in marketing, creating, and delivering the product—an event sponsorship—must be identified and totaled, and a profit margin applied that is sufficient to meet an event's net revenue expectations.

Expenses incurred in selling a sponsorship, or development costs, include sales commissions, sales expenses, and the cost of market research. Obviously, these costs do not provide any value to the sponsor. They do, however, benefit the event organizer during the process of securing business partners and should therefore be factored into the "cost of goods sold" when setting sponsorship revenue goals and pricing benefit packages.

The many and varied expenses that are encountered by the organizer, but ultimately accrue to the benefit of the sponsor, are known as fulfillment costs. Fulfillment costs represent the actual out-of-pocket expenses that an event organizer will incur to provide the benefits to which the sponsor is entitled. The

Development Costs
- Sales commissions
- Sales expenses (e.g., travel, accommodations, printing, videos)
- Market research

Fulfillment Costs
- Complimentary tickets
- Signage and displays
- Program advertising
- Outside advertising
- VIP receptions
- Sponsor gifts
- Sampling and giveaways
- Discounting and couponing

Figure 7-1
Common Sports Event Sponsorship
Development and Fulfillment Costs

most common development and fulfillment expenses encountered by sports event organizers are summarized in Figure 7-1.

DEVELOPMENT COSTS

Sales Commissions

Experienced event organizers may be consummate experts at planning, managing, and executing events and perhaps even outstanding promoters in marketing their events to the public. They are often less adroit, or have only limited time available, in developing the sponsors required to meet their budget's revenue expectations. Their relationships with the event marketing decision makers within the companies most likely to support their events may simply be too limited to successfully reach their sponsorship goals.

This is when sports event organizers seek professional help from the agencies and individuals who specialize in event marketing and maintain more intimate and regular relationships within a wide range of potential sponsor companies. There are a large number and variety of event marketing agencies to be found in *Sports Market Place*, the massive and essential volume of contacts within sports and sports-related organizations available from GreyHouse Publishing (*www.sportsmarketplace.com*). For detailed intelligence on event marketing agencies and news about their current activities, outstanding resources include *IEG Sponsorship Report* (*www.sponsorship.com*) and *Event Marketer* magazine (*www.eventmarketermag.com*).

Event marketing agencies are usually paid a percentage of the gross sponsorship fees they generate, commonly in the area of 15 percent plus expenses. In a well-functioning partnership, the organizer and the agency invest in each other's success. The organizer trusts that the agency is working diligently to bring the sponsors the event needs, and the marketing agency invests considerable time and energy to turn over as much as 85 percent of the revenue it generates to the event. It is therefore not uncommon for the agency to also require a monthly retainer as guaranteed income, usually considered a "draw against commission." In other words, the monthly retainers received by the agency are considered commissions that have already been paid, and are therefore deducted from any final payment due.

If both the agency and the sponsors it develops continue to be associated with the event in future years, the agency generally continues to receive commissions on an agreed-to schedule defined by their contract with the organizer. The agency is usually still entitled to this percentage of future fees that result from its sales activities even if its own relationship with the organizer has expired.

Most event marketing agencies prefer representing established, proven properties with high profit potential. The nature of community-based grassroots events sometimes suggests a more homegrown approach. No matter how lofty the aim, how warm the emotion, or how seemingly attractive the event is to the organizer, agencies are less drawn to events where the sponsorship revenue expectations are low or set unrealistically high. Events with limited geographic appeal are also generally attractive to only the most entrepreneurial marketing agencies or those most interested in local events, because the revenues, and therefore the profits, they can generate are concomitantly limited.

Sales Expenses

The agreement negotiated with the event marketing agency should also define the direct expenses beyond commissions or fees that the organizer will consider reimbursable in connection with the agency's sales activities. Organizers may incur many of the same expenses whether they retain an agency to solicit and sell sponsorships, or market the event to corporate partners themselves. These may include the costs of travel and accommodations to meet prospective sponsors, the preparation of presentation kits or binders, artwork and artist renderings, writers, photocopies, gifts, sales video editing and copies, office supplies, telephone charges, messengers, and overnight couriers and postage, among others.

It is recommended that the agreement negotiated with the event marketing agency include a limit for total sales expenses. This may be accomplished by working with the agency to establish a detailed budget for sales expenses or requiring that individual out-of-pocket expenses beyond a certain limit (perhaps $200 or more) are approved by the event organizer in advance to avoid the potential of subsequent billing disagreements.

Market Research

Many event organizers conduct post-event market research to gauge ticket-buyer demographics, psychographics, buying behavior, price sensitivities, and perceptions of the quality of the event experience. The same research programs can be applied to measuring the effectiveness of sponsorship, advertising, and promotional programs. Responses may be compiled by personal interviews, by the distribution, collection, and tabulation of questionnaires, and through mailed post-event surveys. The results can help an organizer to improve an event's business and marketing plans, validate the program's appeal to participating sponsors, and demonstrate its strength and value to future prospective business partners.

FULFILLMENT COSTS

Complimentary Tickets

As discussed in Play 3, complimentary tickets are free to neither the organizer nor the sponsor. To the event organizer, they represent a lost revenue opportunity. Because complimentary tickets issued to a sponsor reduce the difference between cash received from ticket revenues and an event's gross potential, they actually "cost" the event budget their full face value. Likewise, when a sponsor analyzes the value of a package of benefits, it will regard the market price of complimentary tickets as value received in exchange for its cash or value-in-kind (VIK) payment to the event. For these reasons, it is common for sports event organizers to consider the face value of complimentary tickets as an expense paid in the fulfillment of a sponsorship agreement.

Signage and Displays

The exposure that companies receive in connection with their event sponsorship may include temporary signage on the playing surface or within otherwise conspicuous view of the audience. Corporate identification may be painted or applied directly on the walls, floors, boards, fencing, or structural fasciae of the host facility. Signage opportunities may also include banners located within and outside the event venue, on city street poles and over intersections, at headquarters hotels, and at area bars, restaurants, and attractions. The costs of designing, constructing, painting, printing, and installing corporate signage would not have existed had a sponsor not purchased those opportunities as part of its package. These benefits are therefore also considered fulfillment expenses. If street banners promoting the event would have been created and installed whether or not a sponsor purchased the right to be recognized on them, the expense should already be captured in the event budget and their cost would not be considered a cost of fulfillment.

Temporary signage mounted on specially designed trusses or frames or on structures installed specifically for the event may also be included as opportunities for exposure. As a general rule, if the truss, frame, or other temporary structure to which the signage is attached is to be installed with or without the need to recognize a sponsor (e.g., signage displayed on speaker stacks, on lighting trusses, or camera scaffolds, etc.), only the signage itself and not the cost of the structure on which it is supported should be considered a fulfillment expense. However, if the structure is installed strictly to meet the obligations of a sponsorship agreement, the costs of rent, fabrication, installation, and dismantling the structure would be added to the spreadsheet of fulfillment expenses.

Video screens and matrix message boards on scoreboards or other information displays around the facility can provide high-impact opportunities to expose and recognize a sponsor's association with the event. The costs of creating artwork for the video screens and programming for the electronic message boards should also be included as fulfillment expenses. The actual operation of these facilities, if they are also used for informational or entertainment purposes during the event, such as play-by-play, replays, the posting of statistics, and the airing of highlights, would not be included in the calculation of fulfillment costs.

Program Advertising

Organizers who publish and market commemorative event programs often include the placement of advertising in their sponsor packages. To reduce financial risk, some organizers license the rights to publish an event program to a third party. The publisher, who may pay the organizer a percentage of sales, will absorb the expenses of designing, writing, printing, and marketing the program. In addition to retaining a large percentage of sales revenues, the publisher is typically entitled to sell advertising space in the program to help defray expenses. To control fulfillment costs, event organizers who license their publishing rights should negotiate for a number of complimentary advertising pages, and a discounted rate for any additional space that may be required to fulfill sponsorship agreements.

It is recommended that event organizers assign both the creative and financial responsibilities of actually creating the advertisement to the sponsor. Sponsor companies frequently engage advertising agencies or maintain internal creative services departments that can easily and cost-effectively provide the artwork for an ad, removing the organizer from a potentially lengthy and expensive process of creative development and approval.

Organizers can also "up-sell" space in order to generate additional revenues. In other words, a sponsor entitled to a complimentary half-page black-and-white ad may subsequently agree to increase the size of its space or add color. The difference between the rate for an ad with features the sponsor is already entitled to and the rate for an ad including its new advertising requirements may be invoiced back to the partner as an additional charge.

Outside Advertising

Advertising in newspapers, magazines, and on radio and television (media "outside" of the event venue) that is designed to promote ticket sales or attendance, or increase the broadcasting audience, and includes sponsor names and logos is of great value to most partner companies. Sponsorship agreements can include obligations for an organizer to place consumer or trade advertising, with the more specific objective of overtly acknowledging a company's support of an event. These supplemental ads, which would not have otherwise been purchased, would be considered fulfillment expenses.

Many organizers enter into promotional relationships with media outlets that entitle the event to VIK advertising in return for an agreed-to package of sponsor benefits. In such cases the organizer trades valuable consideration for the VIK advertising, such as complimentary tickets, signage, and other sponsor benefits, for which the event absorbs the fulfillment costs. If the VIK advertising that flows from the media partner relationship is used by the organizer to pursue his or her own marketing objectives (e.g., increasing ticket sales, attendance, and broadcast ratings), only the direct expenses encountered in servicing the outlet need be captured as fulfillment costs (e.g., complimentary tickets, gifts, VIP receptions). If, however, the VIK advertising is used to meet obligations to another corporate partner, these direct costs are considered fulfillment expenses against the gross revenues that accrue from that sponsor's agreement.

VIP Receptions

Access to pregame receptions, post-event parties, and in-venue hospitality suites has become a sponsorship entitlement of increasing appeal and significance, delivering to sponsors exclusive access and entertainment value for their invitees and conferring prestige upon the sponsors in the eyes of their guests. Invitations to these highly desirable special-access opportunities have become a greatly sought-after status symbol. As a result, this is an area that event organizers must guardedly protect, otherwise an uncontrolled expansion of the guest list can cause expenses to quickly skyrocket.

A sponsor's package of benefits should guarantee a specific number of passes to these receptions and parties to ensure that the anticipated overall costs of entertaining the sponsor and its clients do not exceed the budgeted limit. It should not be surprising when sponsors subsequently determine that they will need more invitations or passes to these limited-access events. One or two passes here and there probably don't amount to much added cost to the event budget, although one or two requests often develop into far more significant numbers. Assuming the reception is being hosted in an area where the available floor space will accommodate more guests, the organizer can establish a "buy-in" price to enable sponsors to purchase supplementary passes for their extra guests at a per-person rate. Sponsors can thereby be provided with the additional access they need while the organizer protects the event budget from potentially costly overruns. A helpful and equitable formula used to set a buy-in price begins with the base per-person cost of food and beverage as charged by the caterer, plus gratuities, service charges, and applicable taxes. It is also fair to include an allowance for additional décor, rentals, and overhead costs, inasmuch as more tables, chairs, centerpieces, floral decorations, dishes, silverware, and other decorative elements will be required as the number of attendees grows. A reasonable allowance per person is 10 percent of the estimated costs of adding a table unit (table rental, centerpiece, place setting), plus a small additional charge for general room décor. This sample formula is summarized as follows:

> Supplemental VIP event buy-in price per person
> = ([per person food and beverage cost]
> × [prevailing gratuities and/or service charge])
> × (applicable sales tax)
> + (10 percent of additional décor, rentals, and other overhead costs)

To illustrate, suppose a corporate partner requests an additional 20 party tickets to supplement the 30 to which it is already entitled. The cost of food and beverage, as estimated by the caterer, is $50 per person, plus 18 percent service charge ($9 per person) and 7 percent sales tax ($4.13 on $59), for a subtotal of $63.13 per person. As the event is a stand-up reception, only a small allowance must be added for additional décor and rentals, for which the event organizer adds $6.50 per person, inclusive of taxes. Rounding off, the organizer can set a charge of at least $70 per additional party pass.

The value of establishing this policy becomes more obvious in considering the costs of entertaining even as few as 10 additional guests requested by each of 5 event sponsors—a total of 50 unanticipated, unbudgeted VIPs. Using the example in the preceding paragraph, the organizer would otherwise incur as much as $3500 in unbudgeted expenses to add this modest number of extra friends to the guest list. To each sponsor, however, the effective cost would total only $700. Access to the event is typically what the sponsors are after, and they are often willing to contribute to help defray the expenses of accommodating their additional guests.

Sponsor Gifts

Gifts of sports apparel and collectible merchandise displaying the event's logo are among the requisite staples of sports events. Few sporting events fail to offer their special VIP guests a cap, T-shirt, golf shirt, tote bag, or goody bag containing one or more of these items. Premium collectibles, such as tickets encased in Lucite, wristwatches, crystal paperweights, framed and autographed keepsakes, personalized jerseys, and other commemorative merchandise, are also frequently given to key sponsor contacts as gifts and expressions of gratitude. Organizers should be sure to include the costs of procuring these items in their estimate of fulfillment costs even though they most often fall outside the benefits to which sponsors are contractually entitled.

Sampling and Giveaways

Companies are often granted "sampling rights," the ability to distribute their products or giveaway premiums featuring their corporate or brand logos to the audience and/or athlete participants. Conferring sampling rights does not necessarily mean that organizers are obligated to pay the material or shipping costs connected with this activity, or for the labor required for distribution. The organizer's agreement with the sponsor should clearly define where the financial responsibilities for sampling activities rest.

Before granting sampling rights to a sponsor, the organizer should consult his or her facility lease and the venue's general manager. Some facilities restrict sampling activities to only those sponsors of an event that will provide products that do not compete with their own sponsors. A concessionaire's agreement with the building may also preclude events from sampling food or beverage items that may cut into their sales. It should be noted that these regulations may not be immediately apparent in a reading of the facility lease. Agreements protecting concessionaires' rights may be confidential instruments between the building manager and its food vendors. Some facility leases contain provisions that obligate the event organizer to adhere to the rules and regulations of the facility. To protect themselves against surprises, sports event organizers should not sign a lease agreement until they have been provided with a copy of those regulations. This is often where restrictions on sponsor activities such as sampling and the display of sponsor signage, as well as the stated rights of the event site's concessionaires and merchandisers, may be hidden. The lease may also reveal a charge for the right to sample or distribute sponsor products and limitations as to the product categories that may be distributed as sample items.

It is not unusual for sponsors to agree to cover the direct costs of sampling their products at events. The staff required to distribute the samples may be provided by the sponsor, through the event organizer, by the facility, or contracted for separately by either party, as long as doing so does not violate building regulations or existing labor agreements. Volunteer organizations such as community sports teams, scout troops, and other youth organizations are excellent resources for providing labor for sampling at sports events. These groups usually come with their own adult supervision or leadership and will participate for the novelty and excitement of being involved in the event, plus a donation to their treasury. Another way to minimize the labor costs connected with sampling opportunities is to restrict distribution to the period when the audience is exiting. Ushers and other house staff are usually underutilized at this point and may be redeployed to staff sampling activities at the exits. Thus, the sponsor will incur only the small additional charge for perhaps an extra hour's time per staff member.

Facility restrictions and labor costs for premium giveaways, items that are not samples of the sponsor's product, are similar to those for sampling. Try to avoid distributing commemorative balls, pucks, sticks, or other implements upon entry to the host venue as they could interfere with play or cause inadvertent injury to members of the audience. These items can be printed with event and sponsor logos and are great keepsakes, but they should be distributed to fans upon exiting. Some promotional items, such as rally towels, cheering cards, T-shirts, caps, and other materials that enhance the participatory nature of the viewing experience, require distribution upon entry. Such objects should be of sufficiently soft construction so as not to create a safety hazard on the chance that fans cause them to become airborne during an event.

Secure the permission of the host venue before approving a sponsor's planned premium item to ensure that it does not violate house regulations or the facility's agreement with the merchandiser. In addition, try to avoid approving the sponsored distribution of premium items that are similar to merchandise being sold at the event. Free premiums can compete with souvenir sales and lower the "per cap" (see Play 3) for both the event organizer and the merchandiser.

The financial responsibility of purchasing the sponsored giveaway item should be defined by the sponsorship agreement. Some preparation ("prepping") costs may also be required, an area frequently overlooked by both sponsors and organizers. Posters, for example, must be rolled and bound with elastic bands or inserted into tubes for easy distribution to the fans and to prevent product damage. Plastic bags are often used to package a sample or giveaway item with product information, promotional offers, coupons, or information on future events. Prepping the sample or giveaway item can be executed by an outside company or by a pool of volunteers.

Discounting and Couponing

Corporate partners often activate their sponsorships by offering consumers added value with the purchase of their products—discounts on the price of event tickets. Ticket discounting is an extremely effective tool used to drive customers into a retail outlet selling a sponsor's product. It is also a great way for organizers to enjoy incremental ticket sales. A large portion of a sponsor's event activation funds may be spent on promoting the availability of ticket discounts. Ticket discount coupons may be incorporated into a product's packaging, printed on shopping bags or on the tray liners of quick-service restaurants, or attached to "point of purchase" displays promoting the product and the event. To further encourage product sales, a discount program may require customers to provide proofs of purchase of a sponsor's product to receive their savings at the box office.

Discounts offered through sponsors offer organizers excellent opportunities for incremental ticket sales. For multiday events, they can be employed to encourage improved attendance on nonpeak days and times by limiting the discount to less well-attended weeknights or for matinees. Tickets sold at a discount through sponsor promotions are not usually figured into the costs of sponsor fulfillment, but must be considered during the budgeting process in the calculation of ticket revenues (see Play 3). To anticipate sponsor needs for discount offers, event organizers should set discount prices even before sponsors are confirmed and estimate the number of tickets that will likely be sold at these reduced prices. The usual expectation is for the sponsor to create, design, manage, and execute the advertising, point-of-purchase displays, coupons, and packaging in connection with its discount offer. It is highly recommended that the sponsor agreement articulate the requirement that all materials relating to the event must be reviewed and approved by the organizer before printing.

Some B-to-B and high-end consumer companies activate their sponsorships by offering event merchandise and tickets *gratis* to their most important clients or as sales promotions designed to transform qualified prospects into loyal customers. An automobile manufacturer may want to promote its sponsorship with a free event ticket offer, providing consumers who take a test drive with a voucher redeemable for a pair of complimentary tickets. Or a mobile telephone company may offer free event tickets to new customers who subscribe at its showrooms. In cases like these, the quantity of redeemed tickets (the number of qualifying customers who actually exchange their vouchers for the free tickets and attend the event) is impossible for either the sponsor or the organizer to predict or budget for in advance. Promotions like these can be powerful advertising tools for an event, as well as valuable incentives that sponsors can use to drive prospects into showrooms and transform potential customers into purchasers.

In most cases, however, the event budget cannot accommodate the issuance of what may become a significant number of these complimentary tickets. The sponsor's dealers, agents, or salespeople who control the distribution of the vouchers must also remain accountable for issuing complimentary vouchers only to justifiably qualified customers or prospects. For this reason, organizers can propose that sponsors desiring to distribute complimentary tickets or vouchers in connection with sales promotions, reimburse the event for those actually redeemed by their customers. To make the promotion as cost-effective for the sponsor as possible, organizers may charge the sponsor the deepest discounted rate the budget will accommodate for redeemed tickets or vouchers. This model places the financial responsibility for the redemption of vouchers with the salesperson or dealer, discouraging the distribution of vouchers to anyone other than a qualified customer. The number of vouchers redeemed at the box office also provides the sponsor with measurable results by which to gauge the effectiveness of the promotion. It is strongly recommended that a disclaimer be included on the vouchers that clearly states that they are redeemable only while tickets remain available. Any restrictions on their validity (such as weekdays only, limits to certain price categories, etc.) should also be stated and positioned obviously on the coupons.

The Sales Process

A sports event director can be imagined as the coach of a football team, signaling plays to the quarterback from the sidelines, focusing the team's resources in pursuit of the goal—the sale of an event sponsorship to a prospective corporate partner. The quarterback, the individual or entity empowered to make the snap on-field decisions, is responsible for executing the play. That individual must make his or her way around a line of shifting obstacles and challenges, a defensive squad filled with a prospect's objections, reticence, and apathy. The quarterback may be the staff member responsible for developing sponsors, a volunteer ringing the doorbells of neighborhood businesses, or an event marketing agency retained to take best advantage of its expertise and list of contacts. The very best are armed with an understanding of what sponsor prospects want from their sports event relationships.

The coach calls for plays that probe, test, and retrench, seeking the right way through these defenses. The opening play starts with the creation and presentation of a sponsorship program that lines up a series of benefits designed to provide business solutions to prospective partners. The first appeal to the sponsor prospect may move the ball close to the goal for a long gain, or perhaps at first only a few inches. Deficient intelligence or a poorly conceived presentation may result in a loss, the event's position moved even farther away from the goal. The ever-running time clock creates a sense of great urgency. There is only a limited amount of time available to bring the package into the end zone and to a victorious close. The quarterback reads the field and senses the potential areas of penetration. New plays are tried, strategies are adjusted based on intelligence gained with each attempt, and, eventually, the program presented is strong enough to score a touchdown. Or perhaps every play, no matter how strategic or creative, will fail and the game will have to be pursued with another, more receptive company. Alternatively, as the time ticks down and the final result appears in doubt, the coach may call for a field goal—a smaller sponsorship package to close at least some kind of deal before time runs out—a gain of only 3 points instead of a 6-point touchdown. But 3 points—50 percent of the revenue the coach set out to realize—may be all that is possible to achieve in this game. And it may just be enough to help win the campaign.

In today's event management and marketing game, a USO (understand stakeholders' objectives) philosophy, that is, understanding what sponsors want from sports events, is the essential unpinning to the sales process. This philosophy is suffused throughout the five-step process of selling sports event sponsorships, as described in the following sections and in Figure 7-2: (1) qualify, (2) design, (3) present, (4) revise, and (5) close.

QUALIFY AND TARGET SPONSOR PROSPECT

Too often, event organizers and marketing agencies create attractive but generic presentations featuring a standardized package of sponsor benefits. They blindly dispatch them to all corners of the business community with the expectation that some marketer, somewhere, will find the event and its promotional potential so compelling, such an obvious and perfect complement to its

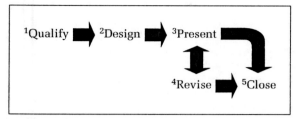

Figure 7-2
Five Steps in the Sponsorship Sales Process

marketing strategy, that it will instantly express interest in becoming a corporate partner. Easily separable levels of benefits define their sponsorship strata—sweeping, ubiquitous benefits for the highest-priced title sponsorship, significant exposure and hospitality opportunities for presenting sponsors, and diminishing levels of signage and ticket allotments for supporting partners. This practice is the classical "shotgun approach" to marketing, scattering shots over a wide area in hope of scoring a hit. The more labor- and capital-efficient "rifle shot approach," a precisely tuned campaign to reach specific target markets, is no less applicable to generating sports event sponsorship sales than it is to consumer marketing.

Most sports event organizers understand the fan base for their sports and events. The marketing agencies and outside consultants they retain to develop sponsorship revenue for these programs require no less familiarity with the product and its audience. This grounding helps marketing agencies and salespeople to recognize the unique opportunities and demographics that can be made available to the right event sponsors and to better match prospects to an event.

The event marketer must narrow the vast universe of potential partners through a series of filters that qualify only those prospects most likely to perceive sponsorship of an event as an effective marketing opportunity and cost-efficient business solution. Figure 7-3 provides a list of questions that can be used to help refine the roster of qualified prospective sponsors. The sales process begins with the selection of target companies that may be approached to support the event. The ideal prospect should be one that shares a common or similar target market with the event, a company whose existing or likely customers are among those expected to either attend or participate. The demographics, lifestyles, interests, and habits of an event's guests or attendees should closely approximate those of the prospective sponsor's customers.

One of the easiest ways to get a sense of a company's target market and, frequently, the types of events they sponsor to promote their products is to visit the web sites of the brand and its parent company. A visit to the Mountain Dew web site (*www.mountaindew.com*), for example, demonstrates the

1. What companies or brands appeal to the same customer demographics and lifestyles as the event?
2. What companies or brands sponsor similar or competitive events?
3. What companies compete with the sponsors of these similar events?
4. What companies sponsor other events that are also supported by your existing sponsors?
5. What is the event's scope, and does it match the prospect company's marketing strategies (e.g., is its interest essentially local, regional, or national)?
6. What companies are launching new products or services that can be promoted by an event marketing partnership?
7. What companies are among those the event organizer is doing business with that may consider cash or VIK sponsor relationships (e.g., vendors, companies represented by volunteer workers or by members of the board)?
8. What companies embrace the same charitable or community-based causes that the event will serve or support?
9. Does the prospect sponsor possess the financial wherewithal to support the event?
10. What is the financial health of the prospective sponsor?

Figure 7-3
Top 10 Qualifiers for Sponsor Prospects

brand's commitment to an active, cutting-edge, youth-oriented culture, as well as many of the sports events that reflect this lifestyle, through colorful, quick-cutting graphics, music, and content. The Sideline Story on page 189 briefly describes this intriguing brand, its target market, and some of the events it sponsors.

Consider the hidden members of your event's corporate family, any entity with a vested interest in the success of your event, such as your organization's suppliers and service providers. It is not realistic to expect that all, or even most, suppliers will be open to providing cash or VIK in return for a sponsorship position. After all, many are in business expressly to generate cash by selling their products and services to the event industry. Some, however, may see the value in reinforcing their partnerships with the event and its organizer for the development of additional business. For those sports event organizations that are under the supervision of a board of directors, advisory board, or other entity composed of community and business leaders, a potential sponsor may already be sitting at your conference table, just a few seats away. Explore how the companies represented by these involved advisors can take best advantage of a more formalized business relationship with the event.

Have you read an article about an exciting new product or service that is being introduced at about the same time as your event? Product launches are usually funded with a temporary growth spurt of marketing dollars. Most com-

Sideline Story—A Youth-Oriented Sports Marketer

Mountain Dew, acquired by Pepsi-Cola in 1964, is a carbonated citrus soft drink brand that has been marketed, according to the company's web site, toward "young, active, outdoor types." The 55 mg of caffeine in each 12 oz. can is roughly 50 percent greater than the stimulant content in Pepsi's flagship cola brand and about half the content in a cup of brewed coffee. Pepsi reinforces its youthful perception in the marketplace with a major sponsorship of both the X-Games and the Winter X-Games, televised festivals of "extreme sports" organized by American cable television network ESPN. The brand's efforts also reach the local, grassroots end of the sports marketing spectrum. In 2002, the brand launched the Mountain Dew Free Flow Tour, a competitive event for amateur skateboarders that visited a dozen skate parks in communities across the United States. Mountain Dew's event marketing efforts, print and outdoor advertising campaigns, and product packaging work together to reinforce the image of a brand that appeals to the most creative, talented, and daring of today's young, homegrown athletes.

panies, along with their advertising and public relations agencies, are always looking for new and unique ways to spread the word about a fledgling product. Sports events can offer new product introduction campaigns the sampling, exposure, and involving promotional opportunities that traditional advertising simply cannot match.

If your event is organized by a not-for-profit entity, is a program designed to improve the community's quality of life, or is a revenue generator for a charity, search for companies that support the same kinds of charitable endeavors. Check the charity's list of major corporate donors, as well as the supporters of similar charities, to generate more leads for your list of prospective sponsors. Cause-related marketing, that is, the generation of funds for a worthy charity, can be a powerful motivator in developing corporate partners. Is the event best positioned as a marketing opportunity, or might it have stronger appeal to a particular sponsor as worthy of charitable support?

The final considerations that should be infused into any process of qualifying potential event sponsors are the analysis of the financial wherewithal and health of targeted companies. Does the prospect company generate sufficient revenues to consider a sponsorship, and if so, at what level of participation? If the company is healthy but has limited resources, a large cash

Sideline Story—Founded to Promote Sports

Many not-for-profit organizations that generate revenues for distribution to worthy community or charitable causes have begun to embrace grassroots sports events, not just as recipients of their funding, but also as marketing tools for the promotion of their own agendas. The Florida Sports Foundation (www.flasports.com), for example, is a private not-for-profit corporation chartered to promote and develop professional, amateur, and recreational sports and fitness activities that support the state's burgeoning sports industry. Among many other endeavors, the foundation stages the Sunshine State Games, an event that not only provides an outstanding training and quality-of-life sports experience for 8000 in-state participants, but also generates a sizable economic impact for the host region. Recognizing the state's attractiveness as a sports destination and the industry's potential for both supporting the business community and adding to tax revenues, the foundation offers event organizers the ability to apply for grants in order to attract sports events that are either bid to interested communities or are completely new. Essential requirements for a successful application are that significant economic impact must be generated for the State of Florida and that any grant award must be integrally necessary to the success of the event (i.e., the event might not be feasible to stage without the grant). As the foundation develops its own sponsors to fund the grants and continue promoting the state as a premier sports destination, organizers are obligated to acknowledge the Florida Sports Foundation as an event sponsor or supporter.

sponsorship is unlikely. Alternatively, a more modest cash sponsorship package, or some combination of cash and VIK, might increase a company's receptivity. What is the state of the industry in which the company does business? If the industry is under economic stress, but the company is at the vanguard, VIK may again help to close a deal. What is the company's financial position—is it profitable or losing money? Is it hiring employees or downsizing staff? It is risky to partner with a company under financial stress because its presence may exclude other, more healthy companies from participating in the event. Slow payment or default by a distressed partner can cause an event to fall short of its own budget expectations.

DESIGN A SPONSORSHIP PROGRAM

It is now time for you to call for the right play that you, as coach, believe will run your team past the objections, reticence, and apathy of prospective sponsor companies. Sponsor revenue expectations projected during the budgeting process should anticipate the scaling of sponsorships into a number of price categories. Although there are many possible models for creating sponsorship tiers, depending on the nature and structure of the event, Figure 7-4 illustrates a generalized pyramidal hierarchy of sports event sponsorships. The model divides available opportunities into four broad levels of participation: (1) Title Sponsorship, (2) Presenting Sponsorship, (3) Category-Exclusive Sponsors (also frequently called "Official Sponsors"), and (4) Non-Exclusive Sponsors and Official Suppliers.

Title Sponsorship

The level of greatest corporate support is title sponsorship, which, when available, is typically held by a single sponsor. Title sponsors can expect to reap the most and most valuable business solutions (i.e., customized package of benefits), as compared with an event's other corporate partners. What they are really paying a premium for, however, is to ensure that their corporate or

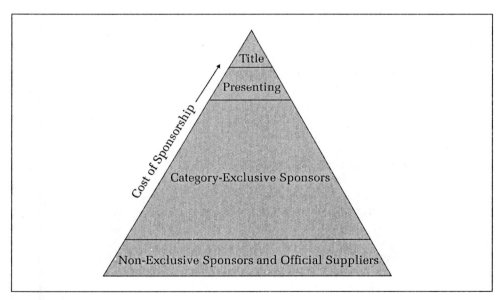

Figure 7-4
Sponsorship Pyramid

brand name is inseparably connected to the identity of the event. Whether motivated by the desire for maximizing exposure to its product's target market, bragging rights over its competitors, or demonstrating its preeminence in the community, title sponsorship can be a powerful, far-reaching tool for the corporate partner. A company that purchases a title sponsorship enjoys the singular benefits of appearing in all advertising, press releases (and, it is hoped, the resulting media coverage), promotions, tickets, signage, and more. Examples of events with title sponsors include the Professional Golfers Association's (PGA) Bank of America Colonial, the Sony Open, and the AT&T Pebble Beach National Pro-Am; college football's McDonald's/Texas A&M Invitational tournament; Major League Baseball's John Hancock All-Star FanFest and Century 21 Home Run Derby, and the National Hockey League's Dodge/NHL SuperSkills competition, to name just a few.

Naturally, inclusion of the company identity in the event title and its graphic incorporation in the event logo clearly and definitively separate the title sponsor from all other partners. This dominant position in the title provides the sponsor with added impact and importance. From the sponsor's point of view, the inseparability of the corporate name from the event identity (e.g., Sony Open) is worth a significant premium. Journalists, as well as other sponsor partners in their own promotional programs, find it difficult to refer to events so named without the title partner's corporate identification.

Most title sponsorships are sold to a single company or brand to maximize impact at a premium price. There are, however, cases in which a pair of sponsors have been combined into a single title deal (presumably, each paying one-half the cost for the top-tier package). The most effective of such programs feature two companies that can partner directly with each other to create meaningful advertising and cross-promotional campaigns. An example was reported in a May 2003 issue of *Sports Business Journal*, which announced that "Ramps and Amps," an 11-city action sports tour, would feature a shared title sponsorship between T-Mobile, a wireless communications service, and Nokia, a manufacturer of cellular telephones.

Presenting Sponsorship

Just beneath the pinnacle of the sponsorship pyramid occupied by a title partner is the presenting sponsorship. Instead of the corporate or brand name preceding the event identity, the sponsor's identity follows the title (e.g., NHL All-Star Weekend presented by Nextel, the Bay Hill Invitational presented by Cooper Tire, the Men's AVP Belmar Open presented by Paul Mitchell, the New York City Cycling Championship presented by BMC Software). This type of participation is generally priced at a lower level than title sponsorship because of the relative ease with which media reports can separate the corporate identity from the event name. The premium value of a presenting sponsorship, however, is in the brand's relationship to the event and its logo, as well as the partner's ubiquitous presence in the promotions and marketing campaigns undertaken by the event organizer. But because the identities are so much easier to separate, it is considerably more difficult to insist that other, lower-tier partners feature the presenting sponsor's name in any advertising or promotion that activates their respective sponsorships.

In the eyes of other event sponsors, the presence of title and/or presenting sponsors can devalue the perception of their own participation. It is wise to disclose all levels of partnership available during the presentation phase, including title and presenting sponsorship opportunities, for two reasons. First, it may entice existing sponsors to consider a greater investment in the event. Lower-level sponsors will also evaluate their event relationship knowing in advance that a title relationship may subsequently be sold and will therefore have a clear and realistic picture of how other corporate or brand entities may enjoy exposure greater than their own.

Category-Exclusive Sponsors

A title and presenting sponsorship can account for a sizable percentage, or even most of an event's sponsorship revenue budget. The largest number of sponsor companies and brands, however, are most often found in the area of category-exclusive sponsors, also widely known as "official sponsors." Because sponsorships of this type are more economically accessible to companies at more modest price levels, events are usually blessed with more of them. Selling a title and/or presenting sponsorship is the ideal of most event promoters. If there are enough category-exclusive sponsors, however, the event can still meet reasonably set sponsorship revenue goals. For this reason, as illustrated in Figure 7-5, the sponsorship pyramid depends on many of these essential building blocks for a respectable amount of both revenue and promotional activation.

Note that the sponsorships in this area of the pyramid are much greater in number and may even account for a cumulatively greater sum in revenue. The category-exclusive building blocks can include any variety of businesses, as illustrated by examples in the figure of those that commonly sponsor sports events. There is, however, an almost limitless opportunity to expand sponsor categories to include companies in many other industries.

Sponsors buy into events to convert the benefits they provide into business solutions. What protects them from their competitors' doing likewise is the exclusivity within their category guaranteed by the event organizer.

It is essential to define exactly what category is being granted exclusivity. Will an automotive company's sponsorship offer exclusivity in regard to cars and trucks, or just cars? Will it preclude the event promoter from pursuing a sponsor relationship with a rental car company that does not feature the automotive sponsor's models? Does the exclusivity extend to auto parts, precluding a deal with an after-market parts manufacturer or retailer? Will an airline partner's sponsorship prevent the organizer from pursuing a relationship with a railroad or bus line? If it is a domestic airline, can the organizer

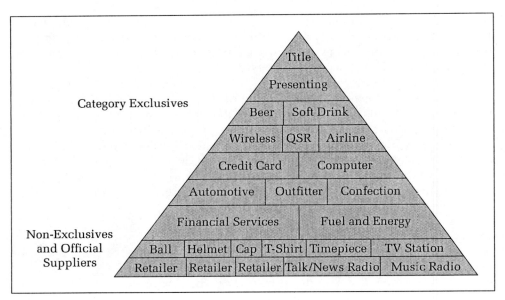

Figure 7-5
Building Blocks of the Sponsorship Pyramid

pursue a relationship with an international carrier? Does a deal with a soft drink company cover soda pop only, or does it include juices, water, milk and dairy drinks, and isotonic beverages as well? If the company neither sells nor distributes these other beverage types, does the soft drink manufacturer's exclusivity still prevent you from selling sponsorships to other companies that sell these products? Does the soft drink deal restrict the promoter from pursuing quick-service restaurant sponsorships with anyone, or with only those that serve that brand?

Obviously, from the promoter's point of view, it is most advantageous to limit a sponsor's exclusivity to the narrowest extent possible, enabling the event to attract sponsorships from a greater number of companies and industry types. From the sponsor's standpoint, the wider the definition of exclusivity, the more valuable the partnership will be. Event promoters often place reasonable limits on areas of exclusivity in the first presentation to prospective sponsors and may negotiate a higher purchase price if additional categories are later requested by a sponsor to make up for the loss in potential revenues.

Exclusivity granted by a sponsorship does not necessarily mean that the company can promote all the products it sells within protected categories. Thus, it is important to define the brands or product lines that are included in the sponsorship. Consider the fictional soft drink company again: Can it promote only its cola or all of its varieties of soda? Will it also be permitted to promote its mixers, juices, waters, and isotonic beverages? Suddenly, a single sponsorship has potential to create a great deal of signage clutter, making it appear that there are many more sponsors than actually exist and devaluing the exposure of other, single-brand sponsors. A May 2003 issue of *Brandweek* reported that Procter & Gamble's sponsorship of the WNBA would extend benefits to seven of its brands, including a deodorant, dishwasher soap, laundry detergent, two shampoos, and a floor cleaner. The cross-promotional opportunities of such an arrangement are undeniable, but the price of a multibrand sponsorship must be adjusted upward to compensate for all of the product categories no longer available for sale by the event organizer.

Category-exclusive sponsors desiring to stand out from their corporate colleagues frequently seek ways of exhibiting more "ownership" of an event, or an association that elevates them in some way above other sponsors. With a little creative thought, the title or presenting sponsorship of a specific event element may be devised. A trophy or award may be created that bears the sponsor's name, such as the Major Indoor Soccer League's "Spaulding Scoring Champion," Major League Soccer's "Pepsi Goal of the Week," and the NHL's "All-Star Most Valuable Player Award, presented by Bud Light." Halftime or intermission entertainment, pre-game festivities, and post-game parties often bear the identities of category-exclusive sponsors. Video or matrix scoreboard programming, event-specific web pages, information centers, concessions areas—nearly any element of an event may each be sponsored by one of the roster of corporate partners, providing them with the sense of ownership they desire.

Some category-exclusive sponsors are less concerned with the ownership of particular event elements than they are with preferential signage locations at the event site, advertising, or hospitality opportunities. For this reason, event promoters should not feel compelled to include title or presenting sponsorship components for specific event elements in every sponsorship pitch. You may be giving away something of little value to a particular sponsor that can help close a deal with another company that places greater emphasis on this type of benefit.

Non-Exclusive Sponsors and Official Suppliers

For financial, legal, or practical reasons, an organizer may desire to offer certain categories of sponsorship on a non-exclusive basis. For example, some local ordinances regulating the sales and marketing of alcoholic beverages bar beer companies from enjoying product-exclusive sponsorships. For community-based grassroots organizations such as local Little Leagues, it may be not practical to have a single law firm, dentist, day camp, pizzeria, or chiropractor involved with an event to the exclusion of all others in its business category. Being able to open the event to as many local businesses as possible, even those that are competitive with one another, keeps the cost of sponsorships to each community partner at a reasonable level, and can help a volunteer organization close many more deals.

Sports Business Journal's editor at large Terry Lefton reported in May 2003 that the United States Olympic Committee (USOC) intended to divide its supplier and sponsorship rights governing official apparel for the first time. Instead of designating a single sponsor or supplier, the USOC subdivided its apparel partners by the elemental activities they would support. Roots, a Canadian sporting goods manufacturer, was awarded exclusivity in the area of providing the outfitting to be worn by American athletes in the opening and closing ceremonies only, whereas its competitor Nike would provide the warmup suits to be worn by the athletes during medal ceremonies.

Media partners, more fully discussed in Play 8, are also good targets for non-exclusive relationships. Stations with sports talk formats and Top 40 music stations, for instance, appeal to totally different demographics. As such, they are not truly competitive with one another. It is therefore often possible to designate more than one "official radio station" for an event, based on the broadcasters' formats.

Any sponsor relationship can be crafted as a non-exclusive partnership, presuming the sponsors are in agreement. This category is useful for generating last-minute revenues after it has been determined that no company wishes to enter into a more pricey, exclusive relationship. It is also useful for smaller businesses and industries that cannot afford participating at an exclusive level. That is why official suppliers are often, though not always, non-exclusive. If it is relatively inexpensive for a supplier to provide its products as VIK to the event (sports equipment manufacturers, for example), the value simply may not be great enough to warrant granting exclusive rights.

A note of caution: once a non-exclusive deal is finalized within a specific sponsor category, it will no longer be possible to accept a competitor's offer to enter into a more lucrative exclusive deal later. To avoid potential lost revenues, be judicious in determining what categories you ultimately decide to open on a non-exclusive basis.

That's Not All, Folks—Create Innovations That Suit Your Event

Although the previously described sponsorship categories are among those most commonly encountered, corporate relationships can take any creative form that a promoter can imagine. Devise new sponsorship concepts to suit your event and organization. For example, an event organizer can establish a partnership in which the sponsor becomes a "guarantor." Guarantors promise to cover cash shortfalls, up to a certain level, at the conclusion of the event to ensure that the organizer remains solvent or the program generates guaranteed revenues for charitable purposes. They can fund this guarantee with a grant or agree to purchase a specified number of tickets, buying and using them outright or donating them to a deserving charity or to worthy recipients such as active military families. Alternatively, guarantors can agree to cover the difference between actual sales and a predefined number of tickets to cover potential losses. A guarantor relationship is best established for events organized by not-for-profit groups or those designed to funnel a significant percentage of their proceeds to charity.

Every sponsor relationship, regardless of whether it takes a traditional or an innovative, unorthodox form, will require some fulfillment inventory (e.g., signage, tickets, ad space, etc.) on the part of the event in exchange for the sponsor's participation. Again, be sure that the inventory each deal consumes is commensurate with the benefits it provides to the event's bottom line.

How to Design a Sponsorship Program

Here is where the USO Principle pays the most handsome dividends. The sports event organizer now has a reasonably good idea of the business wants and needs of the prospective sponsor and knows what resources he or she can offer that sponsor through the event. By matching the menu of event sponsorship resources to the business needs of the prospect, the event organizer is no longer selling just benefits, but *business solutions.*

On a spreadsheet, organize the menu of benefits your event can provide to a sponsor. Then create the number of levels of participation most appropriate to your event. In the example illustrated in Figure 7-6, sponsorships are divided into the four basic levels discussed in this chapter—title sponsor, presenting sponsor, official sponsor (category-exclusive), and official supplier. The latter two categories can be further subdivided into a series of price and benefit tiers, if desired, to provide more options to prospective sponsors. In this example, the levels are simply referred to as "title," "presenting," and "official" sponsors, but there is no magic to the names of the various levels or subdivisions. They can just as easily be called gold, silver, and bronze, or diamond, ruby, and emerald, or identified as suggested by the sport itself (e.g., homer, three-bagger, two-bagger, one-bagger).

The levels are then distinguished by the benefits they include and the degree to which they will be provided, always noting that with benefits come fulfillment costs. Contingent on these fulfillment costs, the organizer's desired return on investment, and the overall revenue goals of the event, a base price can be assigned to each level. In this example, the title sponsorship commands a premium three times that of the category-exclusive sponsorship, and just below twice the cost of a presenting sponsorship, because of the ubiquity of the company name in every reference to, and marketing program for, the event. The difference between the presenting sponsorship and the category-exclusive package is slightly less than double the cost to entice official sponsors to consider upgrading to a presenting position at a reasonable increase in cost. Finally, a minimum value in cash and/or VIK has been set to qualify companies as official suppliers. (These multiples are for illustrative purposes only. Price differences between sponsorship levels are totally at the discretion of each event promoter.)

	Title Sponsor	Presenting Sponsor	Official Sponsor	Official Supplier
Event Identity	TUV/XYZ Sports Event	XYZ Sports Event presented by TUV	Official Sponsor	Official Supplier
Event Logo	TUV integrated into event logo	"Presented by" tag	—	—
Use of Event Marks in Advertising (with event promoter approval)	Yes, in all sponsor's advertising and promotions	Yes, in all sponsor's advertising and promotions	Yes, with official sponsor tag	Yes, with official supplier tag
Line of Sight Signage	10, plus integrated logo appearances	8	4	2
Public Address Ads	10, plus integrated into every PA mention of the event	6, plus integrated into every PA mention of the event	4	2
Video Scoreboard 30-second spots	6	4	2	1
Event Print Advertising	Integrated logo in all	"Presented by" tag in all	Name acknowledgment in 3 full-page ads	—
Event Radio Advertising	Mentioned with event name	"Presented by" tag in all	—	—
Event Television Advertising	Integrated logo in all	"Presented by" tag in all	—	—
Program Advertisement	Back cover	Inside front cover	Full page, color	Half page, b&w
Event Tickets	100 VIP	50 VIP, 50 G.A.	20 VIP, 30 G.A.	4 VIP, 10 G.A.

Figure 7-6
Sample Sponsorship Benefit Grid for XYZ Sports Event

	Title Sponsor	Presenting Sponsor	Official Sponsor	Official Supplier
Pre-Game Reception	100	50	20	4
Post-Game Gala	100	50	20	4
Other Features	Sponsor name printed on all tickets; 10 all-access passes; integrated logo on all event merchandise and staff uniform apparel, street banners and site decor; company rep to present trophies; 50 autographed balls; use of 20′ × 20′ tent for sponsor demonstration purposes; sampling rights; right to host private meet-and-greet reception with athletes; other benefits to be negotiated	6 all-access passes; "presented by" tag on all staff uniform apparel; 25 autographed balls; use of 20′ × 20′ tent for sponsor demonstration purposes; sampling rights; right to host private meet-and-greet reception with athletes; other benefits to be negotiated	10 autographed balls; use of 10′ × 10′ tent for sponsor demonstration purposes; sampling rights; other benefits to be negotiated	2 autographed balls; sampling rights; other benefits to be negotiated
Base Price, as Listed	**$150,000**	**$85,000**	**$50,000**	**$20,000**

Figure 7-6
(Continued)

Remember that you are only organizing a basic framework for sponsorship packaging, as not all of the features of a particular partnership category will be of equal usefulness or value to any two companies. It is therefore suggested that the package price include a margin of contingency to cover unanticipated fulfillment costs. This will enable the promoter to demonstrate some flexibility in providing more value and different business solutions for the sponsor during the negotiating process without necessitating an automatic increase in price.

Promoters must remain flexible as they fashion the available benefits into packages that meet each company's fingerprint-different needs, ever mindful of the revenue and promotional requirements of the event itself. A package designed for a business-to-business sponsor may offer more opportunities for client hospitality, manifest by the inclusion of more tickets in premium locations and an increased number of invitations to VIP receptions. To offset the additional fulfillment costs encountered in accommodating these additional benefits, the organizer may offer fewer advertisements or on-site signage positions. If the fulfillment costs are still greater than were assumed at a particular sponsorship level, the promoter may increase the price of the package originally presented or attempt to use these additional needs as an incentive for the sponsor to consider a higher level of sponsorship.

Event promoters should recognize that the reduction or elimination of certain benefits, such as inclusion of sponsor names in consumer advertising, will have no effect on the bottom line. The advertising will be purchased anyway, regardless of whether the sponsor's name is present. During negotiations, some sponsors will expect that at least some of this decreased value, even though it has no impact on lowering expenses, can translate into a reduced price. Incorporating a fulfillment contingency in the base price may enable the promoter to respond by some amount without imperiling the budget's net sponsor revenue expectations.

Apply your creativity to keeping the sponsorship price down—but net revenues high. If the event is regionally televised and the sponsor is a local company that would benefit less from this exposure, you can reduce the cost of that sponsor's package by positioning its signage in areas not as regularly visible to the television camera. Those positions may be worth a higher premium to a sponsor that values the wider exposure offered by television. Identify other features you can add to the sponsor package that increase its value without increasing fulfillment costs. Is there a special trophy or award that can be given to a participating athlete who embodies the attributes of the sponsor's company or product (e.g., courage, innovation, improvement, style, or leadership)? Can you devise an unusual exposure opportunity or cooperative promotion that combines the event's goals with the prospective sponsor's business objectives? Try promoting an on-line fan poll and ticket sweepstakes on the sponsor's and event's web sites with links to the company's e-commerce page and the event's on-line ticket service.

There are, of course, instances in which the application of the USO approach will result in identifying companies whose business objectives will just never match the demographics, lifestyle characteristics, and opportunities of a particular event. Every effort should be expended to search for synergies before ruling on whether an approach to a financially qualified prospect is worthwhile. The Sideline Story below demonstrates how preconceived notions about a product can be challenged to create sports event marketing opportunities that may not have been immediately apparent.

Sideline Story—Teeing Off to Sell SUVs

The demographics of golf, with its greater than average concentration of high-income, highly educated fans, recreational players, and professional athletes, have long attracted insurance and financial services companies such as Kemper Insurance, American Express, Franklin Templeton, Wachovia, and Bank of America. Purveyors of high-priced consumer goods, such as automotive and computer companies, also find golf a worthwhile event marketing investment. With a broad and lengthy annual schedule of events staged at courses across the country, the Professional Golfers Association (PGA) does not restrict itself nationally to a single sponsor in each category. Rather, a different set of sponsors at a range of different levels may be involved at each tour stop. The 2003 PGA Tour schedule, for example, included events with titles incorporating Mercedes Benz, Buick, Chrysler, Nissan, Honda, and Ford automotive brands and in which category exclusivity applied only to the individual tour stops in which they participated.

A November 2002 issue of *Sports Business Journal* reported on an event marketing initiative by Ford Motor Company to promote its Expedition and Explorer sports utility vehicles (SUVs) through sponsorships of professional golf events. This brand strategy was a noticeable departure from the marketing of luxury sedans, as more traditionally promoted by Ford's PGA-associated competitors. According to a Ford spokesman quoted in the *Journal*, more than one-third of recreational golfers owned a Ford automobile and approximately one-fourth intended to purchase a car over the following year. To differentiate its company from the many other automotive sponsors associated with golf, Ford decided to market its SUVs as ideally suited for both carting around clubs during weekend trips to the golf course and as great vehicles for transporting the kids.

PRESENT THE OPPORTUNITY

The event promoter has now gathered the intelligence necessary to identify the objectives and attributes of the prospective sponsor company or brand. Demonstrating responsiveness and flexibility, the promoter must then line up the appropriate opportunities that the event can offer to achieve a partner's goals. Now it is time to create your own Flying Wedge, the proposal that will smash through apathy by clearly and inarguably illustrating the value the event can provide to the prospective sponsor, and taking possible questions and objections out of the play by anticipating and answering them before they can surface.

The Sponsorship Deck

There are two components to your presentation—the personal, verbal demonstration that a sponsor's marketing wants and needs may be met by your sports event opportunity, and the physical, leave-behind materials that will keep selling well after the meeting has concluded. The written presentation is also widely known as a *sponsorship deck*, an easy-to-read restatement of the most important points of the presentation, accompanied by relevant illustrations, graphs, and charts. An example of a sponsorship deck for a fictional regional multisport tournament may be found in Appendix 6.

An effective sponsorship deck demonstrates that the event promoter possesses at least a basic understanding of the company's event marketing objectives and builds a persuasive case for how sponsoring the event can provide solutions for the company's wants and needs. The deck should contain pertinent and comprehensive information that supports the promoter's arguments, organized in a logical, easy-to-digest format. How the information is presented is a matter of personal preference. I prefer to use short paragraphs, and where possible, I use bullet points instead of, or preceding, the various sections of prose. This technique makes it easy for prospects to scan the deck after the presentation for the information they believe is most salient to their evaluation and ultimate decision.

It is essential that sponsorship opportunities be presented in person. There is simply no way to adequately communicate the excitement of your sports event through the mail. Actually, there is no way to be certain that your mailed or couriered sponsorship proposal, regardless of how well written, will even be opened or read. If it is read, there is no way to respond to questions or to counter objections before opinions are formed. Whenever possible, the sponsorship presentation should be delivered during a live meeting with the company's event marketing decision makers. Remember that corporate marketing executives are besieged daily with sponsorship pitches by event promoters. Mailed proposals do not remain long atop the stacks piled high on their desks; they quickly find their way to the bottom.

The written sponsorship deck is an organized, comprehensive summary of the event marketing opportunity, an outline that is presented in the same order as the verbal presentation. A picture is worth a thousand words, so be sure to include images that illustrate the strengths and visual attractiveness of the event. A well-edited video is worth a hundred times that. Make sure that the video is as brief as possible. One that lasts longer than a couple of minutes becomes boring to everyone but the promoter. It should capture not only the excitement of the event, but also the various ways in which sponsors were recognized and how they activated their relationships.

Be sure to weave plenty of visual aids into your live presentation. If the event is completely new, consider hiring an illustrator to create a series of "artist's conceptions" and floor plans or maps. It is far easier for the prospect to imagine the event if he or she has materials through which to visualize them. If your budget permits, prepare a CD-ROM with the salient points of the presentation, plus electronic images of the supporting visual aids, to leave with the prospect. Alternatively, prepare the presentation as a Microsoft PowerPoint document and burn it onto a disk to leave behind with the printed materials. Make sure the design of the presentation is as exciting and innovative as the content.

If you are meeting at the prospect company's location, try to get permission to set up the meeting room at least 30 minutes beforehand. Bring and display enlargements of photos and artist's conceptions. If you have brought graphics and videos, ensure that the LCD projector for the Microsoft PowerPoint presentation, the VCR, and the computer you will need are loaded, ready, and in perfect working order before the meeting begins. Bring inexpensive gifts of event merchandise to the first meeting, such as T-shirts, caps, and balls or pucks, in sufficient quantity to cover each meeting participant. (Be careful not to bring anything that bears the name or logo of the company's competitor.)

Remember that the deck has to keep selling after the live presentation is over. Make sure it is persuasive, organized, and comprehensive. Leave copies of the visuals behind—pictures, the video and convenient-sized (e.g., 8" × 11½") versions of the artwork. Above all, make sure that the assumptions and promises in the proposal are realistic and that hyperbole is minimized. Experienced corporate marketers have doubtless sponsored sports events that sounded better than they actually were, so assume that their hype detectors are turned to "high."

The points of emphasis to be included in sponsorship sales decks are as individually different as the events they represent. Some may have to include extensive background material to familiarize the prospective sponsor with the audience characteristics of the event or its featured sport. Presentations for reorganized or relaunched events may have to highlight changes in programming, staging, or entertainment value. Some may contain one or a handful of specific sponsorship opportunities, others a menu of opportunities from which the prospect may choose.

Regardless of its ultimate format, there are several basic components of a winning sponsorship presentation, as listed in Figure 7-7, organized in the

1. **Overview**—Capture the tone and significance of the event. Establish the legitimacy of the event and the credentials of the organizer.
2. **Introduction**—Summarize the opportunities presented by the event and the objectives of the presentation.
3. **The Event**—Present a more complete (but concise) description of the property.
4. **The Opportunity**—Include details on how the company can get involved.
5. **Next Steps**—Present the conclusion and a call to action.

Figure 7-7
Basic Components of a Winning Sponsorship Sales Deck for Sports Events

same sequential, interest-building way in which a good novel unfolds. Capture the prospect's attention with the opening bullet points or brief overview paragraph, and then tell this simple story:

> *Coming soon is a compelling and unique sports event. This is the story of what makes it compelling and unique, and how savvy sports marketers can realize their goals by being partners. Your company can be the next to profit by an association with the event. Here's what you can do to get in on it now!*

The **Overview** of a sponsorship sales deck is like the lead in a well-written newspaper story. It should grab the attention of the reader in its opening passage. Communicate genuine excitement and believable enthusiasm—not hype—in your verbal presentation. Establish the attractiveness and legitimacy of the event by portraying its past history and its growth in popularity, scale, and scope. Include brief quotes selected from media coverage of past events that reflect well upon the event. Demonstrate a basic understanding of the prospective sponsor's needs, if known, by describing what makes the event exciting, unique, appealing, and a great opportunity for the business partner. Provide a brief statement identifying the event organizer, the organizer's unique qualifications, and his or her successes in staging this and other events.

Now that you have the reader's attention, launch into a meatier **Introduction.** Demonstrate the attractiveness of the event's audience demographics and lifestyle characteristics. Include graphs, charts, and tables that portray the similarities between the typical ticket buyer or participant and the company's ideal customer. If the event has not yet debuted, describe these audience characteristics on the basis of similar events for the same sport(s) in analogous markets. Disclose the names of past and/or current sponsor companies and brands and, if appropriate, provide examples of how their association with the event proved successful to their marketing efforts.

In **The Event** section, fully describe the program. Provide an organized portrayal of what the event is, where it will be held, and when everything happens. This is the point in the presentation when all the excitement and warmth of your product—the event—should come shining through. If appropriate, include a facilities map, a schedule of activities, illustrations, photographs, and graphics. Again, be sure to acknowledge and showcase images that feature visible recognition of existing sponsors. Describe the program so the prospect can sense the depth of your commitment to your corporate partners. If your description sounds curiously like the copy you might use to promote the event to the potential public audience—it should. Although you are selling a corporate partnership with the event and not tickets, you are still selling.

The event description must be as exciting and intriguing as possible, because it will lead directly into **The Opportunity**. This is where you will present the series of business solutions, entitlements, and benefits the event can provide to the prospective sponsor. If the promoter has a specific role in mind for a particular prospect, it should be fully described as an available option in this section. Otherwise, offer a series of possible customized packages from which to choose. If you know what the prospect wants from an event marketing partnership, demonstrate how the opportunity can help that company to achieve its marketing objectives. With this information, the company's decision-making process may be vastly simplified. Sponsorship packages that offer companies the right kinds of business solutions can then be evaluated on the basis of price and cost-effectiveness.

I prefer to call the last pages of the sponsorship deck "**Next Steps**" instead of "the conclusion." A conclusion implies an ending. If the promoter has done his or her job right, the sales process is just beginning. In this brief wrap-up, the deck should again emphasize the solutions the event can provide. Both orally and in writing, commit to working with the prospective sponsor to find the right solutions for the company if they have not already been presented. Be sure to provide a contact name and information for any questions that might arise after the presentation.

It is rare indeed for a proposal to be so on-target, so intuitively perfect that it is immediately accepted by the prospective sponsor "as is." Be sure to leave enough time during the presentation to solicit reactions and responses, and listen carefully to all questions, comments, and objections. It is likely, however, that a significant number of the companies will simply pass on the opportunity outright. With prospects that seem even marginally engaged, try to determine what features they think are essential and which are superfluous to them. Ask if the sponsorship proposal meets the company's needs, where it may fall short, and what could strengthen its appeal. Sense what level of involvement the company would be most likely to pursue if it did desire to become a partner and determine how the opportunities in the presentation might be better customized for that company's purposes. If you can elicit feedback during the presentation, propose a reasonable time frame for a second, more refined presentation that will better incorporate the prospect's thoughts. If you cannot gain feedback on the spot, propose a date by which you will contact the company for reactions and questions.

REVISE ASSUMPTIONS, THEN REVISE THE PROPOSAL

Taking all questions and feedback into consideration, and adding some creativity, flexibility, and intuition, the promoter should revise the written proposal to incorporate pertinent answers and additional information. This may include additional background and statistics to strengthen the appeal of the event, as well as a revised package of sponsorship features that better meet the business objectives of the prospective partner. Reallocate the fulfillment costs of superfluous benefits to beef up those the company finds more appealing. Reinforce every facet of the presentation—not just "The Opportunity"—to maximize its chance for success. Finally, reassess whether an upward revision in the sponsorship fee is required to adequately cover any new or expanded fulfillment expenses, or a downward revision is necessary to reflect the company's desire for involvement at a lower level. Be sure to clearly identify any new pricing structure during subsequent presentations.

CLOSE THE DEAL

Present the revised proposal, again in person if possible. It is not necessary to orally restate every point of the entire presentation unless requested by the company to update new decision makers in the room. Review only the areas in which revisions were made, linking those changes to the specific feedback provided by the prospective sponsor. Again, ask for questions, comments, and areas of concern. Be prepared to negotiate on the spot if further revisions are requested or required, fortifying benefits in areas of importance and reducing benefits involving features of less apparent significance. This may be your last chance to reach an agreement in principle, so *make it count!* Respond immediately with solutions to the company's challenges. More fine-tuning of the sponsorship solution may be required, and negotiations may eventually become complex and protracted. When it appears that a deal is possible, however, propose sending a letter of agreement to the prospect that will officially summarize the areas in accord. Negotiations will certainly continue once the agreement is sent, but this piece of paper is essential to keeping the deal on track.

The Decision-Making Process

The decision-making process that a company undertakes to evaluate the attractiveness and suitability of an event marketing opportunity can be lengthy and arduous for both parties. After investing a significant amount of time and creativity, and crafting what would seem to be the ideal opportunity, the organizer may still find the result to be negative, often for reasons completely external to empirical analysis. It is therefore important to throw a wide net over the largest number of qualified prospects during the sales process, presuming that there are no rights of first negotiation in force from previous sponsorship agreements. Don't limit yourself to a single company or brand within the same product category. Approach as many as possible to enhance your chances for success. Waiting for one company at a time to evaluate the opportunity and evolve into a sponsor can be a costly mistake.

Present the opportunity to targeted prospects as far in advance as possible. There are thousands of great potential partnerships that wither and die either because there was insufficient time available for the sponsor to fully evaluate the program, or because the company's event marketing budget was already exhausted and committed to other events. The event promoter is competing with dozens of sports and entertainment events for the prospect's consideration, and qualified companies are being approached regularly for every available sponsorship dollar. It is challenging enough to sell an event sponsorship—don't let insufficient lead time be the reason you are shut out.

How early is early enough? If the program is an annual event, it can be very effective to invite the decision makers of targeted companies to attend the most imminent edition as VIP guests. Greet them upon arrival and extend treatment befitting a future sponsor. Make sure that they have access to on-site VIP hospitality, and provide them with some take-home souvenir or commemorative merchandise. Be sure to also invite the decision makers of companies that passed on the opportunity to sponsor the event—if one of their competitors did not subsequently join the event partner family. The quality of the event, the hospitality of the promoter, and the longer period of time before decisions must be made for the following year may persuade them to take another look. Try to set up a meeting to present the partnership opportunity as soon after their attendance as possible.

If it sounds as though you need a year or more to start the process of securing sponsors, that can be absolutely true, particularly for midsize to large sports events and for deals of significant financial value. Simpler community and grassroots events, presuming their income expectations are reasonable, may be funded within a much shorter time frame. Generally, the lower the cost of the sponsorship and the simpler the benefits, the less time is needed to generate sponsorships. For example, a local Little League All-Star game charging a $500 sponsorship fee in return for a few banners needs only enough time to have the banner designed, printed, and delivered. Events that require advertising or promotional fulfillment activities, such as consumer sweepstakes, discount programs, or the creation of commemorative merchandise, need more time to develop.

The Sponsor's Point of View

Sponsor prospects need time to fully analyze the potential advantages of supporting a sports event marketing opportunity. The evaluation period can take weeks or months, and the greater the degree of involvement and cost, the longer the process can be expected to take. A prospective sponsor will evaluate the offer on the basis of whether the event will provide the company with needed and desirable marketing opportunities and whether its marketing budget can accommodate the attendant financial commitment.

In addition to pure cost, an evaluation of the cost-effectiveness of the opportunity will also be of great importance to the sponsor. That is, will spending a given sum of money on this sports event produce a higher level of product sales than if the same sum of money were spent on another activity such as advertising, promotion, or even another sports event? The measure often used in this assessment when product sales are the key determinants is known as the return on investment (ROI). Simply defined, ROI quantifies the number of additional dollars generated in sales for every dollar spent on an event's marketing fees and activation. If the ROI for an event marketing program can yield better results for the dollar than other components of a product's marketing mix, it will generally be regarded as a good buy by the prospective sponsor.

An October 2003 survey by *Sports Business Journal* noted that sponsors have responded to an increasingly challenging corporate economy by becoming more sophisticated, analytical, and demanding with respect to their sports sponsorships. Fully 82 percent of sports league corporate partners surveyed regularly measure the ROI of their sponsorships. Product sales, media exposure, and post-event surveys were cited as among the most prevalent of the multiple methods that sponsors used to evaluate their returns. Most frequently mentioned as a key determinant of ROI were sales, at 82 percent of sports sponsors surveyed, closely followed by media exposure, at 80 percent. Product sales, however, was cited by 49 percent of the companies as the single most important method of calculating their return, with media exposure, at 19 percent of sponsors, coming in a distant second.

Of course, sales cannot be accurately projected before a sports event sponsorship has commenced, only evaluated upon its conclusion. To improve the likelihood of success, savvy sports event marketers measure potential partnerships against the strategies and standards that have yielded them best results in the past. Figure 7-8 provides a glimpse of the criteria that MasterCard International vice president of Global Sponsorship and Event Marketing Robert Cramer uses to evaluate a new sports partnership opportunity.

Many of MasterCard International's ideal event sponsorship characteristics can be applied equally well to sports events of global significance and to regional and community programs. It all depends on sponsors being able to generate an acceptable return on their investment. A corporate partner wants assurances that the respective target markets for the event and its business will be compatible and that a sufficient volume of audience or participants will attend, to whom its marketing efforts will be directed to justify the expense.

Sponsors must also consider the timing of an event. Does the event schedule dovetail with other promotional opportunities (e.g., a Fourth of July sale, holiday shopping, clearances, new product introductions)? Do they already

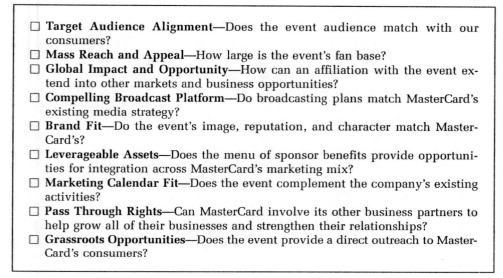

☐ **Target Audience Alignment**—Does the event audience match with our consumers?

☐ **Mass Reach and Appeal**—How large is the event's fan base?

☐ **Global Impact and Opportunity**—How can an affiliation with the event extend into other markets and business opportunities?

☐ **Compelling Broadcast Platform**—Do broadcasting plans match MasterCard's existing media strategy?

☐ **Brand Fit**—Do the event's image, reputation, and character match MasterCard's?

☐ **Leverageable Assets**—Does the menu of sponsor benefits provide opportunities for integration across MasterCard's marketing mix?

☐ **Marketing Calendar Fit**—Does the event complement the company's existing activities?

☐ **Pass Through Rights**—Can MasterCard involve its other business partners to help grow all of their businesses and strengthen their relationships?

☐ **Grassroots Opportunities**—Does the event provide a direct outreach to MasterCard's consumers?

Figure 7-8
MasterCard's Sports Event Sponsorship Checklist

sponsor a sports event that adequately serves their target market at that time of year, making the addition of another program an effort in duplication? Or does the opportunity fit a time of the year when an additional marketing program can help a company create a noticeable spike in sales?

Sports event promoters can provide prospective partners with answers only if they understand the questions. The overarching query will be, "How does this event marketing program offer my business unique and significant opportunity with sufficient and affordable value beyond its intrinsic prestige and attractiveness?"

HOW COMPANIES ASSESS THE VALUE OF A SPONSORSHIP

Except for making sure that the cost of selling and fulfilling the benefits promised to a sponsor do not exceed the revenues required from the relationship, there is no one right way of setting the price of a sponsorship package. Sports event organizers assign a price to a package of sponsor benefits based on how much it will cost them to fulfill their obligations, plus the net profit required to fund event operations. Corporate partners, however, perceive value in terms of measurable sales and exposure opportunities, but also in intangibles such as the reputation of the event. According to IEG Valuation Service managing director Laren Ukman, writing in the second quarter 2002 issue of *Air Shows* magazine, sponsors place great importance on the prestige of an event, audience loyalty, the number of other event partners vying for attention, and the competitive protection offered by category exclusivity. But most of all, they want to be able to credit their event relationship with a measurable increase in product sales and/or an increase in market share.

Because most businesses have many more active marketing efforts in place than just a single relationship with an event, the direct effect of a sponsorship on sales is not always easy to quantify. It is easier to attribute an increase in sales for a small neighborhood business supporting a community sports program where anecdotal feedback from customers is personally received. At the opposite extreme, companies with global reach, spending great sums in support of sports events sponsorships of broad significance, also hope to experience a noticeable increase in sales and capture market share from their competitors. Sponsorship of sports events with national or international prestige, supplemented with wide-reaching, well-funded activation strategies can perceptibly influence sales.

For the vast majority of companies that fall between the small neighborhood concern and the giant multinational corporation, it is difficult to attribute an increase in market share to a single sports event sponsorship or to identify the portion of new sales they helped to develop. It is therefore to the benefit of organizers to devise opportunities that sponsors can use to measurably affect their sales as a result of their partnership. These can include direct sales opportunities at the event and coded dollars-off coupons for products or retailers that may be distributed with tickets upon entry, printed on the backs of tickets to an event, or included with the event program. Organizers can accept proofs of purchase from sponsor product packaging for discounted event tickets or merchandise and work with sponsors to execute cross promotions that demonstrate a direct cause and effect between the event and a product purchase. Any program that adds consumer value to the purchase of a sponsor's product before, during, or after the event can provide direct evidence that an event partnership helped to increase the sponsor's sales, adding great value to the relationship and strengthening the case for continuing the relationship in subsequent years. This is particularly true for B-to-B marketers, for whom sales of products and services as a direct or indirect result of their event marketing activities will typically figure more prominently in their package of sponsor benefits than media and exposure opportunities.

Nextel, a leading wireless communications provider, is a firm believer in the value of using sports events to develop new customers and provide hospitality options to express appreciation to loyal existing users. The company often hosts a Nextel-customers-only hospitality lounge at events, which can be accessed by fans who simply show their Nextel cellular phones. This provides the company's clients with an exclusive hospitality experience and its customer service staff with an outstanding opportunity to entertain a measurable number of subscribers. Michael Robichaud, Nextel's director of Sports and Event Marketing, also measures the number and quality of the customers and prospects who attend the event, as well as the number of trials (sampling of its service) that were conducted on-site. Finally, the company conducts follow-up surveys to measure its customers' opinions on the quality of their event experience. "Nextel has found sponsorships and events an important part of our overall marketing strategy," says Robichaud. "We are trying to distance our business from our competitors by doing things differently. By engaging in aggressive sponsorship activities, we are able to carve out times and opportunities to exclusively deliver our message to our target customers." Through these prospect development and customer appreciation activities, Nextel aims to increase its market share and maintain the loyalty of its existing subscribers.

EVALUATION OF MARKETING IMPACT AND EXPOSURE

Before the event, the projected impact of a sponsor's identification in event advertising, program ads, playing surface and event facility signage, video scoreboard ads, and public address acknowledgments can be estimated on the basis of the number of people who are expected to see these messages, for how long, and how often. During the pre-event evaluation process, the sponsor assigns a reasonable value for each of these exposure opportunities, frequently with historical input from the event promoter. The value of event tickets and hospitality functions are tabulated at least at face value, although sometimes tickets for prestigious, sold-out events are valued at higher rates such as those a third-party ticket broker would have charged to procure the same number of tickets had the sponsor not been guaranteed access. Direct sales and sampling opportunities may also be assigned a subjective estimated value based on projected incremental sales generated by these activities.

According to *Sports Business Journal's* October 2003 survey, 61 percent of sports league sponsors conduct their own analysis of value with in-house personnel. Many companies that support programs with sponsorship fees in the six- and seven-figure range often retain an independent evaluation service before and after the event, such as IEG Valuation Service (*www.sponsorship.com*), the Bonham Group (*www.bonham.com*), and Redmandarin (*www.redmandarin.com*), among many others. These companies measure exposure time and value for a sponsor's logo, name, or product seen on broadcasts and news coverage (see Play 13), as a result of Internet traffic, advertising, point-of-purchase promotional displays, and presence at the event site. Each exposure opportunity is assigned a value per impression, multiplied by viewership, circulation, and web page views, and, in some cases, multiplied again by a factor representing the length of time each corporate message is exposed.

The analysis of sponsorship value includes other key exposure points such as the brand's name and/or logo on event tickets, credentials, staff, crew and athlete uniforms, merchandise, letterhead, directional and welcome signage, street banners, event site entrance treatments, programs, invitations, posters, and many others. Print advertisements, television and radio commercials, ads on the video scoreboard, and public address announcements

1. **Definition of the Event, the Event Organizer, and the Sponsor**
   What corporate entities are entering into the agreement?
   What event(s) or event element(s) does the agreement cover? (This is particularly important for multivenue, multiday, and multiactivity events.)
2. **Identification of the Sponsor Identity**
   How is the sponsor being identified, by the corporate name or by the brand name?
3. **Sponsor Designation**
   How have the parties agreed to recognize the sponsor in both event and corporate communications (e.g., as part of the event title, presenting sponsor, official sponsor, official supplier)?
4. **Exclusivity**
   What product category or categories does the sponsorship extend to?
   What kinds of relationships with other companies are made "off limits" to the organizer by the agreement?
5. **Intellectual Property Rights**
   How and in what form may the sponsor use the event's name and logo?
   How may the sponsor use the event organizer's name and logo?
   How may the event use the sponsor's name and logo?
   What approval process is required for each usage?
6. **Territory**
   Over what geographic territory does the sponsor's rights extend (e.g., community, state or province, national, continental, global)?
7. **Term**
   When does the sponsor partnership begin and end?
8. **Renewal Options**
   Under what conditions may the agreement be renewed?
   Are there exclusive periods of first negotiation or first refusal?
   Are there any price protections offered to returning sponsors?
9. **List of Entitlements**
   Frequently appended to the agreement as a separate schedule. The list outlines all of the agreed-to benefits (e.g., tickets, signage, advertising, hospitality opportunities, etc.) in exacting detail.
10. **Marketing and Promotion Rights**
    What kinds of event-related consumer promotions are permitted by the agreement and over what period of time?
    How may the sponsor use the event in product advertising?
    Is the sponsor entitled to use photographs or video of the event or athletes in its marketing program?
    How many event tickets and what merchandise are permitted to be used in consumer sweepstakes and giveaways?

Figure 7-9
Essential Elements of the Sponsorship Agreement

11. **Consideration**

The sponsorship fee and schedule of payments, whether cash or VIK, must be included.

Fulfillment expenses payable by the sponsor, or optional add-on benefits should also be defined.

12. **Indemnification and Insurance**

Under what procedure will lawsuits stemming from injuries or property damage in connection with the event, sponsor promotions, advertising claims, and other possible causes proceed, and under what state's laws?

To what degree will the event protect the sponsor against legal actions by third parties, and vice versa?

What minimum types and levels of insurance coverage do the parties require of each other?

13. **Cancellation and Default**

Under what conditions, if any, may the agreement be terminated?

What are the promoter's obligations, and the sponsor's rights, if the event is canceled or postponed because of conditions not under the control of either party (also known as forces majeure)?

What happens if either the sponsor or the promoter defaults on its obligations to the agreement or declares bankruptcy?

Figure 7-9
(Continued)

provide additional, easily measured, value. The results generated by these valuation services will also demonstrate that not all signage is created equal. Organizers should ensure that sponsors investing the most in their event enjoy exposure opportunities that are in the most desirable, visible, and valuable locations to the media, broadcasters, and audience.

Finalizing the Deal

The execution of a formal agreement between the sponsor and the event organizer or promoter, drafted and reviewed by competent legal counsel, is highly recommended immediately upon conclusion of negotiations. As a critical legal document, the agreement will include both the negotiated business points of the deal and various legal protections required by both parties. It is not unusual for attorneys representing both parties to identify dozens of further details and ramifications that must be defined (e.g., delivery date for tickets, approval processes, restrictions and limitations on promotions, fee and expense payment schedules, etc.). In addition, there are usually a significant number of necessary legal inclusions relating to insurance, liability, indemnification, cancellation terms, breach of contract penalties, and other safeguards that both parties hope never to have to use but which are necessary to deal with unforeseen issues and emergencies.

Contracts and letter agreements used to finalize sponsorship deals generally remain confidential. Although proprietary and individual to particular event organizers, there are several areas that all sponsorship agreements should have in common, as described in Figure 7-9. This list highlights the most common and essential elements of sponsorship agreements. Many more sections may be added to meet the specific needs of the event and the character of a sponsorship deal.

Now, Service Your Sponsors!

Congratulate your sponsor and the responsible members of your organization on the successful conclusion of negotiations and the execution of your agreement. At this point, the work really begins. Too often, it is during the sales and negotiation processes when event organizers devote the most attention to their sponsors. Fulfilling the sponsorship agreement and investing in the sponsor's successful association with the event is a time-consuming, but rewarding, necessity. It is wise to appoint at least one staff member to serve as an account executive whose key function it is to oversee the event's relationship with its sponsors. This individual should be empowered to ensure not only that the spirit and substance of the contract are met, but also that the sponsors feel appreciated and integral to the success of the event. Organizers should communicate with them often to share new developments and opportunities, to monitor their success, and to ensure they sense their obvious importance to making the event live up to its full potential. Investing the necessary time and effort in helping them achieve their objectives will pay dividends as the event develops and grows in future years.

Post-Play Analysis

The best way to meet the objectives of prospective sponsors is to design a program of event benefits that provides solutions to their business wants and needs. Benefits of sponsorship may include tickets, exclusive-access activities, promotional rights, signage and advertising, and many others. An understanding of what the prospect hopes to achieve through its event association should help an organizer customize an individualized package that contains the most attractive benefits in the right quantities for each sponsor. Organizers should analyze and account for the fulfillment costs of delivering each benefit to ensure that their net sponsor revenue goals remain attainable.

Prospective sponsors should be qualified before being considered potential sales targets. Event promoters should create an organized and persuasive sponsorship deck for presentation to prospects that clearly outlines the opportunities available. Get the prospect's reaction to the presentation and make the revisions necessary to close a deal. Formalize the deal with a contract or letter agreement that clearly outlines the obligations of each party, sponsor benefits and promotional rights, and all financial and legal commitments. Understand how the sponsor will evaluate its success post-event, and ensure that the event meets or exceeds its expectations.

By teaming with sponsors and understanding their wants and needs, event organizers will be better positioned to manage events that will be teeming with sponsors.

Coach's Clipboard

1. An event promoter wants to approach a company with a history of spending generously on sponsorships for similar events. The company's contact, however, refuses to provide any meaningful input on the firm's event marketing objectives and asks that all proposals be mailed before an appointment for any live presentation is considered. How should you proceed in preparing a presentation for this prospective sponsor?

2. A sponsor prospect is presented with an opportunity to be the official software company of a multisport recreational tournament. The company strongly asserts that it requires at least twice the number of premium event tickets and VIP all-access passes, but is unwilling to spend additional money beyond the quoted price of the sponsorship package as originally presented. The promoter thinks that if the tickets and passes are not substantially increased, the deal may not move forward. What course of action do you suggest?

3. A sponsor conducts a post-event evaluation, the results of which suggest that the demographics of the event did, in fact, match those of its target market and that the impact of its exposure met its expectations. The company's sales, however, showed no meaningful increase. What will you do to encourage the sponsor to return next year?

Maximizing and Servicing the Media Partnership

Everything is scrutinized in this business. They talk about your decisions on the air and in print and on talk radio. In this business, what you do is in the paper every day.

—MICHAEL CROWLEY, PRESIDENT, OAKLAND A's,
AS QUOTED IN SPORTS BUSINESS JOURNAL, NOVEMBER 4–10, 2002

The Roman god Janus is most often pictured in profile as a head with two faces. The deity of gates and doors, Janus also represented new beginnings. (Not coincidentally, this is why the month that bears his name is the first of each new year.) Ancient worshipers believed that one must pass through a gate or door before entering new places, therefore the guardian god of doors looks simultaneously in two directions—peering back into the past, and ahead to the new beginning.

To sports event organizers, the media often assume the countenance of Janus. Writers and correspondents look forward to event day, reporting on preparations and controversies and speculating on how competition will unfold. They later look back on the results and provide analysis and perspective on the event's success. The media can be an event's best friend or its worst enemy, and, like Janus, they can sometimes assume both aspects at the same time. Much like the gods of ancient times, as perceived by their followers, the media can entertain well-directed appeals but cannot be controlled. To understand the delicate relationship between an event and members of the media, one must first grasp these key stakeholders' business objectives.

The Two Faces of the Media

A media outlet, whether a newspaper, magazine, Internet web site, radio station, or television network, exists for one primary purpose: to transmit information of interest to its specific target audience. Some of the information and how it is presented—in the form of advertising, promotions, and other joint marketing ventures—is under the direct control of the event organizer. Typically, the more valuable stream of information, in the form of publicity, is under the total control of the media outlet.

The media provides event organizers with an essential platform to publicize and advertise their events, a vital component in the campaign to attract an audience and participants. When coverage of an event is positive, the media can generate the impact, influence, and credibility that advertising alone cannot hope to achieve. Similarly, when its tone of coverage is negative, the impact, influence, and credibility can likewise be so persuasive that even the most creative advertising campaigns will have difficulty overcoming the challenge.

To preserve their objectivity and journalistic integrity, while marketing themselves as providing an attractive platform for advertising and promotion, media outlets most often organize themselves into two separate, semi-autonomous halves. The editorial half is charged with the responsibility of providing informational content by covering news and developing stories and features. This group is typically under the leadership of an editor in chief, who together with his or her writers must compile and communicate information that is relevant and interesting to the outlet's readers or viewers. Event organizers direct their publicity efforts toward this editorial side of the media, presenting and disseminating event information as news, story ideas, and opportunities for coverage before and during the event. Most editors enjoy complete freedom in deciding which stories they believe will be sufficiently compelling to their audience to be written, published, or aired.

In business environments where the press is not financed, managed, or controlled by the government, operating a media outlet can be a very expensive proposition. In addition to selling individual copies and subscriptions, newspapers must sell advertising to cover their costs and generate a profit. Electronic media such as radio, television, and Internet web sites also sell advertising to support their operations, or they charge viewers indirectly through carriage agreements with cable and satellite providers. This second face of the media business is essential to give the editorial staff the freedom and funding needed to pursue their journalistic responsibilities. This is the sales and marketing half of the media partnership, led in the printed media by the publisher. Media outlets sell advertising, create and manage promotions, and pursue event marketing opportunities as vehicles to promote sales, enroll new subscribers, and sell advertising to event sponsors. Event organizers work with the sales and marketing side of media businesses to purchase advertising, create media partnerships, and establish the consumer promotions that will drive ticket sales, attendance, and viewership.

To preserve the objectivity of reporting, an impenetrable Great Wall stands between the two halves of a media organization, particularly in the newspaper business. In the model media outlet, the presence of a promotional relationship between a sports event and a newspaper will not increase the interest of an editor in providing readers with news coverage. Conversely, its absence or a partnership with a competitive media partner will not exclude an event from the editorial assignment calendar. Moreover, an event-media partnership will not provide organizers with a warranty against a lack of coverage or negative stories about the event, nor will it encourage glowing reviews afterward. In the eyes of the editor, if an event makes news, it will be covered, and if it is well organized and executed, it may be covered positively.

Publishers, on the other hand, see more than just the newsworthiness of sports events. They see unique business opportunities that can generate revenue and increase readership. They view events as opportunities to sell incremental advertising and provide promotional platforms to benefit their businesses. Some create "special sections" that add value for readers and profits for the publication through increased circulation and incremental advertising revenue. The publisher and marketing staff are usually the key decision makers on whether to participate more broadly with an event. In addition to generating advertising revenues, their objectives may include increasing readership in their core market and expanding circulation into new markets. Many magazines, particularly news and sports weeklies, are organized along similar lines as daily newspapers. National magazines are difficult to attract as marketing partners, but may be more accessible on the editorial front, assuming the event can generate reportage or stories that are nationally relevant. Generally, magazines with a local focus are much more open to working with event organizers as potential marketing partners.

Like magazines, local television stations and network affiliates are relatively more open to partnership opportunities with sports events than their national counterparts. National networks normally get involved only in terms of providing news stories that are more globally or nationally relevant. There is often a similar separation between the news and sports coverage side of their business, and the marketing and promotional side that generates the revenue to keep them both operating. Where television outlets differ somewhat is in situations in which a network holds the rights to broadcast the event. In such cases, the national broadcaster may engage in promotions that increase awareness of an event for the purpose of increasing viewership of its coverage.

Most business partnerships between sports event organizers and television broadcasters, however, unfold on the local level. The most obvious prospect is the local network affiliate that will broadcast coverage of the event. Although other stations in the market may be approached if the broadcaster passes on a promotional opportunity, it can be more challenging to persuade a television station to promote an event that will be seen on another channel. But if the event is not a broadcast property, nearly any outlet will do. It is best, however, to align the event with a station that is the most watched in the market by the audience you most want to attract. Cable television affiliates are also outstanding resources, so it is wise not to overlook the local sports networks, regional affiliates of national sports networks, or local news channels.

Among potential media partners, radio is one of the most effective in generating local excitement and is frequently the medium most agreeable to promotional partnerships. In the United States, although many stations provide national syndicated programming to their listeners, radio is primarily a local medium. Most advertising is sold locally and is usually far less expensive than television advertising. Radio advertising can also boast a far lower "cost per thousand" than newspapers, as compared with full-page display advertising. (I compare radio spots to a full-page newspaper ad because they are similarly undistracted—there is only one radio ad broadcast at a time and there is only one ad on a full page.)

What an event organizer hopes media outlets will provide—both as partners and as communicators of news—will differ significantly as to the audiences these two partners seek to serve, as well as their respective corporate objectives. To understand what can reasonably be expected from the media, an organizer must comprehend what the two halves of the media business want and need from a sports event.

What the Editorial Side Really Wants from Sports Events

It is important to recognize that because media outlets are typically bifurcated into independently managed editorial and marketing sides, their wants and needs can also diverge along very similar lines. Editors and writers are charged with the responsibility of providing a conduit of information to their readers and viewers and must cover events from perspectives they feel are newsworthy and interesting. To fulfill this mission, those on the editorial side need compelling story ideas, accurate information to help support their reporting, good photo or video opportunities to add visual support to their words, and facilities that will help them cover the event and submit their work to the editor (see Figure 8-1).

Whether the sports event is a community tournament or a multinational invitational competition, event organizers must approach the media in a professional manner that demonstrates an understanding of its members' needs and expectations and represents the organization as competent and knowledgeable. That is, sports event organizers should give editors no excuse to overlook covering an event. An amateurish approach can make a poor impression on members of the media and seriously damage a sports event organizer's overall marketing plan. Diminishing an event's importance in the mind of an editor can jeopardize the placement of essential pre-event reportage and

---

I. Needs Prior to Event Day
- Compelling story ideas
  - Unusual or touching stories about participating athletes
  - Interesting historical points on the event and past athletes
  - Significant business stories (e.g., economic benefits, intriguing or innovative partnerships)
- Accurate and comprehensive information
  - Press releases
  - Media guides
    - Background information
      - Participating athletes
      - Event history
    - Official rules and format of competition
    - Official statistics
    - Schedules of events
  - Access to senior event organizer management for interviews
  - A single point of contact for additional information

II. Needs on Event Day
- Appropriate, comfortable working conditions
  - Workstations with clear view of play
  - Timely access to official and accurate statistics, score sheets, athlete background information
  - Clear, unobstructed positions for photographers
  - Availability of power, phone lines, data lines and fax machines
- Access to organizer management, coaches, and athletes at pre- and post-event press conferences

---

Figure 8-1
What the Editorial Side of the Media Needs from Sports Event Organizers

coverage of the event itself. Because pre-event media coverage provides the public with a strong first impression of an event and, by extension, reinforces the perceived value of attending, organizers should make sure that every contact and communication with the editorial side is clear and confident, accurate and appropriate.

Like sports event organizers, editors and reporters must operate within the boundaries of limited financial resources. On the editorial side, budget constraints are manifest in the amount of space (newspapers, magazines, and Internet) or time (radio and television) that may be devoted to coverage of an event. The amount of space or time allocated to any story is determined by the editor and is a clear manifestation of that person's perception of the event's importance to the readers or viewers. Demonstrate the professionalism of the event and its organization, and convey the importance of the event to the host community with every media contact. "Space in most newspapers is limited. Some organizers, understandably enthusiastic about their ventures, simply fail to realize that others might not share their enthusiasm," notes *Los Angeles Times* sportswriter Helene Elliott. "I think the drama and importance must be inherent. Don't send me demographic studies that men 18 to 34 love this event and so we must cover it. The event should be compelling enough on its own that it doesn't need false hype." Maintain frankness and credibility, as well as reasonable expectations in regard to the intrinsic newsworthiness of your event.

Like sports event organizers, editors and reporters also work against immutable deadlines that must be recognized when planning campaigns to generate publicity. Daily newspapers, television, radio, and Internet media work on daily, sometimes hourly, deadlines, and deadlines for inclusion in weekly media may be only a couple of days prior to publication. Monthly non-news periodicals are sometimes called "long lead" publications. You will need to provide information weeks or months before a particular issue is published, frequently long before pre-event press conferences are scheduled or releases are written. Demonstrate sensitivity to these deadlines by not wasting the media outlets' time. Provide them with the information they want and need *when* and how they want it.

INFORMATION, PLEASE

It is up to the sports event organizer to identify the newsworthy opportunities that exist for media coverage throughout the event planning process and to effectively communicate these possibilities to editors, columnists, and writers. A campaign of strategically spaced press announcements should be planned over the days and weeks leading up to the event, during the event itself, and even afterward, to build interest among the media and, by extension, their readership or viewers—your potential audience. A sample campaign is presented in Figure 8-2 in a generalized, chronologically structured order that will be applicable to many sports events. Organizers may combine any num-

I. Event Announcement
    a. Event Description, Host City, Location, Dates
    b. Logo Introduction
    c. Economic Impact
    d. Charitable Association
    e. What's New
II. Announcement of Participating Athletes or Try-outs
III. Major Sponsor Announcements
IV. Human Interest Stories (may be multiple releases)
V. Ticket Sales Date Announcement
VI. Credential Application Process
VII. "Hard Hat" Tour Invitation (an opportunity to tour the site during set-up)
VIII. Participant Media Introduction
IX. Post-Event Announcements
    a. Official Results
    b. Attendance Figures
    c. Amount Raised for Charity

Figure 8-2
Sample Sports Event Press Announcement Schedule

ber of these announcements into the same release and schedule additional announcements that are appropriate to their event property.

It is most likely obvious that the first communication to the media should officially announce the event. Even existing events with a long tradition in the host city should plan to release a statement announcing the date(s) of the event, location(s), and background information, such as economic impact estimates, if applicable. If the event is launching a new logo, it may be introduced at this time to begin the process of building awareness for the new identity, although a later logo launch is sometimes planned to provide the event with an additional media opportunity at a strategic time. Here, too, an organizer can announce any associated charity that will become the beneficiary of the event, along with historical information on what the event has provided to charities in the past. Don't forget to mention the sale date for tickets if it is known at that time.

The first announcement should introduce the media to the event, concisely describing the competition or program of activities. If the property is an established sports event, this description should also include information on what is new and exciting about the upcoming year's edition. Is the competition format different? Are there new activities or attractions planned for existing or new audiences (e.g., children, families, outreach programs for low-income or at-risk youth)? Do not assume that all media are completely familiar with the event or sport, even those with a long tradition in the marketplace. "Event organizers need to provide members of the media with comprehensive background on the event, easy-to-understand chronologies of the event, and comments from participants, where and when applicable," says Bloomberg News reporter Allan Kreda.

The introductory announcement is of particular importance for events that were open to bidding by prospective host cities. The first announcement is the organizer's best opportunity to excite the local media and, through them, the community and area businesses. Winning the competition to host an event can be big news. Include information on how many other cities competed for the honor and why the city was selected. Include economic impact data (see Play 4) and the number of hotel room-nights event staff, participants, guests, and fans will occupy. If there is a charitable partner or beneficiary of a portion of the event's proceeds, this can be a good opportunity to announce that as well.

DELIVERING THE ANNOUNCEMENT—PRESS RELEASES

There are two primary ways for sports event organizers to provide the media with information before the event—by holding press conferences or sending press releases through the mail, via E-mail, or by fax. Most communication with the media is likely to be by press release, a concise, attention-grabbing missive that provides basic information in convincing, but factual form. Because press releases are most effective when they are as brief as possible (between one and three double-spaced pages), they cannot provide a comprehensive overview of a sports event. They should, however, include as many answers to the "who," "what," "why," "when," and "how" details of the event, heralded by an attention-grabbing headline and subheading.

It is essential that the headline and subhead entice the reader to go further. Press releases are sales documents, though of a more subtle nature than sponsorship decks, for instance. To maximize the chances that a release will become a story, it must be compelling and credible—starting with the headline, subhead, and opening sentences. As Helene Elliott suggests, their credibility depends on their being convincing without any suggestion of hype. Above all, preserve the recipients' perception of your professionalism by ensuring that the release is 100 percent error-free, typographically, grammatically, and factually.

Because some media outlets use the press release as their only source of information about an event, it is important to include one or two quotes from reliable and respected authorities. It is appropriate for one or more points of information to be provided in the form of a quote from the most senior official of the organization staging the event. A second quote may be included from another important stakeholder, such as a participating star athlete, a senior city official, or a representative of the benefiting charity. Don't try to fit every piece of event information into the release; just those items that provide a complete framework outlining what the program is all about. Writers and reporters, however, may want to incorporate more details, quotes, and information beyond those provided in the press release. Be sure to include a contact name, phone number, and E-mail address either just beneath the subheading or at the end of the document. The best stories are almost always generated by writers who look for perspectives that will be unique among those of their competitive colleagues. See Figure 8-3 for a sample press release that officially

---

(Insert Event or Organizer Logo Here)
Leduc Selected to Host
Third Annual Big Street Sports Tournament
More than 1000 Top Amateur Athletes from Across the Nation
to Compete against Hometown's Best This Summer

Contact: Dan Sommer, MNO Sports, Inc.
888-000-0000

The City of Leduc has been named as host of one of the nation's fastest growing street sports festivals in the summer of 2005. The selection of Leduc as the host city for the Big Street Sports Tournament was announced in a joint statement by the mayor of Leduc and MNO Sports of Washington, D.C., the promoter of the event.

The Big Street Sports Tournament will bring more than 1000 top-ranked amateur athletes to compete at Leduc's Civic Sports Complex from July 23 to 27. The visiting athletes will also take on the city's own premier competitors in skateboarding, in-line skating, roller hockey and BMX bicycle contests for all age, gender, and skill levels, ranging from "8 and Under" to "18 and Older" divisions.

"The Big Street Sports Tournament has found the perfect host in the City of Leduc," said Arthur Andrews, executive director of the event. "Action sports athletes from across the country will enjoy the outstanding hospitality for which the city has become famous."

"Leduc has again proven itself to be an active and exciting sports city," said Mayor Angie Arturo. "The Big Street Sports Tournament will attract thousands of families and sports enthusiasts from the local and surrounding communities to watch and enjoy the competitions, as well as to take advantage of a full weekend of great entertainment, interactive activities, and pure fun."

Sports fans and entertainment seekers will be welcome to attend the event free of charge. In addition to the competitions, visitors will enjoy BMX half-pipe exhibitions, an extreme sports video arcade, "kids-only" clinics and activities, free in-line skating and braking lessons, nonstop musical entertainment, a bicycle tune-up area and obstacle course, a street sports product expo, special guest appearances, food concessions, and more.

This is the third edition of the Big Street Sports Tournament, which has been previously held in Providence, Rhode Island, and Orlando, Florida. An average of more than 30,000 visitors attended the festival and tournament in each city.

The detailed schedule of events and additional information for the Big Street Sports Tournament will be released at a later date.

Figure 8-3
Sample Sports Event Announcement Press Release

announces the fictional Big Street Sports Tournament described in the Host City Request for Proposal (RFP) in Appendix 2.

Some sports event organizers will have the budget available to retain the services of an outside public relations agency to help manage the publicity campaign, write press releases, and coordinate press conferences. Others, with limited financial resources and unable to afford public relations assistance, will be faced with the task of creating and distributing their own releases. For organizers working with restrictive budgets, Figure 8-4 provides a brief checklist to consult before distributing the first press release.

DELIVERING THE ANNOUNCEMENT—PRESS CONFERENCES

The first announcement of a sports event and the subsequent issuing of the most meaningful and important event information in succeeding weeks are often communicated at press, or media, conferences. Although holding press conferences can be far more effective in generating media attention than sim-

---

☐ Compile a list of the appropriate story or assignment editors (e.g., sports, business, entertainment, city desk) to whom you would like to send the release at the host city's newspaper, magazine, radio, television, and web-based media outlets. Ensure that all names, addresses, and titles are current and accurate.

☐ News has to be new. Make sure that all information is timely, correct, and not previously announced. Date the release and mail, fax, E-mail, or messenger to every contact on your list on the same day.

☐ Be sure that every word in the release is used and spelled correctly, and that the body copy is grammatically correct.

☐ Include one or two brief but meaningful quotes from the highest-ranking organization official. Quotes should highlight why your "news" is exciting and worthy of coverage.

☐ Always include a company contact name, number, and E-mail address at either the beginning or end of the release.

☐ Generating media interest is a sales process. Be sure to follow up with calls or E-mails to media who do not contact you directly within a few days after sending the release.

☐ Make your first effort your best. If the release results in no media interest, do not rewrite and resend it. Move on to preparing the next announcement as scheduled.

☐ If your release does result in a story, send a brief thank-you note to the editor and writer.

Source: Dollars and Events: How to Succeed in the Special Events Business, by Dr. Joe Goldblatt, CSEP and Frank Supovitz, John Wiley & Sons, 1999.

Figure 8-4
Press Release Development Checklist

ply circulating press releases, they can also be far more expensive. Be reasonable in your expectations. If you truly believe that an announcement is news of genuine significance to the community, it may merit a press conference and may be worth the expense. Will details be revealed that are compelling enough to be worth the time commitment of the media representatives who will attend? It takes far less time for a reporter to read a press release than to travel to, attend, and return from a press conference. (Of course, you will never really know whether a press release has been read.) Are the individuals delivering the announcement(s) newsmakers themselves, worthy of a personal interview or of being captured for later television coverage or in "sound bites" (brief audio clips) for radio reports? Will there be other stakeholders at the press conference whom the media will want to interview, such as participating athletes, coaches, celebrities, or politicians? You should be completely confident that staging a press conference is the correct approach for any particular announcement, as poor media attendance suggests to those who do show up that the message delivered is of little importance. There is only one opportunity to do this right. If the announcing press conference is poorly staged, if there are no new or interesting details revealed, or if few members of the media actually attend, the perception of the event in the market can be seriously damaged.

Recognize, too, that attendance at a press conference means a significant time commitment for editors and their writers. News is happening everywhere, and there are only a limited number of reporters available to cover it all. Make sure their time will be well spent. Start as close to the announced time as possible and make the conference quick, no more than 20 minutes, as illustrated in the sample running order in Figure 8-5.

Press or media conferences are announced by circulating a "media advisory" to the same local contacts that were identified for the distribution of press releases. An advisory is designed to provide enough information to encourage the attendance of media outlets without giving the details that will be announced at the press conference. It should include a general statement describing the subject of the press conference (without inadvertently making the announcement in the advisory), the names of those who will be participating in the announcement, and, of course, where and when the announcement will be made. Again, a contact name should be provided to enable advisory recipients to request additional information, confirm attendance, or to receive press releases in lieu of their attendance. Send the advisory a day ahead of time to enable assignment editors to schedule a reporter or camera crew to cover the press conference.

Select a venue for the press conference that is convenient, and if possible, meaningful to the event. Remember that reporters attending the press conference want little more than to hear the announcement, receive the details they need to develop a story, and then write their articles or reports. They generally will not want to have to endure lengthy commutes, nor will they desire a sightseeing tour of the event facility. If the host venue is conveniently

Time	Item	Duration (mins.:secs.)
10:00 A.M.	Host Welcome and Introduction of VIPs and Tournament Representative	2:00
10:02 A.M.	Announcement of Event by Tournament Representative	3:00
10:05 A.M.	Mayoral Address (introduced by Host)	3:00
10:08 A.M.	Event Description and Details (with video and PowerPoint) by Tournament Representative (introduced by Host)	4:00
10:12 A.M.	Questions and Answers (by Tournament Representative and Mayor)	5:00
10:17 A.M.	Host Wrap-up and Break for One-on-One Interviews	1:00

Figure 8-5
Running Order for a Sports Event Announcement Press Conference

located, by all means schedule the press conference there. If it is difficult to reach, efforts to generate media attendance may be more successful by staging the press conference at a more centralized location such as a downtown convention center, a hotel, or an appropriate local landmark. If the conference is to be held in a facility other than the event venue, try to select a room that will not dwarf the audience. Oversized rooms can give the impression of sparse attendance. If space permits, invite a reasonable number of event staff members and local stakeholders to attend. Their presence will improve the appearance of the conference and may even provide additional interview subjects for the media. Press conferences are usually "limited access" events, so inviting a small number of senior-level sponsor executives, business partners, and community leaders can also provide an exciting bonus that demonstrates gratitude for their involvement. However, try not to exceed the number of media members with the number of guests. Request that nonmedia guests and staff understand that questions to the participants and interview opportunities are restricted to members of the media only.

Some press conferences are held during a morning breakfast or luncheon to enable the organizer to interact with members of the media over a longer period of time. Reporters have to eat too, so this is the one instance when a conference of greater duration is acceptable. Once the meal is consumed, however, the clock begins ticking again. Again, make sure the actual presentation is brief and to the point. Try to schedule the announcement on a day, and at a time, that does not compete for media attention with other sports or special events being held in the community. Check your local newspapers' sports and event calendar sections to reduce the chances of staging the conference concurrently with another activity that can steal attention and reporters away from your message. Avoid scheduling press conferences on a Friday, because Saturday newspaper readership is generally weaker than it is on weekdays. Late weekday mornings or early afternoons are usually best for meeting late afternoon and evening television news deadlines.

Make sure that all media members who attend the press conference sign in as they arrive. Prepare and distribute a press kit that includes the press release, background information, photos, illustrations of the event site, and other appropriate materials that will help reporters prepare their story. Be sure to remember to messenger, E-mail, or fax these items to media outlets that were unable to attend, immediately after the press conference ends. Providing media members with a small take-away token such as an event cap, pin, T-shirt, or tote bag is not inappropriate as long as its actual value is minimal.

Select an articulate host from the community, such as a sports radio personality or disk jockey from a station that appeals to the same target market as the event. The host should introduce a senior organizer executive to deliver most of the information contained in the announcing press release. This segment of the conference should be as brief as possible to enable a guest speaker to be included, such as a city official, the leader of a community host committee, or an athlete. After the guest speaker's brief remarks, the event executive can continue, providing additional event details. The description of the event can be supported by Microsoft PowerPoint graphics and video. If graphics are used to support the presentation, the projector should provide a bright enough picture to be seen clearly without having to turn the lights off in the room. Provide paper copies of the supporting graphics to the media, as well as copies of the video upon request.

When more than one speaker is scheduled, be sure to review each participant's speaking points, the broad topics they will explore, and the statistics they will use in their addresses. It is best to provide each speaker with a brief written explanation of his or her role and the subject to be discussed. Include factual information pertinent to each role to ensure that multiple speakers will not address the same subjects or, worse, provide the media with contradictory information (e.g., expected attendance, economic impact figures, hotel room occupancies, etc.).

The guidelines provided here are most applicable to the scheduling of pre-event press conferences. During the event itself, press conferences are frequently staged to service attending media with pertinent information, official results, and interviews. Technical requirements and a floor plan for staging press conferences are provided later in this chapter.

The Campaign for Attention

Experienced sports event organizers recognize that the announcing press conference or release is only the opening salvo in a campaign to maximize media attention. Publicity, by itself, is not a marketing panacea. It is an essential, but not the sole component of an event's marketing plan and is reinforced by advertising, promotion, and event marketing campaigns. Audiences presume that news organizations are candid, objective communicators of important news, and therefore the information they present is often perceived as more credible than the hype of advertising. Organizers need the media to generate the stories that will impart a sense of believable importance and relevance to their events. Between the first announcement and the day of the event, there may be myriad opportunities to present the media with additional story ideas from a number of different "angles," or perspectives, as shown in Figure 8-2. Create a schedule of opportunities to "pitch" to reporters who had expressed specific interests after the announcing press release or conference. For maximum effect, try to time these efforts to lead up to or coincide with important pre-event milestone dates, such as the first day of ticket sales, the debut of paid advertising campaigns and promotions, or the onset of player or team registration. Other announcements might be timed to generate publicity after the pace of ticket or sponsor sales has ebbed and a little extra boost of public awareness is required.

HUMAN INTEREST STORIES

One of the key focal points for pre-event publicity should be the development of stories about the participating athletes. Putting a human face on a sports competition can make an event more interesting to the potential audience and therefore appealing to reporters like Allan Kreda of Bloomberg News. "To me, the human interest angle always makes a sports event compelling," he observes. "Every event has the ability to produce the unexpected. I go into every sports event realizing that it can provide a drama or situation I've never before encountered." The human perspective on how an athlete prepares for and participates in an event provides the drama Kreda often uses in his reports. "The subtle human stories behind any event are of most interest to me," he adds.

Kreda understands the value of building relationships between his readers, the fans, and the athletes competing in the sports events he covers. The public wants to know who the athletes are, how they came to compete at the event, and why their performance is worthy of the spectators' interest. Roone Arledge, president of ABC Sports from 1968 to 1986, recognized the awesome power of connecting fans to athletes through the use of personal storytelling and revolutionized the way sports events were presented on television. Widely credited as the progenitor of many of the now familiar features of today's sports television landscape, Arledge was responsible for the creation of such landmark programming as *ABC Wide World of Sports* and *Monday Night Football,* and techniques including slow motion replay. While supervising production for ten Olympic Games, he pioneered the practice of interspersing in-depth personal features on world-class athletes within the coverage of their competitive performance. Today, networks embrace this programming approach as a way of riveting viewers to competitions, establishing powerful emotional bonds that involve the audience beyond simple appreciation of athletic excellence.

Sports event organizers should harness this power by familiarizing the media with their events' participants and identifying the human interest stories that may abound. They must identify these opportunities through press releases, advisories, and personal phone calls to editors and reporters, either directly or through the efforts of their public relations agency. Athletes need not be Olympians to have interesting or emotional stories to tell, tales of triumphs over tragedy and courage in the face of personal adversity.

Is there a registration or try-out process for participating teams or athletes? If so, prepare a release or advisory inviting the media to attend, and circulate a press release announcing the final roster of competitors. Are there interesting stories to be told about a local participant who has overcome personal challenges to excel on the playing field?

"Event organizers who have local connections or star performers who have local connections are interesting," observes the *Los Angeles Times*'s Helene Elliott. Are there visiting athletes who have interesting stories or perspectives on the local community to share? Traveling participants also seem to become more interesting the farther they have to journey to the event. Will they spend any time sightseeing or learning about the local culture? Is there a contestant who is poised to break a performance record or personal best time? Perhaps there are teams seeking to end a particularly long championship drought or athletes focused on extending a winning streak. The history of a sports event is frequently best communicated in the words of former athletes. Don't overlook developing stories from the perspectives of event alumni or former greats of the sport.

Although sports event organizers and their agencies can encourage the development of human interest stories by circulating press releases, personal interviews are far more effective. Include an offer to arrange personal or telephone interviews with an individual featured in the release. Reporters often want interviews to be held privately in an attempt to draw out answers or information that other media members may overlook. If you expect an unusually large number of media personnel to desire interviews with the subject, however, a small informal breakfast, luncheon, or reception may be scheduled with the interview subject and interested reporters. Be prepared to stage brief one-on-one interviews immediately after the larger gathering. Television news and sports reporters will want to capture the athlete on videotape to support their stories. Likewise, radio reporters will want to record sound bites to make their reports more interesting to listeners.

Another convenient option for the media is to schedule a dial-in conference call. Your local telephone company can provide a special phone number through which a large number of reporters can listen in, as well as ask questions. Alternatively, a media-only Internet "chat session" can be staged on your web site, or on one belonging to a sponsor, in which reporters type in questions and the subject responds in text. Access to the session can be restricted to the media with password controls and transcripts posted for the public to add publicity value. Media conference calls and Internet chats can be most useful and cost-effective when the interview subject is traveling or lives far from the host city.

BUSINESS STORIES

The benefits and value that an event can provide to the business community should be promoted to both sports and business media early in the campaign. The articles they generate can be particularly useful for attracting local sponsors and promotional partners. "Economic impact stories are always good," notes Helene Elliott. Even if impact figures were released during the announcing press conference, additional statistics can make for interesting reading. Typical minutiae and fun facts may include the number of hotel room-nights expected to be sold as a result of the event, the number of staff members and volunteers who will work on the program, projected attendance, and even the number of media personnel expected to cover the event. Include historical information about the success of the event in previous years and past host cities.

Sponsor announcements are best directed to business writers and trade publications and must be relevant to local commerce or the partner's industry. Is the sponsor celebrating a major anniversary of its association with an event? If so, talk about what has made the relationship so valuable to both parties. Perhaps a major sponsor decided to become involved with a sports event because of the cross-promotional potential with other sponsors. Is there is a new or intriguing special promotion that the organizer or sponsor will execute in fulfillment of their partnership?

Is there something interesting or unique about the sport or event organization? Stories can be pitched that discuss the vigor and longevity of the organization, the growth of the sport or the event's popularity, shifts in fan demographics, the advances in equipment, training, and technology associated with the sport, even the success of the organization's leadership.

COUNTDOWN TO EVENT DAY

As event day approaches, an organizer's need for media attention typically grows exponentially. Publicity over the final few days can help to significantly boost attendance, increase last-minute ticket sales, and, for broadcast events, drive viewer ratings higher. To maximize excitement, pictures best tell the story. Offer the media opportunities to cover preparations as the event moves into its host facility. If the installation of the playing surface or decoration of the event facility can provide good photographs or video footage, be sure to invite the media to capture the occasion. Schedule a media preview or "hard hat tour" to take interested reporters, photographers, and cameramen through the event site (providing there is something to see), or invite them to dry runs, technical rehearsals, or tests of important operational systems. If entertainment is a prominent element of the event (e.g., opening ceremonies, halftimes, closing ceremonies, festivals), invite the media to rehearsals and schedule interviews with the cast or featured performers. For participatory activities, such as sports festivals, allow the media to try these attractions for themselves the day before they are presented to the public. If a sufficient number of media personnel are expected to cover the event, invite reporters to participate in a media competition right on the playing surface. Games or skills competitions can be staged between the media and athlete alumni, with print media against television and radio, or one media outlet against another. Noncompetitive sports events like 10K runs and other amateur events can even encourage the participation of media contestants. An outlet will not only cover the event as it unfolds from a unique insider's perspective, but it may even generate advance publicity about how its representative in the event is training or otherwise preparing for participation.

The arrival of teams or athletes that were previously featured by the press in human interest stories may generate additional photo opportunities. Be sure to include some media availability time in the event schedule to provide access to the most intriguing participating athletes. Opportunities may be scheduled as press conferences with a representative handful of participants just before or after a practice, at a welcome reception, during public appearances, or even during sightseeing tours of local points of interest. Alternatively, media availability time can be scheduled in which the participants are stationed throughout a hotel meeting room or the host venue concourse beneath signs displaying their names, thus guiding reporters to the people they want to interview most. Try to arrange these opportunities at times that will still permit pre-event reporting for last-minute promotion, even if it will appear in the media just an hour or two prior to the competition.

Servicing the Media at the Event Site

As noted in Figure 8-1, media members who cover a sports event expect appropriate, comfortable working conditions and the ability to view the competition from locations conducive to writing or note taking. Of equal importance are access to official statistics and score sheets, athlete and event background information, and the ability to avail themselves of phone lines, data lines, and fax machines to file stories in a timely manner. Members of the media also anticipate being granted behind-the-scenes access to locker rooms, press conference facilities, and other areas where athletes and officials may be interviewed and observed.

MEDIA GUIDES

A printed media guide can provide all reporters with a consistent, uniform presentation of an event's history, pertinent facts, participant information, and statistics. Start with the most basic of information—do not assume that the reporters assigned to cover your sports event or pre-event press conferences are completely familiar with the sport, its organization, rules, participants, or the format of the program.

The lineup, or the order of competition, should be provided to all media members as they arrive or, at the latest, before the event begins. Include a detailed event schedule, packages of statistics, past event results, milestones or records, biographical information on the athletes, and historical background on teams. Competition rules, copies of all press releases distributed since the first announcement, and information on upcoming events should also be provided. Many sports event organizers compile all of this information in the form of a media guide, which may be as simple as a looseleaf binder with section dividers or as professional as a spiral-bound, saddle-stitched, or perfect-bound publication. Media guides are usually published as late as possible to allow for last-minute revisions, which is why looseleaf binders can be particularly useful for events where changes are frequent and inevitable. The appearance and organization of the media guide must maintain a level of professionalism. Design and custom print in color a cover and dividers, number all pages, and include a table of contents for easy access to the information within.

ACCREDITATION

For the purposes of maintaining a safe, exclusive, and professional work environment for the media and to maintain a reasonable level of security for the athletes and others working in nonpublic areas, an accreditation system is strongly recommended. Establishing an accreditation system involves the design and distribution to authorized personnel passes that visually identify the bearers and their affiliation and permit them access to restricted areas. The media accreditation plan must be integrated into an overall system that event security and operations personnel will use to control access to all nonpublic areas of the site for staff, volunteers, vendors, broadcasters, and other authorized stakeholders.

It is useful for staff to be able to visually identify members of the media in order to direct them to the facilities set aside for their convenience, as well as for the distribution of press information. The mechanics of setting up a comprehensive event credential system are more fully explored in Play 14, "Managing for the Unexpected." The process of qualifying members of the media who wish to cover an event and using an accreditation system to manage their activities on the event site, however, is more appropriately discussed here.

Distribute an advisory to the target media listed in your press release database that invites reporters to apply for credentials at least one month prior to the event. Larger and more newsworthy events that anticipate a significant media response should circulate this advisory with even more lead time. Include event schedule information and an application requesting the name of the media member, his or her affiliation, and full contact information. If the event is of the magnitude that the media will be traveling to the host city, you may also include information regarding hotel accommodations.

In democratic societies, it is the right of the media to cover and report on any event that is open and available to the public. It is similarly the right of any event organizer to limit access to the event site to anyone who does not possess a ticket or credential. Organizers should assess the extent to which they can physically accommodate the media before accepting applications for accreditation. Although it is usually advantageous to maximize an event's opportunities for coverage, the number and nature of media members who should be provided with workspace and behind-the-scenes access is completely up to the event organizer and may be limited by available support space and budget resources. It is perfectly acceptable to limit the number of credentials to those who can be accommodated safely and effectively. However, it should be kept in mind that competing media outlets within a particular territory (e.g., the daily newspapers or radio stations in a given market) will demand access that is fair and equal to that provided to their competitors. As a general rule, it is recommended that all bona fide members of the media be accommodated if at all possible. Where the organizer has perhaps a little more leeway in determining whether to provide access is in regard to a media outlet with a small niche readership or a questionable relationship to the event audience. If an organizer has never heard of a certain media outlet that is requesting access, it is strongly suggested that the organizer check into its history (for example, some judgment should be exercised regarding whether some Internet media are truly bona fide media outlets or simply personal web sites). Remember that once you provide someone with a credential for access to restricted areas, you also undertake certain liabilities in exposing participants and staff to unfamiliar or potentially questionable personnel. Members of the media who cannot be accommodated in limited-access work and press conference facilities or who are unfamiliar to the organizer may be alternatively provided with complimentary tickets that do not permit behind-the-scenes access. Although it is highly unusual for reporters to pay for tickets, media members who are not accommodated as previously described are still free to attend the event as ticket holders or members of the public and may subsequently write stories without having to apply for and receive credentials.

Be sure to include a deadline for returning completed media credential applications. It is up to the organizer as to how strictly he or she will adhere to the deadline, balancing the desire for coverage with the necessity to control access to nonpublic areas. As a general rule, the organizer is not obligated to admit members of the media to controlled areas if they appear on event day without having applied for credentials. It is therefore essential that all media outlets that may cover the event have an opportunity to receive and review the advisory and application with sufficient time to respond.

The organizer should carefully review applications and respond to approved applicants with information on where and when credentials may be called for (nonapproved applicants, if any, should also be communicated with). It is recommended that the physical distribution of credentials be delayed until they are actually needed for admission to the event site, so as to reduce the chances of their being counterfeited or duplicated. Credentials should be worn and visible at all times, particularly in restricted areas. A credential may be in the form of a pressure-sensitive printed sticker (acceptable for limited budget, one-day events) or a simple laminated "All Access" card with either a safety pin back or a lanyard to enable it to be worn about the neck (essential for events that are longer than a single day). An example of an event credential is pictured in Figure 8-6.

Figure 8-6
Sports Event Media Credential

As previously mentioned, when a sports event organizer provides a person who is not under the organizer's direct supervision with access to restricted areas, he or she assumes a greater level of liability. Therefore, it is recommended that deterrents to the possible counterfeiting of credentials be considered. For low-budget events, the use of unusual typefaces and the inclusion of multicolor, event-specific artwork can be inexpensive measures, although the widespread availability of desktop publishing and inexpensive scanners and color printers means that a counterfeiter has only to spend a little time to craft a reasonably close facsimile. The application of small holographic stickers, or holographic printing on the credential, is a much better measure for organizers of events with greater security concerns. Printing the credential on special paper with unique weaving is another common deterrent to counterfeiting.

The inclusion of a small head-shot photo of the approved media member on the credential is strongly suggested for major, high-exposure events. Most media outlets are prepared to respond to this requirement and have the ability to E-mail .jpeg or other digital photo files for application to the credential. If such ability is unavailable, the outlet can bring a passport photo to the credential distribution area or small digital photos can be taken by the event's staff and applied to the credential on-site. The best and most secure method of using photo identification is to digitally print the image directly onto the credential. For organizers with more modest budgets, the photo can be affixed to the credential and the entire card laminated to discourage counterfeiters from lifting the photo off and replacing it with another. Be sure to confirm the identity of the individual receiving the credential by requesting a government-issued photo ID or press card before releasing it.

If the event security plan is more complex than simply allowing credential wearers unfettered access to all areas, a color and/or letter code may be included on the face of the credential. This code will provide security personnel with information on the specific areas of access to which the wearer is entitled. It is not generally necessary; in fact, it is preferable not to explain the meanings of the codes to nonsecurity personnel.

The reverse side of the event credential often includes legal disclaimers that transfer the risks of injury during attendance at the event and, as a result of being granted access to restricted areas, to the wearer. The right of the organizer to remove the credential from the wearer for inappropriate behavior should also be included in the notice. It is essential that a qualified attorney develop this protective language.

In addition to providing an exclusive, professional work environment for the media and an essential level of security for the event, the accreditation process will also prepare organizers with an advance understanding of how many members of the media will want to cover the event. Armed with this information, the organizer can install sufficient media center facilities and seating for the number of reporters expected.

Media Center Facilities

As previously mentioned, representatives of the media expect comfortable and appropriate working conditions during the event. Most arenas, stadiums, and other sports facilities have ready-made press facilities designed expressly for this purpose. Others offer a selection of multipurpose rooms or empty spaces that can be allocated and outfitted to fulfill various functions, based on a specific organizer's needs. As you assign spaces to meet your sports event's many requirements, try to keep all the facilities set aside for the media in as close proximity to each other as possible. "The media are creative people and work to daily deadlines," observes Toronto-based media consultant David Job of Media Concepts. "As such, they would prefer to have the logistics flow effortlessly so they may concentrate on their assignments." Be sure to post printed directional signs along the route between the entrance the media will use and all areas to which they require access, including the media workroom, the event office, press conference facilities, the media lounge or hospitality area, the press box or event seating locations, and (if the media will have access) athlete locker rooms.

MEDIA WORKROOM

Media seating at the event should be provided with a clear, unobstructed view of the playing surface whenever possible. Reporters for newspapers, magazines, Internet web sites, and others who must "file" or submit their stories to their editors under tight deadlines should be provided with "tabletop" seating, that is, seats that are located at tables or countertop working surfaces. Draped half-width folding tables can be installed in areas where reporters will be working to provide them with a flat surface for their laptops or writing tablets. Multiple-outlet power bars should be run atop or beneath the tabletops to provide writers with access to power for their laptops and other equipment. Task lighting in the form of small desk lamps should be added if the lighting conditions in the area are not conducive to reading statistics and score sheets. Event-day media also require access to phone lines, either to file a verbal report (in the case of radio) or to upload written stories and digital photography to their editors. One phone line for every three to five media members is suggested, although media outlets can be invited to arrange for dedicated phone lines to be installed at their expense during the accreditation process. To control costs and the possibility of abuse, it is recommended that lines offered by the event organizer restrict access to local and toll-free numbers only. Most media members are accustomed to using credit cards for long distance calls. If a code is required to access an outside line (e.g., "9"), post this information on or near the phone. If the event is televised or if a video feed of the competition is available, place video monitors within convenient view of the media seating sections, as well as in the media workroom and any spaces set aside as press conference areas. A table stocked with multiple copies of past and current event press releases should be visible and within reach of the workroom to provide reporters with memory-refreshing background information. Provide photocopies of pre-event print coverage, as well as transcripts of recent press conferences, if available. It is also recommended that a bulletin board or easel be located near the entrance to the workroom to post the event schedule and transportation information, if such service is provided. A convenient checklist of media workroom requirements may be found in Figure 8-7.

When the media contingent is so large (or the facility is so small) that it is not possible to accommodate all of the media with working space in direct view of the event's proceedings, a secondary media workroom may be constructed behind the scenes. All of the requirements set forth for media seating sections—tables, power, phones, data lines, and so forth—are equally important in these areas, but for such an event television monitors, providing coverage of the event, are absolutely essential.

Members of media expect and demand instant access to information as the event progresses. If they are seated in a single area during the event, a separate localized public address system can be installed to communicate pertinent information exclusively to them. Use the system to announce official results, advise the media on changes in schedule, explain the decisions of judges and referees, update statistics and information on athlete injuries, and communicate post-event press opportunities. Having a media-only public address system is particularly important if an auxiliary media workroom is installed for an overflow of journalists, ensuring that all receive the same information at the same time. In areas where the media tabletops are in public seating

---

☐ Seating with tabletops (preferably with unobstructed view of event)
☐ Multiple power outlets and surge protectors
☐ Telephones
☐ High-speed datalines
☐ Workspace (task) lighting
☐ Television monitors
☐ Small local public address system
☐ Fax machine
☐ Refreshments (preferably in a separate hospitality area)
☐ Rosters and line-ups
☐ Press releases
☐ Media guides

Figure 8-7
Checklist of Media Workroom Requirements

areas, the speakers should be sized, placed, and balanced so that only the journalists can hear the announcements that are directed to them. Most important, be sure to test all systems—electrical, phone, data, and broadcast feeds—several times before the media members arrive to be certain that all are functioning properly.

MEDIA LOUNGE OR HOSPITALITY AREA

Keeping members of the media comfortable is of the utmost importance. Reporters often arrive at the event facility early to grab interviews with arriving athletes and depart late, after the event has concluded, post-event press conferences have been held, and their stories have been written and filed. Provide water, coffee, and soft drinks throughout the day, snacks, and if the budget allows, meals appropriate to the time of day. Most facilities require organizers to purchase food, even in backstage areas, only from their in-house caterers or concessionaires, typically an expensive proposition. If the event is able to bring its own food into the facility, an organizer's options become wider. "For a limited budget, grocery stores make sandwich trays," says consultant David Job. "Whole fruit and beverages can also be purchased and picked up."

If space permits, set up the refreshments in an area separate from the workroom. "Too often, work rooms become social gathering places and noise levels reach points that are distracting to writers who are working on deadline after others may have finished," observes Helene Elliott. "Work rooms are work rooms, period. Set up a separate area, if available, where you have coffee or water and make sure there's a distinction between these areas," she suggests.

To determine what refreshments should be provided, consider what time most members of the media will report to the event site and when most will depart. Estimate arrival at least 30 minutes before pregame player availabilities and departure at least one hour after post-event press conferences to permit them time to file their stories and photographs. Do not assume members of the media will be able to visit concession stands—their job is to cover the competitive event, difficult to do if standing in line for a hot dog. Therefore, provide sandwiches and salads over lunch hours, a hot entrée if they are working through normal dinner hours. Soft drinks (the sponsor's brand, of course), coffee, and light snacks such as pretzels, popcorn, chips, and cookies should always be available.

MEDIA RELATIONS OFFICE

Be sure that members of the media are looked after by knowledgeable staff members or representatives of the event organizer's public relations agency. A media relations office should be located within close proximity of the media workroom to enable reporters access to staff for additional information or special requests. It is recommended that the media relations office be divided into two spaces, one that is separated by closed doors in order to conduct internal confidential conversations with the event director or other senior managers in the event of a crisis or controversy. It is also helpful to have this quieter separate workspace available to the staff for writing and proofreading press releases without distraction or interruption.

The office should be staffed at all times when members of the media are at the event site. Additional copies of press releases and other printed materials provided in the workroom should always be available at the office. The media relations office number should be posted in the media workroom, as well as at the security office and the media entrance. No reporters, camera crews, or any other members of the media should be admitted to the event site without the knowledge of the staff in this media control center. Camera crews should always be escorted through the event site by a member of the media relations staff.

The media relations office is an essential workspace from which to manage media center operations. Desks or draped and skirted tables should be installed to provide the staff with a functional workspace. Install desktop computers and printers if staff will not be using their own laptops and portable printers. Make sure there are at least two telephone sets (more for large-scale events), with multiple lines if possible. Also install at least one high-speed Internet line to enable office staff to access E-mail services, as well as on-line news and sports sites for monitoring breaking developments in local and world news, other sports events, weather forecasts, and on-line coverage of the event itself.

It is also essential to have convenient and exclusive access to at least one mid- or high-speed copier with a collator, a stapler, and a more than adequate supply of copy paper. Install at least one facsimile machine, although large-scale events often maintain two fax machines, one for outgoing and one for incoming transmissions. Install a television monitor that can receive a feed of the event so staff can remain informed of the progress of the contest.

Don't forget one of the most mundane of details—a carton or two of essential office supplies, including folders, paper clips, staplers and staples, writing pads, message pads or Post-its, and any other consumable item that makes an office go (see Figure 8-8 for a complete checklist of media office requirements).

PRESS CONFERENCE AND INTERVIEW FACILITIES

The press conference area provides a focal point for pre- and post-event interviews, for the dissemination of any information that is best delivered by a spokesperson throughout the program, and for any interactive exchange between the media and senior organization management. The press conference facility may occupy its own separate room near the media workroom, or if

- ☐ Easy access from media workroom
- ☐ Desks or skirted 6 ft folding tables
- ☐ Chairs
- ☐ Multiple power outlets and surge protectors
- ☐ Desktop or laptop computers
- ☐ Network or portable printer
- ☐ Phones (minimum of two, preferably with multiple lines)
- ☐ Datalines (high-speed ISP or DSL, if available)
- ☐ Workspace lighting
- ☐ Television monitor
- ☐ Mid- to high-speed copier with collator and stapler
- ☐ Copy paper
- ☐ Fax machine
- ☐ Office supplies
- ☐ Copies of all printed materials

Figure 8-8
Checklist of Media Relations
Office Requirements

such space is unavailable, a draped-off column-free backstage area. Regardless of its location, it should be situated in an area that is inaccessible to the public and as noise- and distraction-free as possible.

A checklist of requirements for a sports event press conference facility may be found in Figure 8-9, and a typical layout in Figure 8-10. Set up enough chairs in view of the stage to accommodate the media expected to cover the event. It is acceptable, but not necessary, to provide tabletop surfaces for laptops or writing tablets in the press conference area. The focus of attention in the room is a stage or dais constructed of risers (raised platforms), commonly available through the event venue, at many hotels and convention centers, or through audiovisual rental agencies. Plan to design a stage that is only as large as required to accommodate the number of participants envisioned. Most stage riser platforms are available in sections of 4-ft by 8-ft, and at heights typically ranging from 18 in. to 36 in. If the interview subjects will most often be standing at a podium, risers that are 18 in. or 24 in. high are probably sufficient, raising the participants high enough to be easily seen by all media members in attendance without seeming to overpower the room. If, instead, the subject(s) will be seated at draped tables, the risers should be set at a minimum of 24 in. in height. It is not uncommon to set the press conference stage with both a podium and draped tables to afford the organizer the flexibility to quickly

☐ Quiet, column-free, limited access space
☐ Media seating
☐ Stage riser(s)
☐ Camera/photographer riser
☐ Skirted tables for stage
☐ Podium (with optional logo)
☐ Pipe & drape backdrop (with optional customized drape)
☐ Public Address System
☐ Table microphones with flashes for interviewees
☐ Wireless microphones for moderator and interviewer questions
☐ Lighting for stage and podium
☐ Video camera & monitors
☐ "Mult" box (allows the media to plug cameras and recording devices directly into the press conference sound system)
☐ *Rear projection screen and projector (optional)*

Figure 8-9
Press Conference Requirements Checklist

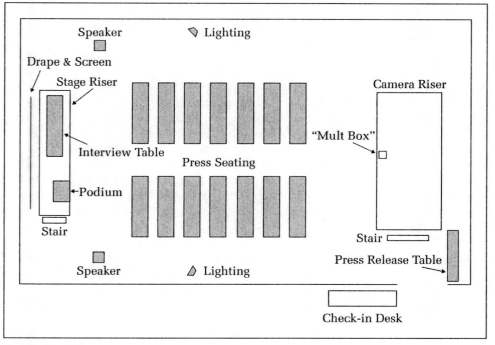

Figure 8-10
Sports Event Press Conference Room Layout

schedule multiple participant interview opportunities and statements without an additional last-minute setup. The podium should be in good, clean condition and include a top shelf for speaker notes. An event logo should be centered, facing the audience, on the top portion of the podium, professionally printed on foam core or Gatorboard to maximize exposure on any television footage taped at the press conference. "Mic flashes," small plastic tiles imprinted with the event's or event organizer's logo can also be attached to the front of microphones on the podium and interview tables to increase visibility.

The microphones should be connected to a high-quality public address system with sufficient speaker cabinets to provide clear, uniformly distributed sound throughout the media seating section. It is strongly recommended that the press conference audio system be installed and operated by a qualified audiovisual equipment supplier who will remain on-site at all times the area may be in use. Be sure that all systems are periodically tested before the media arrive, as well as immediately before any press conference begins.

Drape the wall behind the stage with a dark, nonshiny background. "Pipe-and-drape" units, fabric panels suspended on a frame of sturdy metal pipes, are commonly available from many event facilities and rental companies in royal blue, navy blue, and black. Blue drapes look best in photographs and video. An event logo banner can be suspended from the pipe, centered in front of the drape on a thin monofilament line. One or two additional banners can also be displayed, featuring the logo of the event organization, a title or presenting sponsor, or another essential stakeholder, as desired. Any more than three banners will give a cluttered appearance. Because the reason for affixing a banner to the drape is to increase its visibility in photographs and video footage, it is best for it to be positioned behind and just above the spot where the most important participants will be addressing the media. It should also be of a modest size so that most of the logo will be included in medium-range shots and close-ups. Alternatively, entire panels of drape can be custom printed with "step and repeat" logos to increase the likelihood that at least one logo will make it into each recorded image of the press conference. Step and repeat drapes are like wallpaper—they feature small versions of one or two logos at frequent intervals across the entire surface. Although the logos may not be particularly readable from a distance, they can be very effective in photographs and video.

A "camera riser" may be positioned behind the media seating area, centered on the stage and sufficiently large to accommodate the number of video and still photographers expected. It should be set at an equal height to the stage risers to enable cameramen to shoot over the heads of the seated reporters. Although most members of the media who cover sports events will be equipped with lenses that will capture the close-ups they need from the back of the room, it is also acceptable to place the media riser closer to the stage, as long as those using it will not obstruct the view of those seated.

An audio "mult box" should be located on the camera riser. A mult box is a small, briefcase-sized unit that distributes the sound directly from the press conference's public address system to any plugged-in television camera, radio line, or audio recorder. This small unit is essential to providing the media with top-quality, interference-free sound from the press conference microphones.

Press conference areas should be lit for television coverage. The organizer's audiovisual supplier should be asked to light the stage with a "wash" (an even distribution) of television-friendly light. Lights should never shine directly into the eyes of the participants. Rather, they should be hung from a position 8 ft to 10 ft high, or on lighting "trees" (freestanding poles topped with lighting instruments), and placed at 45-degree angles to the stage's center on either side of the room. Whether hung or placed atop trees, lighting must come from two different positions to eliminate the harsh shadows that can distort or underexpose the resulting photographs and footage.

If a large contingent of media is expected, the organizer may be well advised to install television monitors, at regular intervals in locations distant from the stage, fed by a camera on the photo riser. The same feed can be sent to the video monitors in the media workroom to enable those in the process of writing their stories to cover the press conference as well. If the press conference requires the presentation of event highlights or another videotaped segment, large television monitors are essential. A large projection screen may also be installed on the drape in front of the stage riser if necessary. To avoid having to extinguish the lights during the press conference and to eliminate the chance of the audience inadvertently casting shadows across the image, a rear-projection (RP) screen is the best choice. An RP screen, however, requires a large area behind the stage riser and drape to accommodate installation of the projector at a sufficient distance in order to have the image fit the screen. If space is at a premium, however, installation of large television monitors on carts in strategic locations throughout the room is the recommended option.

Questions from the media can be captured by wireless microphones passed into the audience by event staff members. At least two microphones are recommended, assigned to staff on either side of the room for quick deployment. As these microphones are also tied into the public address system, the questions will be easier to hear within the room and through the recording devices plugged into the mult box.

A Note about Talking to the Media

It is essential to appoint a key contact to serve as a spokesperson for the sports event organizer throughout the event planning process, right up through event day and beyond. All media inquiries and requests for interviews should be funneled through this single individual, who can then schedule other event staff, athletes, and other stakeholders for contact with reporters. Be sure that all event staff and volunteers know the identity and responsibilities of this main contact and that they refer all media inquiries to them. No staff member should provide interviews or insights to reporters before this essential step is taken to ensure that the event organizer speaks with a consistent tone and viewpoint and always provides accurate information. This procedure will also alert the organizer's management of any controversies that may be brewing in relation to the event, its sponsors, or other key stakeholders, as well as any circulating rumors or potential crises on the horizon. The contact will screen and set up interview requests, determining the ideal and most appropriate individual to provide members of the media with the information they require.

Media Coverage and Media Partners

Although journalists' livelihoods are ultimately dependent on the financial health and business performance of the media outlet for which they work, this face of Janus sees not the business and marketing needs of their employer. Conversely, the editorial staff will not expect, nor demand, that any benefits be accorded them as a result of any media partnership between their employer and an event. Journalistic ethics preclude any such expectation. Although great sensitivity must be exercised, it is possible for organizers to demonstrate an appreciation for the partnership. For instance, it is possible to provide a media partner with exclusive story ideas and supporting information for advance publicity purposes (although it is unethical to withhold this information from other outlets if they request it). An organizer can also provide media partners with accreditation for a quantity of writers and photographers in excess of that offered to other outlets, and can provide preferential locations from which photographers can cover the event.

It is essential to ensure that other media outlets covering the event feel no less accommodated in preparing their coverage. Although some feature story ideas and information may be shared with a media partner's editorial staff, it is important to realize that after a story appears in one media outlet, it may no longer be considered news, or newsworthy, by others. Every media outlet wants to be the first to release a story, and it may seem accommodating on the part of the event organizer to provide information to his or her own media partners first (a courtesy to which the media partner will rarely say "no"). It is important, however, that all media in the market feel equally accommodated, appreciated, and integral to the activities in the event's press room. Therefore, if an organizer feels compelled to break a story first to a media partner, that organizer should select the story he or she believes will be of greatest effect to the event's promotional plans, with the least effect on the attitude of the rest of the press. Consequently, writers and reporters will not feel that the organizer is withholding information from them and serving his or her partner preferentially. In most cases, it is best to treat everyone on the editorial side of the media partnership as nearly the same as possible.

Post-Play Analysis

Sports event organizers need the media to help publicize an event from the moment it is introduced, throughout the planning process, and after the day of the event. A campaign of key, newsworthy event announcements and milestones should be scheduled to promote the event at strategic times, such as prior to the first day of participant registration or ticket sales, and with increasing frequency as event day approaches.

The editorial side of the media needs access to reliable and comprehensive information, statistics, and background to enable its members to generate accurate stories. Event organizers must identify opportunities for human interest and business stories to further enhance pre-event coverage.

During the event, members of the media require access to even more information, as well as comfortable working facilities in nonpublic areas that will help them file their stories on a timely basis. Refreshments and meals should be offered at appropriate times of the day during events that require the continuing presence of the media. Visual access to the field of play and free access to the event site are essential in providing a positive environment for the media. Media facilities should also include access to phone lines, high-speed Internet service, and press conference facilities for important announcements and interview opportunities.

Coach's Clipboard

1. Create a publicity campaign for the fictional 10K run in Play 1, including a schedule of key announcement dates. Where should you hold the announcing press conference? What kinds of human interest and business stories will you propose to the media, and how? Where will you place the media office, workroom, hospitality area, and press conference area for this outdoor event?

2. Consider the hypothetical playoffs fan festival in Play 1. How will the publicity campaign for this event differ from the campaign for the 10K run? What kind of pre-event stories might be generated for this event? How should this be managed, given the possibility that the team may not reach the playoffs?

3. Write a press release announcing the aforementioned playoff fan festival. When should this announcement be made, and what should it include?

Activating the Sports Event Marketing Plan

Study the rules so that you won't beat yourself by not knowing something.

—Babe Didrickson Zaharias,
six-time Associated Press
Woman Athlete of the Year between 1931 and 1954

To get their products into the hands of consumers, corporations develop and activate marketing strategies whose tactics include a combination of publicity, advertising, promotion, direct sales, and, yes, event marketing campaigns. To the sports event organizer, the event is his or her product and the consumers may be ticket buyers, attendees, corporate partners, and even participating athletes. Like companies that sell goods to consumers, sports event organizers must be more than just managers and manufacturers. They must also be marketers and promoters, employing various forms of media and mass communications devices to "sell" their events to the public.

The marketing plan fashioned to promote a sports event is composed of the same tools used by consumer companies in varying degrees, as illustrated in Figure 9-1. The proportions of each event's resources that will be dedicated to various components of the marketing plan will vary widely by market and type of event and are totally at the discretion of the organizer.

Play 8 described in detail the infrastructure required to service the editorial side of the media and energize an effective publicity campaign. The core

249

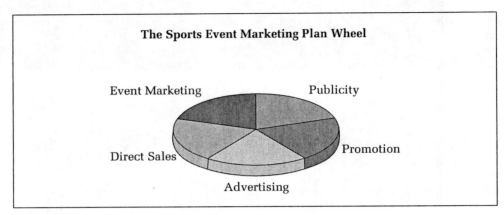

Figure 9-1
The Sports Event Marketing Plan Wheel

attributes of the news media industry, journalistic integrity and a responsibility to report on reality in objective terms, have little impact on the essential truth that a media outlet is also a business, an organization that has to generate revenue in excess of expenses to remain in business. Although some revenues flow from subscriptions and single-copy sales, most of the revenue that maintains print media businesses is the sale of advertising space. Much the same holds true for television and radio. Most of the income for commercial stations flows from advertising time, although some sports television channels also charge cable systems a per-subscriber fee in addition to receiving advertising revenue.

What Media Partners Want from a Sports Event Relationship

Viewed in their most simplified form, advertising rates are predicated on both the number and demographic quality of a media outlet's readers or viewers. Therefore, any opportunity that can increase readership or viewer ratings, or generate measurable incremental advertising, is highly desirable to the publisher or general manager of a media concern. A marketing partnership with the right sports event can present many such powerful possibilities to print and broadcast media.

"Sports marketing offers newspapers the ability to become a part of a local event that typically appeals to families, youth, and ethnic markets," observes Sheri Wish, director of advertising, new business development, multimedia and sports, for the *Los Angeles Times*. "These [audiences] can be somewhat different than the typical core newspaper reader, offering [a media outlet] branding and circulation opportunities to passionate fans and crossing income, race and geographical issues in the marketplace." As previously discussed, event participants, attendees, and viewers can be defined according to demographic and lifestyle characteristics, and by taking advantage of an association with a sports event, a media outlet can reach into new markets composed of loyal, passionate, and motivated fans. To reach them effectively, however, the media outlet must promote its association with the event and provide fans with value not found elsewhere, including expanded coverage and relevant advertising and promotions.

In well-served markets, newspapers, radio stations, local television outlets, and web sites also view themselves as ambassadors of the community, businesses in a unique position to help promote the vigor and vitality of their readership or viewer area. There is no hint of conflict of interest or imperiled journalistic integrity because they will still cover news as news, whether it comments positively or reflects poorly on the condition of the local market. Marketing activity that promotes their community, however, is good for area businesses and increases the relevance of the media outlet as an effective place to spend advertising dollars. The outlet is free to participate as a booster of local business while the editorial side reports on the problems in a community. After all, working behind the scenes to promote economic growth and an improved quality of life directly helps a media outlet's own business. An invigorated market can encourage advertisers to move into the community or seek to do more business there. More business can mean more jobs, more jobs can mean more growth, and more growth means a larger universe of readers. In the long term, attracting more positive attention to the community through marketing efforts is simply good business, and because such efforts are undertaken without the direct involvement of the editorial staff, there is no risk of jeopardizing the outlet's objective journalistic standards.

Publishers and programming executives also know that the excitement that sports events bring to a community can rub off on the companies that take an active role. The media is where potential event attendees and viewers naturally go for information, so establishing a strong, recognizable association with a sports event in the minds of consumers can generate powerful results for both the media outlet and its advertisers. Readership, listeners, and viewers constitute the gold standard on which the media's currency—advertising rates—is based, and sports events can provide outlets with outstanding promotional opportunities that can make a partnership both worthwhile and profitable. Media outlets that become media sponsors can be afforded every benefit befitting their level of participation without endangering the objectivity of their editorial coverage. The greater their financial involvement, whether provided in cash or as value in kind (VIK), the more promotional exclusivities the organizer can offer. For example, a partnership can enable a media outlet to be the sole source for reader, listener, or viewer benefits such as ticket give-aways, sweepstakes, contests, and discounts. At the same time, the division of news media into mutually exclusive editorial and marketing functions helps to protect a sports event from being ignored because of promotional relation-ships with competitor outlets. In a perfect world, media partnerships should not jeopardize the basic editorial event coverage that will be provided by other newspapers or broadcasters.

A formal marketing partnership with a sports event can offer a media out-let many of the same featured benefits that other sponsors enjoy as illustrated in Fig. 9-2, including advertising signage at the event, the ability to distribute copies of a newspaper or special sections created for the event on-site (sam-pling), and the capability of providing special hospitality opportunities for its customers or advertisers. As discussed in Play 6, media partners also seek the ability to offer pass-through rights to advertisers, using event benefits to add exceptional value to their existing marketing efforts to sell more space or time. Running a media outlet is an expensive proposition, so it is reasonable to pre-sume that the decision on whether to pursue a marketing partnership with a sports event will be based on the economics of the deal: Can the company de-rive direct financial benefits from an association with an event or develop new revenue opportunities as a direct or indirect result of the partnership?

- Revenue-Generating Opportunity
  - Advertising
    - Directly from the sports event organizer
    - Incremental advertising from sports event sponsors
- Promotion
  - To increase daily circulation, listeners, or viewers
  - To increase their subscriber base
  - To expand into new markets
  - To promote new writers, talent, or shows
- Advertising
  - Event site signage
  - Inclusion in event advertising
- Category Exclusivity
- Sampling
- Exclusive Hospitality Opportunities for Advertisers
- Pass-Through Rights

Figure 9-2
What the Media Want from a Sports Event as a Marketing and Promotional Partner

What Sports Event Organizers Want from a Media Partner

Experienced promoters know that an event will never reach its full potential through publicity efforts alone. The role of the media-event partnership is to enable both parties to exert more control over the message they want to communicate, control that even the best publicity campaign cannot provide (see Figure 9-3). Typically, the message the organizer wishes to convey is, "Please attend, purchase tickets, or tune in to this exciting event." The message the media partner wishes to communicate will vary with its corporate objectives, but at its core is, "Keep reading or watching this space. We will provide you with news and information on events and other happenings that are of interest to you, as well as with outstanding value (e.g., ticket discounts and other offers) that will more than pay for your copy or time."

Media outlets are no less mercenary about event partnerships than are event organizers, who also evaluate media partnerships from an economic point of view. Simply put, event organizers must also be event promoters to attract an audience and recognize that media outlets are the key suppliers of the advertising space and commercial time they will need to market their properties. Establishing a partnership with one or more media outlets can offer significant event sponsor benefits in exchange for advertising provided on a VIK (value-in-kind), a combination of VIK and cash, or a preferred rate. This type of relationship can help drive marketing costs down for the promoter or expand the budgeted advertising and promotion plan to achieve greater results than cash alone.

In addition to the ability to realize savings on advertising the event, organizers may direct the incremental advertising they must place to satisfy sponsor fulfillment obligations to their media partners. Sponsors also perceive value in placing the advertising that activates their associated promotional

---

- Advertising space or commercial time devoted to promotion of the event
- Intelligence regarding local market sensitivities
- Preferred rates for advertising purchased for sponsor fulfillment purposes
- Promotions designed to encourage ticket sales, increase attendance, and/or encourage broadcast viewership
- Expanded pre-event and event-day coverage to encourage a perception of increased importance
- Provision of added value to attendees (sampling)

Figure 9-3
What Sports Event Organizers Want from Media Partners

campaigns with the newspapers or stations that support the event, adding increased presence and relevance to the media outlet's readers, listeners, or viewers (presuming this audience also complements the sponsor's own target market).

Media outlets represent the most consistent and continuous source of information regarding the past successes and failures of other sports events in the market. Event sponsors come and go, but the media in a given community are often a constant—they are always on hand to cover events and report on them. Archival information, that is, articles written about past events as they unfolded tell only part of the story. Editors and writers can share their unpublished perspectives on what made past events work in their city, or why they did not achieve their full potential. These points of view do not often find their way into the published record, as they do not represent objective reporting but opinions, yet they are no less valid. Although they may represent pure opinion, their perspectives and points of comparison are based on experience and therefore worth serious consideration. Members of the editorial staff are usually not shy about discussing their experiences at events. Usually being limited to reporting only substantiated facts, many actually appreciate being able to share their personal views. Expect and welcome a wide-reaching conversation—how the competition was perceived by the press, the treatment of the media on-site, consumer reaction to the organizer, and the value of the event to the community. Be a sponge! These are the guardians through whom information and perspectives on sports events are filtered and communicated to the public. Few resources will be able to provide better, unbiased feedback.

The members of a media outlet's marketing staff are equally excellent sources of intelligence regarding past events in their community. Their expertise in advertising and promotion can provide added perspective, from a marketing point of view, on where events succeeded and fell short in capturing attention and establishing relevance. This is particularly useful for organizers who are staging an existing event that is new to a given community. Listen and learn from the mistakes that others have made. Potential ticket buyers and event attendees in different markets will behave differently and may respond positively to certain advertising or promotional activities in one town, and negatively to the same marketing endeavors in others.

Experienced marketing professionals in media outlets, like their editorial counterparts, can help organizers decode what has worked best in their community, although their agenda may be totally different. They are in the business of selling advertising space, and an event organizer with marketing needs—and a budget—can be an attractive prospective client. They also recognize that broader promotional campaigns to enhance revenue potential for their newspaper or station can be designed around an event, with its sponsors and business partners generating even more prospective advertising income. This part of the media business is focused on sales, so organizers should not be surprised when a meeting scheduled to explore the marketplace morphs into a sales pitch for advertising space or time.

Selecting Media Partners

Organizers should concentrate their quest for information and insights, and ultimately their event marketing campaigns, on media outlets whose customer demographics and lifestyles match those of the target market of the event. Radio stations are so easily segmented on the basis of their programming formats (e.g., news, talk, sports, urban, rock, soft rock, country, ethnic, easy listening) that the fit between event audience and listeners can be almost intuitive. Magazines and Internet web sites are similarly segmented among obvious populations and interest niches. Daily newspaper readers are less demographically segmented, their readers often defined more along geographic lines in single newspaper markets. However, communities served by multiple newspapers can sometimes exhibit additional demographic segmentation based on the publications' content and style. The *New York Times*, for example, offers as comprehensive a sports section as the *New York Daily News*, but appeals to a higher-income, more highly educated reader. Every outlet under consideration will have a marketing kit available upon request that presents the demographics and lifestyles of its readers, listeners, or viewers, the size of its market, and in many cases, consumer spending behavior. On the basis of this information, and the demographics of an event's target audience, the organizer can select the best media outlets to approach as prospective event partners.

What does a partnership between an event and the media really mean, and what various forms can it take? As discussed earlier, a media outlet can legitimately assume the role of an event sponsor, although its decision to do so will have no bearing on the quality and tone of its coverage of the event. In exchange for enjoying all of the benefits normally accorded to a sponsor, plus others that uniquely meet its specific wants and needs, the media partner may provide the event with advertising space or time, a vehicle for promotional activities, and/or cash.

EXCLUSIVITY VERSUS NONEXCLUSIVITY

The notion of forging a traditional sponsor relationship with a media partner should be familiar by now. It is important to recognize, however, that the provision of advertising by a media outlet without the exchange of cash is no more cost-free to that outlet than complimentary tickets are to the event organizer. Like "free" tickets, "free" advertising is lost revenue potential to the outlet. A media outlet, therefore, expects significant value in exchange for its most attractive and marketable asset—access to potential ticket buyers or attendees through its medium. If sufficient advertising opportunity is provided, the organizer can designate an outlet the "official newspaper" or "official radio station" or provide some other similar partner identification that implies category exclusivity. It is important, however, that sponsorship agreements with media partners do not prohibit the organizer from purchasing advertising from competitor outlets. The pace of ticket sales, sponsor obligations, and other market conditions may require the organizer to place advertising with more than one newspaper, radio station, or television channel; and restricting marketing efforts solely to a single media partner can later prove debilitating. Media partners often seek to protect their investment in an event by insisting on a provision in their sponsorship agreement guaranteeing that advertising placed with competitor media be met with an equal or greater amount of paid advertising with their own outlets.

There are instances when providing category exclusivity to a media outlet makes less sense because the value of advertising, cash, and other assets offered to the organizer is just not sufficient to warrant a sponsorship. In addition, in order to realize an event's sales and marketing objectives, it is sometimes necessary to be able to communicate with equal force to a broader variety of readers or listeners than a single outlet can provide. In such cases, organizers can seek to patch together a number of smaller nonexclusive promotional relationships with a series of media outlets. This approach is most often manifest in the form of a promotional partnership in which limited benefits are provided to a media outlet in return for equally limited VIK advertising, deeply discounted advertising rates, or outlet-specific promotions. The promotional partner may receive a quantity of tickets and event merchandise for use in sweepstakes or advertiser incentives, limited rights to use the event's or organizer's logo, and perhaps some reduced level of on-site presence at the event.

The most effective method of signing a series of complementary nonexclusive media partners is to grant each some exclusivity with respect to one or more event elements. A media partner targeting families or children may be the only outlet permitted to promote a special family ticket package, or authorized to create an event-related educational or skills development program. Such rights may include a sweepstakes geared to the specific interests of radio station's listeners, such as an opportunity to attend a special kid's-only clinic coached by a star player, alumnus, or celebrity. This approach, segmenting media partners by offering them limited exclusivities, provides the event organizer with the option to award others promotional rights to elements more suited to their target markets. For example, a Top 40 radio station may be granted rights to a sweepstakes for a ticket giveaway that includes passes to an exclusive winners-only postgame party. A sports talk station partnered with the same event may conduct a promotion that rewards winners with a behind-the-scenes tour, plus an athlete meet-and-greet session and a visit to the broadcasting booth during the event—all elements of greater intrigue to the hardcore fan.

The strategy of pursuing nonexclusive media partners is becoming increasingly common in the highly segmented radio industry. In a given market, nearly everyone listens to the radio at some time during the day, although perhaps only one or two stations on a given day. Meanwhile, there are dozens of stations from which to choose in a variety of programming formats. Although there is little audience crossover between formats, there is enormous competition between stations that appeal to the same tastes. Therefore, the greatest success will be enjoyed by pursuing radio partnerships that are exclusive only with respect to a station's programming format (e.g., only one sports talk AM station, one Top 40 FM station, one Spanish-language station).

Ownership of stations in the radio industry is also consolidating at an astonishing rate. A sports event organizer may be able to forge a deal with a single company that owns a variety of radio stations within the same community, which can provide a wide range of partners in various formats and great value to both parties. Such a partnership was created between the National Hockey League and Clear Channel Radio, the owner of a large family of stations in South Florida, during the 2003 NHL All-Star Weekend. A group of four Clear Channel stations participated, each popular among a different audience offering distinct demographics. Figure 9-4 lists the partner stations with their key listener characteristics. The combined stations saturated the market with a series of advertising campaigns and promotions specifically appealing to the tastes and interests of the targeted listeners. An All-Star Game ticket giveaway was staged in association with Clear Channel's sports talk station, offering the prize of most intense interest among loyal sports fans. Promotion of the NHL All-Star Block Party, a family-oriented outdoor fan festival, received greater emphasis on the two stations with formats most appealing to men and women likely to have young families, whereas a fan concert starring rock icon Sheryl Crow was more heavily promoted by the station with a contemporary hit rock (CHR) format.

All four of the South Florida–based Clear Channel radio stations listed here were nonexclusive sponsors of the NHL All-Star Block Party in Sunrise, Florida, in February 2003 (see text for discussion):

Station	Format	Demographics
WBGG-FM (BIG 106)	Classic Rock	Men 25–54
WHYI-FM (Y100)	Contemporary Hit Radio (CHR)	Young men and women
WRFX-AM (FOX Sports Radio)	Sports Talk	Hard-core sports fans
WZTA-FM (Zeta 94.9)	Alternative Rock	Men 18–34

Figure 9-4
A Nonexclusive Radio Partnership

Nonexclusive media partnerships are much more difficult to achieve in the print sector than in radio. When there is more than one daily newspaper in a given community, they are almost certain to be highly competitive with one another for readership, advertising dollars, or even attractive promotional relationships with sports events. In cities where a single newspaper monopolizes the available readership, receptivity to participating as a sponsor or promotional partner will vary with the nature of the outlet's marketing objectives, community relations strategies, and its assessment of the event's attractiveness as a platform to achieve its aims. Some such newspapers will desire involvement simply as active supporters of quality-of-life enhancing events in their communities. Others, knowing they face no competition in their marketplace for an event's advertising dollars, will see no value in investing or participating as a media partner.

Television can also offer opportunities for nonexclusive media partnerships, though on a more limited basis than radio. A significant difference between radio and television is that there is a great deal of crossover in television audiences. That is, members of the same target market change channels frequently to view the shows, movies, or events that most interest them at the time they air. Sports events can usually segment their television partnerships into two generally noncompetitive halves—an exclusive "over the air" broadcast partner and an exclusive cable sports channel partner. Of course, if the event is televised, it is most likely that the only promotional partnership possible is with the channel serving as host broadcaster.

Sports Event Promotions

As previously discussed, sponsors often activate their event relationships with consumer promotions that can both support the corporate objectives of the sponsor's brand and enhance the success of the event. Most consumer promotions are supported with advertising in various media placed and purchased by the sponsor. Promotions offered by a media outlet in support of its own partnership with a sports event take the outlet out of the role of middleman and put it in control of event marketing programs that can benefit its objectives directly. Media marketers assign great value to event promotions that can generate a database of readers, listeners, or viewers. For this reason, media promotions are commonly manifest in sweepstakes that require entrants to register by mail, by E-mail, or via an Internet web site. The possibility of winning sports event tickets, unique experiences, merchandise, or memorabilia is a strong incentive for an outlet's audience to take the time and trouble to submit an entry, which can later be compiled into a database for the partner's subsequent direct marketing campaigns. Although the number of entries received is a good indicator of the effectiveness of the promotion, the outlet's ultimate, underlying objective is to use this database to increase subscription sales or ratings.

A promotion that drives visitors to an outlet's web site can be another strong selling point for a media partnership. Most outlets maintain an Internet site that provides visitors with important news and programming information (editorial side) and sells incremental on-line opportunities to their existing advertisers (marketing side). To set the highest possible rates and create the best value for their on-line advertisers, media outlets must generate the greatest possible number of "unique visitors" (an individual visiting the site) and "page views" (how many different web pages an individual downloads during a visit). Event organizers and their media partners will realize the best success when they design their Internet event promotions with these objectives in mind. Don't forget to include links on the media web site to attract visitors to the event's web site, and vice versa. If tickets are required for attendance, be sure to also include a link directly to the site where cyber-visitors can purchase their tickets to the event on-line.

From the sports event organizer's perspective, the most effective promotions, whether placed in the media by other sponsors or as the direct product of a partnership between the event and a media outlet, should be designed as tools to sell tickets or build an audience. Sponsor promotions, although clearly helpful to the organizer's sales and marketing efforts, even if simply as additional exposure opportunities, are primarily designed to promote and sell the sponsor's brand through its association with the event. If the media partner is granted pass-through rights to leverage its event promotion, the marketing message will be subdivided among the various objectives of a potentially great number of partners. Promotions that result from a simple partnership between the media outlet and the event, with no other participating entity, can therefore be the most effective in building an audience.

Organizers, sponsors, and media partners can be as creative as they wish in constructing promotions. It is important, however, for organizers not to lose sight of the key message they wish to communicate or the desired call to action they wish to precipitate. Identify what you want the reader, listener or viewer to do, and the value you are prepared to provide to reward them for doing it. Promotions, whether offered by corporate sponsors or media partners, can be divided into the three general categories, as illustrated in Figure 9-5, according to the key objectives the program seeks to achieve. Tactics employed to fulfill the easy-to-remember "SAT" objectives of sports event promotions are those designed to increase sales (S), build awareness (A), and, for events covered on radio or television, encourage tune-in (T).

SALES PROMOTIONS

The most common promotions designed to generate sales feature cost-saving ticket discount offers. (*Note:* In order to maintain sound financial control over the event's revenue budget, an allotment of promotionally priced tickets should have been included in the calculation of the gross potential—see Play 3). Coupons entitling the bearer to dollars off ticket purchases may appear in

---

Sales
- Discount offers
- Specially priced family packages
- Multiple-day admission packages
- Premium giveaways
- Bounce-back coupons

Key Messages: Value and Urgency

Awareness Building
- Ticket giveaways
- Merchandise giveaways
- Sports trivia contests
- Essay contests
- Press box or press conference access prizes
- Guest columnist or color commentator contest
- Player meet-and-greet opportunities
- School field trips
- Newspapers in Education (NIE) outreach programs

Key Messages: Inform and Excite

Tune-in
- "Watch and win" sweepstakes (i.e., Tune in to see if you're a winner!)
- Insurance prize contests (e.g., million dollar shots)

Key Message: Appointment Viewing

Figure 9-5
Fulfilling the Sales, Awareness, and tune-in (SAT) Objectives of Sports
Event Promotions

print advertisements, on stand-alone retail displays (also known as point-of-purchase promotions—POP), on sponsor product packaging, or downloaded and printed from a partner's web site. To increase the rate of coupon redemption, that is, the number of sales ultimately generated from the promotion, include a web address or telephone number and code that will enable purchasers to conveniently access the discount through on-line and telephone ticket services. The importance of being able to offer consumers a mechanism to take advantage of an offer immediately cannot be underestimated. To enhance the effectiveness of the promotion, try to ensure that as few steps as possible are required and that as little time as possible elapses between receipt of the discount offer and the actual purchasing transaction.

Ticket discount promotions can be designed to achieve any of a number of specialized objectives. Place the fewest possible restrictions on redeeming coupons, except for prohibiting the use of multiple discounts on the same transaction, to increase overall attendance objectives. Alternatively, sales promotions can build attendance for less well-attended periods during multiday events by restricting discounts to weaker mid-week dates or preliminary rounds only, or deepening the cost savings for these harder-to-fill dates. A coupon expiration date set before opening day can be applied to the offer if the objective is to increase the urgency to purchase tickets in advance. Another variation is a "family package" promotion, a multiticket deal that offers a specific number of admissions (typically four or more) at a lower combined price than if purchased separately without a coupon. Package promotions can be particularly powerful tools, as they can also increase the average number of tickets sold per transaction.

For either a cost-savings coupon or a package deal, it is recommended that all discounts be identified as a courtesy made available through a sponsor or media outlet, rather than an offer provided directly by the sports event organizer. Discounting through a sponsor offer is a practice generally accepted even by ticket buyers who have failed to participate in the promotion. Discounting offered directly by the organizer can cause customers who purchased tickets at full price to feel unfairly treated and to seek partial refunds. It is also wise to time the introduction of the discount offer for a date *at least* a few weeks after the sale of event tickets begins. Promotions that result in a discount ticket being purchased by a guest who would have otherwise purchased a full-priced ticket makes little financial sense. Let the first weeks of ticket sales maximize the yield of full-priced tickets sold to the fans who want the best seats, and add the discount promotions to the marketing mix later, when the rate of ticket sales is expected to slow down.

Promotions designed to increase sales can also include the offer of a premium item with every ticket, or with a minimum number of tickets purchased. These offers can create added value for the ticket buyer and, again, may be designed to achieve any number of specific objectives. Advertising in advance that all ticket buyers will receive a valuable premium upon entry to the event (e.g., a bobblehead figure, commemorative patch, pin, ball, etc.) can generate greater overall sales. Events on a more modest budget sometimes offer premiums to a limited number of attendees, such as the first 1000 to arrive. In addition to saving money on premiums, this technique encourages early arrivals to the facility, which has the secondary operational benefit of spreading the flow of incoming guests, as well as increasing pre-event food and beverage sales. To encourage advance ticket sales, the premium item, or a coupon redeemable for the premium at the event site, can be mailed to those who purchase tickets before event day. The cost of the premium can be paid for by a sponsor or promotional partner, directly by the organizer as a marketing or sponsor fulfillment expense, or split between a partner and the organizer. The key to the success of any premium promotion is to ensure that this opportunity is communicated in advance to potential ticket buyers through advertising and other effective marketing platforms so that it has the intended effect of increasing ticket sales.

A variation on this type of promotion that is of particular appeal to sponsors is the opportunity for ticket buyers to receive a "bounce-back" coupon with each purchase. A bounce-back coupon is distributed to attendees at the event site, or via mail with advance ticket purchases, and offers a valuable discount or premium item courtesy of a sponsor if redeemed at a specific location. A consumer electronics store can distribute a coupon at the box office, or upon the attendees' entering the event site, that is redeemable at its retail locations for a deep discount or gift item. Bounce-back offers can also be made during the event, providing discounts or premiums at sponsor-designated locations upon presentation of a used ticket stub. Although such offers may provide exceptional value to an event sponsor and may be worthwhile to create as a cost-free benefit of the relationship, ticket stub bounce-back offers are rarely advertised in advance and therefore do not usually help organizers to sell tickets.

The messages communicated by effective sales promotions are "value" and "urgency." These programs stress value first. By taking advantage of the promotional offer, the ticket buyer or attendee will save money or receive some other valuable incentive such as merchandise, collectible memorabilia, or cost savings on sponsor products or services. To maximize a sales promotion's effectiveness, however, it should also communicate a sense of urgency. The offer should be taken advantage of as soon as possible to ensure that the ticket buyer will be able to fully enjoy it. Expiration dates and a limited number of premium items available "only while supplies last" help to convey such urgency.

AWARENESS-BUILDING PROMOTIONS

Sales promotions work best when building attendance for events that have some history or familiarity among potential ticket buyers and may be less effective for events for which there is a lower level of awareness. The key messages for awareness-building promotions are to inform or familiarize the community with the event and to present salient information in a way that will excite or intrigue, leading people to consider attendance. Although the call to action is "Look over here at this exciting event!" rather than "Get your tickets now!" awareness-enhancing promotions can support attendance-building efforts profoundly, if indirectly. The timing of awareness promotions should be coordinated with the publicity and advertising components of the marketing plan. Publicity efforts can be very effective in generating awareness, and advertising is most efficient in driving attendance. Awareness promotions are, therefore, best timed for introduction once the event's publicity campaign has begun or early in the advertising campaign.

Ticket and merchandise giveaways through a random drawing sweepstakes, a contest of knowledge or skill, and a radio "call in to win" are among the most popular forms of awareness-building programs. To have the intended effect—ultimately promoting the sales of tickets—the mechanism for giving away tickets or other valuable prizes must be associated with communicating the message of ticket availability. To achieve optimal results, the process of registering to win should be surrounded by a campaign that involves the potential entrant in the event and at the same time educates the public regarding what the event is and where and when it will happen. Awareness-building promotions help create what event promoters like to call a "buzz" surrounding an event, that is, a palpable level of excitement building in the marketplace.

Giveaways are highly prized by media sponsors and promotional partners, as they reward their listeners or readers with value and, if the buzz about the event continues to build, can help build their own readership or ratings. Radio stations are particularly effective partners for giveaways, and many are involved with a different giveaway promotion at least weekly. For event promoters, radio campaigns are also highly valued because of the large number of listeners to whom the offer is communicated, plus the number of times the promotion—and the event—is mentioned on the air. Radio hosts can educate their audiences about the upcoming event, and their often enthusiastic delivery can also excite their listeners into entering a contest and ultimately attending the event. Developing a good relationship with the on-air personalities and providing them with the information they need to promote the event is essential to maximizing the effectiveness of a radio promotion and "building the buzz." Consider involving these individuals in the event itself as guest emcees or hosts. Their personal participation in the event is outstanding promotion for both themselves and their station and almost guarantees frequent enthusiastic endorsements on the air.

Sports trivia and essay contests are just two of the many varieties of knowledge- and skill-based competitions that can be used as promotional devices. Trivia contests work equally well as print, radio, and Internet promotions and frequently take the form of entry blank activities for print media or "call in to win" activities for radio. Essay contests, by contrast, are great vehicles for involving students and better-educated fans and are best executed as newspaper or magazine promotions. Entrants can be given a choice of topics or perspectives from which to write an essay of a defined length to be judged by a celebrity panel. (To best manage the judging process, it is recommended that essays be limited in length to approximately 500 words.) As campaigns co-promoted with print or Internet media partners, contests such as these serve to supplement the event's schedule of paid or VIK advertising. As radio or broadcast promotions, they can fulfill the same purpose, but are additionally effective as awareness- and excitement-generating vehicles. The excitement of the contestants who participate live, as well as the enthusiasm of the broadcast hosts, can vividly help to convey the event's relevance to the listening audience.

As stand-alone promotions, or as prizes for winning essay entrants, behind-the-scenes access opportunities are rewards with a high level of perceived value. These limited-access possibilities can include a backstage tour, a visit to the press box, attendance at a post-event press conference, or the ability to serve as a guest columnist, among others. (It is recommended that if the winner is designated a "guest columnist," the qualifying essay or column be posted on the Internet rather than in the newspaper so as to preserve the latter's journalistic integrity.) Meet-and-greet opportunities with athletes before the event, at practices, or during warm-ups can also be particularly attractive prizes.

Effective promotions geared to younger audiences can include school field trips to the event site during nonpublic hours for tours, practices, or a formal educational presentation. These opportunities must be arranged with school districts far in advance to be considered for the academic calendar. Most districts are budgeted for a limited number of trips per year, sometimes only one or two, so the event promoter should contact local educators perhaps as much as a year in advance. Working with a newspaper partner, event organizers can also gain entry into the classroom by developing and circulating academically relevant materials featuring the event as a theme. This, too, is a lengthy, as well as potentially expensive, process and should be created in partnership with the local board of education. Be certain that the schools will accept this material on behalf of their students before spending the time and money to create it. If the program must be sponsored in order to exist, be sure to understand the restrictions the school district or board will place on how sponsors may be recognized, if at all, and what kinds of sponsors might be prohibited. A less expensive and more widely accepted option is to investigate whether a local daily newspaper participates in the Newspapers in Education program. An association with this well-established and highly respected program can further reinforce the legitimacy of the event and its relevance to the local community (see the Sideline Story on page 265).

TUNE-IN PROMOTIONS

For televised sports events and the sponsors who support them by purchasing advertising time on the broadcasts, building viewer ratings can be as important as drawing a live audience. Ratings are based on the number of viewers who tune in to the broadcast live. (Audiences who record the program for later viewing are not factored into television ratings at this time.) Marketing campaigns designed to increase television ratings seek to create "appointment viewing," a desire on the part of the audience to attend the event via television at the time of its original broadcast.

For the most popular of sports programs, events can be relevant and compelling enough by their very nature to generate appointment viewing. The most obvious examples include the astronomically rated NFL Super Bowl and the biennial Summer and Winter Olympic Games. But even these premier mega-events strive to maximize ratings, ever vigilant as to even the most mod-

Sideline Story—Newspapers in Education

In the 1930s, New York City public school teachers, wanting to expand social studies curricula to include daily lessons on current events, approached the *New York Times* to regularly bundle and deliver newspapers for classroom instruction. From these humble roots grew Newspapers in Education (NIE), a program coordinated by the World Association of Newspapers with approximately 700 participating papers in more than 40 different countries. Thousands of schools in the United States offer the NIE program to students from kindergarten to 12th grade through their local newspapers. Publishers have flexibility to design the NIE program content for their own purposes, but in each case, it is designed to expose children to newspapers as a powerful and reliable source of information on current events. This flexibility enables newspapers to feature stories, background information, games, and photographs of events they sponsor or promote in the special NIE supplements they periodically publish. With sports so prominently featured in newspapers every day, providing information on upcoming sports events is directly on-strategy for a print partner's NIE program. Sports event organizers who want to expose their programs to children and their families, have sufficient lead time, and can demonstrate the relevance and appeal of their events to this important audience, should investigate whether their town newspaper offers an NIE program in local schools and, if so, do everything possible to be included.

est slide in viewing popularity. With this strategy, broadcasters can keep their advertising rates high enough to justify the rights fees they pay to the sports event organizer. (For a detailed discussion on the event organizer-broadcasting relationship, see Play 13.) Most events, however, do not have the perceived relevancy of a Super Bowl and need to provide a variety of compelling reasons for the audience to tune in, which is essential to the continued viability of the program as a broadcasting property.

Among the most popular tune-in devices are sponsored "watch and win" promotions that require viewers to respond to some form of prompt during the live broadcast to win prizes. To be effective, the activity must be promoted, advertised, and publicized well in advance of the event. Typically, the more valuable the prize, the more compelling the reason will be to tune in, wait for the cue, and respond. A sponsor may distribute game cards with a serial number, phrase, or other code, along with the instruction to watch for an announcement of the winning variable during the event broadcast. A similar tune-in scheme requires viewers to register in advance through a mailed, E-mailed, or Internet entry form and then tune in to the broadcast for instructions on how the winner can claim his or her prize.

Another promotional device gaining popularity is the "insurance prize" contest. This type of promotion qualifies a sweepstakes winner to compete in a contest of skill for a prize so impressive and valuable that the very fact that an average member of the public—someone just like the viewer—can win is a sufficiently compelling reason for appointment viewing. Although the value of the prize can range from $100,000 to $10 million, the event budget need not set aside such a prohibitive sum to cover the possibility of having to pay an extremely lucky contestant. The organizer can contact an insurance broker to purchase a special policy that will pay the contestant should one win. The premium for the prize can range from 10 to 50 percent of the payout, depending on the insurance company's assessment of the odds of winning. Insurance companies, being in the business of keeping more money in premiums than they pay in claims, will absolutely require input into the contest rules and procedures. Once their requirements are incorporated into the rules, the odds will, of course, dramatically favor the insurance company. But, the possibility of a peer winning a fantastic prize, however unlikely, can create another exciting reason for a person to watch an event.

Effective Sports Event Advertising

Regardless of how talented a sports event's public relations staff may be and no matter how well connected an agency, the ultimate control over what and how much pre-event publicity an event will receive is under the complete control of story editors, who have no other agenda than presenting presumably objective, newsworthy content to their audiences. Although sponsor and media partner promotions provide opportunities to better control the marketing message, the objectives of those campaigns are formed from a composite of event organizer and sponsor partner needs. The event organizer often has a singularly important objective that a promotion, because of its compromised agenda, is less well equipped to achieve. If an organizer, for instance, wants to inform the public that event tickets are about to go on sale, simply circulating a press release means relying on the hope that editors will deem such information newsworthy. (Most will not.) Creating a promotion at this early date diverts attention from the most important fact—tickets are going on sale—and may detract from full-priced ticket sales during the time they are most likely. The only way to be completely certain that the message gets through is to place advertising in targeted media, on either a paid or VIK basis.

By all means, imbue your advertising with creativity and style, but do not sacrifice the effective communication of essential information for originality.

The purpose of effective sports event advertising is to effect a reaction, most often the sale of tickets. Provide all the information and motivation necessary for readers or viewers to want to buy their tickets, and direct them to the most convenient way to make their purchases—immediately. The checklist in Figure 9-6 provides guidelines on the information that is positively essential to include in effective event advertising, as well as additional elements that can be added to enhance the event's position as a "must see" entertainment opportunity. The importance of stating the name of the event and displaying the logo and essential data, such as the date, time, and location, may seem obvious, but it is nonetheless critical to include these items. Be sure to use the day of the week in addition to the date when advertising one-day events to provide absolute clarity to the reader or viewer.

Do not neglect to include an obvious call to action. That is, what do you want to tell the reader, listener, or viewer to do? If the advertisement is designed to inform the public that tickets are now on sale, say so explicitly and make it easy for people to purchase or order them. Include a phone number or web site address so they are able to order tickets immediately or gather the information they need to make a purchasing decision. Regardless of the call to action, provide all of the information required to enable the public to react as desired.

Advertisements for sports festivals and demonstration events in which the competitive elements represent more than one sport, involve sports or athletes

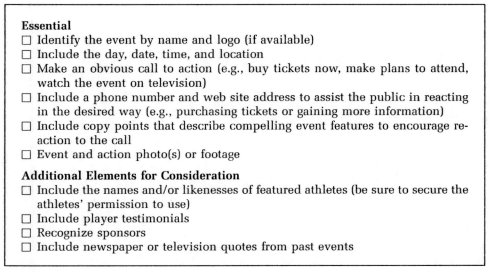

Essential

- ☐ Identify the event by name and logo (if available)
- ☐ Include the day, date, time, and location
- ☐ Make an obvious call to action (e.g., buy tickets now, make plans to attend, watch the event on television)
- ☐ Include a phone number and web site address to assist the public in reacting in the desired way (e.g., purchasing tickets or gaining more information)
- ☐ Include copy points that describe compelling event features to encourage reaction to the call
- ☐ Event and action photo(s) or footage

Additional Elements for Consideration

- ☐ Include the names and/or likenesses of featured athletes (be sure to secure the athletes' permission to use)
- ☐ Include player testimonials
- ☐ Recognize sponsors
- ☐ Include newspaper or television quotes from past events

Figure 9-6
Checklist for Designing Sports Event Advertisements

that are unfamiliar to the public, or are only part of a broader series of attractions should include a list or description of compelling features to promote attendance. Descriptions should be short, imperative sentence fragments, beginning with verbs that emphasize some form of interactivity with the event. Include only the best sales points and those that are perceived as necessary to position the event as an exciting way to spend the fan's day or dollar. Use words like those in Figure 9-7 to spur your target audience into taking your desired course of action.

As influential as these commands might be, nothing is more persuasive than exhilarating photographs and action-laden film or video footage. Communicate the excitement of your event with one or more still images that bring life to your print advertisements. A single dynamic photograph is best for most applications, but multifaceted festivals might be better served with three or four smaller images to more fully represent the broad variety of activities to experience. Try to have your images and copy points complement one another. Use images that communicate a specific story, message, or feeling to the reader.

Be certain that you have the rights to use whatever image(s) you select. The photographers or their agencies must provide permission and will commonly require payment for such use. In addition, any participant or audience member who may appear in a photograph or footage must also provide his or her consent to appear. The permission of athletes and other participants is often secured in advance with a waiver that provides such written consent, or in the case of more notable personalities, should be included in their appearance agreements. Obtaining the consent of members of the audience whose images may be incidentally included in future advertising is obviously much

---

Add these influential words to your starting lineup of descriptive copy points:
- See . . . !
- Experience . . . !
- Watch . . . !
- Meet . . . !
- Win . . . !
- Save . . . !
- Get . . . ! (or Receive . . . !)
- Hear . . . !
- Play . . . !
- Try . . . !
- Cheer . . . !

Figure 9-7
Starting Line-up of Effective Sports Event
Advertising Copy Point Influencers

more difficult. It is strongly suggested that legal language be included on the back of all event tickets and credentials, in a statement notifying individuals that using the ticket and attending the event implies permission for their images to be used in advertising, promotion, and other marketing applications. Free events that do not use tickets should post similar permission language in conspicuous positions at all event entrances to protect against future claims for illegal use of a fan's image. (It is not a bad idea to post this disclaimer even when it is also included on the ticket back.) Finally, individual audience members interviewed on camera or photographed during an event may be asked to sign permission forms at the time their images are recorded for future possible use. Regardless of how audience image permissions are sought, be sure to utilize the services of an experienced attorney to provide the protection required.

What if the sports event is brand new or no images from prior editions are readily available? If it is impractical, or too expensive, to stage photography simulating a past presentation of the event, consider using an action image of a participating athlete in another event. The same permissions, and perhaps additional ones, will be required, and some features of the photograph may require alteration to disassociate it from the other event. (Specifically, avoid images displaying the logos, uniform designs, or other intellectual property of other event organizers or sponsors.) Failing the availability of this option, the databases of stock photography agencies can be searched to identify and acquire the rights to use a suitable image. Today some of the best databases are available on-line, including thumbnail-sized images to help speed and simplify the selection process.

Television commercials should be well edited, exciting, and fast paced. Avoid subtleties and creative images that overwhelm an ad's essential information. Employ the same action words used in print advertising to describe the event's compelling features and attractions, enthusiastically delivered by a professional announcer (or featured athlete). Use up-tempo music to add excitement to the delivery. The rights to use popular music in commercials (known as "sync" or "synchronization" rights) can be very expensive. Less expensive stock music is available through most video editing houses. Promoters will need the same permissions for video and film as are required for still photography and may be able to secure stock footage in the same way stock photography can be obtained. Remember that the information presented in television advertisements is less "sticky" than print ads—you cannot tear out a television or radio ad for future reference. Although it must be memorable, it cannot be expected to impart as much information as a print ad. See Figure 9-8 for more tips on creating your event's television commercial, as well as information specific to advertising in print, radio, and outdoor, or billboard, advertising.

Organizers may be obligated to recognize their sponsors in event advertising. For title or presenting sponsors, recognition integrated within the event

Print Advertising
- Advertise in the newspapers that your target audience is most likely to read.
- Place advertising in the part of the newspaper your target audience is most likely to read (e.g., sports section, entertainment/calendar section, community section). Try to avoid less expensive "run-of-paper" (ROP) ads that will be placed wherever the newspaper has available space.
- Don't count on one placement of an ad as being all you will need to achieve your marketing aims.
- Integrate the timing of promotional advertising placed on behalf of sponsors into the overall advertising campaign.
- Keep the design simple and eye-catching.
- Use still-action photographs reflective of the event's excitement. (Be sure to clear the rights to an athlete's image with both the photographer and the athlete.)
- Remember that print advertisements are excellent reference tools for the readers. They may clip ads out of the paper to retain the information they need, so include as much as possible without cluttering an ad.
- Don't overlook weekly special-interest newspapers and magazines such as community papers, local entertainment weeklies, parent publications, and sports-oriented weeklies.

Radio
- Run ads on stations and programs to which your target audience is most likely to be listening, and at the times of day ("day parts") they are most apt to be listening.
- Include an easy-to-remember phone number and/or web site address for ticket purchases and further information.
- Record a station's disk jockey reading the script with enthusiasm. (You may not be able to use this recording on other radio stations, however.)
- Use upbeat music under the voice-over that captures the excitement of the event.

Television
- Select television programs and special-interest cable shows that your target audience is most likely to be watching at the time they are originally broadcast. (Programs likely to be taped may be viewed after the usefulness of the call to action has expired.)
- Include a screen graphic during the last five seconds of the ad with the event name and logo, day, date, location, and an easy-to-remember phone number and/or web site address for ticket purchases and further information.
- Use footage from previous events that shows action, excitement, and *fan reactions.*
- Include images for which you have obtained rights from both the athletes and the owners of the footage.

Figure 9-8
Sports Event Advertising Tips

Outdoor (Billboards)
- Keep the artwork simple and readable; avoid subtleties. Design billboards understanding that people drive by them at 60 miles per hour, so the copy points should be few, but large.
- Don't try to cram so much information on a billboard that it becomes cluttered.
- Try to include an easy-to-remember phone number and/or web site address to direct passersby to more detailed information.
- Remember that billboards are excellent tools for generating awareness of an event, and less effective as ticket sales generators.

Figure 9-8
(Continued)

name and logo is always expected. Promoters may also have included similar rights for other, or perhaps all, official sponsors to help in their sales efforts. If there is a large roster of sponsors, some definition as to how they should be recognized in event advertising is required to avoid excessively cluttering advertisements. For example, the sponsor agreement can define the size of the ads in which a sponsor will be recognized (e.g., title and presenting sponsor logos in all ads, official sponsor logos in full- and three-quarter-page ads only and listed in type in all others). The promoter can also schedule ads so that a rotation of logos or sponsor names can be established, in which all official sponsors are equally recognized over the course of the entire campaign, but not in every ad. This practice is very useful in minimizing clutter and actually increases the recognition of a sponsor's brand, because when it does appear, it is in the company of the brands of fewer other partners.

The right advertising campaign will be as distinctive as the event it is designed to promote. Determine whether the headlines or copy points should use terminology most familiar to passionate fans of the sport and whether its appearance is the most effective way to reach a particular audience. Sport-specific terminology may turn off the more casual fans and ticket buyers and may be best used in niche publications that appeal more directly to the hardcore audience. Existing sports events such as festivals and demonstrations that target a general, entertainment-seeking audience may include quotes from news coverage of previous editions, a common practice in the motion picture and live entertainment businesses. It is important that the quotes are from sources that will be perceived as credible by the audience. (A creative variation is the use of quotes from past attendees.) Quotes can also be used to reinforce the legitimacy of a relatively lesser known competitive event. Consider soliciting quotes, and permission to use them, from members of the media, players, and other participants that enhance the perception of the event's importance.

SPECIAL SECTIONS

The two faces of Janus in newspapers and other print media—the editorial and marketing sides of the publishing business—delicately converge in the creation of special sections and "advertorials." A publisher may believe that an event can provide an opportunity to sell significant incremental advertising in a stand-alone or pull-out section of expanded coverage. In the United States, freedom of the press guarantees that newspapers can generate any and as much editorial coverage they desire, and therefore they need not be media partners to enjoy the right to publish a special section of expanded coverage. They may also sell advertising to anyone they choose, including those that are competitors to an event's sponsor partners. Sponsors understand that no outside party can have control over a free press, but organizers can still make an effort to enhance, if not protect, their sponsors' association with their event. An organizer might approach newspaper marketing executives to offer introductions to a sports event's sponsors, potentially the best target for selling advertising space in special sections publicizing an event, whether or not the newspaper is a media partner.

For high-profile events in competitive multinewspaper markets, it is entirely possible that more than one paper will undertake the creation of a special section. Care should be taken to provide additional value that supports the special section under development by the event's media partner, including official site maps, detailed schedules of activities, and other exclusive opportunities. Although an event organizer has no obligation to make as much information as readily available to a nonpartner, the publicity value of a special section in a nonpartner newspaper cannot be overlooked. Be sure to provide any information that will help make the nonpartner's special section intriguing reading and a good publicity vehicle for the event. Remember—the quality of any special section reflects on the event. Readers cannot be expected to reason that expanded coverage is poorer in one newspaper because it is competitive with the event's media partner.

ADVERTORIALS

A hybrid concept, the "advertorial," is finding its way into newspapers and magazines with increasing frequency. An advertorial can be a single page, a series of pages, or an entire section of a publication that is at once an advertisement and a collection of feature articles. There is a particular difference between an advertorial and a special section: The event organizer or sponsor purchases 100 percent of the space for the advertorial. The organizer, in turn, can resell advertising opportunities in the advertorial to sponsors or deliver space as part of a sponsor's benefit package. Because all of the space has been paid for by the event, the organizer can write or exert significant control over the editorial copy, inserting articles that best suit his or her marketing objectives. Many organizers commission their own writers or assign their public relations staff to write the articles for an advertorial. For publications that require that their own staff write the copy and are concerned about distinguishing its content from true, journalistically objective editorial, like the *Los Angeles Times*, for instance, the writers assigned by the paper to advertorials are frequently distinct from the core editorial staff.

To ensure that the advertorial's articles will be read by the public, organizers should provide or encourage stories that are no less compelling than if they appeared in editorial sections of the publication. Features should not be copies of press releases. However, because the event has total control over the content, every advantage should be taken to make sure the organizer's message is clear. Decide what you want the readers to do and what you want them to know. Provide every detail that will help them to make the decision you want them to make—to come to the event, watch it on television, or listen to it on the radio.

Event Marketing

Sponsors employ sports event marketing campaigns to promote their products, so why can't event organizers do the same to sell theirs? Strategically scheduled mini-events that provide a taste of the big event to come can excite the public, encourage the purchase of tickets, and generate added publicity coverage. Schedule a fan participatory competition, one that will foster an appreciation for the talents of the athletes featured in the main event. Create an exhibit on the history of the sport being featured and place it in a high-traffic downtown concourse. Consider transforming a scheduled media event into a public opportunity, such as the Top Prospects Preview described in the Sideline Story on page 274.

Rights to these ancillary event marketing activities may be included in sponsor packages or can provide promoters with additional "inventory" they can up-sell to existing sponsors. Be sure that these sponsorships are incremental to the deals required for funding the main event. Event marketing programs either should have been anticipated by the expense budget or must be fully funded by new sponsors or with additional dollars from existing sponsors.

Are there other events, either sports or nonsports events, being staged in the host city that attract a target audience similar to your event's audience? Consider staging a mini-event or a promotional attraction on their event sites to capitalize on the audiences they spend money to draw. Interactive activities—appearances, autograph sessions and photo opportunities with athletes, batting cages, slapshot booths, fan skills or trivia contests, to name just a few—are most effective in creating excitement. A promotional take-away item with

Sideline Story—Top Prospects Preview

Each year, on the day before the National Hockey League Entry Draft, the media are introduced to the top amateurs expected to be among the first players selected. Until 1992, the Top Prospects Preview was a media-only opportunity. To build awareness and attendance at the Draft and to familiarize the public with the future stars of the ice, the preview has been restaged as a free public happening in a central downtown location at lunch hour on the day prior to the big event. Approximately one dozen players are introduced in their junior team jerseys to the public, one at a time, as their brief biographies are read by a guest emcee to an upbeat musical soundtrack. When the last player is introduced, a "prospects class photo" is taken, featuring these future stars in a host of colorful junior jerseys—for perhaps the last time many will wear them before joining the pros.

Members of the media are seated in a roped-off section in front of the crowd, with locations for photographers and video cameras who generate outstanding pictures and footage. The reactions of the crowd behind them only enhance the excitement in news coverage later in the evening. To ensure that members of the media can still gain the one-on-one access to the players they photographed during the preview, an interview and luncheon area is set up in a nonpublic space immediately afterward.

the event date, location, information, and ticket ordering phone number and web site address, is highly recommended. Be creative, and pick an item that represents the sport or event, but if cost is an issue, the item need not be permanent keepsake, such as a refrigerator magnet or key chain. After all, from a marketing perspective, the usefulness of the item expires when the main event is over. Pending the permission of the host event's organizer, the premiums and the activity can be fully or partially funded by a sponsor, and additional elements such as sampling can be included. If possible and permitted, have a supply of tickets available and a mechanism to accept payment.

Are there parades in the host city, street festivals, civic celebrations, special holiday activities, ethnic celebrations, or other activities that bring large numbers of people together? Consider contacting their organizers to create a presence at these festive occasions, presuming the demographics of the audience complements your target market. Fitting into the cultural fabric of the host city is essential; this subject is explored in detail in Play 10.

Post-Play Analysis

An effective marketing plan cannot rely on pre-event publicity alone. Additional tools, including advertising, promotions, and event marketing, must be employed to achieve your event's marketing objectives. Establishing business partnerships with media outlets can help to maximize exposure for an event at a greatly reduced cost. Newspapers and other print media open to participating as partners generally insist on exclusive relationships. Multiple radio and television partnerships can be designed, with exclusivity segmented by programming format. Promotions can be created with both media partners and sponsors that encourage ticket sales or build attendance, generate awareness of the event, or increase ratings for broadcast events. Make sure that event advertising has a clear message, with an obvious and compelling call to action. Consider working with newspapers and other print media to create special sections and advertorials to increase exposure for your event and reinforce its importance.

Coach's Clipboard

1. Create an advertising campaign for the 10K run described in Play 1. Include an introductory ad to solicit participants, and another designed to appear the day before the event to encourage the attendance of spectators. How many times, and when, should each ad run? Write a 30-second radio spot to complement the print campaign.

2. At what other kinds of sports and non-sports events could the organizers of the 10K run stage event marketing activities to maximize spectator attendance? What kinds of activities should they stage, and what kinds of premiums could they distribute to help build attendance on event day?

3. How could the 10K run organizer reach into schools with the NIE program to encourage students to stay physically fit and consider running as a participatory activity? Are there different messages for different age groups? Are there additional activities to appeal to young students, both in schools and in their homes? What kinds of marketing programs (include publicity, promotion, advertising, and event marketing) can be created to target parents that will complement the programs designed to appeal to youth?

PLAY 10

Engaging the Community

On a good team there are no superstars. There are great players who show they are great players by being able to play with others as a team. They have the ability to be superstars, but if they fit into a good team, they make sacrifices, they do things necessary to help the team win.

—RED HOLZMAN (1920–1998),
FORMER NEW YORK KNICKS COACH

Too often, sports event organizers overlook the many resources available in communities that are justifiably proud of the events they stage, as well as those they host. A talented organizer with sufficient resources can stage and promote an event without the active engagement of local government, businesses, or civic organizations. However, ignoring the role the community can play is to ignore the greater impact that can be achieved with the mobilization of these local resources. Some of the same sports event organizers who are aggressive about pursuing sponsorship revenue in a community fail to notice the vast human resources and valuable services often available simply for the asking.

Programs that showcase the talents and athletic prowess of family, friends, and neighbors can be incredibly appealing to elected officials and local governmental agencies. After all, both the "stars" of the event and the people who come to see them compete are members of their voting constituencies. Local politicians strive to represent happy, vibrant communities, and any event that can improve the quality of life in their jurisdictions—within reasonable cost—is welcomed enthusiastically. By extension, the governmental agencies required to support a sports event—police, fire, sanitation, streets, parks and recreation, and others—as long as the organizer's expectations of their participation are within reasonable limits, apply themselves with equal vigor. Although they, too, may cooperate in a selfless community-minded spirit, they also know that their annual budgets are often voted on by the politicians who support the event and those who vote for them.

By the same token, the larger the event and the greater its impact on local infrastructure and municipal services, the more likely that some sectors of the community will come to view it as less desirable, bothersome, or even intrusive. It would be overstating the case to suggest that amateur and professional sports events that draw participants and spectators from an area wider than the local market can develop a love-hate relationship with their host communities. It is true, however, that some constituencies have more to gain from the presence of such events, and others perhaps have a bit more to lose. Sports event organizers should, by all means, accentuate the positive and beneficial aspects of their programs through various marketing and publicity efforts. At the same time, they must recognize the areas of potentially negative impact, realizing that communities are composed of a wide variety of individuals and businesses, each legitimately affected by a sports event in their own particular ways (see Figure 10-1).

Reasons They Like Sports Events	Reasons They Dislike Them
Community pride	Congestion
Quality of life	Crowds
Self-image	Traffic
Promotion of city to the outside world	Noise
Competitiveness with rival communities	Interference with normal business
Showcase of local talent	Security (fear of unruly behavior)
Business opportunities	Setting of precedents (fear of future events)
Retail	Pollution and litter
Hospitality and accommodations	Political opposition from disenfranchised
New business	neighborhoods
Future events	Expenditure of taxpayer funds in support
Tax revenues	of events
Grants for capital improvements	Degradation of existing facilities
Existing facility utilization	

Figure 10-1
How Communities React to Sports Events

Local governments seek and support sports events for a host of emotional and practical, economic reasons, which include instilling community pride and elevating the image and the reputation of their municipalities. The availability of entertainment and recreational options improves the perception of the community's quality of life and keeps its citizens within their hometown borders more often, spending money with local businesses and generating incremental tax revenues. Municipalities are competing not only for spending within their city limits, but also for state, provincial, and federal grants earmarked for building, refurbishing, and maintaining recreational and entertainment facilities. An established history as an active focal point for sports and other entertainment events can position a community as a vibrant, vital hub of economic and tourism activity that is worthy of further funding and development. Finally, do not underestimate the value of bragging rights. Beyond the purely economic competitiveness, politicians, city officials, and even area residents simply like to portray themselves as being from a place that is superior to that of their neighbors.

As explored in Play 4, sports events can generate economic impact across a wide spectrum of businesses, including restaurants, hotels, retailers, ground transportation operators, and other services. The more people an event can attract to a host city, even if only for a day, the greater its impact on the business community, and by extension, the greater the community's support for the program. Keeping the host community's citizens in town raises the excitement level of the event, but also results in their money being spent with local merchants rather than outside the city limits. This helps spike tax revenues for the city and may help fund future capital improvements, not just for event facilities, but also for infrastructure the community uses in everyday life, such as roads, parks, and public spaces. In addition, successful sports events help attract more sports and entertainment events, keeping facilities well utilized and developing an increased flow of consumer spending and tax revenues for the future.

The presence and proportionate importance of each of these motivators varies from city to city, and even from one elected administration to the next. What is almost as sure is that some constituents will be less enthusiastic about the presence of a sports event, although the magnitude of their dissatisfaction and the degree of their ability to obstruct or otherwise affect its planning will differ. Residents living near event venues may be concerned about how both human and vehicular traffic, noise, and potentially boisterous fan behavior may affect their homes and neighborhoods. Businesses may express concern about the added difficulties their employees may encounter in reaching their offices, and some retailers may be anxious about the obstacles their customers may face because of heavy traffic, road closures, or detours.

In almost every community there is likely to be some number of disenfranchised neighborhoods composed of economically distressed families, underemployed workers, and at-risk youth. Cities and developers often place sports facilities in or on the fringe of these areas, taking advantage of initially lower land values and, in some cases, fostering hopes of revitalizing an area to invite more businesses, more jobs, and improved housing. The residents of these neighborhoods may be profoundly affected by sports events staged in immediate proximity to their homes and businesses, suffering from the realities of game day noise and congestion, and if the event is economically exclusionary, from emotional distress as well.

Many of these issues will be lurking beneath the surface and may become apparent suddenly and without warning in local newspaper reports or in statements of various members of local government as a result of discussions held behind closed doors in town and city council meetings. Events staged by organizers coming from outside the community and those that attract participants and spectators from beyond the city limits are particularly susceptible to political criticism and local suspicion. An experienced sports event organizer will identify, acknowledge, and address these challenges early in the planning process to minimize any real or perceived negative impact on the community, demonstrating understanding and a sensitivity to the issues facing all affected businesses and residents.

Identifying the Gatekeepers

The most effective way of identifying community concerns before they surface is to engage local government officials, business organizations, and community leaders early in the planning process. Forge a genuine and functional partnership based on open communication and acknowledgment of each party's respective agenda. Step 1 is to identify the "gatekeepers," the influencers whose opinion and leadership help build consensus in the community. The value of finding and building relationships with a community's gatekeepers is illustrated in the Sideline Story on page 281; although it comes not from sports, but from the world of civic celebrations, it is no less reflective of the influence of gatekeepers and the importance of their role.

Various sectors of the community can throw obstacles in the path of staging a well-conceived sports event, interfering with any number of its logistical component parts, such as venue selection, transportation, parking, or even event marketing and promotion. Gatekeepers are community business or political leaders who can help decode local sensitivities to a sports event before they surface publicly and can help to ease or even eliminate possible areas of frustration for everyone involved. It is important to note that the task is not just to find ways to develop the community's acceptance of the sports event organizer's plans. It is also up to the organizer to incorporate the intimate intelligence provided by the gatekeepers into plans that will serve the local area and its residents well, with a minimum of inconvenience, and with no diminution of any measures required for public safety.

Sideline Story—The Influence of the Gatekeeper

The Radio City Music Hall Productions event team used to call him "Dr. No." The insidious Dr. No was a Philadelphia Police Department senior officer assigned to serve as the liaison to the "We the People" Parade, the nationally televised celebration of the United States Constitution's bicentennial produced by Radio City. One of the largest parades ever staged, the event featured 25,000 marchers and dozens of parade floats, including hand-built, horse-drawn re-creations of those constructed for the original Grand Federal Procession of 1787. Perhaps to a greater degree than any other special event, parades depend heavily on the cooperative and integrated efforts of dozens of city agencies and hundreds of city employees. Without the active participation of the police and the department of streets, it is hard to imagine how a parade might ever occur.

Whether Dr. No understood the significance of this national celebration to the tourism and economic development efforts of the City of Philadelphia to this day remains unknown. What is evident, however, is that he was a skillful master of yielding the powerful word that became his alias and employed it liberally as the answer to nearly every inquiry or request. For the record, it should be stated that the authority and expertise of the local police and fire departments, among other government agencies charged with the responsibility of security and public safety, should generally go unchallenged. These professionals know their city, understand their mission, and are charged with the uniquely weighty burden of protecting the public. This is a partnership in which the rationally exercised authority of the law should be unquestioned.

There came a time, however, when it became apparent that Dr. No's use of his chief weapon had less to do with public safety and more to do with an abhorrence of personal inconvenience and ambivalence toward the event. His refusal to suggest alternatives, make recommendations, or provide feedback that defined the limits to which he was prepared to agree, further supported this perception. (My personal experience is that this is a very unusual attitude among our heroes in blue.) It also became apparent that no operations plan submitted to him would ever be approved, thus seriously endangering the viability of the event and the city's ability to exploit it for their own purposes.

Dr. No unwittingly taught me the value of identifying a gatekeeper. In this case, the keys to the gate were in the possession of an influential deputy mayor who served as City Hall's direct liaison to the We the People 200 Committee, the event's organizer. Our encounters with Dr. No were described to this committee member during a hastily called meeting scheduled to review the operational plans for the parade. Within a day, Dr. No was reassigned, probably to his relief, and a new event liaison appeared whose mantra was more akin to "Let's figure this out together." As we worked more closely as partners, with understanding and respect for each other's needs and responsibilities, the parade drew an estimated 4 million people to Center City Philadelphia to celebrate this landmark date in the nation's history.

As important as gatekeepers are for advance intelligence, organizers should recognize that they are also advocates for the citizens and businesses in their jurisdiction. They will know what kinds of marketing programs will work in their city and what will be received tepidly or negatively. They can advise the organizer whether to ignore an obstacle, work around it, or involve the source of potential criticism more closely in the early stages of planning. They can help identify the true needs of both local residents and industry and show how best to integrate them into the event for the gain of all involved. Figure 10-2 lists some of the most common gatekeepers of the community and where they can be found.

The larger a sports event and more impact it will have on a community's normal operations, the more essential it is to identify one or more highly placed gatekeepers as early in the planning process as possible, perhaps even during the event bidding phase. The local sports commission or the convention and visitors bureau, whose constituencies may have already demonstrated their commitment to the success of the event, can help organizers identify and contact the gatekeepers most important to the tasks and challenges at hand. Certainly, a contact in the office of the mayor, perhaps the city's own chief executive, may be able to provide the highest level of active leadership and personal oversight. Members of city council, or representatives of the analogous body in the community that represents the geographical areas most affected by the event, are also essential partners in gaining the support of the municipality and the citizens living in its environs.

The interest and support of city hall are particularly important to sports events that are not held in the same location each year. Discovering that the community is not behind an event on the highest levels after it has been awarded can be a major disappointment and perhaps even a mortal blow to its eventual success. It is therefore recommended that a letter of support from the appropriate senior local official, such as the mayor, city manager, county supervisor, or metro chairman, be required for inclusion as part of the Request

City Officials
    Mayor and/or City Manager
    Deputy Mayor
    Director of Communications
    Marketing Director
    City Council Representatives for impacted districts
    Executive Director, Convention and Visitors Bureau or Sports Commission
    Police Commissioner or Chief of Police
    Fire Commissioner
Business Development Organizations
    Chamber(s) of Commerce
    Business Improvement Districts or Business Partnerships
    Downtown or Merchants Associations
    Restaurant Associations
Civic Groups
    Rotary International
    Kiwanis
    Masonic Lodge
    American Legion and Veterans of Foreign Wars
Sports Organizations
    Amateur sports federations
    Academic sports organizations
    Grassroots and recreational sports leagues

Figure 10-2
The Sports Event Gatekeepers of a Community

for Proposal (RFP) response. It is important to recognize, however, that city officials are responsible first and foremost to their voting constituents, both residents and business owners. The event's benefits to the community must be genuine and measurable if the involvement of top elected officials is to be expected. This is never more true than during an election year, when officials assume a more political mien, pushing through programs that provide great and obvious benefits to their communities or pulling away from a program at the hint of controversy.

If possible, arrange a meeting with the highest city official possible before the event is awarded or announced. Prepare a presentation of no more than ten minutes—that will probably be all the time he or she has—outlining the event and its benefits to the community. (Don't be surprised if that official is already aware of the program as a result of the bidding process.) Because such busy administrators will want to ask questions of specific pertinence to them within this brief time frame, expect to be interrupted frequently. Emphasize your most important points—how the sports event will serve their city, its residents and businesses—within the first few minutes. Additional information, descriptions, and illustrations may be left behind in a written presentation. The idea is to communicate sufficiently and succinctly with these officials so they are prepared with answers for their constituents' questions and can represent to the community that they have ongoing, constructive, and direct dialogue with the organizer. At the end of the presentation, offer to answer any remaining questions, and in return, ask the official to provide a key liaison through whom all questions and requests to and from his or her office should be channeled. This may also be a good time to further engage city hall with an offer for the mayor and/or an appropriate councilperson to participate as a key speaker in the announcing press conference.

If a meeting with key local government officials cannot be arranged, sometimes simply inviting these senior civic gatekeepers to participate in the sports event in a significant and meaningful way can help to open doors. To illustrate, see the Sideline Story on page 285.

CHAMBERS OF COMMERCE AND MERCHANTS ASSOCIATIONS

Other important gatekeepers are the senior executives representing various sectors of the business community, some of whom may perceive an event as an opportunity, others as an obstacle to their enterprises. The local chamber of commerce represents the interests of area businesses and is responsible for attracting new companies and jobs to the community. Chambers often organize member breakfasts, luncheons, and other regular meetings to impart news, share ideas, and present information on emerging promotional opportunities. Make it a point to meet with the chamber's executive director and marketing director to introduce them to the event and its potential impact on local business. Explore with them the many opportunities—as sponsors, promotional partners, or simply as supporters—for area businesses. Ask whether the chamber would consider accommodating a presentation about the event to their membership at an upcoming regular gathering. Bring promotional materials and giveaways to the meeting, as well as videos and printed summaries that communicate the program's excitement and potential promotional opportunities for business owners. Leave plenty of time for questions and answers and make sure to have a large stack of business cards. Invite feedback and be open to new ideas—you never know where an exciting and new promotional concept will come from (see Figure 10-3). If an opportunity to speak at a membership event is not available, ask to be introduced through the chamber's newsletter or mailings.

Some groups of neighborhood businesses have more specific and localized needs than a chamber of commerce with a citywide constituency can represent. Local not-for-profit organizations with names that contain phrases like "business improvement district (BID)," "downtown association," "merchants association," and "business partnership," among others, concentrate their development efforts on just a handful of streets or blocks. If an event is sched-

Sideline Story—Hockey Hall of Fame Grand Opening

A new Hockey Hall of Fame was due to open in June 1993 in the historic Bank of Montreal building at the busy northwest corner of Front and Yonge Streets in Toronto, Ontario. Among the many celebrations planned was a televised unveiling of the "Honoured Members Wall," an etched glass monument on which the names of inductees to the Hall would be enshrined, a procession of 90 living members to the Hall in convertibles, and the "world's largest face-off," a photo opportunity in which the honorees would pose holding hockey sticks in the broad crossroads, forming an arc around a giant commemorative puck. Two street closures were required to execute the event. First, Front Street would have to be closed to accommodate the parade of convertibles. A few minutes later, Yonge Street, one of the city's busiest north-south thoroughfares, would have to be closed to set up and execute the face-off.

In 1993, however, jurisdiction for each of these intersecting streets was under the control of two different government entities—the City of Toronto and Metro Toronto (the latter was a multicity regional government that merged with the city in the late 1990s, eliminating the distinction and simplifying the staging of events, among other things.) Therefore, a permit was required from each of the two administrations to stage an event in the intersection, but one was reticent to approve the application for reasons unknown. When Canada's then governor general Ray Hnatyshyn accepted an invitation to ride in the lead car and pose with the hockey greats, however, the permits were hurried through.

uled within their area of influence, these local merchants may be among the most interested in exploiting the event to further their own business objectives. They will also be the most concerned about whether the event will create unwanted confusion, congestion, noise, and litter during their operating hours. Marketing and promotional programs undertaken with businesses located near sports event venues can be particularly effective, as both their employees and their customers are accustomed to traveling to and spending time on those few blocks. A business's proximity to the host facility's box office also makes it very convenient for customers and employees to purchase tickets, especially if given a promotional incentive to do so.

- Provide opportunities for official sponsorship. Consider adding a less expensive tier designed expressly for local businesses at national or regional events.
- Place posters or window cards in retailer windows.
- Conduct a window decorating contest—participating and winning retailers can win tickets and prizes for decorating their windows with the sports event theme.
- Request that businesses post welcome greetings to fans and athletes on company-owned electronic message signs and marquees.
- Offer advance event ticket purchase opportunities to participating businesses and their employees.
- Encourage sports event–themed menus at area restaurants and pubs.
- Consider developing cross-promotions with local attractions.

Figure 10-3
Involving Local Businesses

RESTAURANTS

Not everyone views the crowds generated by sports events as a negative. Among the particular business groups that welcome congestion, at least in the form of foot traffic, are restaurants and taverns. Ask the host city's convention and visitors bureau (CVB) to identify a key contact at the local restaurant association. Try to meet with the owners or managers of area eateries and bars to create mutually beneficial cross-promotions that will drive ticket holders into restaurants and their patrons to the box office. Does your event publish an information guide for guests, participants, volunteers, or staff? List participating restaurants that agree to offer dining discounts (e.g., 15 percent off the bill, a free appetizer, or complimentary beverage) to fans and athletes upon presentation of a ticket stub, credential, or coupon. An organizer can further enhance the promotion with in-venue signage, public address announcements, and/or mention in printed programs or in scoreboard messages during the event, adding even more value to the relationship for participating restaurants.

In exchange for the organizer's promotion, these establishments may also decorate their facility, hang posters, offer event-themed menu items, or help promote the program by offering their regular diners coupons redeemable for ticket or merchandise discounts during the month leading up to the event. To maximize exposure for the event at area restaurants, the organizer may agree to provide camera-ready or downloadable logo artwork for the establishments to include on daily menus and welcome banners. A simple one-page permission agreement, drafted by an attorney, that defines how the restaurant may use the logo is strongly recommended for this purpose. The agreement can provide the eatery with the right to use the logo for its own promotional purposes or for decorative uses, presuming an existing sponsorship agreement with another restaurant or chain does not preclude cross-promotions as described earlier. To protect existing or future event sponsors, it is also suggested that the agreement prohibit the restaurant from including any third-party name or logo on banners or printed materials that feature the event name or logo. For example, a banner displaying the phrase "Bob's Restaurant Welcomes the Big Street Sports Tournament" would be completely acceptable under such an agreement, whereas the same greeting from "Bob's Restaurant and Barley's Beer" would be expressly forbidden. In addition, the restaurant should not be permitted to pass through sponsorship rights for any event promotion to a third party, whether paid or unpaid, without the written permission of the organizer. Agree on a reasonable expiration date for the promotion, and make sure that it is recognized in this simple agreement, as well as on coupons and any other printed promotional materials or signage.

AREA ATTRACTIONS AND EVENTS

Events that draw tourists and one-day visitors to a community can be highly desirable for an area's sightseeing and cultural attractions, including local landmarks, amusement parks, museums, theaters, and natural wonders. Cross-promotions similar to those described for restaurants and bars may be pursued with these area attractions. The simplest way of reaching out to attractions is through the local CVB, whose membership roster typically includes the operating entities of the city's most significant points of interest. Develop programs with high-volume attractions that appeal to audience demographics similar to those of your sports event. Concentrate on those that can promote the event or an offer to the most residents and one-day visitors during the weeks leading up to event day. In exchange, the attractions should offer admission discounts to the sports event's fans, guests, participants, volunteers, and staff during the period immediately surrounding the program, most often a few days immediately before and after the event. Attraction offers may be communicated at the event site but are at their most effective when promoted in advance of the planned arrival of inbound guests. As a result of these available opportunities, travelers may determine to extend their stay in the host city to take best advantage of the entertainment, cultural enrichment, and cost savings they can provide.

Consider designing cross-promotions with professional and amateur sports teams in the host city, particularly those with crossover appeal to the sports event's target audience. Offer discounts on advance purchases of event tickets to the loyal fans of major and minor league organizations and the participants in youth and adult recreational leagues. Send event posters to local recreation centers, park information centers, gymnasiums, rinks, and other sports-oriented facilities. Promote group ticket packages to teams and associations that use these venues regularly, and include an information telephone number and web site address. Some organizers offer not-for-profit groups such as junior leagues, scouts, hospitals, and other charitable institutions the ability to purchase a block of tickets at a discounted rate for resale to their membership at full price for fund-raising purposes. (*Hint:* These discounted tickets will show a full price on their face. They should be coded so that in the unlikely necessity of having to provide a refund, box office personnel will know the tickets were sold at a discount. If refunds of fund-raising tickets are determined to be necessary, it is recommended that they be transacted between the charity and the box office rather than with individual ticket holders.)

Be sure to identify the other events and celebrations being held in the host city during the time when your pre-event marketing campaign is being conducted. Sports and cultural events, festivals, civic and holiday celebrations, parades, fairs, and expositions can provide excellent platforms for additional cross-promotions and publicity. Staffing exhibits and information booths or tents at these events can help to raise awareness for your program. In addition, attendees of conventions and trade and special-interest shows that attract out-of-town delegates are always looking for extracurricular activities during their visits. Concentrate promotional efforts on those events that are scheduled during or around the same week as your sports event as great sources for additional attendees.

WELCOMING OFTEN OVERLOOKED NEIGHBORS

Often overlooked opportunities to build an event's relevance and popularity may be available in neighborhoods that are, simply, often forgotten by other organizers. Disadvantaged families and at-risk youth may be found in every city. Extending a welcoming hand to these sometimes unnoticed segments of the marketplace at sports events can provide a host of benefits, including, foremost, the ability to do good works in the community. Activities designed specifically for disadvantaged people can further a host city's own objectives for inclusiveness for the community, develop positive public relations and new fans for an event or sport, and diversify the sport's fan base, among many other benefits.

Providing special access or programming for the residents of lower-income neighborhoods, as well as those most impacted by the event (i.e., those closest to sports event venues) can also help to gain the support of the community and its elected representatives. Organizers can offer exclusive athlete meet-and-greet opportunities, a special luncheon or barbeque with sports personalities, sports clinics, pre- or post-event access to the playing field, or even provide a number of unsold tickets on a complimentary basis to those who cannot afford to buy them. Hosting or sponsoring programs such as these, beyond their purely philanthropic effect, add immeasurable value to the main event in the eyes of city government and the community at large.

Consider, too, the impact of involving the participation of groups serving physically and mentally challenged individuals. Area recreational organizations, charities, and hospitals can assist sports event organizers in identifying these groups and their specific needs. Organizers may discover active local associations serving the recreational needs of Special Olympians and Para-athletes, who can be included either as participating athletes or as guest spectators. Incorporating these inspiring athletes into the program can significantly add to the quality of a sports event. If this option is not within the scope of the event (such as a professional athletic event, for example), consider offering special clinics or workshops conducted by featured athletes, or showcasing their skills during a pregame or intermission demonstration.

Focusing and Managing Community Enthusiasm

Almost immediately after a city or neighborhood has been named as host for an important sports event, a swell of community pride causes leaders and influential citizens to seek outlets for their enthusiasm. Each believes that he or she has a role to play, a contribution to make, and insightful ideas that must be realized. Word quickly spreads about plans for fund-raising dinners, public rallies and parades, concerts and clinics, pickup games and corporate challenges. As unbelievable as it may sound, the actual sports event organizer is frequently among the last to know about these preparations.

Dynamic, involved, and enthusiastic boosters of the community begin to formulate ambitious plans to exploit the event for largely positive and selfless purposes. Those allowed to expand and develop unchecked and without the active involvement of the organizer can drain human and financial resources away from the main event, creating a muddle of mixed marketing messages to fans and potential sponsors. If poorly realized, these additional community activities can even taint the core sports event in the eyes of some segments of the marketplace. Simply put, the more active, interested, and involved a community, the more likely the tendency to want to do too much.

It is in the best interest of the event organizer to channel this enthusiasm, not curb or obstruct it. Consider yourself lucky when a community gets behind an event to the extent that it begins to mobilize spontaneously to support and take best advantage of it. A community's ambivalence, in contrast, can make the road to an event's success much tougher. Reach out and communicate with these fervent and excited souls. Validate the community's desire to become involved and provide focus for their efforts. Demonstrate your USO (understand stakeholders' objectives) sensitivities—show that you understand and support the community's objectives and help it understand yours. Channel its members' energy so that they are working in support of the actual objectives of both the community and the sports event, rather than what they think those objectives should be. Help organize key local supporters into an advisory board to provide you with counsel and insights into the needs of the community. Or engage the most driven and energetic into task forces known as organizing and host committees.

ADVISORY BOARDS

If it is early in the planning process, organizers can form an advisory board composed of influential businesspeople, community leaders, and local individuals whose expertise, contacts, and familiarity with the host city can prove invaluable to event operations. Forming an advisory board creates a legitimate, official group of counselors to the event organization who can be relied upon for valuable advice and insightful recommendations, perspectives on the community, and past event history. Embracing and engaging these leaders pre-empts the formation of any outside ad hoc group, no matter how well intentioned, that may seek to pursue its own agenda in the name of the event. Advisory boards are also useful when the event and its organizing entity have little recognition in the community or among potential sponsors. When it is important to establish the legitimacy of the event and its organizer, the role of the advisory board is of more significance than merely managing and monitoring community activities. Board members should be selected whose presence immediately reinforces the importance and benefits of the sports event to the community—leaders who are trusted and respected by local government, residents, businesses, and the sport. In short, the event advisory board is an organized collection of gatekeepers.

When approaching the individuals targeted for membership on the event's advisory board, be sure their respective reputations in the community are beyond reproach. The host city's sports commission can provide the insights into potential candidates. Be sure the role of the advisory board is well understood by those who are requested to serve. It is a body of experts to give *advice*—not direction, and to provide *recommendations*—not requirements. When an organizer believes the formation of an advisory board would be beneficial to the smooth management and operation of an event, letters soliciting participation should be sent as soon as possible after confirmation of the host city. Explain the significance of the event to the local community and the reason for soliciting the recipient's participation. Allow approximately two weeks to pass before making calls to follow up on the level of interest. A sample letter outlining the roles and responsibilities of an advisory board member appears in Figure 10-4.

It is important to note that the advisory board invitation makes no reference to empowering members to make policy decisions or provide any form of service to the event other than attendance at a monthly update meeting. On the surface, the advisory board will serve as a source of wisdom, but its members' time investment and active engagement can provide influence when

Dear (insert addressee name here):

As you may know, Township Village has been named the host city of the 2005 Major Stick Sports Tournament, an event that will attract 500 visiting athletes and up to 2000 spectators to the Civic Gymnasium. The Major Stick Sports Tournament is in its fifth year, and Township Village has committed to making next February's event the very best ever.

The tournament will provide area hotels with a needed midwinter boost, and local businesses with a unique opportunity to meaningfully enhance their first-quarter marketing campaigns. The event will also generate needed funds for the Civic Gymnasium renovation project scheduled for next summer.

The Major Stick Sports Tournament has requested recommendations from the Township Village Sports Commission for potential candidates to the Tournament Advisory Board. Members will assist us in ensuring the success of the community's participation in the event. The board will convene for a brief breakfast meeting once monthly through February 2005 to review our plans and progress and to gain insights, recommendations, and expert opinions on various topics of interest and impact to the people and businesses of Township Village. An agenda and minutes will be circulated to all members approximately three days prior to each monthly meeting.

As an expression of our gratitude, actively participating advisory board members will enjoy attendance and VIP privileges at the Major Stick Sports Tournament with our compliments.

Please indicate your acceptance of this invitation to participate as a valued member of the Major Stick Sports Tournament Advisory Board by signing and returning a copy of this letter in the self-addressed, stamped envelope provided. We look forward to the prospect of your involvement in this important event for Township Village.

Yours very truly,
Sports Event Organizer

☐ I accept appointment to the Major Stick Sports Tournament Advisory Board.
☐ I am unable to participate at this time.
    (check one)

Figure 10-4
Sample Sports Event Advisory Board Invitation Letter

needed. As the event approaches, members may function as a network of gatekeepers who can help overcome challenges on a case-by-case basis.

ORGANIZING AND HOST COMMITTEES

Organizing and host committees differ from advisory boards in that, at their most effective, they are groups of individuals dedicated to providing time, work, and expertise on specific functions supporting an event (organizing committee) or fulfilling a city's responsibilities as host (host committee). An organizing committee should be ultimately responsible to the event organizer, whereas a host committee may report to a host agency such as the local sports commission or CVB. To use them to the best advantage of all concerned, organizing and host committees should function as fully integrated extensions of the event team.

Properly managed, organizing and host committees can contribute significantly to the overall event organization. At least one senior member of the sports event management team should attend every meeting of the organizing or host committee to ensure that the objectives of this primarily volunteer body and those of the overall event remain well meshed. Unmanaged, organizing and host committees can run amok. A presence at committee meetings demonstrates the organizer's concern and oversight of the progress and quality of work being performed by these community participants. In addition, because such a committee is frequently an ad hoc support organization, it should not be assumed that the responsibilities assigned to and undertaken by it will be successfully or sufficiently fulfilled without vigilant monitoring. The more an event relies on the work product of a committee, the more conscientious the organizer must be in overseeing its activities. It must be recognized that all-volunteer committees require an investment of management's time and energy, and later, expressions of appreciation such as event tickets, party invitations, and recognition gifts. Organizing and host committees for major events may even require full-time professional staff and a budget to finance their operations. In such cases, the financial obligation is usually the responsibility of the host city. In addition, as sports event committees must often supplement their budgets by soliciting sponsorships and donations, the organizer must communicate strict guidelines as to how they may raise funds and from whom, in order to avoid instances in which the organizer and the committee compete for the same needed corporate revenues. Therefore, before forming or requesting the formation of a host or organizing committee, sports event organizers should be completely certain that the need for support truly warrants its creation.

Identify the roles and responsibilities expected of the group, and create an organization plan that defines all reporting relationships. Be sure the sports event organizer is always indicated as the overall authority for the effort, with at least a dotted line relationship signifying host committees that report directly to the local government. Although the specific mission of an organizing or host committee will differ from one event to the next, Figure 10-5 lists a number of the most common areas of responsibility for such committees. This should by no means imply that every committee formed must undertake every role listed, or that other appropriate functions cannot be added to the list.

Notice that each of the functions presented in Figure 10-5 can as easily be undertaken directly by members of the event staff who may already be under

Volunteer Enrollment and Management
  Airport greeters
  Information desk staff
  VIP guest hosts
  Team and athlete hosts
  Courtesy van drivers
  Operations office and message center staff
Experience Enhancement
  Welcoming signage and street banners
  Electronic message boards
  Retail, restaurant, and attraction promotions
Support Services
  City agency liaison
    Police
    Fire
    Sanitation
    Medical
    Parks and recreation
  Transit, transportation, and parking
  Traffic and road closures
Marketing and Promotion
  Business development
  Fund-raising
  Sponsorship
  Sales
  Host city guest management
  Community outreach
    Recreational and grassroots sports group
    involvement
    Charity involvement
    Educational programs

Figure 10-5
Representative Sports Events Organizing and
Host Committee Functions
(subcommittee heads in bold type)

the organizer's immediate control. The formation of a committee, however, is an attractive option when the event budget is insufficient to allow the organizer to contract and pay full-time professionals to manage such functions. These local support organizations may also be formed when the scale of the program is so large or so dependent on local resources that some division of labor between an out-of-town organizer and a local body provides significant cost and management efficiencies. In such cases, committees are often staffed with a combination of experienced, paid event professionals and motivated volunteers. In any case, organizers are well advised to maintain close control over the activities of their supportive committees to ensure that they actually provide what they are charged to contribute, and with the attention to quality and timeliness the organizers would expect of their own staffs.

Host cities should resist the temptation to appoint representatives to the host or organizing committee for the sake of politics or expedience. The best committee is the smallest committee, and any participant who cannot contribute wisdom, work, or experienced perspective to the process will drain precious time and resources and sap the morale of those who invest their time and talents more fully. A committee chairman should be appointed, one who enjoys the respect of the community, who can provide leadership and direction, and with whom both the members and the event organizer can maintain constant communication. The structure of the membership into functional groups should generally mirror that of the event organization. The committee chairman should communicate most regularly with the event director. Subcommittee heads (examples noted in bold type in Figure 10.5) should report their progress to the committee chairman at monthly meetings, but can also work closely with the event organizer's department heads whose operational responsibilities are most similar to their own. Although additional committee members may report to the subcommittee heads, it is recommended that the monthly or semimonthly update meetings be limited to the chairman and subcommittee heads so as to streamline the meeting agenda and maintain efficiency. Subcommittee heads should hold subsequent regular sessions with those assigned to work with them, passing along updates from the last committee meeting and receiving input to present at the next. Committee membership may be composed of city officials, business leaders, and other talented, influential citizens of the community whose interest lies in the improvement or maintenance of the region's quality of life and who have a proven track record of contributing their time, energy, and talents to similar endeavors. The top positions (e.g., the chairman and subcommittee heads with the greatest responsibilities) should be held by the highest-level gatekeepers, wherever possible. Figure 10-6 lists some of the resources to which organizers and host cities can turn for potential organizing committee members.

As discussed earlier, it is often the host city, sports commission, or CVB that will undertake the task of forming a host committee to help the community execute its responsibilities to a sports event without diverting a disproportionate share of city resources from its year-long mission. Thus, it is sometimes impossible or less desirable to prevent political appointments to the host committee. It is important for sports event organizers, however, to make clear to the host city that in order to truly support the objectives of both parties, the committee must be well integrated with the event team and must remain in close communication throughout the planning process.

Position	Resource
Committee Chairperson	Deputy mayor
	City council representative
	Major local real estate owner or developer
	President of local business concern
	General manager of local television or radio station
	Senior partner of local law firm
	Local business personality
Volunteer Enrollment and Management	Sports commission representative
	Convention and visitors bureau representative
	Sports team fan or booster club president
	Community sports program representative
	Community services manager for a local company (preferably a sponsor)
	Representative of a community association with a community services mission (e.g., Rotary, Kiwanis, Lions)
Experience Enhancement	Creative director of a local advertising agency
	Senior manager of a local architectural firm
	Senior manager of an outdoor (billboard) advertising firm
	General manager of a local restaurant or attraction
	Senior manager of a local chamber of commerce
Support Services	City director of special events
	City director of communications or marketing
	Police department community affairs officer
	Parks and recreation department manager
	Transit authority public affairs manager
Marketing and Promotion	Sports commission representative
	Convention and visitors bureau representative
	City director of communications or marketing
	Director of development for a local charity (when the event benefits the charity)
	Senior manager of a local chamber of commerce, business improvement district, or similar group
	Senior account executive of a local public relations firm

Figure 10-6
Organizing and Host Committee Resources

LOCAL PROMOTERS

When a sports event organizer's offices are located far from the host city, it is sometimes practical to work with a local event promoter to execute specific functions of the event operations and/or marketing plan. Organizers pursuing this option should exercise as much care in the selection of a local promoter as they would in pursuing a candidate for a senior management position with their own company. From the public's perspective, the promoter will be indistinguishable from the organizer. His or her reputation in the community, past history, and management style must complement that of the organizer to ensure that both they, and by inference, the event team, will be viewed positively by all stakeholders. Local promoters can be most helpful in marketing and selling event tickets, procuring local labor for setting up, operating, and dismantling an event, and providing insights into local politics and resources. Promoters may be hired on a fee basis, and if they are responsible for managing any cost areas, should be provided with a budget that by formal agreement may not be exceeded without the advance written permission of the organizer. If the promoter is solely responsible for the promotion and sale of tickets, he or she may also be retained on a flat-fee or a fee-plus-bonus basis for achieving certain levels of paid attendance, or remunerated on a commission-per-ticket-sold premise.

Moving Forward

The sports event organization is now in place, and the enthusiasm of the community is focused constructively, via promotional partnerships, on building mutually beneficial business opportunities. Advisory boards and committees of gatekeepers and hard-working volunteers are committed to the success of the community and the sports event to which they are about to play host. Costs are under control, marketing plans are in place, and sponsors are being signed. The production schedule shows that the time remaining is growing short. It is time to get ready for event day, and there is still much left to do.

Post-Play Analysis

Sports events are often staged in a vacuum, with little or no active participation on the part of local government, businesses, or groups that routinely operate in the interest of community service. Many of these sectors of the community recognize that sports events can provide powerful quality-of-life and economic benefits to their region, so organizers who have not engaged the local community on some level may be overlooking a valuable, motivated resource. Organizers should identify the gatekeepers, the influential civic, business, and neighborhood leaders who can provide intelligence on the perceptions of the local market and expedite requests to city agencies and community partners.

Business development groups such as chambers of commerce and neighborhood business partnerships, restaurant associations, and others, can provide an excellent source of exposure for supportive cross-promotions. Consider how to involve lower-income communities, disadvantaged youth, and physically and mentally challenged individuals in the event. Respected members of the community who share an interest in the success of both the sports event and the host city may form an advisory board to provide advice and counsel to the organizer. Task forces composed of local resources, known as organizing and host committees, can contribute counsel, work, and accountability to a sports event organizer. The activities and responsibilities of these committees are overseen by a chairperson or executive director and must be continually monitored by the event organizer to ensure completion to desired standards.

Coach's Clipboard

1. Identify the gatekeepers in your local community who can assist in planning and organizing a meet of visiting amateur swimmers. What obstacles to staging the tournament may arise during planning, and how might one or more gatekeepers advise and help to overcome them?

2. What organizations would you engage to develop cross-promotions and mutually advantageous exposure opportunities for the event described in item 1? How might they help to promote the event, and what would the businesses expect in return? How would these activities impact the event budget?

3. How would you reach out to involve lower-income communities, at-risk youth, and mentally and physically challenged persons in the event? Presuming that entrance to the meet is free, what value can you provide to these sectors of the community that will enhance their experience and further the objectives of the city and the event?

Accommodating and Managing Guests

It is not the critic who counts; not the man who points out how the strong man stumbled, or where the doer of deeds could have done them better. The credit belongs to the man who is actually in the arena.

—THEODORE ROOSEVELT (1858–1919),
26TH PRESIDENT OF THE UNITED STATES

All the plans are in place; now it's time to manage and execute the event. During this period, event organizers put their production and marketing plans into action. "The devil is in the details," it has been said, and this is never more true than in the planning and execution of sports events. It is here that the needs of events vary most. Every event requires clear objectives, a budget, a host venue and production schedule, a marketing plan, and the support of sponsors and other promotional partners. Some events require an understanding of the dynamics of ticket sales, the basics of broadcasting, and the details of technical production. Others require an understanding of the logistical elements of managing participating athletes and incoming guests and fans, still others the fundamentals of working with hotels for event offices, accommodations, and hospitality. Although the remaining "plays" present specialized subject matter that may be more pertinent to some organizers than to others, a working familiarity with all areas of sports event planning is strongly recommended for all.

Selling Tickets

Sports event organizers should view tickets as monetary instruments. Because the physical ticket represents value received by the purchaser in exchange for cash, steps should be taken to protect the organizer and buyer against the possibility of loss, theft, or counterfeiting by unscrupulous opportunists. Event tickets should be generated, only as needed, by a computerized ticketing service or printed by an experienced, bonded ticket supplier. Once received, every ticket should be counted to ensure that the number ordered matches the exact number received. Tickets with specific seat locations or sections should also be checked for accuracy against the seating manifest, a list of every individual seat as defined by section, row, and seat number. Until sold, they should be stored in a secure location, such as a bank vault, safe, or safety deposit box.

Computer-generated tickets do not exist in physical form until printed, and thus require no such antitheft measures prior to sale. They may, however, be more vulnerable to the possibility of counterfeiting. The pervasive availability of desktop publishing software and inexpensive color printing can create an illegal market for phony tickets, which can endanger the financial viability of an event and may put unsuspecting purchasers at risk of being barred admission when the counterfeits are detected. Anticounterfeiting devices that make it easy for organizers to detect a bogus ticket include the application of holographic stickers, printed and embossed foils, traceable serial numbers, complex color printing, and the use of special security paper during the printing process (e.g., the inclusion of metallic threads, watermarks, or images viewable only under ultraviolet light). Many year-round sports facilities now use laser scanners that read printed bar codes on tickets (similar to the zebra-striped SKU codes used by many retailers) at their entrances. Once a unique bar code has been scanned into the reader, no other ticket with the same or an invalid code will be honored for admission. No anticounterfeiting measure will be completely effective against sufficiently motivated persons with criminal intent. (To illustrate, a 1996 report by the U.S. Government's General Accounting Office estimated that $208 million in counterfeit American currency is in public circulation at any one time.) Any measure that makes the creation and printing of counterfeit tickets more expensive and complicated, however, lessens or eliminates the potential illicit profit margin and makes the criminal effort less likely.

TICKET TYPES AND ADMISSION POLICIES

There are two basic types of ticket policies—reserved seating and general admission. Reserved seats guarantee purchasers specific seat locations. Some sports events, most notably those held in professional sports arenas and stadiums, sell their entire inventories as reserved seat tickets, regardless of price level. General admission (GA) tickets, in contrast, enable the purchasers to occupy any available seats on a first-come, first-served basis. GA tickets may be scaled like reserved seat tickets (see Play 3), with different prices for specific sections or levels. They are also sold for events during which members of the audience move around the site or view the event from standing locations rather than occupying seats. Because GA tickets guarantee only admittance, and not necessarily a specific location from which to enjoy the program, managers of facilities hosting sports events that utilize this policy should be prepared for the formation of queues before the doors open, as attendees holding these tickets arrive early to claim the best possible seats or viewing locations. Some events offer both reserved and GA sections, providing for those who prefer the convenience of having specific seats waiting for them when they arrive, usually at a premium price, and enabling others who do not mind planning for an earlier arrival to realize some economies at the sports event. Pursuing a GA seating policy can increase the risk of injuries, particularly if the organizer expects a potential crush of fans racing for the best seats when the facility's doors first open. For this reason, general admission ticketing is not recommended for professional or large-scale sports events. Work with your risk management specialist to determine whether this policy will potentially raise your insurance premiums or increase the likelihood of injuries (see Play 14).

WHEN TO BEGIN SELLING TICKETS

Regardless of the nature of the sports event, whether it is an exhibition game, themed game night, skills competition, track meet, opening ceremonies, fund-raising dinner, or a player draft, selling tickets in advance is an absolute must. Relying primarily on tickets sold as fans arrive on event day, also known as "walk-up" business, can put the organizer at serious financial risk. First, advance sales provide cash flow to cover pre-event expenses and deposits. The funds represented by walk-up ticket sales are not available before the day of the event. Second, advance sales reduce the potentially devastating effects of event-day weather. Attendance is guaranteed by tickets sold in advance if atmospheric conditions threaten, but do not ultimately cancel the event. Fans without tickets, however, have total freedom to decide whether to attend on event day, based on either a whim and or a concern about impending weather conditions. Advance ticket holders have invested their money and will receive no refund unless the event is completely cancelled, so if there is even a small chance that the sports event will go on, they will make the effort to be there.

Creating a sense of urgency is the key to generating advance ticket sales. You want fans to think, "If I do not get my tickets right away . . .

- "I will miss out on attending, because the tickets may be sold out later,"
- "I will not get the best seats, which could diminish my enjoyment of the event," (A reserved seat policy is essential to ensure the best seats.)

- "I won't receive an offered premium item or some opportunity available solely to advance purchasers or for only a limited time."

The "when" of putting tickets on sale is inextricably linked to the "how" of putting them on sale. You must have enough time to inform the public about the event and communicate the availability of tickets to potential buyers. Then you have to make it easy and convenient for them to make their purchases. You must leave yourself enough time to put the word out, let it permeate the market, and have enough time remaining for people to order or purchase and receive their tickets. You also have to give yourself enough time to react to the marketplace with new sales strategies should your initial marketing campaign produce fewer sales than expected.

A sample ticket sales time line for a hypothetical event scheduled for mid-June is illustrated in Figure 11-1. Before a single sale can be made, a ticket manifest must be finalized. The manifest lists every possible ticket number or seat location that can be sold, including standing room and seats identified as having obstructed views. It should also include every location that normally exists but may ultimately be removed from sale because of total obstruction, the installation of cameras, scoreboards, and other operational elements, or any other possible reason that a seat is not expected to be salable. These are known as "seat kills," and it is, of course, preferable to identify them so they may be removed from the manifest of tickets available for public sale well before the first ticket is sold. (Remember that if the tickets for killed seats are included in the event's gross potential, their removal from sale will represent an expense against the budget.) Print the tickets for killed seat locations anyway, just in case plans change later (e.g., camera positions are shifted) and those seats are ultimately unaffected by obstructions.

Note that in the example given in Figure 11-1, the primary public campaign begins on April 1, approximately ten weeks prior to the event. Four

February 1	Finalize ticket manifest
March 1	Past-year ticket buyers, staff, and volunteers receive E-mail, fax, and mail offer for advance tickets purchase before general public
April 1	Marketing and communication campaign begins to promote public ticket sales
April 15	Public ticket sales begin
May 23	Sponsor ticket promotions and second-wave marketing campaign (if necessary) begin
June 15	Event day

Figure 11-1
Sample Sports Event Ticket Sales Time Line

weeks before this date, an offer will be made to those listed in a database of past ticket buyers, staff, and volunteers, presumably the most loyal and likely purchasers. This offer can reward your best customers with preferred seat locations before tickets go on sale to the public, but if this kind of advance accommodation is offered, it is wise not to sell all of the best seats to those included in the presale database. It will be perceived as deceptive and unfair if the only seats available to the very first public ticket buyers are in less than prime locations. A common and fair practice, as applied to this sample event, would be to divide the tickets so that at least some portion of the best available seats will still be accessible to the public on April 1.

Just as important as not setting the "on sale" date too late (i.e., too close to the date of the event) is not promoting tickets sales too early. Events with unusually strong demand for tickets, such as Olympic Games, college and professional championship series (e.g., bowls, "final fours," etc.), and major league all-star contests, do not require adherence to this rule. Organizers for these uniquely successful events often make tickets available six, eight, or in some cases even ten months or more, in advance. For most sports events, however, it is important to time the initial public sale just right. Exactly when that should be will vary, depending on the nature and the date of the event. Note that the first day of public sales for this hypothetical event is in the early spring (April 1). In this case, the organizer believes that the best time to begin selling a warm-weather event is when potential ticket buyers first start thinking about the imminent approach of warmer weather. Attempting to sell the public a far-off, outdoor, warm weather event during the coldest days of winter, when sports fans are in the midst of enjoying indoor and more rugged outdoor events, may prove to be wasted effort. The database of past purchasers, however, can be approached by direct mail and E-mail campaigns at an earlier time. Their loyalty to the sport and their strong, positive memories of past events make them more likely to be future purchasers and perhaps more motivated to procure their tickets ahead of the public rush. In our hypothetical example, this group is granted a one-month window to order their tickets in advance. Although past purchasers may be given more time to respond, if desired, a relatively short advance sale opportunity is recommended, again to increase the sense of urgency. The longer a potential buyer is given to make his or her decision, the more likely the decision will be delayed or, possibly, forgotten completely.

HOW TO SELL TICKETS

As previously mentioned, it is essential to make it easy and convenient for potential buyers to purchase their tickets and to encourage them to act immediately. Today's sports event audiences are no longer accustomed to having to travel to the stadium or arena box office to purchase tickets. If they happen to be attending other events held in the same venue, or live or work nearby, however, the box office is certainly a convenient option that should not be overlooked.

A similar procedure is suggested for ticket sales to grassroots and community sports events that will be held in temporary facilities, or those that maintain no permanent box office. A single, reliably available location with regular business hours should be designated for ticket sales. A local merchant's retail location can be selected and promoted for this purpose. Even if the business owner makes no direct profit from ticket sales, the store traffic created by the sports event purchasers and the resulting incremental sales of the store's retail products can provide a strong incentive to participate as the event "box office." In addition, ticket sales may be promoted on banners and posters on display at the retailer's store, increasing exposure and sales for the sports event to the store's existing shoppers. This option is highly preferable to selling tickets for community sports events out of someone's home, as inconsistent hours of availability will reduce convenience for the potential buyer.

Most twenty-first-century sports fans, however, expect and demand the ability to purchase tickets without ever having to visit a box office. They want instant access to tickets at the time they see the first advertisement or read the first announcement, lest their response to the call to action be delayed or forgotten. Most permanent sports event facilities offer use of their computerized ticket services, such as via Ticketmaster (*www.ticketmaster.com*), Tickets.com (*www.tickets.com*), or a similar system. The fees for transactions using these services are typically shared between the seller and the purchaser and are usually defined in the facility lease agreement (see Play 4). These powerful services also offer event promoters the ability to offer ticket sales over the telephone, at remote locations throughout the host city, and via the Internet. It is wise to include the telephone number and web site address for the ticket service in every event advertisement, promotional coupon, and poster and to provide hyperlinks from the event organizer's web site directly to the ticket service's sales page.

Events that will be held in facilities with no permanent box office can attempt to negotiate an agreement with the dominant ticket services mentioned earlier to sell their tickets. Alternatively, you can take advantage of independent on-line ticketing services and software to manage your own electronic database of ticket inventory, provide fans with a convenient on-line mechanism to purchase their tickets, and maintain access to up-to-the-minute sales reports. Organizers may investigate the software and services offered by companies such as Tix.com (*www.tix.com*), InHouse Ticketing (*www.inhousetickets.com*), and Vendini (*www.vendini.com*), among others. (This mention of representative ticketing services and software does not imply an endorsement or recommendation by the author or publisher.)

Tickets ordered by phone or via the Internet, whether through an event facility's permanent system or a contracted independent service, are usually mailed to the purchaser upon completion of the transaction. If insufficient time remains between the date of purchase and the day of the event to be confident that tickets will be received in time (usually any less than two weeks), they may be printed by the service and left at the venue's "Will Call" window or at the organizer's "Guest Services" desk on event day. If tickets are to be picked up on-site or at the event's offices, it is strongly suggested that they be transferred to the buyer only after presentation of a government-issued photo identification card, such as a driver's license, and a matching signature to guard against possible fraud. Business cards should not be accepted as proof of identification.

Event organizers who can process electronic transactions on their own web sites can also investigate offering fans the ability to output tickets using their own personal printers. This increasingly popular option, which is already offered by many ticket services and sports facilities, provides the buyer with his or her tickets instantly. It also greatly reduces the organizer's costs of handling and shipping tickets.

TICKET BROKERS

Ticket brokers essentially resell tickets they purchase from the organizer, the box office, or from other buyers. The laws governing acceptable business practices of ticket brokers and the maximum fees they may legally charge the public vary widely from one local government to the other. Some may be officially authorized to sell event tickets by the organizer, but by far most operate outside any chain of direct responsibility. Many brokers maintain web sites that list all of the events for which they offer tickets, procured from a variety of sources. Organizers of successful sports events are constantly amazed at the extravagant prices brokers charge for tickets, particularly once the event is officially sold out. As long as the broker does not use the logo, proprietary artwork, or any other intellectual property of the event, there is usually nothing most organizers can do about what many perceive as unduly inflated ticket prices. At the same time, the organizer, having had no direct role in the transaction between the broker and the purchaser, bears no responsibility beyond the face value of the ticket. Therefore, if refunds are necessary for any reason, only the face value of the ticket need be recompensed. Brokers are generally honest, at least to the extent that the tickets they resell are genuine. There are, however, counterfeiters masquerading as ticket brokers who can perpetrate fraud against both the buyer and the organizer. The organizer has no obligation to accept counterfeit tickets obtained from such sources and should encourage those who purchased them to seek the assistance of local law enforcement.

DISTRIBUTION OF TICKETS TO FREE SPORTS EVENTS

Many sports events that embrace a free admission policy may still desire to distribute tickets in advance. Tickets serve as convenient reminders of the event's date and time and can easily be slipped into wallets and displayed under kitchen magnets. Tickets for a free sports event are usually best offered on a general admission basis; reserved seats are not recommended. Free tickets are not usually redeemed at the same rate as priced tickets, as the bearer has exchanged no money or other value for their use. Therefore, organizers often distribute as many as two, three, or even four times the number of free tickets as can normally be accommodated at the host facility in hope of filling it with spectators. This is not possible with reserved seats. It is a near certainty that a reserved seat ticket policy for a free event will result in a significant and noticeable number of empty seats. The exact multiple of free general admission tickets advisable to distribute for a given event should be based on past history, the attractiveness of the event to the public, and the experienced opinions of the facility director, the organizer, and other trusted stakeholders.

Regardless of the number distributed, it is strongly suggested that all tickets include a disclaimer to avoid overfilling the facility, such as: "This ticket is valid for admission on a first-come, first-served basis. The organizer and facility reserve exclusive the right to delay or deny admission based on crowding and concerns for public safety." To guard against overcapacity and to offer admission to fans not holding advance tickets if space permits, it is further suggested that tickets include an advisory that requires arrival at the event at least 30 minutes before it begins. Thus, late-arriving ticket holders may be denied entry if absolutely necessary to maintain safe conditions and the organizer is given the option of admitting non-ticket-holding fans in the final minutes leading up to the event in order to fill empty seats.

Free tickets may be distributed in all of the same ways that promotional material and discount coupons are provided to the community to encourage ticket sales. Point-of-purchase displays in area stores, tickets printed or inserted into newspapers, and print-your-own tickets over the Internet are particularly effective means of dispensing free tickets in the marketplace.

PACKAGING TICKETS

Organizers marketing sports events that are held over a series of days should consider creating packages containing tickets for multiple matches. Packages can include admission for the most attractive event day (e.g., the final round of a tournament) and for one or more dates that are expected to be less popular. This practice can increase ticket revenues and encourage improved attendance during times that may otherwise be expected to draw smaller crowds.

Consider selling multiday tickets ahead of the public offer for individual ticket sales to create urgency and provide the incentive of better seats for those purchasing packages.

Losing Sleep 101—What to Do If Tickets Aren't Selling

Your revenue budget is dependent on ticket sales. A well-placed advertisement has already appeared in the local newspaper, and press releases have been distributed to the media to announce the on-sale date. Yet it is frustrating that advance sales are slower than expected. Is it time to start panicking? Use the decision tree in Figure 11-2 to plan your most appropriate response.

Two courses of action—the reduction of seating inventory and the wide distribution of complimentary tickets, also known as "papering"—are approaches that should be employed after all marketing efforts have failed and the time remaining to sell tickets grows short. Complimentary tickets can still have a small positive effect on the net income of the event (or, in the case of disappointing sales, slightly reduce the net loss) through sales of merchandise and concessions, but will have the greatest effect on perception and public opinion. Simply put, they serve to make the audience appear larger and the popularity of the event greater. The practice of adjusting the reserved seat sales policy to skip every alternate row in the final days before the event [4c] can also make the audience appear larger.

REDUCTION OF INVENTORY [4A]

If large numbers of tickets are expected to remain unsold, organizers may decide to reduce the quantity of empty seats by closing off less desirable seating sections. This enables the organizer to save a small amount of money on the house staff (e.g., ushers, security, cleaning) that would have to service the area on event day. Guests who have purchased tickets in those areas may be moved to unsold seats in higher-priced sections, generally without any complaint from the public.

Events that are broadcast on television are usually seen from one primary direction. Try to fill the areas the television cameras will be facing first. If the event budget permits, cover empty seating sections with fabric or banners containing event artwork to turn a potential eyesore into pleasing décor. Better still, if seats are portable, consider physically removing selected rows and/or sections entirely.

Use this decision tree to plan your response to slow ticket sales. This model presumes that ticket prices are set at reasonable levels and are available to the public by convenient means. It also assumes that advertising and publicity campaigns, as well as the ticket sales date, were not set unreasonably early.

1. Is there still enough time left to sell the remaining tickets? *(YES—go to [1a] and [2]; NO—go to [4])*
   - **[1a.]** Did another sports or entertainment event compete for the fan's disposable income the week the ad was placed? *(YES—go to [1d]; NO—go to [1b])*
   - **[1b.]** Was the public preoccupied by a big news story the week tickets went on sale that diverted attention away from the offer? *(YES—go to [1d]; NO—go to [1c])*
   - **[1c.]** Does the current ad have a clear "call to action," communicate the urgency to buy, have all pertinent information, and have a convenient response mechanism for purchase? *(YES—go to [1d]; NO—go to [1g])*
   - **[1d.]** Is there more than one additional placement of the ad scheduled? *(YES—go to [1f]; NO—go to [1e])*
   - **[1e.]** **Action:** Consider running the ad again, or extending the campaign, and go to [4].
   - **[1f.]** Is the ad placed in print, radio, and/or television in places, at times and on programming the event's target audience will be expected to see? *(YES—go to [2]; NO—go to [1h])*
   - **[1g.]** **Action:** Make adjustments in the ad and buy additional space and/or time, and go to [2].
   - **[1h.]** **Action:** Consider purchasing additional advertising space and/or time in the media most likely to be read, heard, or seen by the event's target market, and go to [2].
2. Have past ticket buyers had time to receive and respond to their advance ticket offer? *(YES—go to [2a]; NO—go to [2b])*
   - **[2a.]** **Action:** Consider making follow-up phone calls or a second mailing to past ticket buyers. Go to [3].
   - **[2b.]** Don't panic yet! Go to [3].
3. Are sponsor promotions offering discounts on tickets already in the marketplace? *(YES—go to [3a]; NO—go to [3b])*
   - **[3a.]** **Action:** Request increased promotion by media partners, if available. Investigate adding other discount admission partners. Go to [4].
   - **[3b.]** **Action:** Don't panic yet! Consider moving up the introduction of sponsor promotions to an earlier start date. Go to [4].
4. Are far more tickets still available than can reasonably be expected to be sold at this point in time? *(YES—go to [4a]; NO—go to [4b])*
   - **[4a.]** **Action:** Consider reducing seating inventory. Close unsold seating or viewing areas in the facility to save on operational costs. Go to [4b].
   - **[4b.]** **Action:** Consider distributing a large quantity of complimentary tickets to deserving groups to make the event day audience appear more robust (called "papering" the house—see discussion to follow). Go to [4c].
   - **[4c.]** **Action:** Consider selling tickets, or distributing complimentary tickets, in every alternate row to make the audience appear larger, and then fill in the empty rows if sales subsequently increase. Go to [4d].
   - **[4d.]** **Action:** Review all other expense areas for potential reductions to compensate for the expected shortfall in revenues.

Figure 11-2
Decision Tree: Response to Slow Ticket Sales

PAPERING THE HOUSE [4B]

"Papering" the house, that is, issuing and distributing complimentary tickets to fill unsold seats is a last-minute, few-options-remaining strategy to make the event venue appear more fully occupied. If widely publicized, this practice can send a message to the public, and to sponsors, that either the event was not popular enough to support paid ticket sales or that it could not justify using a larger facility. It can create dissatisfaction among an event's most loyal guests—those who actually spent money to attend. In addition, once the process of papering the house begins and the availability of free tickets becomes publicly known, the event organizer can usually bid farewell to any possibility of significant incremental ticket revenues. So why do it?

If the event organizer is reasonably certain that all possible avenues to generate additional ticket sales have been exhausted, papering the house effectively can provide a number of advantages. Whether having purchased a ticket or attending for free, audience members also purchase merchandise, concession items, and parking. If the organizer benefits from the sales in these areas, some additional income can be generated from the incremental audience. This is particularly important if budget assumptions require a larger audience to achieve merchandise revenue expectations now that the pace of added ticket revenues appears to be slowing.

A large crowd also creates more fan excitement, motivates the athletes, makes sponsors happier, and makes guests feel that they are attending an event of sufficient importance to have warranted their time and interest. Sparse attendance is almost always mentioned in media reporting. If the program is a multiday sports event, papering earlier rounds can generate more widespread and positive word of mouth, as well as additional ticket sales for later dates. Finally, for a televised event, nothing says "This event is unimportant" more effectively than an empty grandstand.

Deciding to paper the house does not automatically solve these problems unless the strategy to distribute tickets is well reasoned and relatively discreet. The event promoter also has to guard against the most negative possibility of all: Complimentary tickets are widely distributed and the people who receive them still don't show up. Such circumstances say, "Even the people who could have attended for free didn't think it was worth the bother." Unless you are reasonably convinced that papering will generate the audience you need to enhance the overall experience, minimize embarrassment, and increase merchandise and other nonticket revenues, consider other less risky ways of making empty seats disappear, such as closing off and covering seating sections, before committing yourself to this last-ditch effort.

Distribute tickets to groups or through organizations that can be depended on to actually use them. Many communities have programs run through local government agencies that distribute event tickets to low-income and at-risk youth. If you use a ticket service such as Ticketmaster, keep in mind that local sales offices frequently maintain relationships with special charitable programs that can channel tickets to qualified, dependable not-for-profit groups. Blocks of tickets can also be distributed to area businesses through the local chamber of commerce and to hospitality industry employees, such as hotel and restaurant workers, through the convention and visitors bureau (CVB). Distribution of tickets to groups is much more efficient than trying to dispose of tickets one pair at a time. Consider inviting hospital workers, scout groups, and youth organizations. Think of youth leagues and recreational programs focused on the same sport celebrated by the event.

Event vendors may also be able to use tickets for the promotion of their own business objectives. You can host military personnel and their families by working through the public affairs officer at nearby installations, or members of the police, fire, sanitation, and other city departments through the city government or their unions. Try to salvage some positive benefit from the papering effort by selecting one or more of these groups to receive tickets you may not otherwise be able to sell, and issue a press release that turns the donation into a positive publicity story. Again, be sure that the groups to whom you make complimentary tickets available will have the time and ability to distribute them to people who will actually use them, so as to avoid creating sections that, although not empty, are only sparsely populated.

Many of the techniques used to reduce inventory can also be applied to papering. If the event is televised, make sure to concentrate your distribution efforts on the side of the facility facing the cameras to give the appearance of better attendance. Invite the families of technical crews and talent working on the television production to attend as guests of the organizer. If tickets are printed with reserved seating locations, you can also distribute complimentary tickets to seats in every alternate row.

TICKET BACKS

The backs of tickets are often used as marketing opportunities, such as for displaying the logos of presenting sponsors, bounce-back coupons, or promotions for merchandise and future events. Perhaps more important, the ticket back is frequently used for the inclusion of legal language that can cover a multitude of liability issues, including the right to eject the guest for inappropriate behavior, the right to use the purchaser's image in television coverage and future marketing materials, and, increasingly, the acknowledgment that the use of the ticket implies the guest's understanding that attendance at a sports event can possibly result in physical harm in the normal course of competition and presentation. The organizer's legal counsel must assess the need for any messages that should be included on the ticket back and draft all appropriate language. Computerized ticket services use standard legal language on the ticket backs and often do not offer any options for customizing a ticket's obverse side.

Guest Management

The audience of nearly every sports event will include guests who attend at the invitation of the event organizer, the host city, and other stakeholders. These invited guests may include sponsors, broadcasters, and other business partners whose agreements specify a number of tickets to which they are contractually entitled. They may also include individuals whose invitations serve as expressions of gratitude for noncontractual contributions to the success of an event. Tickets in appropriate seating locations should be removed from the event's inventory to satisfy contractual obligations before the first tickets are sold to the public. Other discretionary requirements for special guests should also be estimated before ticket sales begin. Use the information in Figure 11-3 to avoid overlooking some of your most important guest "audiences."

   Note that the figure includes entries for holding both complimentary tickets and tickets "for purchase." High-demand, high-profile, and charity-oriented events frequently invite the majority, or even all, of their guests to purchase tickets. Others invite guests on a complimentary basis to fulfill sponsorship obligations, express gratitude, and extend hospitality to both current and potential future business partners. Often, sponsors and other guests who

	Complimentary	For Purchase
☐ Sponsors, contractual	_____	_____
☐ Sponsors, guests	_____	_____
☐ Broadcasters, contractual	_____	_____
☐ Broadcasters, guests	_____	_____
☐ Host facility	_____	_____
☐ Promotional partners	_____	_____
☐ Players/athletes	_____	_____
☐ Coaches, officials, trainers	_____	_____
☐ Alumni	_____	_____
☐ Celebrities	_____	_____
☐ Host/organizing committee	_____	_____
☐ Local government officials	_____	_____
☐ Influential community contacts	_____	_____
☐ Prospective future partners	_____	_____
☐ Key vendors	_____	_____
☐ Organizer executives and staff	_____	_____
☐ Miscellaneous (house seats)	_____	_____

Figure 11-3
Guest Audience Checklist

are invited on a complimentary basis have additional needs, and the organizer fulfills these requests on a "for purchase" basis.

Sponsors and broadcasters often make up the largest percentage of guests. Be sure that every agreement defines the exact number of complimentary tickets each partner is entitled to receive, as well as how many may be purchased in addition. Review every agreement before tickets go on sale, and remove the required number of tickets from inventory. Figure 11-3 also suggests entries for sponsor and broadcaster "guests," that is, key partner contacts to whom the organizer would like to extend additional, personal courtesies without their attendance counting toward the contractually obligated allotment.

Key host city officials who play a direct or indirect role in the success of an event may also be invited to attend, but do not be surprised if they refuse an offer of complimentary tickets. Many local laws prohibit municipal and state employees from accepting gifts in excess of a certain value. As a consequence, you should take no offense when some government employees offer to purchase their tickets and others simply respond that they are unable to attend. Gifts of event tickets are also excellent expressions of gratitude for host or organizing committee members and influential community contacts who have proved helpful in the planning, marketing, and execution of the event. Don't overlook potential future business partners in the host city. Consider inviting the key marketing executives of both local and national companies headquartered in the area who may be solicited for future event partnership. Finally, has next year's sports event already been awarded to a new host city? Be sure to invite key contacts and gatekeepers from that community to witness event operations firsthand and begin to spark their interest and excitement.

Value-in-kind (VIK) deals with vendors and media partners frequently involve the transfer of event tickets, which should also be held back from the manifest prior to public sale. The organizer may also wish to invite key vendors who have provided outstanding service or unusual value to the event. Keep a reasonable supply of "house seats" on hand, tickets in good viewing locations for last-minute requests and invitations. It is wise to reduce this quantity as the day for the event gets closer, periodically returning unused house seat tickets to the inventory available to the public. By the day before the event, all but perhaps a handful of unassigned house seats should have been used, or released for public sale.

Feel free to expand the form in Figure 11-3 to include columns that note the number of tickets needed for ancillary events, such as parties, receptions, workshops, clinics, and player practices. The organizer would be best served by maintaining the form on a Microsoft Excel spreadsheet or, preferably, in a guest management database using Microsoft Access software or a proprietary database program, as described later in this chapter.

CONFLICT SEATS

Keep a quantity of tickets available on game day for "conflict seats." These tickets are actually used to *resolve* conflicts, such as reseating guests from areas that may have become unexpectedly obstructed by such elements as lighting towers, trusses, cameras, scoreboards, staging or decorative props. Tickets for seats that the organizer is able to identify in advance as obstructed-view locations, as well as standing-room tickets, should be sold with their limitations printed or stamped on the ticket front at the time of purchase, so conflict seats are not generally used for reseating these guests. Other uses for conflict seats include reseating guests upset by belligerent neighboring fans, reseating bearers of duplicate tickets for particular seats (a rarity with today's computer-generated tickets), or any number of discretionary purposes deemed appropriate by the front-of-house staff. Conflict seats are typically not returned to the box office for public sale, as they may be required at any point during the event. The host facility can recommend an adequate number of conflict seats to hold, based on its size and experience.

Guest Management Systems

A system of guest management encompasses more than the simple compiling of an invitation list, sending invitations, and assigning tickets to those who accept the offer. Whether the needs of guests are maintained on index cards, in a loose-leaf notebook, or in an electronic database, organizers must constantly monitor and manage these requirements, right up to event day. Administering the guest management process efficiently is of paramount importance. Money, goodwill, and reputation are at stake when inviting and hosting these influential individuals. Current sponsors and business partners expect a flawless sports event experience in recognition of their participation, and the generation of future business may in part depend on the organizer's exhibiting his or her proven guest management skills and capabilities.

The larger the guest list, the more imperative it is to organize the guest management process electronically. This will give the organizer the ability to access information easily, eliminate duplicate invitations and ticket assignments, generate management summaries, and include a more comprehensive record of information for each invited guest, such as portrayed in Figure 11-4.

The guest management database includes a record of each individual invited. These individuals are frequently divided into "audiences," categorical descriptions of the types of organizations they represent. Typical audience categories include many of those listed in Figure 11-3, but may be expanded or subdivided as the event and its guest list require. If the database is particularly

```
 1 Audience
 2. Name
 3. Title
 4. Company
 5. Address
 6. Phone
 7. Fax
 8. E-Mail
 9. Assistant Name
10. Date Invitation Sent
11. Date of Most Recent Follow-Up
12. Date Response (RSVP) Received
13. # Tickets Invited
14. # Tickets Provided
15. Comp or Purchase
16. Payment Information
17. Seat Location
18. Ancillary Event Tickets
19. Date Tickets Mailed
20. Pickup Authorization (i.e., who is al-
    lowed to pick up this guest's tickets)
21. Ground Transportation
    a. Arrival Information (airport, flight,
       time)
    b. Departure Information
22. Hotel Room Type
23. Hotel
24. Other Guests in Room
25. Credit Card
26. Gift
27. Invited By
28. Notes
```

Figure 11-4
Guest Management Database Record
Composition

large, the management of individual audiences may be divided among the event staff members who most often interact with those invited to attend (but cross-reference all lists of invited guests to avoid duplications).

The guest database is a powerful, permanent record that can also increase future efficiency, serving as the basis for compiling invitation lists for subsequent sports events as well. For these reasons, it is important to include as much information in each record as possible. Request that invited guests provide the data for items (or "fields") 2 through 9 to ensure that you have the most up-to-date contact information. Track the invitation process in fields 10 through 12. If a follow-up letter, phone call, fax, or E-mail is sent because no response was received by the requested deadline, indicate the most recent attempt at communication in item 11. Fields 13 through 17 initially indicate how many tickets are being held, and ultimately provided, for the guest, the seat locations assigned, whether they are provided gratis or on a paid basis, and whether payment has been received. If tickets to additional events, such as parties or hospitality programs, are to be provided, the number required should be inserted in item 18. It is recommended that separate fields be assigned for each ancillary event, providing the organizer with the flexibility of inviting each guest to only the activities desired.

In cases where sports event tickets are of significant monetary value, the organizer may be advised not to mail tickets to the invited guests, but, rather, request that they pick up their tickets on-site, either at the box office "will call" window or at an organizer's "guest services desk." Tickets may be lost in transit, and the use of overnight delivery or bonded messenger services can add considerable operational expenses. Some guests who have received their tickets in advance may arrive at the venue with their tickets still atop a dresser or left in their hotel rooms. Be sure to have access to the database and vouchers ready at the guest services desk on which to copy the seat locations for guests who arrive without their tickets.

It is also wise to establish a policy regarding who will be permitted to pick up a guest's tickets. It is recommended that guests pick up their tickets personally, upon presentation of valid photo identification such as a driver's license or passport. Many important guests, particularly celebrities, government officials, and senior executives, may find it inconvenient or undesirable to pick up tickets themselves. A representative may be identified to the organizer and authorized in advance by the guest, via fax or E-mail, to receive tickets in his or her place (field 20). This representative should also produce acceptable identification and sign a log or receipt upon acceptance. As previously stated, business cards alone should never be accepted as a valid form of identification or authorization.

The guest management database can also assist in the administration of transportation systems (21) and hotel accommodations (22–25), as well as any other special program or privilege, such as the distribution of gifts to selected guests (26). Any additional information that suits the organizer's purposes may be included in the database, such as the name of the staff member who invited the guest (27), along with miscellaneous notes of interest (28).

The great power of an electronic guest management database is manifest in the organizer's ability to sort information by any individual field. Management reports can be generated identifying only "Players and Athletes," or just those guests requiring hotel rooms, individuals invited on a complimentary basis, or those invited by a particular staff member. In addition to the use of off-the-shelf software options such as Microsoft Excel spreadsheet and Microsoft Access database programs, there are a host of more specialized electronic solutions. These include on-line event registration services and web-based software, some incorporating modules for the management of guest accommodations, such as those available from Cvent (*www.cvent.com*), ePly (*www.eply.com*), Kavi (*www.kavi.com/solutions/*) and 123 Sign-Up (*www.123signup.com*). (This mention of these on-line and software suppliers does not imply an endorsement or recommendation by the author or publisher of this book.) These companies primarily service corporate and association events, but some of their services are easily adaptable to small and mid-size sports and recreational events, particularly for the registration of athletes and teams.

MANAGEMENT OF ATHLETES AND PLAYERS

For most sports experiences, there simply is no event without the athletes. Players and athletes should be managed like the most important of VIP guests. Make them feel appreciated, and their enthusiasm and excitement, their professionalism in meeting the media and other important guests, and their physical performances will shine through. The players, whether they are a group of 10-year-old track competitors, a team of college footballers, or members of a professional hockey club, are the ultimate ambassadors for their sports and the events in which they compete. They are the attraction the public comes to see and, in most instances, represent everything that is positive and good in sports. Therefore, no discussion on guest management would be complete without including these most important guests—the athletes and their own guests and families. Manage them with the respect and treatment they deserve, and they will come prepared to compete with clear and focused minds.

What athletes want most of all is to perform to their highest potential. Try to make the event a memory of a lifetime, if not only for their performance, then also for the experience. Make sure that their families feel the admiration as well. Consider staging special events just for them. Allow families to attend practices, and provide them with the best viewing areas that can be made available. If player appearances at additional sponsor or fan events are part of their participation, transport the players to the event facility in style. Ensure that they arrive early enough to stay on schedule, but not so early that they sit around waiting to participate. Make certain that there are healthful refreshments available in an attractively decorated waiting area ("green room") before their appearance. Try not to schedule players for so many appearances, or for such lengthy durations, that they tire before their athletic performance. Respect any physical routines they must adhere to leading up to the event (e.g., practices, aerobic workouts, weight training) before scheduling other activities.

Sports event organizers who require athletes to make special appearances should also consider hosting a private reception, postgame meal, or party, or open a hospitality lounge that is exclusive to players and their families, an oasis from the frantic atmosphere surrounding most events. Use the same guest management system to track the arrivals, departures, hotel accommodations, ticketing, and gift needs used for your most important guests. You may even add their uniform and equipment needs, ground transportation requirements, and ancillary event appearances as additional fields in the database.

COMMUNICATING WITH GUESTS

Communicate with your guests to ensure that they have all pertinent event information before they leave home and when they arrive at the event. Send a confirmation letter with preliminary event information after receiving an indication of their attendance. Include instructions on how to book rooms at the event's headquarters hotel, information on ground transportation options in the host city, and a hotline number for last-minute changes to arrival plans. Create a password-controlled web page that guests can access for up-to-the minute information on event developments and reprints of pre-event newspaper coverage. Publish a welcome package to be given to the guest upon checking in at their hotel or when they pick up their tickets, including a convenient pocket-sized event information guide containing final activity schedules, event office locations and telephone numbers, transportation schedules, dining and entertainment options, and discounts offered by local businesses. Open an information desk in each headquarters hotel lobby. In short, never leave the guest in a position where he or she neither knows the answer to a question, nor how to get one.

Hotel Management

Sports events that draw participants and guests from outside the host community must usually enter into a relationship with at least one host hotel. Hotels start to make their money on "heads in beds," but those heads also have mouths that eat in their restaurants, drink in their bars, and talk over their telephone systems. Guests work on rented high-speed DSL lines in the hotels' sleeping rooms, attend dinners and parties in their ballrooms, and use audiovisual services in their conference facilities. Moreover, a hotel's catering department provides meal and refreshment services to all of these functional areas.

WHAT HOTELS REALLY WANT FROM EVENTS

Most hotels want to attract groups that they know will fill sleeping rooms and generate restaurant and catering revenue. Sports events, like corporate conferences and conventions, that can fill as much as 70 to 80 percent of their total capacity are most welcome if they bring major food and beverage events, such as parties and dinners, along with them. Hotels rarely offer more than 80 percent of their rooms to a single group, so as to reduce their risk in case of a poor turnout and to ensure that they have a supply of guestrooms for what hotels call their "transient" guests—their loyal and frequent business travelers. In addition, many hotels have contractual agreements in place that guarantee a certain number of rooms to airline crews, visiting guests or transferring employees of local corporations, and members of other organizations year-round. The more long-term contracts a hotel has in place, the lower the percentage of rooms it will be able to make available for the guests and staff of one-time events.

Hotels are in the wagering business. They bet on the success of an event by agreeing to hold a certain number of rooms for the group's use. However, they do not want to commit to holding rooms for an event if the organizer is not equally, and contractually, obligated to use them. To improve their odds of success, hotels routinely investigate an event's "pickup history," the number of rooms the organizer has actually used in the past as compared with the number that were originally held, by calling previous host cities and properties. A high percentage of actual usage makes an event highly desirable and will encourage the hotel to offer an organizer a greater number of rooms. A poor pickup percentage may cause a hotel to either offer fewer rooms or pass on participating at all. Hotels want event organizers to constantly monitor their expected needs and to advise them as early as possible if the program will not require as many rooms as were requested. If a hotel holds rooms for a sports event that do not materialize into occupancy by guests, they want to be compensated for lost business.

WHAT EVENTS REALLY WANT FROM HOTELS

Organizers are also in the wagering business. They want to ensure that the selected hotels will hold the number of rooms they will require to accommodate their athletes, guests, and staff at the lowest possible level of financial risk. They want the best available accommodations at the lowest possible rate, and polite, attentive service for their guests. The quality of a sports event's selected host hotel reflects directly on the overall event experience. Athletes and guests who encounter accommodations of poor quality or inferior service will have equally poor memories of their attendance at the event.

Sports event organizers also need places to work. They require hospitality suites to meet and greet their guests, as well as rooms for participant registration, ticket distribution, transportation dispatching, and information dissemination. If the event is being held in a city distant from their home offices, they will want to convert some hotel meeting rooms into full-service offices, with workspaces that feature telephones and data lines, fax machines, computers, printers, and copiers.

Some sports events require too many rooms to be accommodated in a single hotel. Although guests may be dispersed among multiple host properties, organizers most often concentrate their functional offices and staff in one "headquarters hotel." When organizers need to use more than one hotel, they prefer them to be adjacent to one another, or within a reasonable walk, to avoid having to allocate funds to shuttle guests and staff between more distant properties. If a large number of hotels are required, organizers prefer they be located in clusters to similarly minimize shuttle transportation costs.

Unless the event is limited to using a specific property because of a sponsorship agreement with a particular hotel, organizers should inspect as many hotels as possible to compare overall quality, rates, service features, and business policies. The local CVB or sports commission can save the organizer's staff a significant amount of time by coordinating inspection visits, or "site surveys," of hotel properties that it believes meet the stated needs of the event, from overall quality to guest room and space availability and the interest of a property in being considered as a host hotel. During a site survey, which will average 1½ to 2 hours, the organizer will have an opportunity to evaluate the hotel on a wide range of criteria, such as those that are listed in Figure 11-5 and described in the following section.

EVALUATING AND NEGOTIATING WITH HOTELS

Among the first characteristics to evaluate is the geographic desirability of the hotel's location. Is it adjacent to, or reasonably close enough to the event site to provide participants and guests easy access? If the hotel is not close to the host facility, the organizer may need to establish a shuttle transportation system. Transportation systems are most cost-efficient when a single bus or van within a fleet may be used for multiple trips. The farther the hotel(s), the fewer round trips each vehicle will be able to make per hour, and the greater the number of vehicles that will be needed. Is the hotel in an attractive location within the host city or on the edge of an economically depressed area? Sometimes it is preferable to sacrifice proximity to the event site for a more pleasant or attractive location.

Based on both personal visual inspection and ratings of independent hotel evaluation services (e.g., Mobil Travel Guide, Automobile Club of America, Fodor's Travel Guides, etc.), is the property of a quality and reputation that will reflect well on the sports event? How well is the property maintained, and when were the guest rooms, meeting rooms, and public spaces last renovated? Will some invited guests require a more elegant hotel, and others a more value-oriented property? If so, should the group be split in two or more subgroups, based on their price and quality sensitivities?

Is the hotel prepared to hold an adequate number of guest rooms, suites, and meeting and reception rooms for the event's guests? Until a hotel has a signed contract for the rooms, it will place them "on hold," a nonbinding

☐ Geographic location
☐ Overall hotel quality (via independent ratings and visual inspection)
☐ Suitability of rooms
☐ Sufficient rooms and suites available on 1st hold
☐ Room rates
☐ Suite rates
☐ Complimentary room ratio
☐ Function space availability
☐ Function space rates
☐ Telephone and data line installation charges
☐ Business center services
☐ Shipping & receiving charges
☐ Room service hours
☐ Health club facilities and charges
☐ Room drop charges
☐ VIP amenities
☐ Sponsor sensitivities
☐ Newspaper delivery
☐ Valet parking availability
☐ Parking rates
☐ Hotel-controlled television channel
☐ Signage policies
☐ Supplier exclusivities (e.g., audio-visual, security, rentals, decorators)
☐ Deposit and payment schedule
☐ Cancellation policy
☐ Attrition policy

Figure 11-5
Host Hotel Evaluation Checklist

agreement to provide the rooms until a specified deadline date for a final contract—unless someone else signs a contract first. The total of all rooms reserved over all pre-event, event, and post-event days is called a "room block." It is standard practice for a hotel to contact event organizers holding rooms that are not yet contracted if another group expresses interest in contracting over the same period. The hotel usually offers the organizer an opportunity to formally commit to using the rooms in the block before entering into a contract with another party, but will release the hold if the organizer does not agree in a timely manner. It is also standard practice for hotels to put a "second hold" on rooms, which will entitle the second group to automatically claim the rooms should the first decide to release its hold or fail to enter into a contract.

What percentage of the rooms will be paid for directly by the event, and what percentage by the guests? Are the rates within an acceptable price range for the purchaser? Few groups pay the standard "rack rate" for sleeping rooms. The more rooms an organizer will commit to using and the more catered events they will hold at the hotel, the more negotiable the room rate will become. Will suites be required by the event for important sponsor guests, celebrities, athletes, performers, or senior executives, and are a sufficient number of adequately sized suites available? Hotels usually offer a number of complimentary rooms for the organizer's use based on the number of rooms actually used. This ratio, which is somewhat negotiable, is usually in the area of 1 complimentary room for every 45 to 50 paid rooms (suites are often counted as two or more rooms). Try to negotiate an additional room or suite on a complimentary basis for one or more of the organizer's top executives and a number of free upgrades to higher-priced rooms, subject to availability.

Does the hotel offer an adequate amount of space for the various hospitality events (e.g., dinners, luncheons, parties, award ceremonies, and meetings) the organizer wants to host at the property? Is there sufficient space for event office needs over the dates required for setup, pre-event preparation, and the post-event dismantling period? Every hotel has a standard rental rate for its meeting and ballroom spaces, but many will waive these rates if the event commits to a large enough number of guest rooms or a guaranteed amount of catering over the course of the stay. The cost of meeting room rentals can be a considerable, but often avoidable, expense and is often a strong enough reason to select one hotel over another as a suitable host.

The installation of telephone and data lines in hotel meeting rooms can also be surprisingly expensive. Negotiate the best possible installation rate per line, and request the ability to make local and toll-free long distance access number calls at no cost. Organizers can purchase prepaid telephone cards or use telephone credit cards at a fraction of the cost of hotel long-distance charges, particularly if toll-free access is complimentary. Internet access over high-speed data lines, such as DSL and T-1 services, are becoming increasingly essential to sports event organizers using web-based guest management systems or requiring remote computer access to their home office servers for retrieving E-mail. These services are also much more time-efficient than dial-up modems and should be seriously considered for hotel-based event offices. Although many hotels now offer high-speed Internet access from guest rooms for a flat daily rate, the installation of DSL and T-1 lines in meeting rooms will likely incur an additional installation charge.

Have staff travel with laptop computers, if possible, to avoid the high costs of renting desktop units. Rent printers if necessary, but make sure they arrive with the CD-ROM disk that contains the proper printer driver codes for installation on the laptops. Productivity and efficiency will be greatly increased if the budget can accommodate the rental of copiers, facsimile machines, and printers for the hotel-based offices, rather than having to rely on the hotel's business center. Guests, particularly sponsors and other business partners, however, will often require access to the hotel business center for many of these services, as well as for shipping, overnight couriers, and the use of computers. If your needs do not warrant the costs of installing equipment in your meeting room office, try to negotiate preferred rates and extended hours of operation for the business center.

Are there charges for receiving event materials shipped to the hotel and delivered to the meeting rooms? If these charges cannot be negotiated away, will the hotel agree to a flat or maximum daily fee for received packages and faxes? Are there service charges for shipping materials from the hotel as well? Will the hotel permit courier and freight companies to pick up prepaid shipments without a service charge?

Room service hours, where available, should be compared with the times that guests and staff will most likely make use of in-room dining, particularly during late hours after non-meal events have concluded. Hotels will often extend hours at the organizer's request if the property can reasonably expect to profit from this accommodation. Are high-quality health-conscious menu items that appeal to guests available? Some hotels may offer to provide special late-night, event-themed items and healthful food selections, promoted on special in-room menus during the event. Sports events generally attract health-conscious athletes, fans, and guests, so access to fitness facilities is also usually expected. Is there a facility located on the property with a sufficient quantity of aerobic and weight-training equipment in good working order, or is there a health club nearby with which the hotel has an access agreement? Is there a charge for using the facilities, and if so, can it be negotiated to enable event guests to enjoy the privileges on a complimentary basis? If the facility is not available 24 hours a day, is it open at times that are reasonable when compared with the event schedule? Can extended hours be negotiated?

Organizers may be planning to communicate with their guests by delivering information packets, letters of welcome, or newsletters to their rooms. Surprise gifts such as T-shirts, caps, or a basket of sponsor products can await guests returning to their rooms after the event. Most hotels charge a fee for these "room drops," which can range from $1.00 to $3.00 per delivery, depending on the size or weight of the items delivered.

A less expensive alternative is to staff a guest information desk in the lobby of the hotel for the distribution of daily information. In addition, most hotels will not charge for the distribution of information packets to guests upon check-in. The organizer can request that the hotel recognize a certain number of the most important guests with special welcoming amenities, such as the delivery of a themed basket of goodies, a plate of dry snacks, chocolates, fruit, beverages, or a souvenir cap, pennant, or T-shirt. Most hotels will agree to offer these warm welcomes to a limited number of the event's guests, as identified by the organizer, at the property's expense. Make sure that the hotel is aware of sponsor sensitivities so that it does not greet sponsor guests with a basket of their competitor's products. Be aware of the hotel's own sponsorship agreements, although most hotels will agree to serve a sports event sponsor's products even if they have existing agreements with a competitor company.

Will the hotel deliver newspapers to the event's guests each morning? Can the organizer specify a particular newspaper, such as the event's print partner? Are valet parking and self-parking options available, and if so, at what cost? Try to secure a number of complimentary parking spaces for staff vehicles or courtesy vans, in convenient locations if possible.

Is there an available channel on the hotel's in-room television system for the organizer's own programming? Some hotels permit organizers to run videotapes of past sports event highlights, present information on Microsoft Powerpoint slides, and offer other entertainment or information to all guest rooms on an open television channel. There is usually a charge for this service.

What are the policies regarding decorative, informational, or directional signage in the hotel lobby, on the building exterior, and in other public spaces? Some hotels will permit freestanding signage that posts event and transportation schedules and directs guests to various event offices. Will the property permit the organizer to hang decorative welcome banners, display trophies, and outfit front desk staff, bellpersons, doorpersons, and waitstaff in event caps, golf shirts, or jackets? Some hotels welcome this level of staff participation, whereas others will restrict staff to wearing lapel pins.

Finally, are there exclusive suppliers that the organizer must use inside the hotel property? At minimum, hotels generally insist on providing all food and beverages and telephone services on their campuses. Does the hotel require union electricians to distribute power or to install lighting for parties and hospitality events? Is the organizer obligated to use the in-house audiovisual company, or can needs be bid out to others? In-house vendors with exclusive rights to provide these services will almost always be more expensive than those who must compete with companies that can be brought in from the outside. Can the organizer hire an outside security company to protect the event's guests and assets, or must all security be arranged through the hotel?

ATTRITION AND CANCELLATION CLAUSES

Perhaps the most sensitive and financially risky points of negotiation are the hotel's policies on room attrition and cancellation. An attrition penalty is incurred when the number of guest rooms used by an event falls below an agreed-to percentage of the contracted number. Cancellation penalties, of course, are encountered if the organizer cancels the entire agreement after the contract is signed.

As previously discussed, the hotel wants to assume the least risk of being left with unused, non-revenue-producing sleeping rooms, and the organizer wants to take on the least risk in having to pay for them. Hotels generally refuse to be bound to hold rooms without defining financial penalties for organizers who cancel their agreements or fail to fill all or the vast majority of rooms they contract. Although the penalties may seem unusually onerous, this is a necessary business practice for the hotel. Consider this, sports event organizers: Would you allow another business to hold event tickets indefinitely without paying for them, understanding that even though there is demand for those tickets, there is a chance they will be returned unused and unpaid for? Hotels need these safeguards to maintain their business; at the same time, event organizers need to minimize the financial risk of encountering cancellation or attrition penalties.

As a result, hotels will generally pressure organizers to get contracts signed, and organizers will try to delay executing formal agreements as long as possible. This dynamic is sometimes reversed when an event is of such great regional, national, or international importance that a city expects a large influx of travelers who are not part of the organizer's room block, or when a particular hotel is strongly desired by an organizer because of its quality, convenience, or value. In these cases, the organizer will want to protect a room block at preferred rate, while some hotel managers resist, preferring to fill their rooms with individual travelers, presumably at a more lucrative room rate. As surprising as it may sound, some hotels simply prefer not to participate in sports event group bookings, or will hold only small-sized room blocks, because they operate at high percentages of occupancy and at rates they need not negotiate.

Once a hotel contract is signed, it indicates that both parties are betting on the success of the other. It also means that the organizer is fully aware of the potential financial impact of the prevailing attrition and cancellation clauses. Thus, when it is time to execute an agreement, be sure the event is unlikely to be canceled or postponed and that you hold only those rooms that you truly believe will be needed. Penalty provisions aside, a hotel contract actually works in the sports event organizer's favor—it does not permit the hotel to cancel or reduce the size of the room block. It may, however, allow the organizer to periodically reduce the size of the room block by a specified percentage without penalty on defined deadline dates well in advance of the event.

Be particularly vigilant in regard to how cancellation and attrition penalties are calculated. Some are calculated on the total number of room-nights held during the contract period, or on the quantity of rooms contracted for what is called the "peak-night," the night when the number of a sports event's guests is at maximum. Some agreements will demand payment not only for the unoccupied rooms, but also for an estimated amount of lost income from food and beverage operations. Organizers should attempt to assume only the risk for the rooms themselves, as the amounts of lost income from food and beverage operations are simply assumptions that cannot be substantiated. Most attrition penalties are activated when the total room pickup falls below 80 to 90 percent of the contracted room-nights, a percentage that the organizer should attempt to reduce as much as possible during negotiations. Smaller and more upscale hotels, however, frequently insist on an even greater percentage of pickup, some as high as 100 percent. These penalties will be assessed during the settlement of the bill after the event.

Cancellation penalties, however, are payable immediately upon termination of the contract. The percentage of room revenue for which the organizer is responsible will increase at contractually defined deadline dates, beginning as low as 10 percent of room revenue upon execution of the contract, increasing to 25 percent perhaps a year in advance, then periodically to 50 percent, 75 percent, and up to 100 percent if the rooms are cancelled just before event day. Again, the contract proposed by the hotel may suggest that penalties include estimated food and beverage income, which the organizer should attempt to negotiate out of the agreement. If dinner functions, parties, and other hospitality events are included in the contract, some hoteliers will attempt to include some portion of the projected revenue for these functions in the cancellation penalty. Event organizers should resist this inclusion, as no expenses are incurred against these programs by the hotel until very close to the event (i.e., the hotel does not purchase food or contract labor for the hospitality function until just days before it occurs).

An essential element to include in the contract relating to cancellation and attrition is a provision stating that if rooms are released by the organizer and subsequently resold by the hotel to other groups or to the public, the value received for those rooms will be deducted from the organizer's penalty. Requesting this inclusion is reasonable and puts no one at a financial disadvantage, as the hotel suffers no financial hardship if the rooms that were contracted, but unused by the organizer's group, are eventually sold to others. Without this provision, the organizer would remain totally unprotected against attrition, but the hotel could enjoy the benefits of essentially being paid twice for the same room.

DEPOSITS

Like many business agreements, hotel contracts often include a request for a nonrefundable deposit of 10 to 20 percent of the total value of the rooms on hold upon execution of the contract. If paying this deposit is unavoidable, it can be applied to satisfying the event's "master account," a tally of all charges that will be paid by the organizer during settlement of the bill after the event. The size of the deposit is frequently negotiable if the organizer can produce evidence of an excellent credit history, or if most of the room block will be paid for directly by the event's guests.

It is advisable to set up a master account regardless of who is paying for the guest rooms. The organizer can specify which staff or guest rooms should be billed to the master account. It is recommended that organizers authorize only room and tax charges for these rooms so that incidentals, such as room service and restaurant charges, shop purchases, pay-per-view movies, laundry, telephone, and other fees, are paid by the occupants and selectively reimbursed after a thorough review of their expense reports. Master account charges may also include fees for catered meetings and receptions, telephone installation and event office costs, delivery and room drop charges, business center usage, and other operational expenses.

Managing Hotel Operations for Sports Events

Once the hotel contract is signed, the property's sales department will take a less active role in the event, replaced by convention services and reservations department representatives who will remain in contact with the organizer on a daily basis. The convention services contact will work with the organizer on the assignment and installation of office, hospitality, and reception facilities and will often coordinate the event organizer's catering needs.

The reservations department will work with the organizer to manage the room block and guest registration. Many organizers prefer to manage the room block by requiring guests to arrange for hotel accommodations through them (the organizers). This is particularly useful when a number of host hotels are involved. The organizer can assign guests and participants to the hotels that are most appropriate for them, or can distribute the audience to properties that require the greater number of occupied rooms to avoid attrition penalties. It is also the best way to identify the guests who have indicated their intention to attend, but who have failed to make reservations. Event staff can contact these individuals to determine their housing needs as the deadline date to release the sleeping rooms approaches.

The organizer will then generate a "rooming list" for the hotels through the event's guest management database, updating the hotels with changes throughout the pre-event period. Be sure to work with the reservations department to ensure that the rooming list has all of the information it requires, and to determine how best and often to inform them of the inevitable changes to the list.

If guests are given the responsibility of making reservations directly with the hotel(s), provide them with a code that will identify them as belonging to the event. The hotel can then provide a rooming list to the organizer, indicating who has made reservations within the block. It is essential to regularly and vigilantly compare this list with the names in the guest management system to ensure that all event guests staying in the hotel have identified themselves as belonging to the block. Those who make reservations in their assigned hotel but are not identified as event guests may not be credited to the room block, which may result in the assessment of an otherwise avoidable attrition penalty. Organizers should provide guests with a reservation deadline well ahead of the key date to release rooms, as defined in the hotel contract. Fix a response deadline that is at least two weeks ahead of the release date to give event staff an opportunity to contact those who have not yet appeared on a rooming list.

Finally, it is standard procedure to provide gratuities to hotel employees dedicated to the success of your event. The hotel sales manager can recommend the customary range of cash gratuities that may be offered to the convention services manager, catering managers, bell staff, and others.

Hotels and organizers have a common objective, ensuring that their guests enjoy the best possible sports event experience. The hotel's convention services department will create a resume of important information for the entire hotel staff regarding the event's operations at the property, which the organizer should review for accuracy. The convention services contact will also schedule a "pre-con" (preconvention) meeting a few days before the majority of the event's guests arrive. Among those invited will be key organizer personnel and the property's departments heads (e.g., housekeeping, security, bell staff, room service, front desk, etc.) to ensure a direct and consistent flow of information between the two partners. The pre-con meeting is an excellent forum to express appreciation for the staff's hard work to come and to surface any questions or concerns about the hotel service encountered to date. If the event has any policies regarding athletes or other guests (e.g., no autographs), this is the appropriate forum in which to communicate them. Leave the staff feeling excited, appreciated, and committed to success, and the organizer's guests will enjoy their stay as much as the event itself.

Post-Play Analysis

Marketing campaigns should focus on selling tickets in advance to enhance attendance and revenues. Design these campaigns to establish a sense of urgency, but allow enough time for the public to respond. Set a ticket policy—reserved seats or general admission—that best serves the needs of your sports event. If tickets do not sell well, a number of options may be considered to make the event venue appear more full, including the reduction of seating inventory and the distribution of complimentary tickets, also known as "papering." Be sure to remove tickets required for business partners, athletes, and invited guests from those to be sold, before sales begin.

Keep track of all guest needs by establishing a guest management system that works best for your event. This database will indicate whether guests have accepted their invitations and what tickets they will receive to which activities; it will include arrival information, accommodations assignments, and more. Athletes and event participants can often be managed using the same system, adding special activities, perquisites, and equipment needs as additional fields that are customized just for them.

Communicate with your guests and ensure that they have all pertinent event information, such as activity and transportation schedules, dining and entertainment options, maps, and important telephone numbers. Consider publishing a guide, as well as an Internet page, to provide easy access to the essential information required during their visit as well as ahead of time. Carefully evaluate hotels under consideration as host and headquarters properties. Negotiate the best contract possible, and hold only the number of rooms you are reasonably sure you will use. Financial penalties for using far fewer rooms than contracted, or for canceling a hotel deal, can be significant.

Coach's Clipboard

1. Ticket sales for a national skateboard competition, which were brisk at first, have slowed dramatically. Approximately 50 percent of the available tickets have been sold, but the budget had estimated 70 percent. With two weeks remaining until the event, what plans should be considered to balance the budget and fill the venue? Assume that one half-page advertisement is already scheduled to appear in the local newspaper on the weekend of the event.

2. A regional track and field event is best viewed from a section of existing bleachers that is open to the public. What viewing options can be considered to accommodate the attendance of sponsor guests?

How would you begin to design a similar area on a public beach for a surfing competition?

3. A beachfront resort hotel would provide excellent accommodations for important guests traveling to the host city for your event, but the director of sales resists negotiating for preferred rates or anything less than 95 percent pickup before an attrition penalty begins to apply. Although guests will be responsible for their own charges, the organizer will remain liable for the unoccupied rooms. The event venue is located 20 minutes away by shuttle bus. What options should you explore to minimize the event's financial exposure?

Presenting Your Event

There is no separation between sports and entertainment, as far as I'm concerned . . . merge them together and create something unique.

—ROBERT JOHNSON,
OWNER OF THE NBA CHARLOTTE BOBCATS,
AT THE 2003 INTERNATIONAL CONFERENCE ON SPORT AND ENTERTAINMENT BUSINESS

Crafting the Sports Event Presentation Plan

Today's sports event organizers recognize that audiences have certain minimum expectations when they attend a sports event. When people come to watch their favorite athletes, they expect to be able to see every moment and nuance of the performances and to share in the emotional excitement. They come to participate vicariously in the players' victories, to demonstrate their admiration with displays of appreciation, approval, encouragement, and support through hearty applause and throaty cheers. To enhance their sense of participation and enable them to react with knowledgeable enthusiasm, audiences want to be able to visually comprehend, evaluate, and judge the progress of the contest. They want as much information as possible, rosters, official results, statistics, and the other interpretive data that can enhance and enrich their viewing experience. Finally, they also want to be entertained. They want to feel they are personally involved and witnessing something unique and important,

To meet the minimum expectations of the audience, sports events must be presented so that fans are . . .

- Able to see the competitors they came to watch
- Able to visually comprehend the progress of the event or competition
- Kept informed of official results and critical information
- Kept excited and entertained

Figure 12-1
Basic Requirements of Sports Event Presentation

perhaps even historic. Regardless of the eventual outcome, a sports event must present an experience worth the fan's entertainment dollar.

It is not coincidental that the basic requirements of the live sports experience summarized in Figure 12-1 embrace philosophies that are similar to those underlying the way an event is presented on television. Sports event broadcasts inject the viewer into the competition, establishing an intimacy between the audience and the athlete. Cameras remove distance, capturing the facial expressions that register accomplishment and disappointment, achievement and frustration. Announcers describe the progress of play, provide insightful analysis, and project opinion as to how the athletes and their coaches can respond to competitive challenges. Videotape replays reverse time to allow both announcers and audiences to dissect and evaluate a team's, or athlete's, performance. Hosts familiarize the viewer with the athletes, provide pertinent background information, present statistics, and summarize the event upon conclusion. Exciting music, colorful graphics, and the skillful direction of camerawork keep viewers sufficiently engaged and entertained to ensure that they remain glued to their television screens even during commercial breaks.

Whether they are televised or not, the most entertaining sports events are those that embrace the same production values, logical flow, and minute-to-minute attention to detail as a well-planned broadcast. Craft the event as though you were planning a live show on the world's largest 360-degree television screen, and then add the extra elements unique to the live entertainment experience that can enliven the athletes as well as the audience. Give the event a sense of worth and importance by creating an environment of excitement from the moment the audience enters the event facility, through the pre-event entertainment and ceremonies, and during the competition itself. Remember that audiences experience sports events in a multisensory way. The sounds of a sports event can be as important as its sights in raising the level of enthusiasm and enhancing the entertainment experience.

To fully capture the active involvement of the fans, the competitive activities at a sports event may require the support of technical systems including lighting, sound amplification, and video image magnification (or "I-Mag"), among others. The same technical support systems may also be used to entertain the audience with ceremonies and entertainment elements before, between, and after the competitions.

Ceremonies and Entertainment Elements

Every event has its own personality, every sport—even new and emerging ones—its own traditions. For some sports events (e.g., football, hockey, basketball), organizers want to get the crowd loud, energized, and excited. For others (e.g., golf, figure skating, tennis), a more conservative atmosphere is acceptable and appropriate. In almost every instance, however, opportunities abound for celebrating the featured sport, setting an exciting tone for an event, and making unique, lasting impressions with emotional opening ceremonies and pre-event festivities, intermission entertainment, and post-event finales (see Figure 12-2).

Many sports events, particularly those involving teams of athletes, are presented on large playing surfaces, and in some cases, before large audiences. The playing surface, the natural focal point for an event, can also serve as the stage for ceremonial and entertainment segments, as long as they do not affect the quality of the surface for the competition. Regardless of how impressive the entertainment, the actual competition is what the audience has come to see, and the safety of the athletes and quality of the surface are paramount as compared with any other consideration.

- Pre-event live musical entertainment
- Opening ceremonies
- Introduction or entrance of athletes
- Presentation of colors and national anthems
- Sport-specific ceremony (first pitch, tip off, face-off, coin flip)
- Recognition of past champions and event alumni
- Appearances and participation by celebrities and dignitaries
- Video highlights
- Halftime and intermission entertainment
- Live musical performances
- Post-event presentation of awards and trophies

Figure 12-2
Presentation and Ceremonial Elements of Sports Events

PAGEANTRY

Most sports events are presented on a 360-degree stage, surrounded by an audience that may be dozens to hundreds of feet distant from the action. Because it is difficult to establish an intimacy with the athletes from such prodigious distances, most of today's large arenas and stadiums have installed large video displays to simulcast the action, deliver information, and provide replays. These screens, known by such brand names as Sony Jumbotron or Mitsubishi Diamondvision, bring the action and the personalities of the athletes into sharper focus for the live audience. The large size of the playing surface and the extraordinary distance from the audience create a similarly challenging environment in which to entertain and excite audiences before play and during intermissions. Pageantry—colorful, large-format entertainment with an emphasis on music and mass movement, sometimes supported by special effects such as lighting, lasers, and pyrotechnics—is a popular solution in professional and top-tier amateur sports for these reasons.

AMATEUR ENTERTAINERS

An enormous budget is not required to inject the colorful and exciting pageantry that can give even the most homegrown sports programs the feel of a big event. The area's best high school and college marching bands can provide musical entertainment that can energize and inspire the crowd. Drill teams and kick lines can perform acrobatic and dance sequences that add a visual dimension to the thunderous presence of the band. For even greater impact, organizers can combine local bands or drill teams into a massed band, or a larger dance line, for an even grander presentation. Add colorful, waving flags of symbolic significance to the event (flags of countries, states or provinces, sports teams, or schools, and customized designs made especially for the program) for great, inexpensive props that can measurably increase the visual excitement on the field. With the exception of custom banners, you don't even have to buy the flags, poles, or holsters. Most items can be rented from a regional flag retailer. Drill teams and youth sports teams, groups of people who are used to working together as an organized unit, can be mobilized as flag and prop holders and marchers.

Using existing groups to provide large numbers of amateur performers is a manageable and efficient approach. Groups often come with their own infrastructure; members are used to following the instructions of their coaches, teachers, or the other adult supervisors who routinely coordinate and manage their activities. They usually have an established procedure for relaying information to their members and are familiar with traveling, or at least arriving and marshaling, as groups. It is obviously easier to manage four coaches, each responsible for 25 team members, than 100 individual performers. Each participating performer should receive, review, and sign a simple one-page waiver prepared by the event's attorney, protecting the organizer against liability claims in case of injury or accident and granting permission to use the performers' images in event photography, video coverage, and broadcasting (for a more detailed discussion on participant waivers, see Play 14 and Appendix 8).

Treat amateur entertainers with the same respect and consideration you extend to those who are being paid to perform. Ensure that plenty of water is readily available at all rehearsals, as well as in staging areas, and that restroom facilities are easily accessible. If rehearsals or call times require participants to be on the event site throughout the day, be sure to provide light meals or snacks or reasonably long enough meal breaks for them to be able to find food elsewhere. The feeding of cast and crew members is a perfect opportunity to involve a food or restaurant sponsor. Where possible, the best practice is to provide food for cast, crew, and staff members on-site when events or rehearsals are located in areas that offer few dining options. Rehearsals usually cannot restart until all cast members have returned, so it takes only a few late-returning participants to hold up an entire show.

CELEBRITY ENTERTAINERS

Organizers of major sports events are incorporating entertainment provided by well-known bands and celebrity performers with increasing regularity. Musical performers who appeal to the same target audience as the featured sport can add significant excitement to pre-event, intermission, and even post-event festivities. Their celebrity stature and amplified sound can help bridge the physical distance between the event and the audience. Keep in mind that a performer's fee is not related to the length of his or her appearance. To professional performers, the time investment is nearly the same whether they play a single song or a full 90-minute concert. They still have to travel to the event, set up their gear, participate in a sound check and rehearsal, perform, and then travel on to the next stop. Their fees may be negotiable to some extent, but do not expect costs to be significantly reduced because of the brevity of their appearances.

Well-known musical acts are best procured through their national booking agency. You can usually identify the agency on the act's web site or on the liner notes of its latest compact disk. For the right price, performers will appear virtually anywhere as long as they are not on hiatus or working on an album. When a band takes a break from touring, its members disperse and it is very difficult for their management to reassemble them.

Artists' fees can be very expensive, but that is only the beginning of the costs that can be incurred when booking recognizable talent. After receiving notice of the initial asking price, request a copy of the act's contract and rider. The rider is a list of all of the extra requirements that must be covered by the organizer, including the number of people for whom travel must be provided and at what class of service. The list typically includes members of the act, as well as backup singers and musicians, the manager, the road or tour manager, sound director, lighting director, and, often, others. Some acts additionally require such personnel as bodyguards, hairdressers, makeup artists, and wardrobe supervisors, and their riders will indicate whether the specific individuals to fulfill these roles must travel with the artists or may be provided on-site by the sports event organizer. The rider will also contain specific information about the act's requirements for hotel accommodations, meals, post-event hospitality, and complimentary event tickets. Minimum production requirements are also provided in an accompanying technical rider, usually specifying the size of the stage, audio equipment, lighting, musical instruments (often referred to as "backline"), and other performance-specific needs.

Negotiate the fee and the rider at the same time, as it is the totality of an act's costs that is important. You may still be able to meet an artist's minimum fee requirements while reducing the expenses of fulfilling the rider, or partially cover the rider costs with a reduction in the fee.

There are areas of negotiation illustrated in Figure 12-3 that may be applied to the contracts for professional artists. Remember that most talent contracts and riders are generic documents. Other than including the date, location, the name of the buyer, and the length of the performance desired, they are not generally customized by the agency to the needs of a particular show or sports event. As a result, the contracts that organizers receive are generally designed to be applicable to events in which the act is performing as a solo or featured concert attraction. Sports events usually use professional artists in a much more limited way, integrated as an element of a much broader event. As such, their tour management may relax a significant portion of the technical requirements, such as the size of the stage or the supporting lighting, sound, and special effects. With fewer technical requirements, the organizer may also

---

- Talent Fees
- Air Travel
  - Reduce the number of people traveling
  - Convert a number of airfares at first and business class to coach
  - Seek to include sponsor-provided tickets
- Hotel
  - Reduce the number of people traveling
  - Reduce the number of suites required
- Meals and Snacks
  - Reduce or buy out
- Technical Rider
  - Reduce technical requirements (e.g., stage size, lighting, special effects, audio) to levels appropriate to the event and its host facility
- Complimentary tickets

Figure 12-3
Commonly Negotiable Talent Contract and Rider Terms

be able to successfully reduce the number of technical personnel who must travel with the artist to the event.

The meal requirements outlined in the artist's rider are often exhaustive. To simplify event day logistics, especially in temporary event facilities that are not equipped for fine catering, organizers can propose a flat fee payable to the artist that will enable the act's tour management to provide the meals desired on its own.

Finally, most artists will require a number of complimentary tickets to the event for their management, important business clients, and perhaps even the local members of their fan club. As the event is not a typical concert, the organizer can usually negotiate a reduction in the number of tickets normally required by an artist.

Put the counteroffer to the agency in writing, but do not be surprised if it does not respond immediately. The agency will have to confer with the artist's management before accepting any reduced fee, and with the act's tour manager to discuss any alterations to the rider. Acts in high demand may also deliberately delay in responding in hope that a concert promoter or an event in another location will offer them more money for their appearance. It is not unusual for popular performers to refrain from accepting the terms of a counterproposal until 90 days before an event, when it becomes apparent that no more lucrative offer from another party for the same date is likely. Therefore, be sure that your counterproposal includes an expiration date for accepting the offer. Although it may not inspire a performer's management company to act with any greater speed, it does enable the organizer to approach alternative acts after the expiration date has passed.

HOSTS AND ANNOUNCERS

Sports events frequently require a public address announcer to welcome and communicate with the audience, relaying official scores and fulfilling marketing obligations to sponsors. A pleasant-sounding, authoritative announcer with a smooth, professional delivery will capture the attention of the audience and lend an air of importance to both the festivities and the competition. The best sources for announcers are local radio and television stations, which can provide another exposure opportunity for a sports event's media partners. Make sure the announcer becomes familiar with the pronunciation of each of the participant's names to ensure that he or she can present all announcements with authority, sincerity, and confidence.

Some events also lend themselves to involving a host or emcee in addition to the public address announcer. Unlike the unseen announcer, a host has a visible presence and provides at least some of the focus of attention when speaking with the audience. A host can provide a more personal touch to welcoming the audience, interviewing players, coaches, and dignitaries, and delivering scripted monologue for pre-event and intermission festivities. Like a television color commentator, the host can add dimension and drama, information and insights, enthusiasm and entertainment value to both the pre-event ceremonies and the contest itself.

If you want to add ceremonies and entertainment to your sports event, knowing what resources you can reach out for will help inspire your planning. But before contacting potential performers and other event participants, you have to know how you will use them and what you will want them to do. It is now time to begin the production planning process.

Production Planning

Planning the presentation and production of sports events is a complex process that often requires the appointment of an event producer or presentation director (sometimes called a game operations director). This individual is charged with the responsibility of developing the program's creative approach, working with technical specialists to arrange for sound, lighting, staging, and other presentation tools, and ultimately overseeing the day-to-day details of event production. Once the producer has a reasonable understanding of the missions of the sports event's presentation and how they will be achieved, the planning starts with the preparation of lists—lots of them, including contact lists, rehearsal schedules, production schedules, cast lists, wardrobe lists, prop lists, audio and music play lists, video lists, and event rundowns. These documents help the producer to organize his or her thinking, identify required purchases, and communicate expectations to the cast, production staff, and crew. Developing and maintaining these many lists ensures that no detail goes unconsidered by the presentation director and that every facet of the production is communicated to the entire presentation team. Figure 12-4 provides a summary of

☐ Event Rundown
☐ Script
☐ Production Schedule
☐ Rehearsal Schedule
☐ Contact List
☐ Cast List
☐ Wardrobe List
☐ Props List
☐ Music Play List
☐ Audio Equipment List
☐ Video Elements List

Figure 12-4
Essential Sports Event Production Document
Check List

the most essential production documents, most of which are explored in detail in the following sections.

EVENT RUNDOWNS

The key event presentation tool is the "rundown," or running order, a document that outlines the precise details of how an event will unfold. The document is divided into rows that represent "segments" or "scenes," descriptions of a major event activity, and columns that provide fine detail as to what occurs within each segment. A complete sample event rundown appears in Appendix 9, a small portion of which is represented in Figure 12-5 for the purposes of the discussion that follows.

During planning meetings, and in the midst of the event itself, it is simplest and most expedient to refer to a production segment by its sequentially assigned item number. It also removes the possibility of error in case some segments are similarly titled. Following the item number is the time column, indicating the precise time of day that each segment will begin. It is advisable to synchronize all of the presentation staff's clocks and watches to "official event time" at least one hour prior to the entrance of the audience. Digital stopwatches that display the time of day to fractions of a second are highly preferred over analog timepieces with sweep second hands. If the event is televised, the official time is set by the broadcaster, as networks must time their programming and breaks with the highest level of precision.

#	Time	Segment	R/T	Description	Audio	Video/ Scoreboard
1	7:00:00	**House Open**	0:30:00	Audience enters. Lights at preset levels. Gobos in corners. Stage managers to get players out of locker rooms at 7:25:00.	PA mic: Welcome and sponsor recognition (Pea Pond Mills, Pete's Pies, Faroff Airlines, Metro Daily News) over music CD #1	Event and sponsor logos in rotation; welcome; sponsor logos during recognition (Pea Pond Mills, Pete's Pies, Faroff Airlines, Metro Daily News)
2	7:30:00	**Player Warm-Ups**	0:20:00	Players enter and warm up on field. Lights on full.	Music CD #2	Event and sponsor logos in rotation; welcome

Figure 12-5
Setting up an Event Rundown

Official network time may be confirmed by a quick visit to the broadcaster's production truck.

The running time (R/T) indicates the amount of time required to complete each segment. In the preceding example, the running time is expressed in the most common form for televised sports events—"hours:minutes:seconds." Rundowns are easiest to customize and maintain on a Microsoft Excel spreadsheet, enabling the event organizer to apply formulas that automatically calculate the next entry in the time column based on the running time in the previous row.

The next column gives a description of the activities occurring within the segment. The description should be detailed enough to provide a general sense of how the event site will appear to the audience, as well as any details regarding what should be set up during this time period in preparation for the next segment. In this example, the field will be lit at some predetermined level specifically designed to create a desired theatrical effect as the audience enters. During the same segment, stage managers, the individuals responsible for the movement of people and materials on the field, will ensure that players are moved from the locker rooms with ample time to begin their warmups as scheduled in segment 2.

Columns for rundowns can be customized for the specific needs of a particular sports event. Most will include an "audio" column that describes what the audience will hear during the segment. As will be made more apparent by referring to the complete rundown in Appendix 9, the audio column indicates whether the sound the audience should hear will come from a tape, a compact disk, a particular microphone or computer "file server" that will store event music in a digital format for instant retrieval and play. Servers are especially useful when flexible, immediate access to a large library of music is required, and is often used to react to specific game or event situations.

A column may also be added for "video" if there is a large screen in the event venue. Many companies also rent screens that may be installed especially for an event, either on a freestanding scaffold or mounted on the back of a tractor-trailer. Presentation directors for events of more modest scale can rent video projectors and screens, video walls, or projection televisions, as appropriate for the size of the event and whether it is held in daylight, at night, or indoors.

The video screen can be used to simulcast broadcast coverage of the event or images from cameras operated solely for the consumption of the live audience. Providing live coverage to the screens is commonly called "I-Mag," or image magnification. Although including I-Mag coverage of an event can be expensive, there are few presentation tools that can establish better intimacy and participation between the athletes and their fans. Preproduced video highlights of past events, features on participating athletes, and special music videos can also be presented to add great entertainment value for the fans. Animations and still graphics can be designed to display player close-ups, background, trivia, and informative statistics. Sponsors also consider the ability to run commercials or display their logos on the screen as offering highly desirable exposure opportunities. Videos may be run directly from tape or stored in a file server for instant access. The same column on the rundown can be used to describe the images displayed on the scoreboards or electronic message boards (also known as matrix boards), if available and appropriate. The sample event shown in Appendix 9, for example, takes place in a facility that is equipped only with a matrix board.

The running order must be kept current and distributed to all production staff with the date and time of revisions noted on all pages. A general announcement noting the date and time of the final revision should be communicated to all production staff before the event begins, to ensure that all possess the correct, definitive version.

SCRIPTS

The rundown defines the specific information that is required for the script, the document that contains the exact words to which the host or announcer must give voice. Scripts are best prepared with a heading on the top right side of the page showing the item number from the running order, as well as the segment description (see the sample script page in Figure 12-6). Center the name or role of the individual who will read this portion of the script. Print the script in large, double-spaced type, and underscore or bold the key points of emphasis. This will also help to immediately identify the contents of the script page without having to read all of the copy.

Like the running order, the script must remain current with the date and time of any revision, noted as a footnote on all pages. Be sure the public address announcer and/or host has an opportunity to review the script—even if not completely finalized—before event day to enable that person to make his or her own notes, investigate pronunciations of names, and be familiar enough with the copy to deliver it confidently, enthusiastically, and error-free.

It is best to provide the script to the announcer in a loose-leaf notebook to allow the insertion of revised pages when changes are made without having to replace the entire script. Use a different color paper for sheets replaced each time a series of script revisions are released, and match the prevailing running order with the same color paper.

Scripts often include contractually obligatory sponsor acknowledgments and commercial announcements, usually delivered during the pre-event period, intermissions, and breaks in the action. Throughout a sports event, however, the audience is often waiting expectantly to know what's going on. Identify for the announcer those moments and situations during the competition when it is appropriate to relay information to the public. Think of how you watch a sports event on television—the announcers tell you everything you need to know. Why should your paying customers receive any less information? Such information

---

(1) HOUSE OPEN

ANNOUNCER

WELCOME TO THE FIVE COUNTY FOOTBALL TOURNAMENT, presented by

PEA POND MILLS. TODAY'S EXCITING EVENTS ARE ALSO BROUGHT TO

YOU BY:

PETE'S PIES. MADE FRESH EACH DAY RIGHT IN PETE'S OWN KITCHEN.

BRING YOUR TICKET STUBS FROM TODAY'S EVENT TO A PETE'S

LOCATION NEAR YOU FOR A 15% DISCOUNT OFF A FRESH PETE'S FRUIT

PIE. FRESH PIES FROM FRESH PERSPECTIVES, THAT'S PETE'S . . .

AND BY **FAROFF AIRLINES.** FAROFF IS GOING YOUR WAY WITH 15

FLIGHTS DAILY FROM FIVE COUNTY METRO AIRPORT. CONNECTING

YOU WITH AMERICA FOR YOUR NEXT TRIP, THINK FAROFF . . .

Figure 12-6
Sample Script Page

may include upcoming matches, official results, explanations of judges' or referees' decisions, important statistics, records that have been broken. Establish a protocol as to when those announcements may be delivered—during play or only during a break in the action. Video screens are also often used to communicate important information when it is deemed inappropriate or too intrusive to deliver it orally.

PRODUCTION SCHEDULE

If the event rundown is the key tool for the actual presentation of the event, the production schedule is its analog for the staff responsible for preparing the physical site. The production schedule outlines all of the preparatory activities at the event facility. A sample production schedule is provided for illustrative purposes in Figure 12-7.

Five County Football Tournament Production Schedule

Day/Date/Time	Activity	Location
Friday, September 9		
9:00 A.M.–12:00 P.M.	Phone and data lines installed	Room 156
1:00 P.M.–6:00 P.M.	Production office equipment (fax, copier, printers) delivered	Room 156
Saturday, September 10		
2:00 P.M.–5:00 P.M.	*Calhoun vs. Kennedy H.S.*	Stadium field
6:00 P.M.–11:00 P.M.	Production office set up	Room 156
Sunday, September 11		
9:00 A.M.	Security begins—credentials required	All areas
9:00 A.M.–6:00 P.M.	Banner and signage installation	All areas
Monday, September 12		
9:00 A.M.	Production office opens	Room 156
9:00 A.M.	Distribute walkie-talkies	Room 156
10:00 A.M.–5:00 P.M.	Clean and set up locker rooms	Rooms 142/144
Tuesday, September 13		
9:00 A.M.–5:00 P.M.	Load-in and install lighting	Stadium field
	Load in and install sound	Stadium field
7:00 P.M.–11:59 P.M.	Focus lighting	Stadium field
Wednesday, September 14		
9:00 A.M.	Balance sound system	Stadium field
9:00 A.M.–12:00 P.M.	Paint field markings and 50 yard line logo	Stadium field
9:00 A.M.–2:00 P.M.	**No staff or crew permitted on field!**	
9:00 A.M.–3:00 P.M.	Media workroom and lounge set up	Rooms 136/138
6:00 P.M.–11:00 P.M.	Technical rehearsal	Stadium field
Thursday, September 15		
4:00 P.M.–8:00 P.M.	Ceremony rehearsals	Stadium field
7:00 P.M.–11:00 P.M.	Equipment trailers arrive	Gate 5
8:00 P.M.–11:00 P.M.	Technical rehearsals	Stadium field
Friday, September 16		
8:00 A.M.–3:00 P.M.	Team practices and photos *(No stadium audio!)*	Stadium field
3:00 P.M.–7:00 P.M.	Ceremony rehearsals	Stadium field
7:00 P.M.–9:00 P.M.	Dress and camera rehearsal	Stadium field
Saturday, September 17		
6:00 A.M.	Television news trucks arrive	Gate 5
8:00 A.M.–4:00 P.M.	Team practices and photos *(No stadium audio!)*	Stadium field
4:30 P.M.–5:45 P.M.	Ceremony rehearsals	Stadium field

Figure 12-7
Sample Production Schedule

Saturday, September 17		
6:00 P.M.	**Doors open!**	
7:00 P.M.	Opening ceremonies begin	
Sunday, September 18		
8:00 A.M.–10:00 P.M.	Tournament play	
Monday, September 19		
8:00 A.M.–6:00 P.M.	Load-out all equipment and offices	
6:00 P.M.	All walkie-talkies returned	Room 156

Figure 12-7
(Continued)

CAST LIST

Management of the event's noncompetitive participants and performers can be facilitated by a cast list, as illustrated in Figure 12-8. The cast list is a roster of the various individuals or groups, organized by their roles or functions as defined in the running order. The names that constitute each unit appear in the next column, followed by the key contact for each. Note that the marching band in this example is made up of a total of 150 members from two dif-

Five County Football Tournament
Cast List

Cast Unit (#)	Name(s)	Key Contact	Coordinator
Marching Band (150)	Maxwell High School Band	Ethan Jacobs	Ryan Holzer
	Nathaniel High School Band	Harold Matthews	Ryan Holzer
Flag bearers (50+3)	Andreas High School Drill Team	Catherine Arthur	Tiffany Richards
	McJames High School Drill Team	Jean Shirley	Tiffany Richards
USMC color guard (4)	U.S. Marine Corps— Quantico	Capt. Mitch Field	Marc Levine
Army parachute team (5)	U.S. Army—Fort Bragg	Lt. Erwin Edwards	Marc Levine
Lieutenant governor (1)	Lieutenant Governor Jill Samuels	Art Frank	Bill Haufreitz
Coin toss celebrity (1)	Senator Jackson Litvak	Katerina Daniels	Bill Haufreitz
Anthem singer (1)	Donna Andrea	Donna Andrea	Bill Haufreitz
Announcer (1)	Rob Roberts	Rob Roberts	Bill Haufreitz
Trophy presenter (1)	Phil DeBasquette (sponsor)	Maria Marconi	Bill Haufreitz

Figure 12-8
Cast List

ferent high school bands. The key contacts in this case are the band directors of the schools.

Also notice that although the flag bearer unit requires 50 participants, 3 additional drill team members are included in the cast list. These extra individuals are "alternates," cast members who will attend all rehearsals with their units, so that they can easily replace those who drop out of the event because of illness, schedule conflicts, inadequate rehearsal attendance, or subsequent disinterest. Alternates are strongly recommended for amateur performing groups in which the number of participants is critical. In this example, there are 50 flag bearers, each holding a flag emblematic of one of the United States. To have 49 states represented would be unacceptable; therefore, it is important to include alternates in case a member of the unit fails to attend the event for any reason. The marching band, however, requires no alternates, as missing members would not be as noticeable. (*Note:* Marching bands that perform intricate field formations, as is often the case during football game halftimes, may require alternates to eliminate the possibility of visible gaps in their routines.) Alternates, when required, serve a very critical function. However, as they may not participate in the actual ceremonies if ultimately unneeded, the organizer may assign them to other roles during the event that require little or no rehearsal preparation.

The cast list identifies the key contact for each unit, the person to whom information should be directed for each group that constitutes the cast. Data such as the person's phone number, E-mail address, and mailing address should be included in the event's contact list. The final column on the cast list denotes the talent coordinator (TC), an event staff member directly responsible for all aspects of the participation of specific cast units. Depending on the complexity of the program, the talent coordinator can serve other roles on the event staff as well. For example, the TC responsible for the participation of sponsors in event ceremonies can also serve as the individual responsible for sponsor-driven functions, such as fulfillment and guest management. A TC should attend all rehearsals for his or her assigned unit and serve as the primary conduit of information to the group's key contact. The TC should be the person the group seeks out upon arrival at each rehearsal and on event day. Although a TC can be assigned to more than one group of participants, care should be exercised to avoid assigning one TC to groups that may participate simultaneously in sectional rehearsals that are held in separate locations (see "Sectional Rehearsals," which follows shortly).

Scheduling Rehearsals

Rehearsals are essential to the smooth operation of any event. Even the most simple and straightforward presentation should be meticulously rehearsed to ensure smooth and professional execution. Several types of rehearsals may be required, including sectional rehearsals, technical run-throughs, and dress rehearsals, as illustrated in Figure 12.9.

Five County Football Tournament Rehearsal Schedule

Day, Date	Time	Location	Rehearsal	Units
Saturday, September 10	9:00 A.M.–12:00 P.M.	Calhoun H.S.	Pre-show sectional	Marching Band (150) Flag Bearers (50+3)
Sunday, September 11	4:00 P.M.–6:00 P.M.	Calhoun H.S.	Pre-show sectional	Marching Band (150) Flag Bearers (50+3)
Monday, September 12	4:00 P.M.–6:00 P.M.	Calhoun H.S.	Pre-show sectional	Marching Band (150) Flag Bearers (50+3)
Wednesday, September 14	4:00 P.M.–6:00 P.M.	Calhoun H.S.	Pre-show sectional	Marching Band (150) Flag Bearers (50+3)
Thursday, September 15	6:00 P.M.–11:00 P.M.	Five County Stadium	Technical rehearsal	Announcer
	4:00 P.M.–5:30 P.M.	Five County Stadium	Announcer rehearsal	Marching Band (150) Flag Bearers (50+3)
	6:00 P.M.–8:00 P.M.	Five County Stadium	Pre-show rehearsal	Announcer Parachute Spotter (1)
Friday, September 16	8:00 P.M.–11:00 P.M.	Five County Stadium	Technical rehearsal	Athlete Stand-ins (50) USMC Color Guard (4) Celebrity stand-ins (3)
	3:00 P.M.–4:00 P.M.	Five County Stadium	Entrance of athletes rehearsal	
	4:00 P.M.–5:00 P.M.	Five County Stadium	Color guard and celebrity blocking	
	7:00 P.M.–9:00 P.M.	Five County Stadium	Dress and camera rehearsal	Marching Band (150) Flag Bearers (50+3) Announcer Parachute Team (5) Athlete Stand-ins (50) USMC Color Guard (4) Celebrity Stand-ins (5)
Saturday, September 17	4:30 P.M.–5:00 P.M.	Five County Stadium	Anthem singer rehearsal	Anthem Singer (1)
	5:00 P.M.–5:15 P.M.	Five County Stadium	Celebrity blocking	Lt. Governor (1) Coin Toss Celebrity (1)
	5:15 P.M.–5:45 P.M.	Five County Stadium	Trophy presentation rehearsal	Trophy Presenter (1)
	6:00 P.M.	Five County Stadium	**Doors open!**	

Figure 12-9
Rehearsal Schedules

SECTIONAL REHEARSALS

Units that perform at sports events ceremonies may have different rehearsal requirements, based on the complexity of their participation or the precision of their performance. A marching band that must execute several different formations while playing, for example, will require a larger number of rehearsals than, say, the announcer. A series of sectional rehearsals expressly for the marching band, and the flag-bearing drill team members who must be integrated into the band's field formations, has been scheduled in the hypothetical example illustrated in Figure 12.9. In the early stages, it is not important for the band to practice on the same field on which they will ultimately appear. To enable the technical staff to install the sound, lights, and other equipment needed at the hypothetical event venue, these first sectional rehearsals are scheduled at a nearby high school.

Sectional rehearsals may be conducted with or without sets, staging, or props. It is wise, however, to simulate the position of any staging or obstacles (e.g., lighting towers, added bleachers, risers, or constructed sets) that will be present during the event with traffic cones and construction tape to familiarize members of the cast with their locations throughout rehearsals. Later sectional rehearsals should include the actual props, sets, and technical production elements, and if feasible, are best held in the venue in which the ceremonies will take place.

BLOCKING

Blocking is the process of determining entrances, movement, and positions during sports event ceremonies, as well as the exiting of all participants, props, and staging in sequential order. Blocking is best planned on the actual performance space, but may be simulated elsewhere. The first blocking run-through need not be done with the actual participants present. Stand-ins may be positioned and repositioned until the presentation director (and television director, if appropriate) is satisfied with the ceremony's flow and appearance. If stand-ins have been used, a final blocking run-through should be scheduled with the actual participants if at all practical.

The importance of rehearsing the entrance and exit of each unit cannot be overstated. Blocking will help to identify potential areas of congestion and confusion at entry and exit points and can indicate the length of time required for participants to move from their point of entry to their performance area, and then back out again. Blocking diagrams, such as those depicted in Figure 12-10, may be drawn and distributed to cast members and staff to graphically demonstrate the proper movement of the cast, sets, and props on the field; these are particularly helpful tools for complex ceremonies that involve large numbers of participants.

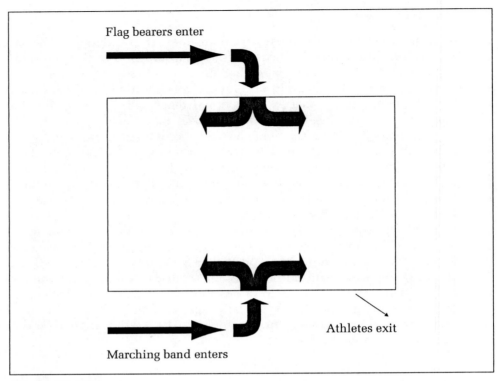

Figure 12-10a
Blocking Diagram 1

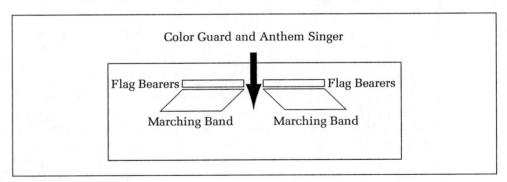

Figure 12-10b
Blocking Diagram 2

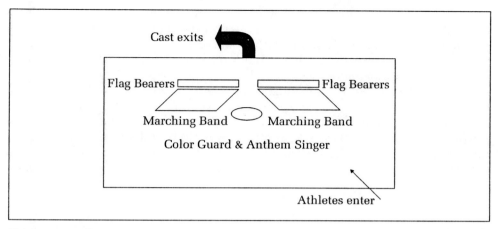

Figure 12-10c
Blocking Diagram 3

TECHNICAL REHEARSALS

The designers and technicians responsible for lighting, sound, video, and special effects need time to work toward perfecting their event day presentation. Technical rehearsals are conducted to make sure that all of the equipment functions properly and creates the desired result. This is the time when the presentation director can make adjustments in lighting, sound, video, and other effects before the participants arrive for the rehearsals that will combine the cast with all of the technical elements. As such, technical rehearsals can be conducted only in the actual location where the event will take place. In addition, if the sports event is being held outdoors during any time when the sky is not completely dark, it will be important to conduct technical rehearsals at approximately the same time of day as the actual presentation to evaluate the effect of both the intensity and angle of sunlight on the visibility of added lighting, video, and other visual effects.

DRESS REHEARSAL

The final rehearsal is often called the dress rehearsal. This rehearsal should run through the event from start to finish in real time, that is, without stopping. This will help the presentation director to verify the timings on the rundown and make adjustments accordingly. The dress rehearsal should involve every participant in the ceremony, although it is not uncommon to have dignitaries and celebrities represented by stand-ins. Dress rehearsal is the last, best time to see how the ceremonies will unfold exactly the way the audience will see it on event day. It is final confirmation that the production plan is as accurate as possible. For events that are broadcast on television, it is often also the best opportunity for the broadcast director to stage a simultaneous camera rehearsal to maximize the quality of the show.

If an event's production is particularly complex, it is strongly recommended that one or more event run-throughs be scheduled in "stop-and-go" fashion. These are extra run-throughs of the entire program, held a day or two prior to the dress rehearsal and involving all participants (or stand-ins) and technical departments, during which the presentation director may stop the rehearsal, request adjustments, provide direction, and restart the segment. Stop-and-go run-throughs should be scheduled to take no less than twice the expected running time of the event to accommodate the pauses in rehearsal.

Technical Tools of Sports Event Production

Often, in addition to the ceremonies and entertainment of an event, the competition itself will require the installation and operation of technical systems such as sound and lights. Fulfilling their most basic objectives, a sound (or audio) system is responsible for communicating verbal information and musical entertainment to the audience, and lighting maintains optimal conditions for safe play and visibility for the audience. At minimum, the design of these technical systems must support and never impede the competitive activities. This essential mission, often expanded by the theatrical needs of ceremonies and entertainment, is further explored in the following sections.

SOUND

Surprisingly, sound is one of the most often overlooked production elements at sports events. Even many of today's largest professional sports facilities have permanent installations that are substandard in terms of how well they amplify and distribute sound throughout the venue or the range of sound they can reproduce. Many use loudspeakers that are well suited to project the range of the human voice but are incapable of reproducing the wide range of bass and treble tones appropriate for playing live or recorded music. If music is integral to the entertainment of the audience, be sure to test any existing permanent systems for the quality of sound they can reproduce, using various pieces of music with as wide a range of tones as possible. Orchestral soundtracks such as John Williams themes and digitally recorded pop and rock tunes can clearly demonstrate the degree of a sound system's versatility.

Also test how well the sound is distributed throughout the audience. Sound reaches spectators in a "line of sight" fashion. That is, if you are in an area where you can see the front of the speakers, then sound should be able to reach your ears without the distortion of first being reflected off another surface. The system should be balanced so the volume and tone of the sound is essentially the same, regardless of where a listener sits. A system has an insufficient number of speakers, or is unbalanced, when the volume in one area is very loud, but low, distorted, or inaudible in others. In addition, determine whether the sound should be projected onto the playing surface, the benches, or the athlete waiting areas. If so, additional speakers may be required, as many facility's systems are designed to amplify sound only into the audience and not onto the playing surface.

If the existing sound system is not up to required standards, work with a qualified audio designer or rental agency to supplement the number of speakers or add the right kinds of speakers to produce clear, distinctive sound. Sometimes, however, it is best to start over and install an entirely new temporary sound system that will operate independently from the permanent one. Audiophiles are familiar with the two major types of speakers (although there are more): woofers for low, bass tones, and tweeters for higher-pitched sounds. Woofers are typically housed in larger speaker cabinets to achieve their characteristic deep and resonant tones. Without woofers music can seem shrill and even irritating. Tweeters are needed to provide the clear, high tones that prevent the sound from seeming muffled. Do not be surprised if your audio company installs what looks like single-speaker cabinets. Frequently, the two types of speakers are housed in the same cabinet for smaller facilities.

Speakers project sound from amplifiers that receive audio information from a number of sources. The voices of announcers, hosts, and live performers are received from microphones that are either hardwired (have a cable that runs to the amplifer) or wireless. Wireless microphones, also known as "RF mikes," transmit the sound over a radio frequency (hence the "RF" abbreviation). RF microphones can simplify the staging of an event by allowing the performer to be located anywhere on the stage or the playing surface without trailing a microphone cable. It is wise, however, to have backup mikes available (preferably a hardwired backup microphone) in case of a failure of the wireless system or unanticipated interference from another RF source. Note that there are usually many other pieces of electronic equipment at a sports event that will use radio frequencies, such as walkie-talkies being used by the event and facility staff and cameras and microphones being used by broadcasters, to name just a few. There may also be RF users outside, but near the venue, such as transportation dispatchers and others. It is therefore important that the frequencies of all these users are coordinated to ensure that the sound system broadcasts the signal from only those sources desired without interference from others on the same frequency.

Recorded music may be played from compact disks, digital audiotape (DAT), or from a digital source such as a computer server programmed to store musical tracks. Music loaded on a computer server system such as Click

Effects (*www.clickeffects.com*), or other professional playback and disk jockey programs, offers the great advantage of being able to access any desired piece of music instantly from a large library of songs. The software and technology required for music editing and storage of an enormous library of music have become inexpensive and widely available even to the home use market. At the time of this writing, a small Apple iPod device with 15 gigabytes of hard disk storage, sufficiently large to store as many as 3700 different songs, can be purchased for less than US $350. Adobe Audition (formerly Cool Edit Pro) is a widely used PC-based program for editing music and adding effects, capabilities available a few years ago only in a professional sound studio, which sells for less than $300.

The sound from all audio sources is cabled to a mixing position, a console from which an operator can select the microphones, disk players, tape players, video sources, or computer servers (each dedicated to its own "channel") to be turned on, and those to be turned off. The mixing position can also blend the sound received from each channel to achieve the desired combination of sounds, such as an announcer's voice and a selection of music, in proper balance. The console should be located in the audience to allow the operator mixing the sound to experience the volume and balance between channels just as the audience does.

One of the unfortunate characteristics of the sound generated by large-scale pageantry is that it may be difficult for participants to hear themselves and the other sounds of the event around them. Figure 12-11 provides a list of helpful staging and production hints relating to sound at sports events that can help to reduce the confusion.

LIGHTING

Lighting needs can be divided into three major categories—competitive necessities, television requirements, and theatrical or ceremonial needs. In this regard, the organizer's first and most important mission is to ensure that the lighting is sufficient for the safe execution and viewing of the sports competition, with no areas of shadow that can affect the quality of play. Lighting must come from more than a single point to avoid the casting of shadows. Further, lighting sources must be elevated so that they do not create blind spots on the field by being projected from an area in the athletes' direct line of sight.

Televised sports events require a more powerful level of lighting for coverage of the competition. Most sports event stadiums and arenas that are home to organized professional, semiprofessional, or college teams are already equipped with lighting that will serve most television needs. Competitions held in venues that are infrequent sports event hosts and temporary outdoor facilities, however, may require added lighting for both general event and television lighting. Companies such as Iowa-based Musco Lighting (*www.musco.com*) can provide permanent and temporary installations. Their portable

- Be sure the public address system design includes speakers facing the performers, and that the volume can be controlled separately from the rest of the facility's speakers. Most permanent sports venues have a minimal number of speakers, if any, facing the playing surface. Add speakers if necessary to achieve this objective.
- For their members to perform in synchrony, directors and conductors of marching bands, choirs, and any other large performing group must be visible to their units. The directors are often positioned on elevated platforms, scissors lifts, or atop sturdy folding ladders.
- To keep a number of performing groups synchronized and playing to a pre-determined tempo, many presentation directors employ a "click track," an electronic metronome that may be fed to the conductors, band directors, and orchestra musicians through headsets. A click track is never heard by the audience.
- Professional and celebrity bands and singers will require floor monitors, small wedge-shaped speakers that face the performers, set on the front of the stage risers. The monitors will enable the performers to hear themselves, as well as any prerecorded musical tracks.
- Marching bands, choirs, and other multipoint sources are extremely difficult to amplify by natural means to a pleasing blend of sound, especially when there are far more instruments or voices than microphones, and when there is a limited amount of time to set up, balance, and remove the microphones. It is not uncommon to record these performers during a rehearsal or in a studio, and to have them play live in accompaniment to their recording. This will provide the audience with full, true-to-life sound, and is also called playing "live to track."
- Be sure to obtain the proper clearances and licenses for any public performance of music. The playing of recorded music for nondramatic public purposes, even background music during the audience's entrance, requires a music license from the organization that represents the holders of the copyright. In the United States, most music is represented by one of three major licensing associations—the American Society of Composers, Authors and Publishers, or ASCAP (*www. ascap.com*), BMI (*www.bmi.com*), or SESAC (*www.sesac.com*). You can check these organizations' web site, or the recording artist's compact disk, to determine which licensing group to contact. All rights in Canada are handled through a single entity, known as SOCAN (*www.socan.ca*).
- The use of music performed live must generally be cleared directly by the publisher of the work, unless the artist who recorded it is also the performer. Professional performers can be expected to have cleared the music in their usual repertoires.
- The publisher of a work must also clear the use of music on video programming played during an event. The right to use music on the soundtracks of video presentations is often referred to as synchronization, or "sync," right. The publisher may charge a few hundred dollars for one-time use at a live event, up to several thousand for a broadcast event.
- Broadcasters maintain their own master licenses for the use of music during their coverage.

Figure 12-11
Sound Advice: Staging and Production Hints for Sports Events

systems are often mounted on trucks and are effective at distances of up to 1000 ft. Temporary units may also be ordered with their own generators, equipped with booms to elevate lighting to as much as 150 ft high.

Various types of lighting instruments and techniques can be applied to the presentation of a sports event, adding theatricality and excitement to opening ceremonies, athlete introductions, entertainment and anthem performances, intermission fan promotions, and more. Before designing the lighting for ceremonies and entertainment, determine how the lighting to be used for competition and television purposes is controlled. Television lighting, and most competition lighting, is so bright that little in the way of theatrical lighting will be seen unless the lighting used for television and the competition is turned off or dimmed. Many of today's top indoor sports venues have installed electric shutters on their television lighting, which enables the facility to be temporarily darkened without actually extinguishing the lights. These shutters may be used for only a limited time, in some cases up to 15 or 20 minutes, to keep the lights behind them from overheating. Older facilities use lights that, once extinguished, must cool down before they can be relit, a period that can take up to 15 minutes. A noticeable amount of time may pass after the lights are turned back on for them to warm up to the temperature required for television coverage. The event's lighting designer should consult with the facility manager and test the house lighting for this "restrike time." There are also lighting systems that proclaim the ability to restrike to the levels required for television coverage almost instantly. It is strongly suggested that any permanent lighting system not using shutters be tested for the time required for restoration to full intensity after being turned off.

Theatrical lighting can be divided into two major types—fixed and movable instruments. Fixed lighting is clamped in a stationary position, focused on a single nonmovable location. Leko lights and par cans are all of the fixed variety. Lekos are spotlights that can be focused sharply on fixed areas of variable size. The lamps in par cans look like automobile headlamps and basically function in a similar way, illuminating a larger area with a general "wash" of light. A sheet of colored gelatin (also known as a "gel") can be installed on any of these fixed instruments to create light of the desired shade and intensity. Color changers or scrollers, a series of gels either manually or automatically operated, can also be installed in front of these fixed instruments. Strobes are specialized fixed lights that can blink once like a blinding flash of lightning, or at variable, sometimes rapid rates of speed to create stop-motion effects.

Dozens of stock patterns and custom-built logos can be projected by installing "gobos" on the lighting instrument, stencils that are cut from metal or etched on glass. Glass gobos can be fabricated in full color or, less expensively, in a single tone (with color added by a gel), if desired. The effects they can provide can be striking in either fixed or movable lighting systems. Sports event presentation directors can order custom gobos to project the logos of an event, the organizer, or the sponsors on the playing surface and other locations throughout and even outside the venue.

Movable lights, which can create more dynamic and exciting effects than fixed instruments, are further divided into manually operated and computer-controlled instruments. Follow spots are large spotlights that can be moved manually by an operator to follow the action during player introductions and entertainment performances. The use of computerized, or intelligent, lighting, however, allows the most exciting effects to be achieved. The beams from a large number of lights may be moved in many directions at once, colors changed, the size and shape of the beams varied, gobos revealed and rotated. Different looks can be preset for the audience's entrance, athlete introductions, ceremonies, anthem performances, intermissions, and exits. The lighting designer "records" these settings into a computer and can cause an entire segment's look to change dramatically with the press of a single button.

The production schedule may have to provide the designer with a significant amount of time to point and focus fixed lights in their desired positions and to program the complex looks that intelligent lighting can generate. As focusing must be done in darkness, the programming of lighting for events held outdoors must be done at night.

LASERS

A laser emits an intense beam of light that can be narrowly focused, bounced off mirrors, or filtered to create colors, prisms, and cloudlike patterns. The output of a laser is best seen when the atmosphere contains moisture, as minute water droplets reflect the light to create the brilliant beams. For this reason, the use of lasers often requires the use of fog or haze machines. A laser can be used to generate an arrow-straight beam focused on tiny mirrors located across the event facility, with the resulting reflections aimed at additional mirrors to give the appearance of a great number of beams. Audiences often think they are seeing many laser beams when they are simply seeing a single beam split into dozens of reflections. Lasers can also be programmed to project logos or create animated effects when projected against a flat surface. These laser graphics are actually produced by a single beam tracing the artwork at a very high rate of speed, which is why laser images seem to flicker as the design being drawn gets more complex. Lasers create a great amount of heat and must be located where they can be cooled by a running water source. They must also be projected onto areas away from the audience to avoid potential eye injuries to spectators.

VIDEO AND PROJECTORS

As is true of audio, there are two ends to a video system. On one end is the source of the images, such as the television feed of a live broadcast, a sports event's dedicated cameras, and the playback of recorded materials and computer-generated animations. Recorded video can be played from videotapes, laser disks, DVDs, or as is becoming increasingly popular, from computer servers. The great flexibility offered by instant access to a desired video clip has made storage of video images and animations on a computer's hard drive a most attractive alternative to sports presentation directors.

On the other end is the medium on which the images are made visible to the audience. The various sources are cabled to a video switcher that enables an operator to select the images desired and change from one image to another by a desired effect, such as a cut (an instant change from one camera or image to another), a dissolve (a gradual fading out of one image as another fades in), or a wipe (an animated effect that removes one image and replaces it with another). In a darkened indoor facility or an outdoor venue at night, video images may be projected on white screens. A projector is positioned either in front of or behind the screen. Rear projection (RP) screens are often preferred to eliminate the chance of shadows created by members of the audience or cast. The disadvantage of rear projection is the amount of space required behind the screen for the positioning of the projector so the image fills the surface. The distance between the screen and the projector is known as the "throw," and the larger the screen, the greater the throw required. Rear screen projection is also best when the audience views the screen only from the front. Fans who watch anything projected on an RP screen from behind will see a mirror image. It is also important to remember that to avoid casting shadows on the image, the area between the projector and the screen cannot be used for entering cast members, participants, or athletes, or the movement of any backstage crew.

Video projectors have become less expensive and more versatile in recent years. Projectors using liquid crystal display (LCD) technology can automatically switch from front screen to rear screen imaging without special lenses, and electronically correct the phenomenon of "keystoning," a common form of image distortion caused when the projector lens is not exactly centered on the screen. (A keystoned image may look wider at the top of the screen, for example, than at the bottom, or vice versa.) If projectors are to be used, it is recommended that two projectors be simultaneously focused and the images synchronized on the same screen, if the budget permits. This will provide an important backup system in case one projector fails. As viewed by the audience, a failure would cause the image to appear to dim slightly rather than go completely dark.

Most major sports and entertainment events have switched their loyalties to light-emitting diode (LED) screens, large television screens that require no projector. Sports event audiences will recognize Jumbotron, Diamondvision, Daktronics, and other brand names as representative of this type of display. As a group, these screens are sufficiently bright to present sharp and colorful images in sunlight as well as in the dark. If the facility does not have an LED video screen, and the event budget permits, a temporary installation can be arranged. If the staging plan will accommodate it, consider using a mobile, truck-mounted screen to eliminate the labor costs of unloading, installing, and removing a rented unit. The companies that rent such trucks also provide an on-board control room complete with video switchers, tape decks, video servers, slow motion recorders, character generators (machines that can add graphics, such as player names, statistics, and other typed information to an image), and even cameras to feed images to the screens, providing great cost efficiencies.

Video projection and broadcast images are unforgiving of lapses in clarity and the quality of footage. Household VHS tape will appear fuzzy and indistinct on a projection screen. Try to use a professional "broadcast quality" format and grade of tape, such as today's industry standard Beta SP. Although it is more expensive to purchase Beta SP tape and to rent compatible playback equipment, this format is the least costly of the many emerging varieties that are now being used for high-end digital and high-definition recording. As digital and high-definition television become more mainstream, formats like Digital Beta (also known as Digi-Beta), D-2, and D-3, and their likely successors may become more common, but for the moment are extremely expensive and the tape machines more difficult to find. If you are using an existing control room at the event facility or renting a truck-mounted screen, make sure that the tape format you choose is compatible with this equipment. The technologies for capturing, editing, storing, and projecting video are evolving as rapidly as ever. For a wonderful on-line resource to stay current on new and evolving facets of this fast-paced production tool, visit *http://videouniversity.com*.

PYROTECHNICS

Pyrotechnics, more commonly known as fireworks, can punctuate an event with spectacular color and heart-stopping sound. Fireworks displays can be designed to last just a few brilliant seconds as a visual and auditory climax for the closing moments of an event, or to provide a visually rich and thunderous pageant of 20 minutes or more, synchronized to a musical soundtrack. In short, fireworks almost always imply a feeling of celebration.

The catalog of aerial pyrotechnic effects, those launched into the air by electronically controlled mortars or rockets, is extremely varied, their names often reflective of their visual impact. It is easy to imagine the effects created by Yellow Chrysanthemums, Red Comets, Split Comets, Ring Shells, Stars, and Roman Candles, to name just a few. The size of the shell's burst is determined by the size of the shell—3 in. (diameter) shells are among the smallest and least expensive; larger shells in popular use can be 8 in., 10 in., 12 in. or more. Shells that create a loud noise upon exploding include a "report charge," although many can be designed to display without this loud *bang*.

Ground-based fireworks, such as pyrotechnic fountains, do not launch shells into the air and are therefore the effects of choice indoors, because the position and height can be more precisely designed and regulated. Small shells can also be suspended from roof beams on nonflammable cables to provide a controlled indoor "aerial" display. Graphics, such as logos and line art, can be executed in fireworks called set pieces, or pyrographics. These ground-based displays can create a brilliant finale moment, virtually burning an event's or sponsor's brand image into the memories of thousands of spectators.

A gas flame projector uses a burner that releases and ignites a flammable natural gas, producing a bright orange flame and a ball of heated air that is perceptible for hundreds of feet. Obviously, it is important to keep all flames and pyrotechnic effects away from athletes, fans, staff, equipment, and décor that can ignite or be functionally affected by their heat or the by-products of ignition. Gas effects usually burn clean, with no visible smoke or debris. Pyrotechnic devices, however, can leave behind ash, pieces of shell casings and ignition assemblies, and chemical salts and invisible gases that can irritate or injure if they come in contact with members of the audience, cast members, or athletes. They also create smoke, which can produce additional irritation and obscure the playing surface for both live and television spectators. The effects of smoke are particularly noticeable when using pyrotechnics indoors, as it often takes the host facility's ventilation system a significant and noticeable amount of time to remove it.

Pyrotechnics should be designed and fired only by experienced, licensed fireworks companies and technicians. These professionals will be familiar with the safety requirements governing the use of pyrotechnics and gas effects as recommended by the manufacturer and the American Pyrotechnics Association or other national bodies. They will file for all needed permits (be sure to plan far enough in advance to accommodate this application process) and arrange for the necessary test firings that are universally required by local fire marshals. Be prepared to produce certificates of fireproofing for all banners, sets, props, and other materials near the firing and spectator areas, as well as proof of liability insurance. Also make sure that the amount of smoke and debris generated will not interfere with the quality of the playing surface or the comfort and performance of the athletes.

AUTOCUE

Participants who deliver speeches at an event, as well as hosts and emcees who are visible on camera, can be supported with a device called an autocue or teleprompter. This equipment is composed of a large television monitor supported by a special word processing program that scrolls through the script as the speaker reads. Because the autocue is positioned just below or to the side of the camera that will capture his or her image, the speaker is able to read from the monitor's screen while appearing to be looking into the camera or straight ahead. Because users do not have to consult a written script or note cards, or memorize an address, they will appear more professional, confident, and believable when using an autocue device.

Supovitz's Theory of Event Flow

Like nature, live events abhor a vacuum. When nothing is happening, audiences lose interest and begin thinking about being elsewhere. The television industry is quite familiar with the tenuousness of its hold on an audience. There are rarely even a few seconds in which there is a total absence of movement and sound. If there is a gap of just a few moments, viewers know that someone has made a mistake. Take a cue from our broadcasting brethren, and *produce live events as though they were television shows.*

The running order and script reveal the visuals and words that will be used to support a sports event, but not necessarily how well they are stitched together. The cueing, or the second-by-second timing of how the event flows from one segment to the next, should be perfected during rehearsals. Be on the lookout for times when absolutely no visual or aural information is being exchanged during ceremonial elements, as well as during competition. Such a gap may last only a few seconds, but the excitement of the audience and the momentum of the competition can quickly dissipate during that time and may require great effort to restore.

If an event is to be broadcast, embracing this philosophy will make the live event far easier to translate to television. Even if it is not, today's audiences are accustomed to fast-paced, multisensory experiences and constant access to compelling information, thanks to both the Internet and advances in sports event coverage. Many professional basketball, baseball, football, and hockey teams direct their everyday games in this manner, but this theory suggests that other sports events, including amateur and grassroots programs, can be easily and cost-effectively executed in the same way.

To continuously engage the audience, have the hosts conduct player interviews, play upbeat music, or stage promotions and contests that give away prizes. Start these elements as soon as a pause in the play begins, and cease just as the contest resumes. Fulfill sponsor obligations for public address announcements, but include a background of appropriate music. (Think of these as your commercials.) Play exciting and inspirational music as athletes are introduced. Program fan participation activities between matches or during intermissions. Have a band perform, screen music videos, provide replays of highlights from the competition in progress, announce or show statistics. Cue these elements tightly together so that as one finishes, the next begins. Don't just make the event as good as if you were watching it on television—make it better.

Sports purists often decry the loss of conversation between members of the audience, and the cultures of some sports require more sedate surroundings. Although producers should design the most appropriate presentations for entertaining their core fans, the notion of tying event elements closely together is no less valid. There should always be something for the audience to do or discover when competition is not in progress, even if the experience is in another location to which the audience has to direct its attention. Having activities and entertainment planned elsewhere on the event site, but not in the area of the athletic competition, is a good alternative for events whose culture frowns on noise where the sport is being played. In such cases, provide activity at corporate hospitality pavilions, public food areas, or an on-site fan festival.

Some sports events, of course, are already television presentations. Producers who embrace the notion of designing their events as though they were television shows are well positioned to work side by side with their television counterparts and will be able to balance their needs with the unique requirements of this important medium. See Play 13 to better understand the needs of our broadcasting stakeholders.

Post-Play Analysis

Sports events are entertainment experiences. Audiences want to be able to support their favorite athletes or teams, comprehend the progress of play, be kept apprised of important information, and be entertained. Pageantry provided by marching bands, drill teams and kick lines, and other large-format performing units can add significant scale and excitement to pre-event ceremonies and intermission periods, their large-scale visuals and sound filling the often substanial void between the audience and the playing surface.

Sports event presentation directors, or producers, manage the production by generating important planning documents, including an event rundown, production schedule, cast list, wardrobe list, and rehearsal schedule, among others. These essential tools help to organize the myriad details that must be managed in preparing the facility for event day. Consider all of the presentation tools that can help to excite, entertain, and inform the audience, including lighting, sound, video, and special effects such as lasers and pyrotechnics. The use of each must be designed for maximum effect without affecting the quality of the playing surface.

Coach's Clipboard

1. An action sports competition featuring skateboarders, BMX bicyclists, and in-line skaters is scheduled for a community stadium of 5000 seats. The competitors include participants from the community and invited athletes who are coming from a significant distance. Create brief pre-event, intermission, and post-event ceremonies that will excite the audience and familiarize attendees with the fame of the visiting athletes. Include an event rundown and rehearsal schedule in your plan.

2. What kinds of technical equipment, both for the competition itself and for presentation purposes, will be required to produce the event described in item 1? Create a production schedule to organize the facility for deliveries, installations, rehearsals, and dismantling of the event.

3. Your sponsors have requested recognition beyond signage at the host venue for the event described in item 1. What exposure opportunities can be offered to partners during opening ceremonies, intermissions, and during the competition itself? How can you use various technical presentation tools to provide a unique impact for your top sponsors?

Working with Broadcasters

You're never as good as the praise and you're never as bad as the criticism.

—GARY BETTMAN,
COMMISSIONER, NATIONAL HOCKEY LEAGUE,
IN SPORTS BUSINESS DAILY, OCTOBER 9, 2002

Mass media such as television, radio, and, to an increasing extent, the Internet, can provide sports event organizers with the incalculable benefit of broad geographic exposure. The ability of a broadcast to make an event available to an exponentially larger audience can position a sport like no other promotional tool, achieving a degree of instant accessibility and fame and, in time, helping a sport to establish its cultural relevance. A sports event broadcast places the organizer in a superior competitive position, enabling him or her to attract more and better athletes and teams and to package sponsorships at prices far greater than those expected for nontelevised events. Even incidental television exposure can have an effect on a sponsor's sales, and a guarantee of a viewing audience for a company's commercials, signage, and products is a major selling point for a potential sponsorship. As discussed in this chapter, such an outstanding and enhanced exposure opportunity is difficult to achieve and, on a number of levels, is becoming increasingly costly to execute.

Sideline Story—Sports Television: Where It's Been, Where It's Going

College baseball enjoys the distinction of being the first sport ever featured on television. A single camera on the third base line made history when it transmitted images of a 1939 match between Columbia and Princeton Universities for the very first time. It was a featherweight boxing championship that anchored the first network sports broadcast on the *Gillette Cavalcade of Sports* on NBC. Neither pugilist Willie Pep nor opponent Chalky Wright could possibly conceive of themselves as pioneer athletes back in 1944, especially when there were only 7000 functioning television sets in the United States. But it was apparent even then, in the waning years of World War II, that corporate sponsorship of televised sports events would be necessary to cover the considerable costs of putting them on the air.

Decades later, rights fees would make up most of a broadcaster's expenses in covering sports events. In 1970, networks paid the National Football League $50 million for the right to broadcast its games, and by 1985 those fees had risen to $450 million. How high is up? In 1998, the NFL's broadcasting rights were sold in an eight-year package for $17.6 billion.

Realistically speaking, the vast majority of the sports events currently being staged will never enjoy broadcast coverage. Only a select few will ever be attractive enough for broadcasters to invest the time and capital needed to cover them or for sponsors and advertisers to purchase the commercial time to make the venture financially viable. Even fewer will be so universally appealing that the broadcaster will invest beyond its costs of simply producing the program to add a rights fee payable to the event organizer for the opportunity to feature it on television or radio. By all indications, as the twenty-first century opens, television rights fees for any but the most popular sports events may have finally peaked.

What Broadcasters Want from Sports Events

For the most part, broadcasters are in the business of making money while serving their viewing audiences. They earn the greater part of their revenues by selling commercial time or collecting subscriber fees from cable and satel-

- Profit potential
- Viewers
  - High ratings and market share
  - Exclusive, compelling, and superior programming as compared with that of their competitors
- Commercial sales potential
  - Cash commitments from event sponsors
  - Programming that attracts other paying advertisers
- Exclusivity
  - No other real-time coverage by other television broadcasters
  - No other mechanism for fans to receive live pictures or video (e.g., Internet)
- Opportunities to provide high production values to viewers
  - Intimate, unobstructed camera positions
  - Coverage opportunities that provide unique, behind-the-scenes access

Figure 13-1
What Broadcasters Want from Sports Events

lite operators. Additional revenue potential is realized by providing various forms of in-program recognition to broadcast partners, usually associated with programming elements such as replays, score clock graphics, or even virtual signage (superimposed artwork of a sponsor or brand logo that appears to be at the event site, but is visible only to the television audience). In short, the potential to make a profit by televising a particular sports event is generally the motivation for a broadcaster to desire covering it (see Figure 13-1).

VIEWERSHIP AND RATINGS

For most broadcasters, profit potential is driven by how many viewers they can attract to a sports event. The more viewers it can attract, the more the broadcaster can charge its advertisers. In the United States, two standards are used to measure the quantity of television viewers—Nielsen ratings points and market share. Through a variety of data collection methods, including instantaneous electronic monitoring and submission of written diaries by participating families, Nielsen Media Research assigns television rating points that represent the number of households that watched a particular program within a specified area (another media research company, Arbitron, provides similar ratings information for radio). In this nation of an estimated 106 million households, one national Nielsen rating point is equivalent to 1 percent of the total, currently an approximate 1.06 million households. Rating points are also compiled on a market-to-market basis, the value of which vary depending on the local population. A single rating point earned for a broadcast in a city of 2 million households, for example, would represent an estimated 20,000 households (again, 1 percent of the market). Ratings for nationally telecast events are compiled on both national and local levels, the data for which can help disclose to organizers and sponsors which regions are stronger and which are weaker for a particular sport or event. For example, a sports event with a national rating of 1.7 (1.802 million households) can present a much more impressive rating of 5.8 in a host city of 1 million households (58,000 viewing households), and yet only a 1.1 score in a more distant city of 4 million (44,000). Sports events that are televised in only a single local market, of course, do not generate national ratings.

After an event has aired nationally, two sets of ratings are released. The first, called "overnight ratings," represent a national estimate based on electronic viewing data gathered solely from the country's largest markets, released within hours of a broadcast. National ratings are released several days later after more complete data have been collected and analyzed from all surveyed markets across the country. Depending on the nature of the event and the consistency of its appeal, national ratings may vary from overnight data by as much as a full rating point or more.

Nielsen also subdivides ratings across several demographic categories to assist sponsors in better targeting their advertising purchases. Ratings can be tabulated strictly for male viewers of ages 18 to 34, for example, a highly prized market for many sports event advertisers. Low national ratings, however, are not always indicators of weak programming choices. Depending on the sponsor, national rating points may be less important than local ratings in their most important geographic markets, or exceptionally good viewership among their products' target demographics (specific age groups or gender, for example).

Another common reference point used in determining the effectiveness of a program in attracting television viewers is a number that represents the "share of market." The number often quoted as a "share" is the percentage of televisions tuned to a particular program as compared with all of the televisions being watched during the same time period. Programs that are scheduled to air late at night may generate only modest ratings (because many people are asleep), but a strong share of market (because a large number of those who are awake and watching television are viewing a particular event).

COMMERCIAL SALES POTENTIAL

From the broadcasters' perspective, the profit potential of covering a sports event is almost always dependent on the ratings it can be expected to generate. Their ability to identify a past event's ratings performance among various demographic characteristics determines how much they will be able to charge for commercial time. They can also use a more detailed demographic analysis of the ratings to target companies that want to position themselves to the types of viewers a sports event attracts.

The most likely companies to purchase commercial time on a sports event broadcast are the sponsors who already enjoy a business relationship with the organizer. Many corporate partners will have already planned to "activate" their event sponsorship with the purchase of commercial time. Other companies will have spent their budgets, assuming that their on-site signage will already be highly visible during the event broadcast and that no additional purchase of commercial exposure is necessary. Overall, however, the attractiveness of broadcasting a sports event increases with the receipt of commitments to purchase commercial time from current event sponsors.

The broadcaster will also evaluate the program to determine whether it has enough appeal to persuade new advertisers that are not sports event sponsors to consider purchasing commercial time. If event sponsors do not elect to participate as advertisers, the broadcaster will want the flexibility to sell the opportunity to any company willing to spend the money—even those who are competitors of the event's sponsors. It is a good practice, in most cases, for organizers to ensure that their sponsor contracts provide exclusivity only at the event site. Agreements should, however, guarantee sponsors the right of first refusal on opportunities to purchase commercial time on any event broadcast that may subsequently be scheduled. That is, the organizer's agreement with the broadcaster would obligate it only to present event sponsors with an opportunity to buy commercial time before offering the same deal to the sponsors' competitors. If a sports event sponsor waives its right to purchase commercials on the broadcast, or fails to respond within a certain amount of time, the broadcaster would then be permitted the latitude to approach competitor companies. There are, however, many major events that offer broadcast advertising as part of their sponsorship entitlements, in which cases such exclusivity may be preserved. These packages are generally priced expensively and may include the purchase of broadcast advertising as a sponsor fulfillment item.

EXCLUSIVITY

Broadcasters who have invested the considerable capital required to produce televised coverage of a sports event want assurances that their rights to exclusivity are protected. They will vigorously defend their rights against any other mechanism by which a fan can visually consume the event, in whole or in part, on other television stations or even over the Internet. Any simultaneous transmission of the sports event within their viewing territory will detract from their ratings and make it more difficult to sell advertising at the highest possible rates. The presence of radio broadcasters and still photographers is usually not problematic for the broadcaster, but videographers, even those desiring to record only pieces of the event for news coverage, can create significant issues for the rights holder. Quite simply, the broadcaster will want to be the exclusive source of all video footage for news highlights, sports magazine shows, and any other programming. The presence of the organizer's dedicated video cameras recording the event for archival or promotional purposes, as well as the host facility's I-Mag camera crews, are usually not excluded by rights holder exclusivity.

Organizers should be open to welcoming video crews from other media outlets, but must limit their access to defined areas with no view of the playing surface, such as news conference areas and other back-of-the-house areas, to preserve the rights of the host broadcaster. (Enabling members of the media to videotape segments of the competition if there is no host broadcaster is completely at the discretion of the organizer.) The broadcaster may also wish to be protected with respect to any video simulcasts of the sports event on the Internet. Streaming video images and audio on the organizer's web site, however, is a great way to expand the event's reach globally if broadcast coverage is limited to only a modest geographical region. Because global access includes the region where the broadcast may also be seen, the rights holder may require that Internet coverage be delayed from just a few minutes to as much as an hour to give the rights holder the window of exclusivity it needs to generate ratings.

OPPORTUNITIES TO PROVIDE HIGH PRODUCTION VALUES

If a broadcaster has ascertained that providing coverage of a sports event represents a viable business proposition, its next objective is to ensure that the product it can deliver to the viewers is of the best quality possible. In general, producing television coverage of a sports event is an expensive proposition. It requires an enormous expenditure in labor for on-air talent, camera operators, electricians, video editors, sound engineers, graphics designers, and drivers, among others. Cameras and production trucks with video and audio control rooms must be rented or moved to the event site, scaffolds for anchor positions and studios built, lighting and audio systems installed, videotaped features edited, and host scripts written. With all that effort and expense, broadcast producers want to make sure they can position cameras in locations to cover the event from the best and most intimate of perspectives.

With the rare exception of those who well understand that excited audiences make for exciting television, in setting their agendas producers sometimes neglect to take the quality of the experience for the live audience into account. They want their cameras in the best possible locations, regardless of the visual obstructions they might create for those who may have purchased tickets for seats immediately behind their equipment. For this reason, it is best to know the camera locations before tickets are put on sale. The seats immediately behind the cameras may be removed from public sale ("killed") or made available to the broadcaster for entertaining its own complimentary guests. Broadcasters also want unlimited access to athletes before the event to conduct interviews and provide behind-the-scenes glimpses of the event. Both are perceived to add great value to the viewing experience. As a general rule, if unfettered access will not interfere with the operation of the event, the safety or performance of the athletes, or the quality of the viewing experience of the live audience, there is no good reason not to grant these broad rights to the broadcaster.

What Sports Event Organizers Want from Broadcasters

Sports events can provide broadcasters and their viewers with outstanding entertainment, but in today's business landscape, it is clearly a buyer's market. For their part, organizers desire the greatest and broadest exposure possible for their sports events. From a brand positioning perspective, this exposure provides legitimacy and validation that the event and its featured sport are relevant enough to merit broadcast coverage and offers them outstanding opportunities for self-promotion (see Figure 13-2). Television exposure does not come without a potential downside, however. Televised programs must be sufficiently compelling to ensure that the local paying audience will still come to witness the event live. Clearly, tickets cost money, and attendance costs time in commuting to the event, parking, and returning home. Television, however, provides no-cost access to the event and the convenience of never having to leave your home. Recognizing this reality, the National Football League routinely blocks television coverage within local markets in which tickets for games have not sold out. The convenience and absence of cost in consuming a sports event on television is yet another reason to ensure that the live presentation of the event is even more exciting and provides greater value than the broadcast version, as discussed in Play 12.

- Greatest and broadest exposure possible
  - Establishment or reinforcement of the event's cultural relevance
  - Promotion of the featured sport and event
  - Increased value to existing and potential sponsors
    - Easier to sell sponsorship
    - Ability to charge higher prices
  - Coverage in a time slot when the most viewers can watch the event
- Coverage provided by the broadcaster with no or few incremental costs to the event
- Rights fees

Figure 13-2
What Sports Events Want from Broadcasters

The exposure provided by television coverage also makes an event more relevant and attractive to potential and existing sponsors. The positions granted by the organizer for sponsor signage at the event site becomes even more significant, those with the greatest probability of being seen on television commanding higher fees or included only within premium priced partner packages. Presuming that sponsorships are priced competitively for the expected number of viewers, television coverage generally makes events far easier to sell to potential sponsors.

Broadcaster–Sports Event Business Relationships

In addition to realizing increased sponsorship fees, sports event organizers hope to profit from rights fees paid by a broadcaster. At the very least, they want to enjoy the remarkable benefits of television exposure without experiencing any net increase in their costs. Agreements with broadcasters should define what fees, if any, would be paid to the organizer and which expenses would be assumed by the broadcaster. These parameters define the four basic relationships between broadcasters and the sports events they cover, as listed in Figure 13-3.

Event organizers who represent properties with an extremely high perceived value, typically those of global or national importance, often offer broadcasting rights to interested bidders in exchange for a cash payment, or rights fee. A broadcaster who purchases the rights to televise an event (the rights holder) is confident that the program, by virtue of its expected ratings and viewer demographics, will appeal so strongly to advertisers that it will be able to charge the high rates for commercial time that will cover its production costs and the rights fee and still leave a profit. There are, however, precious few sports properties that can command such significant rights fees.

Other events are attractive enough for broadcasters to consider airing, but are not expected to generate sufficient profitability to enable them to offer the

> - Fee-based Rights Holder
> - Fee-free Rights Holder
> - "Time Buy" Provider
> - Owner or Co-Owner

Figure 13-3
Broadcaster Business Relationships with an Event

organizer a rights fee. Some event organizers will nevertheless award the rights to the broadcaster on a no-fee basis to take advantage of the broadened exposure for promotional purposes, as well as for the incremental value a broadcast will generate with respect to sponsor fees. Organizers may also be able to negotiate receiving a commercial spot or two on a complimentary basis in no-fee deals, which can in turn be used for their own advertising, resold to a sponsor, or included in a high-end sponsorship package. Sports events that can provide no-rights-fee programming for smaller, niche broadcasters may be the wave of the future as professional sports teams begin testing the market for the introduction of their own proprietary regional sports networks (RSNs). The National Basketball Association's (NBA) Memphis Grizzlies, for example, announced in October 2003 its intention to launch its own sports channel. With $10 million in start-up costs and a limited number of basketball games as anchor programming, the network immediately announced that it intended to offer area promoters the ability to air high-profile regional sports events on its channel, but that no rights fees would be paid.

If broadcasters pass on the opportunity to televise a sports event, all hope is not lost. Organizers can negotiate with broadcasters to purchase a time slot in return for a flat cash payment and then produce and air their own coverage of a sports event. These productions can air live or be re-edited in a compressed form for later broadcast. Entering into a "time buy" relationship releases the broadcaster from all risks of having to generate viewers and advertising revenue, placing those responsibilities squarely on the shoulders of the organizer. In return for the purchase of airtime, the organizer will usually receive all of the available commercial time, perhaps minus one or two spots the broadcaster will hold back for promoting other programming. The organizer, in turn, can sell the commercial time to sponsors and other advertisers, either independently or through a third-party marketing agency. Alternatively, the value of the commercial time can be included in the fulfillment costs of event sponsorship packages, a benefit perceived to be of great value to business partners.

Obviously, time buys are risky propositions. The organizer will have to assume the significant financial risk of purchasing the airtime, as well as the costs of producing the event for television—basically all of the expenses the broadcasters themselves were unsure of being able to offset through their own marketing efforts. Before committing to a time buy, event organizers are well advised to confirm the time slot being purchased in writing. The advertising rates, or the value of commercials granted to sponsors, that an organizer will be able to charge to offset costs will depend on the customary advertising rates charged for other programs during the time and day an event will air, the overall interest in the event among the viewing public, and the channel on which it will air. Production costs will remain the same whether a program airs at 1:00 A.M. on a Monday evening or 8:00 P.M. on a Thursday. The value and attractiveness of the airtime—and the rates that can be set for advertising—will obviously be much greater for the latter time slot than for the former.

Sideline Story—ESPN's X Games

In 1995, ESPN, the most popular all-sports cable channel in the United States, staged the first Extreme Games (*www.expn.com*) across four cities in Rhode Island and Vermont before an estimated 198,000 spectators. This eight-day multidisciplinary tournament included nine competitive action sports, such as windsurfing, bungee jumping, and mountain biking. The following year, ESPN announced that a new winter sports festival would be added to the already familiar X Games brand starting in 1997. By 1998, the X Games franchise went truly global, the organizers staging an Asian X Games exhibition in Phuket, Thailand, during which qualifiers advanced to the Summer X Games in San Diego. Although ESPN does not release attendance figures, reports suggest that at its peak, as many as 275,000 spectators attended the summer games and more than 80,000 attended the winter edition. More significant, these various X Games events and qualifiers provide ESPN with hours of television programming in direct event coverage and for incorporation into magazine show features. As both the organizer and rights holder, ESPN can assert total control over the event schedule, invited athletes, featured sports, sponsorships, and staging.

Time buys have become somewhat more affordable as the cable television industry continues to subdivide into increasingly smaller special-interest and niche viewer markets. That does not necessarily mean, however, that the economics of producing a sports event for special-interest cable channels are becoming more attractive. Dozens of regional and specialty sports channels are now available as partners, many of whom are hungry for new and inexpensive programming, and new broadcasters are entering the marketplace regularly. The limiting factor, of course, is the number of viewers that smaller, niche broadcasters can attract and the concomitantly reduced advertising rates that organizers can charge sponsors to offset the production, even with cheaper airtime costs. Although production costs will be the same no matter where the program airs, the smaller the potential viewing audience offered by the broadcaster, the less valuable the commercial time will be. Therefore, another important point to negotiate in a time buy agreement is the channel's willingness and ability to promote the event telecast with free commercial spots in the days and weeks leading up to the program, as the most likely audience for a televised event may be the viewers already watching that channel.

With increasing regularity, broadcasters themselves are becoming event organizers and owners of original sports programming made expressly for television. ESPN's wildly successful X Games franchise, featuring both cold- and warm-weather competitions, provides these broadcaster/owners with sports events over which they can exert total control. They can feature the sports they think their viewers most want to see, eliminate those that rate as less popular, and convert advertisers into event sponsors, rather than the other way around.

Working with Broadcasters

In most cases, broadcasters are engaged in the sole business of broadcasting events, not staging them. A close working relationship between the organizer and the rights holder based on an understanding of each other's objectives is essential to ensure a positive and beneficial outcome for all involved. It has earlier been stated that events should be presented just the way they would be seen on television to keep the live audience energized and engaged. Similarly, broadcasters want to capture the excitement and dynamism of the live event experience to keep viewers from changing channels to other programming alternatives. "Through my experience, I have found that live event coordination and television producing are in many ways similar," observes Canadian Broadcasting Corporation sports producer Sherali Najak. "In television one of my jobs is to extract the passion and emotion an event can create," says Najak. If a sports event is televised, the organizer should work cooperatively with the television producer to find ways to help the viewers feel as though they are there, and perhaps even wish they were. "I always find that because events are so detail oriented and time-consuming to organize that the execution and planning of the event often takes priority over the thrill and amazement that television tries to cover," he asserts. "This can't be manufactured, but certain steps can be put in place to give the event a chance to tell its own story."

If the organizer has done his or her job well, the live audience will feel the pulse of excitement from the moment they arrive. The event environment is loaded with visual and auditory cues that something special is about to happen, and its audience will react vociferously at predictable points in the running order—when athletes first enter, for example. For live broadcasts, try to coordinate the timing and staging of these focal points with the broadcaster so that the television production can also take best advantage of them, rather than taking the risk that viewers will be watching a commercial when the most climactic moment occurs. Live audiences enjoy the sense of participation in an event; let these people know when the television audience is joining the event and prompt them to demonstrate their excitement at that very moment.

The broadcaster and presentation director should also remain in communication during the competitions themselves to coordinate the points at which commercial breaks will be taken, preferably during a pause in the action. Many sports that are regularly televised in real time have adopted protocols that determine when television breaks can be taken, and delay the resumption of play until the broadcaster has returned from airing their commercials. The competitive cultures of other sports totally preclude stopping play for commercial breaks, and as a result the broadcaster must decide whether commercials will air only during intermissions or during unpredictable and potentially decisive moments in the competition.

Keep in mind that when a sports event is televised, there is no real "backstage." Anything and everything can be captured on television or videotape unless specific instructions regarding access are communicated to the broadcaster. Clearly establish whether a broadcaster's cameras will have access to the athletes' locker rooms, and if so, during what periods. Can the broadcaster's personnel enter the locker room pre-event to tape interviews? Will they be able to broadcast live from the dressing rooms during intermissions, or can they be limited to a location outside the door? What kind of access will they be permitted post-event? Dress the nonpublic areas in which cameras will be permitted to shoot with event banners and posters for additional logo exposure.

Make sure that either the organizer or the host facility has determined what kinds of production trucks and trailers the broadcaster will require for its coverage of the event and has identified the locations where they will be positioned. A truck contains all of the technical equipment required for producing the coverage, and the positioning of cameras often determines its location. Ascertain how cables will be routed between the truck and the cameras. If they are run through public areas, determine whether they must be hung from the ceiling or placed beneath temporary cable chases to ensure that athletes or fans will not trip over them.

INTEGRATING AUDIENCE NEEDS

When dysfunctional relationships develop between sports event organizers and their broadcasting counterparts, the reason is often a lack of the basic understanding that there is really only one audience being served by both parties. When a difference of opinion emerges between the live presentation director and a television producer, it is far from unusual to hear this argument: "To whom would you rather promote your product—the few thousand people here or the millions watching on television?" The right answer is the one often least expected: "Both!"

Organizers are responsible for delivering value and an emotional payoff to the loyal fans of their sport to keep them engaged, entertained, and ready to pay to return for future events. Unless there is respect for the needs of an event's core audience, loyalty is bound to wane and disinterest is sure to result. These hard-core fans are the same people who will later watch television coverage of events they cannot attend; thus, ultimately, even television viewership will ebb because of such cavalier neglect. Keeping fans coming back is as much a ratings concern for broadcasters as a financial one for the organizer. Simply put, a full event venue also makes for good television. Nothing says, "This event is not important enough for me to spend time watching it" more than empty grandstands seen on television. The organizer must provide good reasons for the live audience to keep coming back for future events.

Broadcasters have concerns similar to those faced by sports event organizers, but with a significant added challenge. Like organizers of live sports events, they must keep members of their viewing audience entertained and their interests served at all times to keep them tuning in to future events. Broadcasters' concerns are more immediate and acute with respect to a sports event broadcast, however. A fan who has already invested capital, time, and effort to pay for a ticket, give up a day or evening, and travel to see a sports event live has far greater staying power than one who is watching from home. A person at a live event will remain attentive to the event a far longer period of time, even if the contest proves disappointing, than a viewer with ready access to a remote control. Television producers must be concerned with attracting and holding their audience on a minute-to-minute basis, lest the viewers switch to alternative sports programming on another channel. Understanding this important stakeholder's key objective is paramount to the future business of the sports event organizer—potential ticket buyers are *watching the event on television*. Organizers should do everything possible to help television producers keep their coverage interesting, informative, and entertaining. Give them the unique access they need to bring the viewer closer to the athletes and the sport. Make sure they do not miss a second of the action. Work closely with them on developing new camera positions to give viewers totally new perspectives on the coverage of your sport.

Similarly, sports broadcasters should also take note—prime television viewers are *watching the event live*. The most likely viewers of coverage of future sports events are seated in the grandstands. Work with the live producer to bring replays, player features, and interviews to the fans in the stands. Fans like to associate with others who are devoted to their favorite sport. Demonstrate your own knowledge, respect, and loyalties to the sports they love, and they will devote their allegiance to your coverage and on-air talent as well.

Glenn Adamo, the NFL Network's vice president of production and operations, and veteran of sports broadcasts ranging from regional regular season contests to Olympic competition, is a master at working closely with live sports event producers to achieve mutual objectives. He notes five areas of "Must Do's" for sports event organizers when working with broadcasters (see Figure 13-4).

1. Communicate during planning
2. Integrate timings and other broadcasting needs
3. Remain flexible
4. Rehearse together
5. Communicate during events

Figure 13-4
Adamo's Top 5 Broadcasting "Must Do's"
For Sports Event Organizers

"ONE EVENT—ONE AUDIENCE"

Sports event organizers must let the broadcaster know what activities are being planned before live coverage is scheduled to begin. Pre-event fan activities can provide outstanding footage (known as "B-roll") that can be integrated into taped features to air during event coverage, or at the opening of the broadcast. Make sure that the broadcaster is offered an opportunity to send a camera crew and reporter to all press conferences and other media events, the best times to capture interviews with the athletes. Engage the broadcast producer in discussions regarding the development of the event rundown so that he or she can plan everything from camera positions and commercial breaks to segment timings and scripting. Familiarize the producer with every aspect of the event to ensure that the show can portray the sport with the impact and imagery presented to the live audience. If organizers strive to stage the event with the precision of a television production, the only way to ensure that both parties remain in step is to integrate their timings so that each understands what the other can expect as the event unfolds. "Timing is always underestimated," says sports producer Sherali Najak. "Five seconds of a dead house can be a lifetime on television. It's magical to the viewer when events or introductions happen exactly on cue without a second of silence or hesitation." As both Najak and Glenn Adamo can attest, there may be two productions being presented simultaneously (i.e., television and live), but there is still "one event—one audience."

To achieve this unity of purpose, both parties must remain flexible and understanding of each other's objectives throughout the planning process. A segment may have to be moved to provide a broadcaster with time to break for a commercial, another may have to be shortened or lengthened to accommodate other requirements and realities. Broadcasters, similarly, should maintain some flexibility to ensure that the event does not lose its focus or momentum for the live audience. "Remember, the event producer has spent days and even weeks planning his execution so it is perfectly timed for his purposes. Asking the producer to "scrap" his show for TV will not work," says

Adamo. "A producer can be flexible but needs you (the broadcaster) to also understand his issues."

In this spirit of "understanding the stakeholders' objectives" (USO), accommodating commercial breaks cannot result in a total cessation of activity for the live audience. While the broadcaster is fulfilling its advertiser and sponsor obligations, the organizer can likewise use the opportunity to do the same for his or her own. Sometimes, however, the momentum, especially in regard to pre-event entertainment activities, must continue to keep the audience engaged. It is helpful for the broadcaster and the live presentation director to agree in advance on what segments can be missed and over what period of time. Providing broadcasters with an opportunity to review rundowns, scripts, and other presentation plans well in advance gives them an opportunity to create their own rundowns and surface challenges, requests, and requirements during the formative stages of planning. If the organizer and the broadcaster craft the rundowns together, the presentations are more likely to appear seamless, both on television and at the sports event venue.

CAMERA REHEARSALS

There is only one way to test whether these integrated timings will, in fact, work to the benefit of both audiences—that is, by having the broadcaster and the event director rehearse all critical segments together. For example, decisions should be made in advance as to whether the broadcaster will use the event's announcer or its own during athlete introductions, and how they will be covered by the cameras, whether hand-held cameras will be temporarily permitted on the playing surface, and at what pace they will progress to accommodate the needs of television. For the live event audience, athletes can be announced more rapidly, but if the introductions are being planned for television, a pace must be established to allow for smooth direction of the cameras and the announcers. Staging a camera rehearsal for segments such as this is by far the best way to establish such parameters. The athletes themselves are rarely available for these essential rehearsals. Use stand-ins to simulate the timing and assist in the blocking of player introductions and other important ceremonial elements for the purposes of both the live event producer and the broadcast producer. Schedule joint rehearsals far in advance—like the producer of the live sports event, the broadcast producer has many more rehearsals that must be staged during the time leading up to the program (e.g., host rehearsals, and rehearsals for tape cues, animations, and graphics).

The camera rehearsal will also establish whether the lighting conditions planned for various segments will be conducive to television coverage. Live presentation directors love to stage events in the dark. Light and laser shows are at their most dramatic and emotional when they are executed with theatrical effects in an otherwise completely dark facility. For television, however, dark environments are horrendously limiting. The impact of a light show on a television screen does not approach the excitement it generates in the facility. As wonderful as they might be live, light shows often appear indecipherable on television, so these theatrical openings are frequently the points in the rundown at which broadcasters will be doing something else.

Moreover, television directors don't like concentrating on a single shot for a long time. The response of the audience at a sports event and during pre-event introductions is a great visual opportunity for television directors. If the fans are in total darkness, the director will have difficulty portraying their enthusiasm at key moments in the broadcast. To give broadcasters an option to show enthusiastic audience reactions, consider partially lighting fans in selected seating sections during times and segments when the rest of the audience is otherwise in the dark. Broadcasters should demonstrate the lighting they plan to use during various theatrically illuminated portions of the event. Thousands of dollar's worth of lighting and special effects can be ruined by floodlights used during an unanticipated interview at the edge of the playing surface or in an anchor position overlooking the field.

Installing temporary television lighting in indoor facilities that are not specifically designed for television can offer its own challenges. Simply put, lights are hot. "Temperature is something I never thought about till I saw all the lights it takes to put on a television event in a large [indoor] venue," observes the CBC's Sherali Najak. "If the audience is too warm (or too cold), then it affects the perception of the product. Many of the shows we do are in excess of two hours. The audience starts fidgeting (in the heat) and becomes disinterested in the production of the show. I always make it a rule to cool down the house right up until show time." Not only can lighting affect the comfort of the audience, it can also dramatically impact the performance of an athlete. Make sure that the air-handling system of the host facility can adequately cool or vent the heat from the indoor environment. If it cannot, temporary air-conditioning units can be rented, albeit at a high cost.

THE IMPORTANCE OF COMMUNICATION DURING THE EVENT!

Close and regular communication between the organizer and the broadcaster must extend well beyond the planning process. It is also essential to maintain open lines of communication throughout the event and broadcast as they progress in real time. The game presentation director should appoint an individual on staff to maintain contact with the producer in the television truck during the event to receive the concerns of the broadcaster, as well as to communicate any required changes in timings by either party. Accidents happen during events, and aberrations in timing, order of competition, and athlete appearances, among other variances, are to be expected. "If your show, or theirs, goes awry, you need to be able to communicate in order to execute the integration without embarrassment," observes Adamo. Install a private line (PL) phone or other wired device between the truck and the presentation director's control room to maintain a flow of communication during all phases of the event. Know when the broadcaster has, in fact, departed the event site to accommodate a commercial and, definitely, when viewers have returned, to ensure they miss no part of the action. Communicate the substance of judging and referee's decisions to the broadcaster so that viewers are as well informed as the live audience. Make sure that the broadcaster has access to all essential information to make the broadcast genuine, authoritative, and reliable.

Post Play Analysis

Broadcast coverage of sports events can exponentially increase the audience that witnesses a competition and can provide tremendous additional value to event sponsors. To present a viable business opportunity to a broadcaster, sports events must be able to generate revenues in excess of production costs and any rights fees that may be paid to the organizer. As a result, very few events become broadcast properties, as compared with the total number staged. Alternatively, sports event organizers can invest in a "time buy," the outright purchase of time from a broadcaster. In exchange for a cash payment, the organizer typically receives the inventory of commercials available during the time of the broadcast, which the organizer can resell to sponsors or other advertisers. The organizer, however, must pay the costly expenses of production and, in the case of taped events, for the postproduction editing of the event.

Sports event organizers and broadcast producers can create a seamless production by embracing the "one event—one audience" concept. The future viability of both the sports event and its broadcast coverage depend on simultaneously serving the needs of both the live and television audiences. The parties should communicate with each other regarding their plans before the event and exhibit reasonable flexibility to ensure that the needs of both the live program and its televised counterpart are met. Rehearse important television moments with broadcast cameras operating, and be prepared to make adjustments to enhance their coverage. Keep the lines of communication open throughout the planning process, and establish a system for real-time communications during the event broadcast to minimize the effect of accidents, mistakes, and oversights and to inform the broadcaster of all pertinent developments.

Coach's Clipboard

1. Both national and regional broadcasters have decided not to take advantage of the opportunity to televise a top-tier skateboarding competition. The event's presenting sponsor is keenly interested in having the event featured on television, but the organizer has no available funds to risk buying the time on the regional sports network that is willing to air it for a price. What can the organizer do to

improve the chances of the event's being broadcast? What other options exist if television broadcast coverage remains elusive?

2. A television producer has been assigned to cover your one-day track-and-field event just two weeks before the races will be held. A pre-event ceremony has been scheduled and publicized to begin at 3:00 P.M., with the first race stepping off at 3:20 P.M. During the first conference call to review the event rundown, the broadcaster indicates that for its purposes, the first race must begin at 3:08 P.M. What options are available to you as the sports event organizer?

3. A major news event has suddenly preempted live television coverage of an organizer's sports event in progress. What kinds of risks may the organizer be subject to, and what protections should the organizer have in place to minimize the financial impact?

Managing for the Unexpected

I don't believe in superstitions. They're bad luck.
—*Former New York Mets manager Bobby Valentine,*
as quoted in Sports Illustrated, *May 6, 2002*

As game day approaches, the countless hours of intense and detailed planning have laid a solid foundation for an entertaining, smooth-running, and rewarding experience for the athletes, audience, sponsors, and staff. Regardless of how simple a sports event may appear to be, rest assured that there will be dozens of unfulfilled details and inadvertent omissions that will come to light in the final days, hours, and minutes, from just about every direction. Some may even become evident as the event itself progresses, a natural by-product of a detail-laden, multidisciplinary process. It remains the sports event organizer's job to predict, project, and plan for these issues and challenges before they present themselves, and to establish a plan to deal with those that nevertheless emerge unexpectedly.

Risk Assessment and Management

Every sports event carries elements of risk—and lots of them. Athletes may be injured in the course of competition or as a result of accidents in noncompetitive circumstances. A spectator can fall from the bleachers at a community

379

activities field, or an errant ball can cause unintentional physical harm. Organizers add risk factors for almost every benefit they offer their audiences and any accommodations they make for the athletes. Despite meticulous planning and all good intentions, a caterer can unwittingly serve tainted food, trusses supporting lighting can tip and fall, loudspeakers can become detached and drop to the ground, a bus or van carrying participants can become involved in a traffic accident. Fireworks can drop smoldering debris on unsuspecting people or damage parked cars. Spectators can wander into non-public areas, trip on cables, or fall down stairs. In short, absolutely anything can happen.

The comforting news is that although organizers cannot totally eliminate the possibility of an injury or damage to property as either a direct or indirect result of a sports event, they can exercise the good judgment and sensitivity required to evaluate and manage risks and greatly reduce the potential of their occurrence. An essential resource for incorporating this philosophy into all phases of sports event planning is *Event Risk Management and Safety,* by Peter E. Tarlow (John Wiley & Sons, 2002). In this book, Tarlow outlines a formalized risk management process, which is summarized and expanded in Figure 14-1.

ANALYZING RISK EXPOSURE AND POSSIBLE OUTCOMES

Identify the many areas in which an event and its various participants, spectators, stakeholders, and organizations may be placed at risk. Issues can be separated into three broad categories: (1) areas that may affect the health, safety, and security of spectators, staff, and participants, (2) financial and legal issues that can threaten the ability of the organizer to complete the event, and (3) potentially catastrophic occurrences that can cause the event to be canceled completely (see Figure 14-2 for a summary of the discussion that follows).

---

1. Identify areas of risk exposure and the likelihood of their occurrence.
2. Project possible outcomes flowing from areas of risk exposure.
3. Determine possible remedies.
4. Act on feasible remedies to prevent possible outcomes.
5. Identify possible reactions to potentially unavoidable crises.
6. Formalize crisis management and communications procedures.

Figure 14-1
Risk Management Process

A careful and thorough evaluation of the areas listed below can help sports event organizers manage potential risks that may impact the safety of the public and participants, as well as the financial health of the organizer.

Safety and Security
- Crowd Control
  - Queuing of early-arriving spectators
  - Sufficient points of ingress and egress
  - Sufficient front-of-house staff for directing and providing information to guests
  - Emergency evacuation plan
    - Dissemination of instructions and information to staff and the public
    - Clearly marked emergency exits
  - Protection of athletes and playing surface from spectators
- Security of Assets and Property
  - Lockable storage and office areas to prevent theft of equipment and materials
  - Adequate security personnel to safeguard equipment and materials that cannot be protected in lockable areas
- Public Safety
  - Policies regarding banned materials and substances at the event site (weapons, alcohol, bottles, cans, drugs, etc.)
  - Degree of audience screening upon entering the event facility (e.g., magnetometers, wands, bag x-rays or searches)
  - Inspection of vehicles entering restricted areas
  - Policies regarding sales and consumption of alcohol at the event site
  - Accreditation process and system
    - Background checks of staff, freelancers, and volunteers
    - Security for points of accessibility to nonpublic areas
  - Physical condition of the event venue
    - Public areas (e.g., entrances, exits, concourses, seating areas)
    - Playing surface (including team benches, dugouts, etc.)
    - Backstage and locker room facilities
    - Parking facilities
    - Lighting conditions
  - Accessibility to emergency medical personnel and facilities
    - Athletes
    - Staff
    - Public
- Presentation Elements
  - Lasers, pyrotechnics, and other special effects
  - Safety procedures during darkened periods

Financial and Legal Issues
- Labor Disputes

Figure 14-2
Managing Sports Event Risk Factors

- Unavailability of required labor
- Picket lines and protests
- Legal Challenges
  - Court injunctions
  - Failure to secure required permits
  - Intellectual property right infringements
  - Criminal investigations
  - Civil suits
- Bankruptcy
  - Organizer
  - Host facility
  - Other stakeholder (e.g., vendor, sponsor, broadcaster)

Cancellation Scenarios
- "Acts of God"
  - Weather conditions
  - Flooding
  - Earthquake
  - Power failure
  - Structural damage to, or collapse of, host facility
- Catastrophic Political or Cultural Events
  - Global or national tragedy
  - Acts of terror
  - War
  - National day(s) of mourning

Figure 14-2
(Continued)

Although the areas of concern may seem as limitless as the imagination, the probability of such risks occurring may range from the infinitesimal to the quite possible. It is the responsibility of the organizer to ensure that all plans minimize the risk potential to the greatest degree possible through a process of thorough self-examination.

SAFETY AND SECURITY

Next, project the possible outcomes that can develop from areas of potential risk. Some may simply create nuisances that can affect the enjoyment of those in attendance; others may pose the potential for more serious health and safety concerns. First and foremost, the safety and well-being of all who attend a sports event, from participants to spectators and staff, are of paramount importance. With all other considerations treated as secondary, determine whether you, the organizer, and the facility are providing a sufficiently safe environment for the event, from the time and point of arrival until departure.

Sideline Story—Protecting Event Participants

If you think a violent incident involving spectators and athletes cannot happen at your sports event, consider this abbreviated, but sobering, chronology:

- On April 30, 1993, 19-year-old tennis star Monica Seles was stabbed in the back by a spectator who charged through the grandstands and jumped into a courtside rest area while she waited for her next game to begin at the Hamburg Open in Germany. Rushed to a nearby hospital, Seles recovered, but would not play again for 27 months.
- During the last game of the 1995 NFL New York Giants' season, fans launched dozens of hard-packed, icy snowballs onto the field, striking and knocking a San Diego Chargers assistant unconscious. The team identified 75 season ticket holders and their guests as being among the perpetrators and revoked their ability to renew their accounts for the following season.
- The playing field was abandoned for a half hour after fans at a 2001 Cleveland Browns football contest against the Jacksonville Jaguars began throwing beer bottles onto the field. The game was halted with only 48 seconds to play, following a disputed call by the officials. The game was completed after the stadium had been almost entirely emptied.
- In 2002, fan violence erupted in the stands during a game between the Washington Redskins and Philadelphia Eagles. Police attempted to control the crowd by using pepper spray, which drifted toward the Philadelphia bench and into the players' faces, causing respiratory symptoms and vomiting among team members.
- In April 2003, Chicago's U.S. Cellular Field (formerly Comiskey Park) witnessed an attack on first base umpire Laz Diaz when a fan leaped onto the field and attempted to tackle the official during the eighth inning of a game against the Kansas City Royals. This was the fourth time the game was halted that night while stadium security rounded up fans running onto the field. Just the previous season, Tom Gamboa, then the Royals' first base coach, was assaulted by a fan and his 15-year-old son on the very same field.

In September 2003, in an effort to reduce threats to athlete security and the incidence of injury, the New York City Council overwhelmingly approved legislation that imposed penalties of as much as $1000 in fines and one year in prison on fans who illegally enter playing surfaces at professional sports events.

Have plans created an environment that will encourage fans to arrive extremely early and rush into the facility when the doors first open (first-come, first-served general admission seating, for example)? How early will spectators arrive, and will they begin crowding around the entrances to get the best possible viewing locations? How early should the facility plan to queue the spectators into orderly lines? (These types of crowd control issues can also exist on the day event tickets are first put on sale at the box office.)

How early should the public be admitted to the facility on the day of the event? Will there be sufficient time and front-of-house labor to ensure that all arrivals can find their seats before the event begins or within a reasonable period of time? Are trained, informed personnel available to keep crowds moving, to direct spectators and answer questions? Is there pre-event entertainment to encourage early-arriving guests to take their seats, rather than rushing in from the concourses as the competition begins? Are there obstacles, either physical objects or security presence, between the spectators and the athletes to protect them from the activities or enthusiasms of one another?

Are concessions open to enable fans to purchase refreshments and merchandise while they wait for the event to begin, or to occupy them during breaks in play? Is alcohol being served to adults who present the required proof of age? How late into the event will alcohol be served, and are there trained personnel among the concessions' staff who can determine whether a spectator's reasonable limit of consumption has been reached?

Most permanent event facilities maintain a written evacuation plan in case of fire and other extreme conditions or credible threats to public safety. Become familiar with the plan and under what circumstances it may have to be implemented. What procedures are required if an evacuation becomes necessary? How will the public know the best routes to vacate the building? What role does the event's staff play during and after the facility is being cleared?

Does the celebrity status of the sports event's participants require the separation of the public from the competitors to ensure their safety? What can happen if the event's accreditation plan is compromised and a fan accesses a nonpublic area? Is there a plan to screen those arriving at the facility and to search bags and other carried items to ensure that no one enters with materials that can be used to intentionally—or even accidentally—injure participants and other spectators? Does the screening system create long waiting lines at the doors, or are there adequate personnel and entrances to handle the numbers of spectators expected? Do plans also call for athletes and support staff to be screened and searched?

Does the event's system of designing and distributing credentials discourage the possibility of counterfeiting? Is there an approval process in place that requires review or oversight of the list of credential applicants before they are approved, so as to control the number and nature of those receiving them? Does the system of soliciting and hiring staff, freelancers, and volunteers include some form of background or reference check? Do event staff drivers or vendors providing transportation services have valid and appropriate licenses and acceptable safety records, or a history of traffic violations?

Is the event facility in good physical condition, or are there areas that require upgraded lighting or the removal of potential sources of injury? Have temporary event venues been designed to permit the flow of people through safe, well-lit areas? Have cables and temporary wiring been distributed in such a way as to eliminate or minimize the possibility of ensnaring or tripping passersby? Are lighting towers and other upright structures sufficiently weighted down or secured with guy wires to keep them from upending in wind or as the result of a collision? Are the poles and pegs for tented areas secure and weighted? Are tower and tent guy wires strung in areas away from public access? Are there sufficient restroom facilities, and are they serviced regularly? Is there sufficient parking or nearby access to mass transportation systems to accommodate participants and spectators? Are there sidewalks present, or is there a clear path off the street from parking areas to the event venue? Are shuttle buses a safer alternative to move spectators onto the event facility's property?

Is the playing surface in good condition, or are renovations required to guard against athlete injuries? Are there holes, grills, or depressions in the surface that must be filled, capped, or repaired? Is there a clear, unobstructed path between the locker room or athlete preparation areas and the playing surface? Will there be easy access for both athletes and spectators to medical personnel, equipment, and supplies, and a system in place to direct help to where it is needed? Is an ambulance on-site for dispatch of an injured or ill person to a hospital or clinic? If not, how long will it take for emergency vehicles to reach the event venue, given the traffic conditions at various times on event day?

Are there presentation elements that can pose a threat to safety, such as pyrotechnics, flame effects, lasers, or trusses or towers containing lighting and sound equipment? Has the design and installation of all technical elements been executed or supervised by professional, experienced personnel? Are all potentially dangerous special effects stored and displayed in areas that are at a sufficient distance from the public so as to minimize any possible mishap? Have experienced, licensed riggers installed all equipment that is suspended over the playing field or spectator viewing areas?

FINANCIAL AND LEGAL ISSUES

Safety is of the utmost importance, but there are other areas of risk that can affect the conduct of a sports event. Are the contractual agreements governing workers at the event facility, hotels, and major vendors in full force and effect, or is there a possibility of a strike, lockout, or work slowdown due to labor unrest? How could the potential of labor actions affect the safe and smooth conduct of the event? Is there a possibility of a picket line or protest being staged outside the event facility, and what effect will the presence of protestors have on spectators or other labor groups associated with the event?

Have legal challenges been filed against the event, organizer, or host facility? Is there a claim being levied against any stakeholder associated with the event that may cause the program to be postponed, delayed, or altered in any way? Are all required permits secured or in the process of review? Have all appropriate licenses for the public performance of music, video, or design elements been acquired, or do any outside parties claim intellectual ownership of the event or any element contained therein?

Are any stakeholders, including the organizer, facility, major sponsors, vendors, or media partners, in particular financial distress? Are any in imminent danger of filing for reorganization or bankruptcy? How much cash in deposits or progress payments has the organizer already paid to, or received from, financially shaky stakeholders, which may therefore be at risk of partial or total loss? Are there legal actions pending against any stakeholder that has failed to meet past contractual obligations?

CANCELLATION SCENARIOS

What kinds of occurrences can cause the event to be canceled or postponed? Is the event's successful completion subject to favorable weather conditions? At what minimum and maximum air temperatures may the event proceed? Is an outdoor contest subject to the existence of dry field conditions, or may it proceed regardless of precipitation? What extreme precipitation conditions could cause the event to be subject to cancellation or postponement? What effect would high wind conditions have on competition?

What is the likelihood of a weather postponement at that time of year? If the event must be postponed, is an alternate "rain date" provided for in the facility lease? Is it practical to move an outdoor contest to an indoor location? What additional costs would the organizer have to bear to hold the event on an alternate date? Will the organizer be liable for issuing refunds for rescheduled or canceled games? What is the financial exposure associated with a total cancellation? In addition to refunding ticket revenues, what portion of sponsorship, broadcast, and other revenues will have to be returned? What extreme weather conditions might cause cancellation or postponement of indoor events—a blizzard, ice storm, hurricane, damage stemming from tornados, or flooding due to torrential rains? Is the event facility in a seismically active zone prone to earthquake activity? Does the venue have its own power-generating capability, or is it subject to even the remote possibility of power outages? Is there adequate illumination of the playing surface and spectator access areas in case a daytime event must be delayed until after sunset? Are there local curfew ordinances that require the event to be completed by a specified time?

How would the organizer react to the great unknowns of catastrophic political or cultural events, such as a global or national tragedy, acts of terror, or the sudden outbreak of war or epidemic? Would the event continue to be held on a national day of mourning following tragic circumstances? These issues, and their sometimes financially serious consequences, were once thought to be far-fetched in the United States, but the events of September 2001 and those that followed have brought such unthinkable possibilities into sharp focus.

Remedying and Responding to Risk Exposure

Considering the many potential areas of risk exposure and analyzing the impact of the dozens, or even hundreds, of hypothetical circumstances that could befall a sports event will help organizers to crystallize possible responses before the intense pressures of necessity and immediacy prevail. Some answers may seem patently obvious. For example, if an unsafe structural condition exists in the facility, it is the responsibility of the organizer to bring it to the attention of the venue owner and request or demand its repair. Conditions that are insufficiently safe or secure should be reinforced, removed, or repaired before they present clear threats to safety. Access to non-public areas should be obstructed or manned by security staff. Challenges to maintaining positive cash flow in the event of default by a sponsor can be mitigated in advance by securing letters of credit from a bank or investors. Options for issuing refunds in case of a sudden, unavoidable cancellation are best considered before fans start lining up at the ticket window, when there is still time to determine how cash can be made available, given the enormous financial impact such an eventuality can have on the organizer.

The answers to other hypothetical questions may be less obvious, requiring great forethought and the application of sound, ethical, and responsible judgment. It is impossible to predict, for example, how outside events beyond the control of the organizer might affect the safe conduct of the event, or even the advisability of opening the doors to the public at all. These are the concerns for which insurance was invented.

LIABILITY INSURANCE

In its most basic form, an insurance policy is issued by a company that agrees to assume the financial risks of unforeseen, unfortunate, and even cataclysmic occurrences on behalf of the organizer in return for a fee (the premium). Depending on the amount and type of protection an event organizer chooses to procure, a significant portion of the budget can be spent on satisfying insurance premium expenses.

At minimum, event organizers should procure liability insurance to protect themselves from direct expenses and legal actions that may result from injuries to spectators, athletes, and volunteers. Proof of insurance against property damage is also essential and will be required by many event facilities, sponsors, equipment rental companies, and other business partners to help protect their own assets against risks related to the event.

"Policy forms are nonstandard in nature and are often specifically tailored based on the type of event, duration, and the ability to postpone and/or reschedule," says Bill Bannon of BWD Group, an agency based in Lake Success, New York, with expertise in sports and entertainment insurance. Organizers should investigate coverage options for sports events early in the planning process, not just to ensure that an adequate budget is set aside for this purpose, but also to guarantee locating the protection needed at the lowest possible cost. "The insurance marketplace for coverage of sports events is small and specialized," Bannon notes.

The amount of liability insurance that should be procured for a sports event is both a budgetary and a business decision based on its size and complexity. Most event liability policies should carry minimum protection of U.S. $2 million per occurrence, although larger events and those that are deemed to present more risks to spectators or participants should seriously consider policies offering coverage of $5 to $10 million per occurrence, or even more. Most policies have an aggregate ceiling as well, limiting the total amount of coverage per event to a stated figure. Just as with personal auto, medical, and home owner's insurance, a deductible will usually apply. That is, the organizer will be responsible to pay the deductible amount to satisfy claims against an event before the policy's protections begin providing the balance.

Check the policy carefully to determine whether additional insurance coverage is advised. Will the organizer retain the services of independent transportation contractors or will staff members be required to drive vehicles for deliveries and on official business? In the latter case, special automobile coverage should be obtained. Are alcoholic beverages being served? Liquor liability insurance is strongly advised in such cases. Are checkroom facilities being provided for spectators' coats and bags? Coat check insurance is available to protect against theft or loss of furs and other expensive personal effects. Is the organizer serving food or selling merchandise? Consider product liability insurance to guard against the risk of tainted food or injuries and accidents related to souvenirs (even miniature bats, balls, sticks, and flags on sticks can hurt bystanders or become missiles). Working closely with an experienced attorney and insurance agency is essential to identify the types and limits of coverage that are advisable for a particular sports event.

The need to procure insurance for participating athletes will depend on the nature of the event, participating governing organizations, and other factors. As a general rule, such an insurance policy must be in effect, or be obtained, whenever an athletic competition is staged. Organizations such as USA Cycling, for example, offer approved event organizers the option to purchase insurance through its own broker or to act independently as long as the coverage meets its minimum requirements. Coverage is especially recommended for exhibition activities such as alumni games, amateur invitational tournaments, and celebrity games, among others. Athletes who do not train daily for regular competition are especially susceptible to injury.

Make sure your own vendors are carrying adequate insurance as well. Legal actions against an uninsured vendor working on an organizer's behalf can cause the supplier to go out of business, leaving the organizer exposed to pay 100 percent of a plaintiff's damages. Proof of coverage, in the form of "certificates of insurance" that include definitions of their policy limits, can easily be obtained from vendors. Check all of your leases and agreements for requirements to name the host facility, sponsors, vendors, and other stakeholders as "additional insured" parties. Your insurance company will issue a certificate that identifies the party requesting coverage as also being covered by your insurance. In return, your attorney and insurance broker will help you to identify any of your business partners who should also name your organization as an additional insured. Commonly, these will include event facilities, as well as vendors in "high-risk" businesses, such as rigging, lighting, and pyrotechnics companies, and others.

CANCELLATION INSURANCE

Cancellation insurance recompenses an organizer for event expenses if the program is unable to proceed or to be held at all. The various, often necessary, forms of cancellation insurance can be very expensive and may be subject to a number of significant restrictions and limitations imposed by the insurer. Because policies vary, it is wise to work with an insurance agency to shop and compare the coverage available and the premiums charged by a number of different insurance companies. Cancellation coverage can be used to repay sponsors and ticket buyers, satisfy vendor invoices, and fulfill other financial obligations, which will protect the organizer from the possibility of economic ruin due to unlikely and unforeseen circumstances. The premium charged is usually a percentage of the total amount covered, which can range from the amount needed to protect gross receipts to the amount required simply to recompense the organizer for irrecoverable expenses. A provision should also be included to cover any reasonable expenses an organizer may encounter in an attempt to prevent a cancellation, whether or not that attempt is ultimately successful. An organizer cannot simply cancel a sports event and expect the insurer to honor a claim. The policy will define specific acceptable reasons that an event may be canceled, many of which are listed in Figure 14-2.

Cancellation insurance premiums have increased dramatically since 2001, and areas of coverage have narrowed or become better defined. Availability of

Section 102(1)(A): Any act that is certified by the Secretary (of the Treasury), in concurrence with the Secretary of State, and the Attorney General of the United States (i) to be an act of terrorism; (ii) to be a violent act or an act that is dangerous to (I) human life; (II) property; or (III) infrastructure; (iii) to have resulted in damage within the United States, or outside the United States in the case of (I) an air carrier or vessel described in paragraph (5)(B); or (II) the premises of a United States mission; and (iv) to have been committed by an individual or individuals acting on behalf of any foreign person or foreign interest, as part of an effort to coerce the civilian population of the United States or to influence the policy or affect the conduct of the United States Government by coercion.

Figure 14-3
Definition of "Certified Act of Terrorism" (Federal Terrorism Risk Insurance Act of 2002)

insurance protection for "certified acts of terrorism," for example, is now guaranteed in the United States as a result of the Federal Terrorism Risk Insurance Act of 2002 (see Figure 14-3 for the government's definition of certified acts). For an additional premium, many insurance policies can also offer coverage against "noncertified acts of terrorism," basically defined by the same circumstances, but without the Treasury Department's official certification. Insurers can offer different levels of coverage for noncertified acts based on occurrences within certain distances from the event venue (e.g., 250 miles), or within a specified time before the start of an event (e.g., seven days). Both time and distance variables are frequently negotiable, but the better the coverage, the more expensive the premium will be. The location of the host facility will also be considered when the insurer sets the premium. Generally, sports events held in major cities are considered by insurance companies as more likely targets than those staged in less populated areas.

Additional protections can be added to cancellation insurance policies at the organizer's request and expense. Sponsor revenues dependent on television coverage, for instance, can be insured against preemption due to matters of national attention, such as breaking global news stories and tragedies. An outbreak of a virulent communicable disease can also cause spectators, sponsors, and athletes to reconsider their plans to travel to a host city for a sports event. According to the Canadian Broadcasting Corporation, the impact on the local economy in Toronto, Ontario, during the SARS outbreak of 2003 topped an estimated C$1 billion. The effect on travel and tourism alone was expected to reach in excess of $570 million. As a result of such catastrophic losses, communicable diseases are now often excluded from regular cancellation coverage, requiring the negotiation of additional premiums.

Sideline Story—Global Unrest Fuels Jumps in Insurance Premiums

A March 2003 story by Jay Weiner in the *Minneapolis Star-Tribune* attributed unusual increases in insurance costs at the Metrodome, the city's 64,000-seat indoor stadium, to the war in Iraq and a worldwide increase in terrorist activity. Although the Terrorism Risk Insurance Act of 2002 formed a temporary partnership between the U.S. government and the insurance industry that guaranteed the availability of insurance coverage against losses resulting from acts of terrorism, the costs of obtaining this insurance can be extremely high (although the potential costs of not being covered can be far greater). Insurance premiums for the Metrodome reportedly doubled from 2001–02 to 2002–03, from US$250,000 to more than $500,000, including $150,000 for terrorism coverage alone. According to the article, in larger cities, insurance premiums increased by an even greater factor. An insurance expense that had already reached a seven-figure amount more than tripled at a sports complex in Northern New Jersey.

WEATHER INSURANCE

Weather insurance is another type of coverage to carefully consider for outdoor events that can be affected by such meteorological effects as rain, snow, temperature, high wind speeds, and fog. This type of cancellation protection specifies under what conditions the insurer will honor claims to recover expenses. "This coverage is typically written on an all-or-nothing basis," says BWD Group's Bill Bannon. "If specified unwanted conditions occur at the location as determined by the closest National Weather Station or an on-site independent weather observer, the policy would pay the limit purchased." Typical measures include how much rain and snow must fall over a defined period, sustained wind speeds, and trigger levels for extreme temperatures. These specifications are negotiable according to how much the organizer is willing to spend. A policy that will honor claims for events canceled because of rainfall of 4 in. over two hours immediately before the event will cost less than one that protects against 2 in. during the same period. If it seems to you that purchasing insurance is more like wagering than the usual process of making a sound business decision, you are not mistaken. Insurers want to improve the odds that they will be able to keep your money and reduce the probability that you will collect on a claim. Nevertheless, cancellation coverage is often essential for ticketed and sponsored events to avoid the possibility of financial disaster due to weather. Some sponsors will actually require the organizer to carry cancellation insurance to ensure that their marketing investment will be repaid if the event is not ultimately executed.

WAIVERS (RELEASES)

Simple, single-page documents designed to provide sports event organizers with limited, but specific protections from legal actions are called waivers or releases. Signed waivers are usually requested from individuals who will engage in some participatory aspect of a sports event, such as amateur athletes, performers, volunteer staff, promotion contestants, and participants in certain physical demonstrations and activities. An experienced attorney should craft an organizer's waiver that is most appropriate for the type of event and the protections desired. A parent or legal guardian must sign waivers required from minors. Waivers should include language indemnifying the organizer against claims arising from injuries that result from participation in the event. A participant's receipt of the document implies acceptance that some level of risk is involved in his or her event experience, and the person's signature essentially acknowledges that he or she has taken this into account when making the decision to participate.

Another common purpose of the participant waiver is to provide agreement that the image of the signatory at the event is the property of the organizer. This grants the organizer permission to use a participant's image in video footage and photography for live or recorded broadcasts, advertising, promotions, and printed materials. The participant will not be paid, nor will that person's further permission be required if his or her image is used in any of these or other materials. This language is also frequently printed on the backs of sports event tickets to remove the risk of legal challenges to the future use of the audience members' images in these same materials. Many sports event organizers also post similar consent language on large posters prominently displayed at the host facility's entrances to further reinforce their ability to use audience images in broadcasts of the event.

ACCIDENT RESPONSE

The presence of first aid personnel such as qualified first aid practitioners, emergency medical technicians (EMTs), and physicians is essential to protect the safety and well-being of all in attendance at any sports event. Sports events are inherently risky, especially for participants in athletic competition, but also in some respects for the spectators. It is strongly recommended that wherever possible an ambulance be present or accessible to the event site for the timely transfer of injured persons to full-service medical facilities. At minimum, an ambulance service or nearby hospital should be identified and be made aware of the event in case rapid dispatch of an emergency vehicle is needed. All staff and volunteers should be familiar with the procedure and mechanism to summon early response medical assistance to the scene of an injury.

If an accident occurs on the event site, whether involving athletes, spectators, staff, crew, volunteers, or vendors, make sure that affected parties are referred to first aid personnel whether or not there appear to be any injuries. An incident form should be filled out to provide full contact information for an affected party, as well as a description of the injury, the location, and the circumstances surrounding the occurrence (see Figure 14-4). If possible, the facts recorded on the report should be reviewed and verified by the injured party. Most permanent event facilities have a standard incident report form and will provide the organizer with additional copies for his or her files and possible future reference. The accuracy and comprehensiveness of this document are essential, as it will certainly play a role of major importance in any future legal action.

ACCREDITATION

Event credentials and the access they provide to nonpublic areas are neither a right nor perquisite to be automatically granted to staff, stakeholders, or important guests. Although they are often perceived as such, they are first and most importantly a method of controlling access to areas of the event venue that require a measure of security. They can help an organizer improve security at an event by prohibiting unauthorized access by the public into sensitive locations such as the area around the playing surface, player benches and sidelines, locker rooms, media facilities, and other areas over which operational control is essential. The form of the credentials should not be designed until their end purpose and the method by which they will be distributed are clearly defined (see Figure 14-5).

The accreditation process begins by defining the areas of the event facility that require restricted access and determining how strictly those areas must be controlled. Make copies of the event facility floor plan, and separate public areas from those to which access should be limited. Note where checkpoints will be required—the points at which credentials must be presented to security personnel for access to restricted areas. Make sure that there are no other ways of gaining access to these restricted areas (i.e., back doors, elevators, staircases) without first encountering a checkpoint.

The simplest credential system is one in which only a single level of access is indicated—an "All Access" credential. For many events, however, different levels are required to provide extra security and crowd control measures. It may be desirable, for example, to more strictly limit access to the locker room corridor from all but few essential event personnel. The area immediately surrounding the playing surface might be off-limits to all members

(Event, Organizer, or Host Facility, Name)
Incident Report Form

Date of Incident: _____

Name of Person Assisted: _____

Home Address: _____

Local Address (if different from above): _____

Phone (Day): _____ (Night): _____

E-Mail: _____ Male/Female: _____

This person is _____ a guest _____ staff member _____ volunteer _____ event participant

_____ other (describe): _____

Emergency Notification Contact and Number: _____

Description of Injury or Complaint: _____

_____

Location of Incident (as detailed as possible): _____

_____

_____

Details of Incident (use back of form if additional space is required): _____

_____

_____

Assistance Provided and Actions Taken: _____

_____

_____

Name of Responding Individual: _____

Signature: _____ Date: _____

This form must be submitted to the Event Operations Office as soon as possible following an incident.

Figure 14-4
Incident Report Form

☐ Define areas of access.
☐ Identify levels of access.
☐ Design credential (anticounterfeit, photo, code).
☐ Create and communicate application procedures.
☐ Validate and distribute.

Figure 14-5
Checklist for Designing a Sports Event
Accreditation System

of the media except authorized photographers and television camera operators, requiring a different level of credential.

The overall design of all accreditation, regardless of access level, should look essentially the same to enable security personnel to identify bona fide credentials at a quick glance (see sample credential in Figure 8-6). The best practice is to visually distinguish credentials that provide special access with a band of a specified color and a large letter or number code that can immediately confirm its status to security personnel from a distance of several feet. Post a chart at each checkpoint that identifies, for both security staff and credential bearers, the color bands and codes that are permitted to pass into the adjacent restricted area. This practice eliminates confusion and obviates the need to print the exact significance of codes and color bands on the credentials. Because the egos of credential holders must often be considered, it is frequently best not to label credentials with access level codes that are obvious in hierarchy (e.g., A, B, C). Finally, remember that working representatives of police and fire departments do not require credentials to gain access to event facilities.

Like event tickets, credentials should be designed and printed so they may not be easily counterfeited. The bearer of a credential has more privileged access to an event site than a ticket holder, and a breach of security by someone with a bogus credential can have incredibly serious results. For this reason, it is strongly recommended that credentials include the name and affiliation of the wearer and photo identification that is sealed onto the card under a plastic laminate. Without this precaution, it is easy for a recipient to pass his or her credential to another person and for the photo to be replaced. Design elements such as embossed metallic logos or holograms, and special papers with colored or metal threads, are also common anticounterfeiting devices.

To further reduce the possibility of counterfeiting, it is recommended that credentials be distributed at the latest possible moment, preferably at the actual event site on the first day they are required. Whenever possible, however, credentials should be prepared in advance. To speed this process, passport photographs of the recipients can be mailed to the organizer ahead of time or E-mailed as "jpeg files." Credentials must be picked up in person. A valid government-issued ID card, such as a driver's license or passport, should be presented as proof of identity before the credential is released. Prepare a log listing all who have received their accreditation, and require a signature beside each name to indicate that the credential has been picked up. Credentials should be worn about the neck or clipped to clothing in a visible location at all times to identify the wearer as authorized to be in restricted areas. As an added security measure, it may be advisable for some staff, vendor, and volunteer personnel to undergo background checks. This is of particular importance for individuals who are not well known to the organizer, but may be placed in proximity to star athletes, celebrities, and dignitaries.

AUDIENCE SECURITY

Is your event of sufficient public importance or visibility to consider screening all who enter the venue? Should members of the audience and those entering through the loading docks, employee entrances, and the media gate be subject to scans with electronic wands, bag searches, and x-rays, or required to pass through magnetometers (metal detectors)? Although these measures can increase the sense of security at an event, they can significantly delay the entrance of the audience if insufficient security staff or equipment is applied. Nevertheless, they can also prevent the possibility of criminal activity, and their presence may even reduce the premium for liability insurance.

The sense of a safe and secure environment is essential to the enjoyment of the audience. Are security staff members within easy reach of all seating areas in case of an altercation between members of the audience? Are trained security personnel on the lookout for pickpockets, thieves, and shoplifters? Are they in radio contact with a supervisor in case additional assistance is needed?

Reacting to Emergencies

Risk assessment and management methodologies can be very effective in reducing the chances of accidents and emergencies, but they cannot completely eliminate their possibility. Despite thorough planning and the remedying of their most probable causes, incidents beyond the control of the organizer may still occur. Prepare to meet these challenges head-on by establishing a chain of command and a crisis communications plan.

ESTABLISH A CHAIN OF COMMAND

Sports events are fast-moving environments, where unpredictable situations can develop from any quarter—among the athletes, the audience, or the staff. Things happen quickly and must be responded to rapidly, responsibly, and authoritatively. Establish a chain of command that identifies the decision makers who are empowered to manage areas of responsibility, and define the limits to their authority. Determine the kinds of issues that should be communicated further and immediately to the most senior members of the organization and how they can be reached. The most important document in managing the operations of an event is a contact list—a list of event and organization staff with accompanying addresses and E-mail, telephone, fax, and mobile phone numbers. The length of this document may make it difficult to carry around at all times. An effective way to ensure that all personnel have the most important information on event day is to condense the list into a roster of mobile phone, event office, and facility office numbers on a small laminated card, two-sided if necessary. Issue a pocket-sized version to all staff, or punch a hole in the top so they can be attached to the lanyards holding credentials.

Sideline Story—An Emotional Exhibition

On September 20, 2001, U.S. president George W. Bush addressed his nation, a bit more than a week after the terrorist attacks on New York and Washington that killed more than 3000 people. As the intermission began between the second and third periods of an NHL preseason exhibition match in Philadelphia between the hometown Flyers and the visiting New York Rangers, the arena suspended its usual intermission programming to provide live coverage of his speech on the Jumbotron. The president was still speaking when the players reentered the ice, and at the voiced insistence of the fans, the game was delayed until the 36-minute address had concluded. During this extraordinarily emotional period in the nation's history, the league, the teams, and the players agreed that the game should be declared over immediately after the address even though only two periods had been completed, ending in a 2–2 tie. In an unprecedented moment that demonstrated everything that is good about sports, the opponents lined up to shake hands before more than 19,000 emotional and inspired fans.

CRISIS COMMUNICATIONS PLAN

A written communications plan should be developed to formalize the procedure the organizer will use to manage major challenges internally and the method by which the media and the public will receive information in case of a crisis. The plan should outline the step-by-step process by which a potential crisis will be identified, managed, and communicated (see Figure 14-6).

The organizer will have already completed the first part of this exercise—the identification of potential crises—during the risk assessment process (see Figure 14-2). Beyond those conditions listed, the organizer must be prepared for the totally unexpected as well. Identify in writing the ultimate decision maker who will ascertain whether an event should be canceled, postponed, continued, or in any way altered. Some organizations require those decisions that can affect their financial health or public image to be made by the board of directors; however, convening a quorum can often be impractical, as crises often develop quickly and responses may be required just as rapidly. It is recommended that only a single decision maker be designated, if possible. If the organization's bylaws require board approval, this individual may be the chairperson, who will act in the interest of the full board and in consultation with the event director or president of the organization. Select a second-in-command to take the decision maker's place if this person is incapacitated, missing, or otherwise inaccessible.

Top-level officials may make up, at least in part, the Crisis Assessment Task Force, a small, select group of experts with whom the decision maker will consult in case of an emergency. At minimum, the individuals in charge of security and operations, the event facility, media relations, and broadcasting should be included in this group of consultants. The function of the task force is to receive information and analyze any developments related to the crisis, and make recommendations to the decision maker. It is suggested that this group be kept as small in number as possible to streamline discussion, consultation, and decision making.

☐ Identify areas of crisis potential.
☐ Identify the decision maker(s) and crisis assessment task force.
☐ Establish a command center.
☐ Identify critical stakeholders.
☐ Assess appropriate responses.
☐ Create a media communications plan.

Figure 14-6
Checklist for Designing a Sports Event Crisis Communications Plan

Sideline Story—The Space Shuttle *Columbia* Disaster

During final rehearsals, just hours before the pregame ceremonies were to begin for NHL All-Star Saturday in February 2003, the space shuttle *Columbia* disintegrated over Texas at a height of 200,000 ft. The shuttle was due to land at Cape Canaveral, only 200 miles north of the host arena in Sunrise, Florida. In the early hours after the tragedy, there was scant detail and no confirmation from NASA as to whether anyone had miraculously survived, or whether the debris had caused catastrophic damage to towns in Texas and neighboring states along the shuttle's trajectory. Time was growing short, and I could not wait for official news before evaluating plans for our event in every detail. I had to move, and fast. If the impact of the disaster included devastation on the ground, the event might have to be canceled completely. Assuming the tragedy was restricted to the unfortunate souls on board, however, the production staff was quickly assembled in the arena. Production director Steven Hubbard arranged to hang black drapes from the arena's upper level fasciae in four corners. A moment of silence would be written into the script. A military color guard was already scheduled for the pre-event ceremonies. Our scriptwriter, John Kannengeiser, would contact the public affairs officer in charge of the guard's appearance to ensure adherence to protocol regarding the display of the American flag on a day of national tragedy.

The opening ceremony was originally planned to include a series of giant "postcards from Florida" projected onto the ice. The lighting director was to ensure that images of Cape Canaveral or the space shuttle were not included. Every second of video and screen graphics was reviewed. One feature, an animated logo for the Dodge/NHL SuperSkills competition, featured stars dashing across the night sky, leaving comet trails very similar to the images of incandescent falling wreckage that millions of viewers had just seen on CNN. Our video director and his staff moved quickly to render an entirely new animation without this potentially evocative and disturbing imagery.

Our game presentation director, Sammy Choi, pointed out that the opening ceremony preceding the player introductions drew heavily from space imagery. The more we thought about it, the more we realized that 75 percent of the already heavily rehearsed show was no longer appropriate. The opening ceremonies featured enormous projections of rotating stars, with a video of NHL players skating against a night sky. The hockey all-stars on video were to transform into constellations of shooting stars falling to the ice surface in lasers and lights to a soundtrack of Moby's "We Are Made of Stars." Regardless of how hard everyone had worked to develop, design, and rehearse these spectacular effects, there was a unanimous opinion that hockey players appearing to fall from the sky would be too reminiscent of the morning's tragedy. Our lighting designers, David Agress and Paul Turner, who had been awake all the previous night focusing the original show, worked feverishly to reconstruct a light show that would be as spectacular as possible, just not as obviously themed.

It was also our plan to treat fans to a colorful, celebratory fireworks show as they exited the arena. After a day filled with repetitive replays of explosions in the upper atmosphere on every television channel, we decided to quietly cancel this surprise event element. After all was said and done, however, our assumption remained that people bought their tickets to be entertained, and if they chose to attend, their expectations were that we would entertain them. If we had any doubt about whether all this self-examination was necessary, it vanished when just minutes before the event I received a phone call at the timekeeper's bench from a reporter at Associated Press inquiring whether we had reconsidered any of our plans for the presentation.

Remember that there is usually more than a single decision and response required in managing a crisis. There may be many second-to-second judgments required as an emergency and its aftereffects develop. Identify a command center to which appointed members of the Crisis Assessment Task Force and the decision maker will report when an emergency becomes apparent. This facility should be in a secure area, out of public view but within easy reach of those who will require access. The control center should be equipped with a number of hardwired telephones in case of a failure of the cellular telephone or walkie-talkie network. Installation of a computer, printer, and fax machine is also recommended.

The courses of action formulated in the command center may also affect the businesses of important event stakeholders. It may be appropriate to alert some of these stakeholders to the crisis and the anticipated responses before members of the media or the public are apprised. If an announcement is determined to be of sufficient importance to communicate to the media, consider whether a limited number of top sponsors and broadcasters should be informed simultaneously, or immediately before the media, so they can prepare their own required responses to the crisis.

In the case of a major emergency, you probably will not have to worry about calling the media to inform them—they will already be calling you. Select a spokesperson to provide members of the media with a consistent source of information and communication. Who that spokesperson should be can depend on the nature and severity of the crisis; however, credibility and authority are key. The greater the potential impact of the crisis, the higher into the organization you may want to reach for the spokesperson. If the media are already on-site, convene a press conference and prepare a release with consistent information for immediate distribution upon completion of the session. If the media are not on-site, circulate announcements via a press release with a contact name and number for further inquiries. The contact should not be the spokesperson, but someone who will screen and prioritize calls and schedule interviews for that person. A press conference may be subsequently scheduled at a time and place the media can attend. Identify the cause for concern (e.g., athlete injury, potential cancellation/rescheduling of the event, etc.) and state how and when the organizer will respond (if known at that time). The spokesperson should make only truthful statements of fact and offer no speculation. If details regarding the crisis and its response continue to develop and additional information should be given at a later time, provide an estimated time frame to the media as to when they might be updated.

Acknowledging the World Condition

Globally significant events, whether developing in the host city, or hundreds, even thousands of miles away, can affect an organizer's plans and program. In the days following the tragic terror attacks on the World Trade Center and the Pentagon in 2001, dozens of amateur, college, and professional sports events were canceled or postponed. As emphasized throughout this book, sports events are very public reflections of our culture, and as such must sometimes mirror society's moods and expectations as they exist outside the arena. After a respectful pause in the staging of many sports events to reflect on the tragedies of the period and to make necessary adjustments in security procedures, play was resumed, often preceded by "moments of silence." Flags flew at half-staff, black bunting draped the walls of many arenas and stadiums—in later days replaced with red, white, and blue—intermission sponsor promotions were replaced with the singing of "God Bless America." As a gathering of human beings with common interests (i.e., fans of a sport or team) and values shared by all people, a sports event is also expected to provide opportunities for public reflection (see the Sideline Story on page 399).

Few world events can match the horrors of September 2001. But other tragedies of cultural significance can develop at any time. It is important for organizers to demonstrate their own sensitivities, as well as those of their nation and local community, when such things happen. Carefully review all aspects of the event presentation plan—ceremonies, production elements, public address announcements, decorative elements and advertisements—to ensure that no inadvertent lapse of judgment is apparent to the participants or members of the audience when such unfortunate circumstances occur.

Applying sensitivity in the wake of a tragedy is simply common sense. It is, one hand, incumbent upon sports event organizers to entertain their guests and ticket buyers. To do any less would be a disservice to their loyal, paying customers. On the other hand, difficult times call for a candid assessment of how appropriate a celebration of sport may be in light of the world condition. Here's hoping you never have to make such decisions. But, in case you do, be prepared to act quickly and decisively.

Communications

From both operational and risk management perspectives, there is an essential need for information to be exchanged continuously between the event director and various areas of responsibility. Communications systems—walkie-talkies, Clear-coms, cellular telephones, RIM (wireless E-mail) devices, private line (PL) communicators, and others—provide much of the connective tissue that keeps an event together and running smoothly.

In 1949, United States Air Force captain Edward A. Murphy, an engineer working at Edwards Air Force Base, inspired the now-infamous and oft-quoted Murphy's Law: "If anything can go wrong, it will." Murphy was working on an air force project, charged with the responsibility of determining how much sudden deceleration a human being might be able to survive in a crash. Inspecting the device that would be used in the experiment, Murphy found it wired incorrectly. When he expressed his annoyance at the technician who installed it ("If there's a way to do it wrong, he'll find it," he fumed), his famous namesake principle was immortalized.

My own corollary to Murphy's Law relates to what I have too often experienced as the most common source of grief in the execution of special events: "The area with which you can not communicate is the place where things will inevitably go wrong." Events are living, dynamic organisms where challenges are presented in real time and must be solved before the audience or athletes can notice them. So, as you plan your event, consider Supovitz's Corollary, perhaps as appropriately expressed in the vernacular of Sun Tzu, author of *The Art of War:* "You have already lost control in the area where a pathway of communication does not exist."

Sideline Story—"What We Have Here Is a Failure to Communicate"

The 100th Army-Navy Game was held in December 1990, just weeks before the deployment of graduating cadets and midshipmen from West Point and Annapolis to the Persian Gulf for Operation: Desert Storm. The modest budget for its halftime show belied its importance as a patriotic tribute to the armed forces personnel already on station and those in the stadium who would soon be joining them to liberate Iraqi-occupied Kuwait. At the show's climax, country-western star Lee Greenwood performed his hit "God Bless the U.S.A.," as a full 300 ft wide American flag covered the entire field at Philadelphia's Veteran's Stadium, held off the ground by 300 midshipmen from the U.S. Naval Academy standing around and beneath the massive banner. (As a gigantic single-piece flag, proper protocol would not permit any part of the standard to touch the ground.)

To communicate with the midshipmen without having to rent radios, two audio cues were devised. A cannon blast would indicate that it was time to unfold the flag across the field. At the conclusion of the song, and after an expected rousing ovation, the unseen midshipmen beneath would wait for a second cannon blast to begin re-rolling the flag.

As expected, the song brought the entire stadium of people to their feet. The producer, standing beside the cannon, cued the blast midway through the piece, and the flag began to unfurl majestically. At the very moment it reached its full length, a second cannon report was heard, fired by an excited group of cadets on the opposite sideline, and the flag began to disappear as quickly as it had been revealed, to the surprise and dismay of the producer. It had never occurred to the organizers that at a stadium filled with military personnel, cadets, and midshipmen, there might exist more than one cannon.

You are simply not in control of your event if you do not have a system of communication in place that will provide instant contact to and from every area where decisions must be made and directions transformed into action. It is sometimes tempting to skimp on walkie-talkies and phones to avoid cost, when in fact, not being able to communicate with event staff members, and their not being able to communicate with the event director, can result in the entire budget being wasted on a completely failed event. Consider how improved communications would have avoided difficulties in the Sideline Story on this page.

It may not be possible to provide communication devices for staff in every location. However, every staff member, volunteer, or participant should know how to reach someone in a position of authority and responsibility. There should likewise be a way to reach each and every individual empowered to execute a job at an event. For event participants, this pathway of communication may be through an area supervisor or stage manager who can relay messages and information between the event director and the coaches, athletes, or cast.

The most common devices in use for event site communications are two-way radios (or walkie-talkies) and Clear-com systems. Two-way radios are advantageous because they are wireless, giving the wearers mobility throughout the event site. Test the radios well in advance to determine if there are any areas in which transmissions cannot be heard. Such "dead spots" are common in indoor facilities, where radio signals have difficulty penetrating concrete walls. Consider working with your radio supplier to install a repeater antenna, a device that essentially receives the transmission and then re-broadcasts it to hard-to-reach or more distant locations.

Walkie-talkies are radio frequency (RF) devices, as are wireless microphones and remote television cameras. There may be many groups that have independent two-way radios in the same facility, such as the production staff, broadcasters, front-of-the-house staff, transportation dispatchers, parking lot staff, and even entities outside in the immediate area, such as taxis and delivery services. Work with your radio vendor to "clear channels," ensuring that the communications system used by each group does not interfere with any other. The most illuminating "Sideline Story" illustrating the results of a failure to provide clear channels of communication may be the Old Testament tale of the "Tower of Babel." Interference between different communication groups using the same radio frequencies can prove confusing and disastrous. It can also render the pictures and sound from wireless television cameras and microphones useless.

Closed-circuit wired systems, such as Clear-coms, are commonly used in areas where continuous and simultaneous two-way conversations are required. Users of walkie-talkies, of course, cannot hear anyone else when they are talking. Clear-coms, however, operate more like telephones. Both parties can hear each other continuously. Wireless Clear-com stations are also available for users who require more mobility.

Tie Down the Details

Another way to manage for the unexpected is to make sure that all staff members and stakeholders have a clear understanding of all event details before the actual program takes place. Schedule a "tie-down meeting" two to five days before the event, and invite both event staff and representatives of each functional area and agency (e.g., marketing, public relations, insurance, information technologies, etc.). The meeting should systematically review the schedule of events, the production schedule, the event rundown, issues concerning the athletes and the competition, transportation systems, communications, sponsorship fulfillment plans—any and every detail that should become common knowledge to the event staff. During this meeting, staff members should feel free to ask questions, request additional information, and surface issues and challenges. Therefore, the larger and more complex the event, the farther in advance of event day you will want to schedule the tie-down to permit sufficient time to make adjustments based on issues that will come to light during the meeting. Be sure to communicate any changes to the plan made after the tie-down meeting. Prepare and distribute an Event Manual that contains all of the pertinent information and schedules discussed.

Volunteers and event-day staff should have an orientation meeting that is a more condensed version of the tie-down. They should also receive a Volunteer Manual, an easy-to-access reference book that provides all appropriate information.

Post-Play Analysis

Subject all aspects of the event to a thorough risk assessment and management process. Identify areas of risk to athletes, spectators, and staff, as well as financial risks to the organization. Project possible remedies to potential crises flowing from these risks, and take actions that will reduce the likelihood of their occurrence. Procure liability insurance, and if necessary, event cancellation insurance to reduce the financial burden on the organization in case of accidents, emergencies, and circumstances that could cause the program to be canceled or postponed. Prepare to respond to emergencies by establishing a chain of command and a crisis communications plan.

Be sure to have a system available for communication between the event director and major areas of responsibility. It is impossible to control an event or respond to the unexpected without the ability to communicate. Information is power, and its accessibility the best defense against confusion. Schedule a staff tie-down meeting and an orientation for event-day staff and volunteers to review event details and surface conflicts and inaccuracies. Circulate an event manual containing all pertinent schedules, contacts, and information, to be used as an easy reference tool.

Coach's Clipboard

1. You are organizing a marathon race through a major downtown area. Analyze and list the risks you will most likely encounter. What kinds of insurance coverage should be secured?

2. Your marathon's budget is dependent on having 75 percent of its revenues derived from sponsorships. The presenting sponsor, who was to provide 50 percent of total sponsor revenues, has filed for bankruptcy and will default on its final payment. How will you, as organizer, continue to pay the bills? What steps might have been taken during the event planning process to avoid this crisis?

3. Create a crisis communications plan for the marathon. Who should be included in the crisis assessment task force? Where is the best place to locate the command center? How will you respond if threatening weather appears likely to turn dangerous during the course of the event?

PLAY 15

Reviewing the Game Tapes

I firmly believe that any man's finest hour—his greatest fulfillment of all he holds dear—is that moment when he has worked his heart out in a good cause and dies exhausted on the field of battle—victorious.

—VINCE LOMBARDI, HALL OF FAME NFL COACH, 1913–1970

The final moments on the score clock have expired, the final heats have been run, and the tournament champion has been crowned. The crowds have gone home, the athletes' buses have pulled away, and the equipment, décor, and added seating have all been disassembled and removed. Congratulations are in order for the event's managers and staff, and sincere gratitude due all those whose participation and hard work have contributed to an event that was rewarding for the athletes, fans, sponsors, host city and facility, broadcasters, and the organizer. But the work is far from over. There are people to thank, bills to pay, and opinions to solicit before the time comes to consider staging the event all over again.

Post-Event Publicity

Stage a press conference after the event has concluded, with statements by key stakeholders and interviews with winning athletes and team members. Although the press coverage that can be generated after the event can no longer help an organizer sell tickets, it can help develop recognition and revenues in the long term. As soon as the event has concluded, be sure to circulate press releases with the official results, attendance figures, milestones and records broken, and any amounts that may have been raised for charity.

Collect both pre- and post-event news clippings from newspapers and magazines, and tapes of television coverage, reports, and interviews, for archival purposes as well as for circulation to sponsors and other stakeholders. If your sports event is worthy of only local media attention, a staff member or volunteer can likely accomplish this mission throughout the planning process. If stories are expected to be generated beyond the host city, however, consider hiring a newspaper clipping and television monitoring service to ensure that you will receive copies of stories regardless of where they appear.

Recognition

Try to budget recognition for key staff members, volunteers, and vendors, especially those who invested effort far beyond expectations (see Figure 15-1). A small keepsake can go a long way toward making sure that those who have worked countless hours, or gave freely of their time, feel appreciated. An event team develops into a family. The stresses and rigors of event planning, management, and execution can have the same effects that challenges have on a real family—the experiences its members have encountered together can either bind them inseparably close or drive them irreversibly apart. As the extended family parts at the close of an event, a party—even if it's just pizza and soda pop—can help to seal the relationship forever.

- Post-Event Party
- Gifts
  - Game ball or puck
  - Poster
  - Tickets encased in Lucite
  - Crystal paperweight with event logo
  - Photo album
  - Wall plaque
  - Highlights video or copy of the event broadcast
  - Goody bag
- Personal and signed note of thanks from senior management

Figure 15-1
Common Forms of Post-Event Recognition

Settlement

Enjoy the accolades, but there are almost certainly bills left to pay and perhaps even some revenues to collect. The process of receiving, reviewing, and paying invoices, collecting money yet to be received, and fulfilling all remaining obligations is called the "event settlement." The more complex the event, the longer the process can be expected to take. Like the organizer, the host facility, the hotels, and the major suppliers will receive invoices for materials procured and labor expended during the process of preparing for their own involvement in the event. It is not uncommon for facility and hotel settlements to take a few weeks, or even several months, to complete. Be sure to review every charge and compare the terms of leases, contracts, and letter agreements to make sure that all costs are within the understandings they outline. There may also be charges that should have been sent directly to other stakeholders such as sponsors and broadcasters. If possible, have these charges deducted from the settlement and invoiced directly to these third parties, unless they were arranged for or requested by the organizer on their behalf. In the latter case, it is often more appropriate to pay the charges and then invoice the stakeholders. Finally, if you have amortized capital expenses, don't forget to carry the proper percentage forward to future events.

Postmortem

Within a week or two of the end of the event, conduct a series of postmortem meetings with staff, sponsors, and stakeholders. This extremely valuable process can help isolate areas and circumstances that were executed less well than planned, and recognize the success of those elements that achieved their goals and objectives. Annual events should begin planning their next edition no later than the end of the last, so use the postmortem less as a critique of what has passed and more as a springboard for that which will follow.

Conduct post-event meetings with broadcasters and other stakeholders as well. A candid discussion of the triumphs and tribulations of their respective experiences can help the organizer improve his or her performance in the future. Recognize sponsors' and other partners' participation with special gifts and collectible items from the event that can adorn their lobbies and offices, vivid reminders of their association with the program. If sponsors have agreed to support the event only until the most recent edition has concluded, this is the perfect time to renew their relationship. Come prepared to learn how you can better meet their objectives, and reconfirm their commitment before their excitement can wane. Don't be surprised, however, if they prefer to await the results of any marketing research or event promotions they may have conducted.

If you have conducted marketing research among your fans and spectators, share the results with your partners and ask that they do the same for you. The event family does not end with the staff and volunteers. It extends to your best partners as well. Stay in touch throughout the year and discuss plans for future events. Engage these partners in the planning and development process, and they will feel involved, invested, and embraced.

The Future of the Sports Event Business

A number of years ago, a colleague came into my office, flush with frustration and seemingly at the end of her patience with a new crop of interns. "Why is it that our interns get dumber every year?" she vented. "They don't," I replied. "Interns will always come to a project with no knowledge of what we do. The gap between your own knowledge and experience and theirs keeps getting wider because you're growing as a professional. They will always come as new students of the industry."

Twenty years ago there were only a handful of institutions of higher learning that offered degree programs in sports business, even fewer that trained students for careers in event management. A recent special report on sports education in the *Sports Business Journal* listed 114 colleges and universities in North America now offering a sports management major. Intern and entry-level job applicants are not as often arriving with degrees in psychology and biology, work experience in banks and real estate offices. They often arrive with a firm grounding in the history, philosophy, and practice of the industry, armed with skills and understandings that their predecessors of two decades ago had to make up in drive and determination alone.

The discipline of special events parallels the sports industry, with its exciting growth as a dynamic entertainment business. Today interns and graduates are no longer arriving as blank slates. They come to us with fresh perspectives and refreshing questions, new ideas and no less drive and determination. Among those of us who may serve as their mentors, the wisest will be listening as much as they teach.

The Game Ends . . .

Sports events are massive consumers of time, labor, and capital. They can be hard on the physical, mental, and emotional state of those who compete, plan, promote, manage, sponsor, broadcast, publicize, present, and otherwise participate in these uniquely exciting and stimulating environments. Everybody wants the same thing—a successful event that is a positive experience for everyone it touches. Sports events can engender an infectious passion and intense conscientiousness in all who are involved. It is a competitive environment, to be sure. Everyone wants to record his or her personal best—the best athletic performance, the best promotion, the best event presentation.

If my own experience is any guide, there will be countless mornings when you will arise before the sun after a seemingly endless string of 18-hour days. You may stumble toward the shower and, with what seems like every remaining ounce of your strength, turn on the hot water. You may let the water stream down your body while leaning motionless against the tile as time seems to stand still, the battle joined to fight the fatigue and clear the cobwebs from your mind. You may at this point ask, "Why am I doing this to myself?"

Under the circumstances, it may take a while for the answer to come. Then, the event is finally under way, the fans are cheering, and the athletes are giving it their all. Your own heart is pounding and the adrenaline is surging through your bloodstream. In a rush, it is suddenly done and the energized crowd leaves abuzz, still cheering, laughing, singing, and reminiscing over memories just moments old, but lasting a lifetime.

Then you'll think back to that morning shower, and smile inwardly.

"Yeah . . . that's why!"

Event Expense Budget Worksheet

ACCT. NO.	EXPENSES	BUDGET	FORECAST	ACTUAL	VARIANCE	COMMENTS
1000	**Player Costs**					
1001	Player Appearance Fees					
1002	Player Prize Money					
1003	Player Gifts					
1004	Player Travel, Air					
1005	Player Travel, Ground Transfers					
1006	Player Travel, Hotel					
1007	Player per Diem					
1008	Player Scheduled Meals					
1009	Player Guest Expenses					
1010	Uniforms and Equipment					
1011	Insurance					
1012	Officials					
1013	Officials, Travel Expenses					
1014	Trainers					
1015	Trainer Expenses					
1016	Medical Staff					
1017	Ambulance					
1018	Player/Athlete Transportation/Parking					
1050	**Ticketing Expenses**					
1051	Capital Replacement Fees					

ACCT. NO.	EXPENSES	BUDGET	FORECAST	ACTUAL	VARIANCE	COMMENTS
1052	Sales and Amusement Taxes					
1053	Box Office/Ticket Processing Labor					
1054	Remote Ticket Fees					
1055	Credit Card Commissions					
1056	Ticket Printing					
1057	Group Sales Commissions					
1058	Mailings, Creative					
1059	Mailings, Printing					
1060	Mailings, Postage					
1100	**Facility Expenses**					
1101	Facility Rental					
1102	Facility Labor					
1103	Carpenters					
1104	Electricians					
1105	Laborers					
1106	Riggers					
1107	Cleaners					
1108	Field/Ice Maintenance Crew					
	Front of House (FOH) Staff					
1109	Ushers					
1110	Ticket Takers					
1111	Security					
1112	House Supervisors					
1113	Medical/First Aid					
	Presentation Crew					
1114	Scoreboard					
1115	Video and Matrix Crew					
1116	Stagehands					
1117	Spotlights					
1118	Changeover Crew					
1119	Miscellaneous Facility Labor					
1120	Bleachers/Additional Seating					
1121	Playing Surface Prep Expenses					
1122	Game-Required Equipment					
	Crowd Control Barriers/Barricades					
1123	Rope and Stanchion					
1124	Barricades					
1125	Fencing					
	Power					
1130	Utility Costs					
1131	Generators					
1132	Power Distribution					

ACCT. NO.	EXPENSES	BUDGET	FORECAST	ACTUAL	VARIANCE	COMMENTS
1133	Water					
1134	Waste Receptacles and Dumpsters					
1135	Portable Toilet Facilities					
1140	Arena Décor and Signage					
1141	Tenting					
1142	Flooring and Carpeting					
1143	Pipe and Drape					
1200	**Guest Services**					
1201	Invitation Design and Printing					
1202	Invitation Postage					
1203	Guest Management Expenses					
1204	Guest Transportation					
1205	Guest Gifts					
1206	Guest Hospitality					
1207	Complimentary Tickets					
1208	Information Guides					
1209	Directional Signage and Info Desks					
1210	Hotel Lobby Décor					
1211	Hotel Staff Gratuities					
1213	Hotel Attrition Contingency					
1300	**Event Operations**					
1301	Temporary Staff and Interns					
1302	Volunteer Staff Expenses					
1303	Staff Travel Expenses					
1304	Staff Meals or Per Diem					
1305	Staff Wardrobe/Uniforms					
1306	Site Surveys/Planning Trips					
1307	Pre-Event Planning and Tie-Down Mtgs.					
1308	Event Location Office Rent					
1309	Event Location Office Furnishings					
	Event Location Office Equipment					
1310	Computer and Printer Rental					
1311	Copiers and Fax Machines					
1312	Televisions and VCRs					
1313	Phone Lines					
1314	T-1 Lines					
1315	Phone Equipment					
1316	Phone Service and LD Charges					
1317	Event Location Office Supplies					
1318	Radios					
1319	Cellular Phone Rental and Service					

ACCT. NO.	EXPENSES	BUDGET	FORECAST	ACTUAL	VARIANCE	COMMENTS
1320	Accreditation					
1321	Postage and Overnight Services					
1322	Storage					
1323	Shipping and Trucking					
1324	Liability Insurance					
1325	Event Cancellation Insurance					
1326	Legal Services					
	City Services					
1330	Police					
1331	Sanitation					
1332	Fire					
1333	Other City Services					
1334	Permits					
1335	Miscellaneous Op. Costs					
1500	**Marketing/Promotion**					
1501	Logo Development					
1502	Advertising Agency and Creative					
1503	Advertising Agency Expenses					
1504	Advertising, Print					
1505	Advertising, Radio					
1506	Advertising, Outdoor					
1507	Posters and Handbills					
1508	Public Relations Agency					
1509	Public Relations Agency Expenses					
1510	Telephone Information/800 Service					
1511	Street Banners, Design and Printing					
1512	Street Banners, Installation					
1513	Airport Greeting Signage					
1514	Promotional Items (caps, pins, T-shirts)					
1515	Miscellaneous Marketing					
1600	**Media Expenses**					
1601	Press Conferences					
1602	Media Pre-/Postgame Meals					
1603	Media Center F & B					
1604	Media Tabletops, Phones, etc.					
1605	Photocopier/Fax					
1606	Media Office Expenses					
1607	Media Guide					
1608	Photography					
1609	Media, Miscellaneous					
1610	Media Gift					

ACCT. NO.	EXPENSES	BUDGET	FORECAST	ACTUAL	VARIANCE	COMMENTS
1700	**Sponsor Fulfillment Costs**					
1701	Agency Commissions					
1702	Sales Expenses					
1703	Banners and Signage					
1704	Complimentary Tickets					
1705	Hospitality					
1706	Sponsor Gifts					
1707	Other Fulfillment Expenses					
1800	**Broadcasting**					
1801	Broadcast Expenses					
1802	Airtime Purchase					
2000	**Production Costs**					
2001	Stage Risers and Platforms					
2002	Set Design					
2003	Set Construction/Rentals					
2004	Set Refurbishment					
2005	Lighting					
2006	Audio					
2007	Props and Flags					
2008	Draping					
2009	ClearCom					
2010	Video Production					
2011	Video Projection					
2012	Production Management Fees					
2013	Production Management Expenses					
2014	Production Labor, Installation					
2015	Production Labor, Rehearsal and Event					
2016	Production Labor, Dismantle					
2020	Equipment Rental					
2025	Talent Fees					
2026	Talent Expenses					
2030	Costumes and Wardrobe					
2031	Floral					
3000	**Associated Events and Programs**					
3001	School/Educational Outreach					
3100	Welcome Party					
3200	Closing Party					
3300	VIP Hospitality					
3400	Spouse Program					

ACCT. NO.	EXPENSES	BUDGET	FORECAST	ACTUAL	VARIANCE	COMMENTS
4000	**Other Expenses and Adjustments**					
4100	Amortization of Prior Year Assets					
4200	Deferral of Capital Assets—5yr.					
4300	Deferral of Capital Assets—3yr.					
4400	Contingency					

Total Expenses

APPENDIX 2

Sample Host City Request for Proposal

MNO Sports Events, Inc.

Request for Proposal to Host the
Big Street Sports Tournament
Summer 2004

MNO Sports
123 S.W. Second Avenue
Biggtown, MD 00000
© September, 2003

Request for Proposal
Big Street Sports Tournament

Contents

I. Introduction

MNO Sports is pleased and excited to offer communities with an active interest in world-class amateur sports events and festivals the opportunity to host a proven, exciting, and crowd-pleasing concept in amateur street sports: **The Big Street Sports Tournament.**

The Big Street Sports Tournament will attract thousands of families and sports enthusiasts from local and surrounding communities, free of charge, and participating amateur street and extreme athletes from throughout North America for a full weekend of entertainment, interactive activities, tournament play, and pure fun, including . . .

- Age-Bracketed Skateboard Competitions
- BMX Half-Pipe Exhibitions
- In-line Skating Demo Zone
- Extreme Roller Hockey Rink
- Street Sports New Product Expo
- "Kids Only" Clinics and Activities
- Bicycle Tune-Up Area and Obstacle Course
- Extreme Sports Video Arcade
- Special Guest Appearances
- Nonstop Musical Entertainment
- Food Concessions
- . . . and more!

The Big Street Sports Tournament is totally new for 2003, with more to see, more to do, and more to enjoy than ever before. Your city can capitalize on the expanding interest and phenomenal growth in street sports within your community and beyond, by participating as the host of this world-class street sports festival and national invitational tournament.

II. The Big Street Sports Tournament: A New Tradition Continues

The Big Street Sports Tournament enters its third year in 2004, combining visually exciting, heart-stopping athletic demonstrations by top street athletes with an invitational tournament matching local amateur players with visiting teams from across the continent in all age, gender, and skill categories, ranging from "8 and Under," all the way to "18 and Older" divisions. The tournament draws approximately 1000 top amateur athletes from all over North America, accompanied by their friends and families. Past host cities include Orlando, Florida, and Providence, Rhode Island.

This document has been prepared to provide prospective host cities with uniform and comprehensive guidelines and specifications to assist them in the preparation of a proposal to host the Big Street Sports Tournament. For your ease of preparation and to assist us in the evaluation process, a questionnaire is included which, when complete, will form the core of your proposal. The questionnaire must be completed and requested materials attached for successful consideration. You are, however, welcome to append any additional information to the questionnaire that you believe will present your community as the best possible host for the **Big Street Sports Tournament.**

Please submit your proposal by November 15, 2003, to the address noted on the last page of the questionnaire. Once all proposals have been received, MNO Sports will analyze the submissions and determine whether site visits will be required prior to final selection of a host city.

If you have any questions regarding this document, or the preparation of your proposal, or wish to receive a copy of this document via E-mail, please do not hesitate to contact Nathaniel Jacobs, Vice President, MNO Sports at, (202) 000-0000, or by E-mail at *njacobs@mnosports.com.*

III. Event Schedule

The next available edition of the **Big Street Sports Tournament** will be held on a single weekend in the summer of 2004. A potential host city should select first- and second-choice weekends that are the optimal dates for staging the event in its community.

Most inbound participants and their guests will arrive on Friday evening. The host city is welcome to provide a hospitality reception sponsored by a local restaurant for arriving players, if desired.

The public is welcome on the event site beginning with the first tournament games at 8:00 A.M. on Saturday. The site will close at 7:00 P.M. Saturday, reopening at 8:00 A.M. Sunday morning, and remaining open until closing ceremonies conclude at 6:00 P.M. Sunday evening.

Special events and entertainment will be scheduled throughout the weekend at times to be determined.

IV. Role of MNO Sports

MNO Sports will work closely with the host city, its designated agencies, and local corporate partners to ensure that the **Big Street Sports Tournament** offers a positive and rewarding program for all visitors, athletes, sponsors, and business partners, while providing a major sports showcase for the host city.

MNO Sports will . . .

- Design, manage, and produce the Big Street Sports Tournament at its own expense
- Install, operate, and dismantle all event attractions, equipment, and other elements
- Work with the local sports commission, convention and visitors bureau, or other authority to promote and publicize the event on a national basis
- Manage the tournament invitation and registration process

- Work with area hotels to provide attractive, reasonably priced accommodations for visiting athletes, fans, and event staff
- Promote extended visits to the host city and local points of interest to visiting athletes and their families in their invitations and registration packets, as well as in web links for E-mailed materials
- Provide benefits to the host city as outlined in Section VII

V. Role of the Host City

The host city will play a prominent role in helping to shape the character of the **Big Street Sports Tournament.**

A. EVENT SITE RECOMMENDATIONS

It is an objective of MNO Sports to attract the largest audience possible for the event. The ideal event site will provide a minimum of 50,000 usable[*] sq ft of space in a location demonstrably familiar to the local community as a major event site and/or one that regularly experiences high pedestrian traffic during a weekend or featured event.

Up to seven (7) performance and street sports competition areas will be installed on the event site, requiring level footprints of clear, flat, unobstructed blacktop free of pot holes, street lamps, utility poles, planters, and manhole access covers. This space is required to accommodate the playing and demonstration surfaces, team benches, and spectator viewing areas. Competition areas range from the smallest at 30′ × 50′ to the largest at 110′ × 160′.

Preference will be given to event sites that reflect the unique culture and qualities of the host city.

B. EVENT SITE SERVICES

The host city will ensure that the site is delivered in clean condition to the event before the scheduled onset of installation. The city will maintain sanitation during and after event hours and will supervise cleaning of the site immediately after the removal of event elements by MNO Sports at no cost to the event.

The host city will schedule sufficient police, fire, and emergency medical service coverage during the event, as well as during installation and dismantling operations, to protect the health and safety of the public, participants, and event staff. Adequate overnight security staffing by either bonded guards, or on-/or off-duty police is essential. These requirements will be provided by the host city at no cost to MNO Sports.

[*]Required gross square footage may be greater to avoid the presence of street lamps, medians, planters, or other obstructions.

C. HOTEL RECOMMENDATIONS

Approximately 350 quality and competitively priced hotel rooms will be required on peak nights. The following is a preliminary schedule of room requirements:

	Mon.–Thurs.	Fri.	Sat.	Sun.	Mon.–Tues.
Rooms	10	350	350	350	10

Host hotels will also make available the meeting rooms or function space required for the management of the event during the days listed here at no cost. To be considered as a prospective host hotel, function space should be put on a tentative hold per the following schedule:

Office	Min. Sq Ft	Occupancy
Operations Office	1500	7 Days prior through 2 days following event
Event Storage	1500	7 Days prior through 1 day following event
Gift Bag Distribution	1500	7 Days prior through 1 day following event
Sponsor Hospitality	1500	1 Day prior through final event day

The event headquarters hotel will permit event organizers to place welcome and directional signage in the hotel lobby area and on the exterior of the building in mutually agreed-upon locations. The event will be permitted to staff an information desk in the lobby of the hotel, within line-of-sight of the guest registration area.

The headquarters hotel(s) will provide a total of 30 complimentary room-nights for pre-event planning trips, the fulfillment of which will be administered by the local convention and visitors bureau.

During the event and for up to four (4) weeks prior, a discounted "staff rate" will be available to event staff, up to a maximum of 80 room-nights. Hotels will agree to provide the event with a rebate of US$10 per room-night occupied by visitors assigned to the event room block during the periods listed earlier, excepting the discounted staff rate rooms as defined herein.

Although the host city should identify hotels that are interested in being considered as a headquarters hotel after they have reviewed these specifications, MNO Sports will negotiate and contract with any and all required local hotels directly.

D. PROMOTION AND PUBLICITY

The host city will undertake all efforts to publicize the event in advance to promote attendance. The promotion plan should combine advertising on local television and radio and in local magazines and newspapers, as well as provide additional promotion through the installation of street banners, outdoor advertising, Internet web sites of local interest, and other mechanisms. MNO Sports will consider—but must approve—all proposals for media partnerships (e.g., the naming of one or more media outlets as **"the official television station (radio station, newspaper, etc.) of the Big Street Sports Tournament"**).

Please enclose with your proposal any letters of support and/or interest from media interested in participating as promotional partners for the event, containing commitments to provide advertising time or space.

E. WELCOME SIGNAGE

The event will look favorably on proposals that include welcome signage installed to greet inbound players, sponsors, and special guests at airport locations, and on street poles in major business districts and near headquarters hotels, and approaching the event site, over key intersections, or on outdoor advertising billboards. Sponsor identification may be included, following the guidelines discussed in Section F. (Note: MNO Sports may, at its sole discretion, require inclusion of the national presenting or title sponsor(s) of the event in the design of all welcome signage wherever local sponsors are included.)

F. LOCAL SPONSOR PARTNERS

The event maintains an impressive list of sponsors entitled to marketing and promotional rights at the Big Street Sports Tournament (see Attachment A for the roster as of the date indicated).

MNO Sports will consider—but must approve of—any local sponsors and the package of entitlements to be proposed by the host city. The sponsors may provide either cash or value in kind to the host city to offset the latter's expenses. This notwithstanding, MNO Sports maintains its rights to procure local sponsorships or value-in-kind arrangements at its sole discretion. The host city will retain all revenues from local cash sponsorships from the agreements it generates, providing they are approved in advance by MNO Sports. All costs in fulfilling said sponsorships will be borne by the host city. The event is appreciative of trade or value-in-kind deals provided by the host city that can provide additional value to the event. MNO Sports, however, cannot provide cash payments or commissions to the host city for such donated goods and/or services.

Notwithstanding the above, MNO Sports will not approve local sponsorship deals with companies who, in MNO's sole opinion, are competitive with the event's current or prospective business partners, as listed in Attachment A.

G. HOST CITY FEE

There is no fee to submit a proposal for consideration as host city of the Big Street Sports Tournament. A $10,000 fee will be paid to MNO Sports by the selected host city that is awarded the event, due upon execution of a letter agreement between the host city and MNO Sports covering the event. This fee is not refundable if the host city cancels its participation for any reason after the letter agreement is executed. MNO Sports may waive the host city fee if, in its sole opinion, the host city is providing exceptional value in equipment, products, or services that will benefit the event beyond the minimum requirements of this Request for Proposal.

H. VOLUNTEER STAFFING

MNO Sports will provide all management and paid staff for the event. The host city will be required to provide approximately 30 volunteer staff per event day to work under the direction of MNO Sports for the proper, safe, and efficient operation of the event. The host city should specify how it will assist MNO Sports in the solicitation of volunteer staff. Each volunteer staff member will receive an event cap and T-shirt both for his or her use on-site and as a take-home memento. Meals and refreshments appropriate to the time of day will also be available to working volunteer staff.

I. FOOD VENDOR MANAGEMENT

The host city will be responsible for the identification of licensed, reliable, and experienced food vendors for the event site. MNO Sports will be entitled to a $75 fee per vendor per location. The host city may assess an additional fee to be paid by vendors to offset its expenses.

J. KEY POINT OF CONTACT

The host city should identify a key staff person to serve as a high-level liaison between the local government and the event director. This key contact will interact directly with the municipal departments required to successfully stage the event, expedite any and all local permitting requirements, and ensure that the event complies with all applicable municipal ordinances, where appropriate.

K. AVAILABILITY OF EVENT EQUIPMENT AND SUPPLIES

The host city should identify any event equipment and services it will agree to make available to the event at no cost.

The following items are essential to the operation of the event, and their provision at no cost to the event would significantly improve the chances of a successful bid. Please enter the quantity of items available on the questionnaire included in Section IX of the Request for Proposal form:

- Bleachers
- Dumpster
- Folding chairs
- Folding tables
- Forklift
- Golf and utility carts
- Ice and ice storage
- Power generators or access to power sources
- Shuttle buses between player hotel and event site (may be municipal transit vehicles)
- Staging platforms and/or risers
- Temporary restroom facilities
- Tents and canopies
- Waste receptacles
- Water trucks

VI. The Ideal Event Site

The recommendation of an appropriate, attractive, and highly desirable event site is among the most important considerations in preparing a successful event proposal. As previously discussed, it is a mutual objective of the event organizers and the host community to attract the largest local and inbound audience possible for the event, and one that showcases the unique aspects and culture of the host city. Therefore, the ideal event site will showcase the unique aspects and culture of the host city and will possess a combination of many of the following attributes:

- An area in, or adjacent to, a normally high pedestrian traffic flow during the operating hours of the event
- An area in, or overlooking, landmark or nationally recognized buildings, scenery, skylines, or natural wonders
- A flat, smooth, and well-maintained paved surface, with sufficient drainage and contiguous space to accommodate the various playing surfaces and entertainment areas, plus safe pedestrian flow through all areas of the event site (as determined by the local fire marshal)
- A player equipment drop-off location and visitor access to nearby free or reasonably priced parking and/or mass transportation
- Visitor and participant access to on-site or nearby restroom facilities (or the ability to install portable restroom facilities, provided by the host city at no cost to the event)
- Sufficient weight-load capacities to enable fully laden tractor-trailers to park and off-load at the event site. (*Note:* Several decorated trailers will remain on the event site for the duration of the program.)
- Complete access for installation beginning Thursday afternoon at 5:00 P.M., and completion of dismantle by Monday morning at 8:00 A.M.
- No rental charges, permit fees, or other financial obligation payable by the event to the city and/or private owner of the property
- No broadcast origination fees or media restrictions in the case of live or taped telecasts or news coverage
- Permission for the sales of event merchandise to the public with no additional charges levied against gross proceeds other than normally payable local and/or state or provincial sales taxes
- No site-specific sponsor exclusivities that conflict with the business partners of the event as described in Attachment A.

VII. Host City Benefits

HOST CITY DESIGNATION

The host city will be able to use its designation as **"Host City of the Big Street Sports Tournament"** in all advertising, promotions, and publicity prior to, during, and for one year following the event, with each such use subject to the approval of the MNO Sports.

USE OF MARKS

The host city will have the right to incorporate the logo of the **Big Street Sports Tournament** into all advertising and promotional material, as well as in the production and distribution of premium items, with such use subject to the approval of MNO Sports.

PROMOTIONAL OPPORTUNITIES

The host city will have the opportunity to utilize the event to promote tourism or in other marketing campaigns undertaken by the local government and its agencies among both participants and visitors. Opportunities may feature the inclusion of a premium item in visiting player gift bags, city attraction and restaurant maps, coupon books, product samples delivered at check-in for visiting players, and the inclusion of a special promotional brochure in the player solicitation package sent to potential participants during the team application process, with all such materials and use subject to the approval of MNO Sports.

The event organizer will promote the host city on the **Big Street Sports Tournament** Internet web page at *www.bigstreetsports.com* in banner advertising, pre-event features, and coverage of the event.

All printed and electronic materials designed to promote the event will prominently feature the host city, including press releases, participant applications, and advertising.

EVENT SITE BENEFITS

The host city will receive significant and prominent recognition at the event site on signage boards located throughout the area, and in scheduled public address announcements.

The host city will receive a 10' × 10' tent on-site for its own exhibition purposes for the duration of the event. Alternatively, the host city may utilize its own existing structure for such purposes, which may exceed the 10' × 10' footprint, subject to the approval of MNO Sports.

The host city may enter one athlete or team in each amateur tournament event at no cost. This opportunity may be used for internal or promotional purposes, at the discretion of the host city.

DATABASE ACCESS

MNO Sports will make the database of all tournament participants and MNO Sports-run sweepstakes entrants, if any, available to the host city for post-event marketing purposes, as permitted by law.

PLAYER VISITS

The event organizer will make 2 one-hour appearances of five visiting street sports athletes available to the host city, for attendance at a city-run reception, hospital visits, or other opportunity to be mutually agreed upon.

VIII. Attachment A

Big Street Sports Tournament Partners
(as of August 30, 2003)

The following companies are the national sponsors of the Big Street Sports Tournament and are entitled to exclusive promotional benefits in connection with the event. Additional national event sponsors may be confirmed by MNO Sports at any time without notice. The host city may seek to secure local sponsors in product categories other than those listed here, with the prior approval of MNO Sports:

Soft Drink Company
Isotonic Beverage Company
Bicycle Company
In-Line Skate Company
Skate Wheel Company
Skateboard Company
Safety Equipment Company
First Aid Supplies Company
Quick-Service Restaurant Company
Cell Phone Company

Note: In an actual RFP, the names of real sponsor companies would appear here.

IX. The Big Street Sports Tournament

Request for Proposal Response Form

Prospective host cities are invited to prepare their proposal in any format desired; however, a fully completed Request for Proposal Response Form should be included as the first section of the submitted document. An electronic version of this form is available upon request. To receive a copy via E-mail, please contact Nathaniel Jacobs at *njacobs@mnosports.com.*

Please submit all applicable forms and accompanying materials by November 15, 2003, to the name and address noted on the last page of the Response Form.

I. Contact Information

Host City: _____

Applying Entity (e.g., CVB, Sports Commission):

_____

Primary Contact: _____

Title: _____

Address: _____

_____

Telephone: _____ Fax: _____

E-Mail: _____

Weekend(s) applied for:

1st Choice: _____

2nd Choice: _____

The applying city agrees to all terms as outlined in the bid specifications for the Big Street Sports Tournament. _____ Yes _____ No.
(If "No," please attach a detailed description of exceptions.)
Are there other city festivals or events scheduled on the same weekend(s) or on the weekends immediately prior to, or following these dates? _____ Yes _____ No
(If "Yes," please note or attach further information.)

II. Proposed Event Site

Site Name: _____

Site Owner: _____

Event Site Contact Name: _____

Contact Phone: _____ E-mail: _____

Please attach a description of how the proposed event site fulfills "The Ideal Event Site" characteristics described in this RFP (include photos, floor plans, and elevations, as available).

Seating Capacity: _____

Price Breaks: _____

Taxes and Fees on Sales of Tickets: _____

Labor and Union Exclusivities: _____

Hourly Labor Rates (including benefits and management fees):

    Ushers: _____

    Security: _____

    Electricians: _____

    Carpenters: _____

    Riggers: _____

Catering Exclusivities: _____

Merchandise Exclusivities: _____

Concessions Exclusivities: _____

Other Restrictions: _____

III. Hotel

Hotels participating in the bidding process must hold space on a first option basis until the determination of a host city is made. Please complete one hotel form for each property participating in the bid.

Hotel Name: _____

Total Number of Rooms: _____

Total Held for Event on a 1st Option Basis: _____

Proposed Room Rates: Single: _____ Double: _____

Tax Rates on Sleeping Rooms: _____

Year of Last Sleeping Room Renovation: _____

Year of Last Public/Function Space Renovation: _____

If selected, the hotel agrees to provide function space in the quantity, and as described in this RFP: _____Yes _____No

Please attach description of any exceptions or exclusions.

Hotel Contact Name/Title: _____

Phone: _____ Fax: _____

E-mail: _____

Contact Signature: _____

IV. Host City

City Services Liaison: _____

Title and Phone: _____

Convention and Visitors Bureau Contact: _____

Title and Phone: _____

Availability of Event Resources (see Section V.(K)):

Item	# Available	Comments (e.g., size)
Folding tables	_____	
Folding chairs	_____	
Staging and/or risers	_____	
Power generators or access to power	_____	
Bleachers	_____	
Portalettes	_____	
Golf and utility carts	_____	

Water trucks   _____

Forklift   _____

Dumpster   _____

Waste receptacles   _____

Ice and ice storage   _____

Tents and canopies   _____

Shuttle buses   _____

Regional Population: _____

Average Household Income: _____

Effective State and Local Sales Taxes: _____

Additional Non-Hotel-Related Taxes: _____

Proposed Media Partners:
Please enclose letters of interest or support.

Print: _____

Television: _____

Radio: _____

Other: _____

Source of Volunteer Pool: _____

Please submit all applicable forms and accompanying materials no later than November 15, 2003, to:

Nathaniel Jacobs
MNO Sports
123 S.W. Second Avenue
Biggtown, MD 00000
njacobs@mnosports.com

Request for Proposal Evaluation Form

Sports Organization
Event Name

RFP Evaluation Form

Selection Criteria	CITY A	CITY B	CITY C	CITY D
Contact Name and Title	_____	_____	_____	_____
Contact Phone	_____	_____	_____	_____
Contact E-mail	_____	_____	_____	_____
Agree to All Bid Specifications? (Yes/No)	_____	_____	_____	_____
Exceptions:	_____	_____	_____	_____
	_____	_____	_____	_____
Other Events Scheduled within Time Period	_____	_____	_____	_____
Event Site Information				
Name of Event Site	_____	_____	_____	_____
Location of Event Site	_____	_____	_____	_____
Size or Seating Capacity	_____	_____	_____	_____
Contact Name and Phone	_____	_____	_____	_____
Meets Ideal Event Site Requirements? (Yes/No)	_____	_____	_____	_____
Exceptions:	_____	_____	_____	_____
	_____	_____	_____	_____

Selection Criteria	CITY A	CITY B	CITY C	CITY D
Effective Taxes on Ticket Sales	____	____	____	____
Other Fees on Ticket Sales	____	____	____	____
Labor and Union Exclusivities	____	____	____	____
Hourly Rates (including benefits and management fees)	____	____	____	____
Ushers	____	____	____	____
Security	____	____	____	____
Electricians	____	____	____	____
Carpenters	____	____	____	____
Riggers	____	____	____	____
Catering Exclusivity?	____	____	____	____
Merchandise Exclusivity?	____	____	____	____
Concessions Exclusivity?	____	____	____	____
Hotels				
Hotel Name (# Rooms)	____	____	____	____
Overflow Hotel (# Rooms)	____	____	____	____
Room Rates	____	____	____	____
Tax Rate on Sleeping Rooms	____	____	____	____
Will Hotels Meet Min. Requirements? (Yes/No)	____	____	____	____
Exceptions	____	____	____	____
	____	____	____	____
Host City				
Will Host City Provide Support Required? (Yes/No)	____	____	____	____
Exceptions:	____	____	____	____
	____	____	____	____
Size of Market (population)	____	____	____	____
Average Household Income	____	____	____	____
Effective State and Local Sales Taxes	____	____	____	____
	____	____	____	____
Letters of Support Included	____	____	____	____
	____	____	____	____
Additional Pertinent Information	____	____	____	____
	____	____	____	____
	____	____	____	____
Evaluator Comments	____	____	____	____

APPENDIX 4

Facility Selection Survey Form

Proposed Event: _____

Date(s)/Time(s): _____

Load-in Date(s): _____

Load-out Date(s): _____

Facility: _____

Facility Address: _____

_____

Key Contact: _____

Title: _____

Phone: _____

Fax: _____

E-mail: _____

Date Availability for Load-in: _____

Event Date(s): _____

Date Availability for Load-out: _____

Available Seating by Scale/Level:

   Total Manifest: _____

Manifest by Break: Section: _____ Tix: _____

    _____ Tix: _____

    _____ Tix: _____

    _____ Tix: _____

    _____ Tix: _____

Build-Out Options?   _____

Rental Costs/Terms: _____

Tax Rate on Tickets: _____

Capital Replacement Fees on Tickets: _____ paid by _____

Other Service Fees on Tickets: _____ paid by _____

Credit Card Processing Rate: _____

Other Box Office Fees: _____

Merchandise Contact: _____

Exclusive? _____ Terms: _____

Caterer Contact: _____

Exclusive? _____

Event Promotion Services: _____

Hourly Labor Rates:

    Electricians: _____ Union: _____

    Carpenters: _____ Union: _____

    Riggers: _____ Union: _____

    Stagehands: _____ Union: _____

    Decorators: _____ Union: _____

    Security: _____ Union: _____

    FOH: _____ Union: _____

    Medical: _____

    Scoreboard/Video Crew: _____

Estimated Conversion/Cleaning Costs: _____

Facility Notes:

Locker Rooms: _____

Dressing Rooms: _____

Marshaling and Storage Areas: _____

Scoreboard/Matrix/Jumbotron: _____

Media Facilities: _____

Parking Facilities: _____

Available Equipment (quantity/cost):

Tables: _____   Tablecloths: _____

Chairs: _____   Risers: _____

Phones: _____

Data Lines: _____

Forklifts: _____   Barriers: _____

Pipe and Drape (lgt/ht/color): _____

Crowd Barriers (lgt/type): _____

Other: _____

_____

_____

_____

_____

_____

Sponsor Exclusivities and Restrictions:

_____

_____

_____

_____

_____

_____

_____

Hospitality Options:

_____

_____

_____

Other Notes:

_____

_____

_____

APPENDIX 5

Sample Facility Event License Agreement

This Facility Event License Agreement is provided for illustrative purposes only, and is a representative composite inspired by a variety of actual contracts. This document is not intended for use in its current form as a legal instrument between a potential facility licensee and the licensor. A number of additional legal details may appear in actual Facility Event License Agreements. Event organizers and facilities should retain the services of competent and experienced legal counsel for the process of creating, negotiating, and agreeing to any contract, including a Facility Event License Agreement.

XYZ Entertainment Center
Event License Agreement

This agreement (the "Agreement"), made and entered into on this _____ *st* day of _____, 200_, by and between *XYZ Sports & Entertainment, Inc. ("XYZ")*, a Florida corporation, and hereinafter referred to as **Licensor,** and for the use of *XYZ Center (the "Center"):*

JKL Sports Events, Ltd.
123 S.W. Fifth Avenue
Cityview, FL 30000
954-000-0000 (Tel); 954-000-0001 (Fax)
Harold Matthews, President

Hereinafter referred to as **Licensee.**

The Licensor and Licensee hereby agree as follows:

1. EVENT (THE "EVENT")

Event Name/Description: _____

Move-In/Rehearsal Day(s): _____

Event/Performance Days and Times: _____

Move-Out Day(s): _____

Ticket Prices: _____

Estimated Gross Potential: _____

Move-In, Rehearsal, Event, and Move-Out Days shall collectively be referred to as the "License Period." Use of *XYZ Center* in excess of the time described herein may result in additional charges to the Licensee.

2. LICENSE FEES

(a) The Licensee agrees to pay to the Licensor the following License Fees (the "License Fees"):
  1. Basic License Fee: *$30,000*
  2. All other fees referenced in this Agreement, including, but not limited to the Television Origination Fee and Souvenir Merchandise Fee;
  3. All such additional fees, charges, and other amounts payable by the Licensee, including, but not limited to, event staff service charges, food and beverage service charges, cleaning, maintenance, and conversion charges.
(b) The Licensee agrees to pay all taxes levied on the License Fees or as a result of the Licensee's use of the *Center* including, but not limited to, admission taxes, amusement taxes, and sales taxes on the ticket price.
  The Licensee agrees to pay *$15,000* as a nonrefundable license deposit. The deposit is due and payable upon the return of this executed Agreement.
(c) The Licensee will be responsible for paying in full the amount of the Licensor's actual costs on settlement in accordance with the provisions herein. The Licensor will, upon request, provide the Licensee with estimates of projected Event costs. Such estimates are reasonable attempts at identifying costs made in good faith by the Licensor based on information provided by the Licensee and are not binding on the Licensor.
(d) The License Fee has been determined based on the Ticket Prices and Estimated Gross Potential as defined above. In the event that the Actual Gross exceeds the Estimated Gross Potential, the License Fee shall increase by *0.5%* for each *1.0%* positive difference between the Estimated Gross Potential and the Actual Gross. Regardless of the Actual Gross, the License Fee will not be decreased.

3. LICENSE AREA

(a) The Licensor hereby agrees to grant to the Licensee the nonexclusive right to occupy and use the following areas (the "Licensed Areas") of the *Center* during the

License Period: *the Center bowl, concourse, locker rooms, and all other non-office spaces in the Center.*

(b) No other areas shall be occupied by the Licensee unless authorized in advance in writing by the Licensor. The Licensor reserves the right to license or use all areas of the *Center* not expressly assigned to the Licensee during the License Period for any purpose whatsoever.

(c) The Licensor shall have the right to the free access of any and all areas of the *Center* including, but not limited to, the Licensed Areas at all times during the License Period.

4. SERVICES TO BE PROVIDED BY THE LICENSOR

(a) The Licensor shall provide lighting, heating, air-conditioning and water, as installed at the time of this agreement, and at such times and in such amounts as shall be necessary in the Licensor's sole opinion, for the comfortable use and occupancy of the *Center.*

(b) The Licensor will provide equipment, staffing, or services for this Event including, but are not limited to, ushers, ticket takers, security, police, ticket sellers, conversion crew, cleaning staff, carpenter(s), laborers, electrician(s), riggers, and emergency medical personnel. The Licensor retains the right to determine the appropriate number of personnel necessary to properly staff the *Center* and protect the public.

(c) All utilities, including, but not limited to, electricity, water, gas, telecommunications, cable television, data and Internet service and other equipment and services needed by the Licensee, must be ordered through the Licensor.

5. EVENT TICKETS

(a) The Licensee acknowledges that the Licensor has an exclusive agreement with *Ticket Service, Inc. ("TS"),* a computerized ticket service company, whereby the Licensor/*TS* will jointly act as exclusive agents and be responsible for maintaining control over the inventory, distribution, and sale of all tickets for the Event through the Licensor's Box Office and *TS* outlets.

(b) Regardless of whether tickets will be sold on a reserved-seat or general admission basis, the number of tickets printed shall not exceed the maximum capacity of the *Center,* which the Licensor shall determine in its sole discretion.

(c) The Licensee acknowledges that tickets purchased by telephone, by mail order, at *TS* outlets, and through the Licensor's Will Call Office are subject to service charges payable to *TS* and/or the Licensor in addition to the basic ticket price.

(d) The Licensee shall pay to the Licensor all applicable credit card service charges, based on gross credit card revenues, including applicable taxes, of *two and a half percent (2.5%).*

(e) Following the Event, the Licensor shall provide to the Licensee a full report of ticket sales by the Licensor/*TS* for the Event, and prepare the Preliminary Settlement Summary. The Licensor shall then pay to the Licensee the proceeds of all tickets sold by the Licensor/*TS,* less (i) The total of all applicable taxes, service charges, and Facility Usage Fees (currently *$0.50* per ticket) and (ii) The total identified by the Licensor as owing pursuant to this Agreement.

(f) The Licensor shall provide to the Licensee a Final Settlement Summary 30 days after the final date of the Event indicating any adjustments due to either party to this Agreement.

6. COMPLIMENTARY TICKETS AND PASSES

The Licensee shall provide to the Licensor *sixty (60)* complimentary tickets for the event, in locations to be selected by mutual agreement, the value of which shall not be included as part of the proceeds from ticket sales.

7. REFUNDS

(a) As a result of cancellation or postponement of the Event, *TS* and the Licensor shall refund the ticket price of any unused tickets, and may in accordance with *TS* and/or the Licensor's policy refund applicable service charges and/or handling fees at the point of purchase.

(b) In the event that part of the Event is canceled or postponed, Licensor may in its sole discretion determine what, if any, portion of the ticket price shall be refunded.

(c) Any amounts forwarded to the Licensee by the Licensor with respect to ticket sales shall be returned immediately to the Licensor after the Event has been canceled or postponed.

(d) The Licensor shall retain the right to make ticket refunds for cause or maintaining the public faith. This right shall include, but is not limited to, seats blocked by equipment of the Licensee, its broadcasting partners, or sponsors, when exchange for comparable locations is not possible.

8. MERCHANDISE AND PROGRAM SALES

(a) The Licensee or the Licensee's designated agent(s) shall have the exclusive right only during the Event to provide souvenir merchandise and programs to the Licensor for sale by the Licensor on behalf of the Licensee.

(b) At the conclusion of the Event, the Licensor shall return all the unsold souvenir merchandise and programs provided by the Licensee or the Licensee's designated agent(s). The Licensor shall retain a commission of *20%* of Net Revenues on merchandise and program sales, less all applicable taxes and credit card commissions.

(c) Notwithstanding Section 8a above, the Licensor retains the exclusive right to operate and maintain its concessions, store, and concourse merchandise kiosks during the Event to sell souvenir merchandise and programs not related to the Event, and without any payment due to the Licensee.

9. ADVERTISING AND SPONSORSHIP

(a) The Licensor retains the exclusive right to conduct, sell, and retain all revenues from all advertising and promotion whatsoever in and about the *Center* including, without limitation, on the public address system, video screens, main scoreboard, auxiliary scoreboards, matrix message signage, display signage, posters, banners, and promotional displays during the Event and without approval by or payment to the Licensee. The Licensee shall not obstruct or cover any such advertising or promotion.

(b) The Licensee shall not display or grant to Event sponsor(s) or others any right to display advertising at the *Center* without the prior written consent of the Licensor, and which consent may be withheld for any reason.

(c) The Licensor consents to and grants the Licensee a limited license to use the logo and name *XYZ Center,* as applicable, in Licensor's approved typeface as the site designation for the Event in advertising and other material promoting the Event. All such usage shall be subject to the Licensor's prior written approval and shall be accompanied by applicable trademark notifications as designated by the Licensor.

(d) The Licensee shall not permit the distribution of any free samples or promotional merchandise, programs, food, beverages, or printed material of any kind at the *Center* during the Term without the prior written consent of the Licensor, which consent may be withheld at the Licensor's sole discretion.

10. VIDEO AND/OR AUDIO REPRODUCTION

Licensee and Licensor hereby agree that there shall be no electronic media exploitation of the Event whatsoever without the prior written permission of the Licensor. The term "electronic media exploitation" shall be defined as the exploitation of the Event, whether on a live, delayed, or other basis, through any means of signal distribution including, but not limited to, broadcast television, basic or premium tier cable television, direct-by-satellite television, pay-per-view television, radio, basic or premier tier Internet service, or home video.

Notwithstanding the foregoing, the Licensee grants to the Licensor the right to record and utilize video or audio/visual excerpts from the Event for historical or archival purposes, or for the purpose of marketing the *Center* to other potential licensees.

11. LABOR AGREEMENTS

Licensee shall not perform any work or employ any personnel in connection with the Event except if such work or employment conforms to labor agreements to which the Licensor or its contractors are a party.

12. FOOD AND BEVERAGE CATERING SERVICE

The Licensor reserves the exclusive right to provide all food, beverage, and catering service outlets within the *Center,* including alcoholic and other beverages, and to retain all revenue derived therefrom.

13. INSURANCE, INDEMNIFICATION AND DAMAGES

(a) The Licensee agrees to assume, defend, indemnify, protect, and hold harmless the Licensor and its affiliates, shareholders, officers, and employees against any and all claims or causes of action arising or resulting: (i) from the use, occupancy, or licensing of the *Center* by the Licensee, its contractors, subcontractors, exhibitors, or other invitees or persons attending the Event; or (ii) out of any personal injury or property damage occurring in or upon the *Center* due to any contravention of the provisions of the License, the said rules and regulations, or any applicable laws, rules, regulations, or due to any negligence or willful act by the Licensee.

(b) The Licensee shall obtain and maintain, at its own cost and expense, for the duration of the License Period, a Comprehensive Public Liability and Property Damage Insurance policy along with the required Workers' Compensation, Automobile Liability, and Umbrella Liability coverages. A certificate of insurance shall be provided to the Licensor a minimum of thirty (30) days prior to the starting date of the Event. The Licensee shall name the Licensor and its respective shareholders and officers as additional named insureds on the insurance policy. Such insurance shall be provided by a comprehensive general liability insurance policy including personal injury, contractual liability, cross liability, and occurrence property damage with a combined single limit of at least $5,000,000 for each occurrence.

(c) The Licensee shall not make any alterations of any kind to the *Center* without the prior written consent of the Licensor, which consent may be withheld in the Licensor's sole discretion. The Licensee agrees that if the *Center* is damaged by the act, default, or negligence of the Licensee, or any person admitted to the *Center* by the Licensee or Licensee's agents, then the Licensee shall pay to the Licensor upon demand such reasonable sums as shall be necessary to restore the *Center* to its original condition.

14. FORCE MAJEURE

None of the parties shall be in breach of this Agreement if the performance by that party of any of its obligations hereunder is prevented or preempted because of an Act of God, accident, fire, labor dispute, riot or civil commotion, act of public enemy, governmental act, or any other reason beyond the control of that party. In any such event, this License shall terminate and the Licensee and the Licensor shall each only be responsible for their own expenses.

15. OBSERVANCE OF LAW AND PUBLIC SAFETY

(a) The Licensee, its employees, agents, and all other persons connected with its use of the *Center* shall comply with all laws, statutes, regulations, and all requirements of governmental and regulatory bodies.

(b) The Licensee will obtain all necessary permits, licenses, and approvals relating to the use of and the conduct of the Event in the Licensed Areas and provide the Licensor with satisfactory evidence of the licenses and approvals.

(c) The Licensee will obtain at its expense the right to use any patented, trademarked, or copyrighted materials, dramatic rights, or performance rights used in the conduct of the Event.

(d) The Licensee agrees that it shall not use any pyrotechnic devices without the prior written consent of the Licensor, which consent may be withheld at the Licensor's sole discretion. If such consent is granted, the Licensee shall comply with all laws, rules, regulations, criteria, and policies of all federal, state, and municipal authorities or agencies applicable thereto. The Licensee shall deliver all supporting documentation confirming the Licensee's compliance with the above requirements at least fifteen (15) days prior to the first performance of the Event.

16. TERMINATION

(a) If the Licensee is adjudicated bankrupt, or adjudged to be insolvent, or a receiver or trustee of the Licensee's property and affairs is appointed, or the Licensee is in default of any of its obligations under this Agreement or pursuant hereto, then this license may at the option of the Licensor be canceled by delivering to the Licensee notice to that effect.

(b) Upon any termination, the Licensee shall immediately pay to the Licensor the License Fees as liquidated damages, together with all costs, losses, expenses and damages, as determined by the Licensor. Deposits and payments received are non-refundable in all instances including, but not limited to, a termination.

The Licensor:
XYZ Sports and Entertainment, Inc.

By: _____

The Licensee:
JKL Sports Events, Ltd.

By: _____

Sample Sports Event Sponsorship Deck

D.E.F. SPORTS & ENTERTAINMENT

An Introduction to
SportsFest:
A Mid-States Regional Multisport Festival
presented to
Mid-States Car Dealers Association

August 2004

An Introduction to
SportsFest 2005

Contents

I. SportsFest—An Overview

Midsummer weekends in the Mid-States Region have changed since the introduction of SportsFest in 1998.

Since then, SportsFest has annually provided the region's children and their families with an exciting, highly anticipated weekend of wholesome fun and friendly competition, enveloped in a festival atmosphere featuring great entertainment, fantastic local food, and a midway filled with interactive exhibits, intriguing displays, thrilling rides, and involving activities.

More than just a sports festival, SportsFest is a celebration of our region's diverse cultural heritage, our active lifestyle, and our vibrant business community.

More than 50,000 active, entertainment-seeking families are expected to ***Get into It*** by participating in SportsFest 2005, returning to enjoy their favorite sports events, plus a host of new programs, activities, and entertainment.

SportsFest is a favorite location for local television and radio news, a magnet for dozens of live remotes throughout the weekend. The event also generates significant newspaper coverage throughout the Mid-States Region.

SportsFest provides participating businesses with outstanding opportunities to reach a large number of the region's active consumers, introduce new products, host important customers, and demonstrate their support of community recreation programs. The Mid-States Regional Car Dealers Association (**MSCDA**) can drive qualified buyers into its members' showrooms, conduct test drives right on the event site, and explore additional options for a wide variety of promotional opportunities at the Mid-States Region's most anticipated sports and active lifestyle festival.

The net operating proceeds of SportsFest 2005 will be donated to the Mid-States Region Sports Council for the redevelopment of recreational facilities, the acquisition of new sports equipment, and the funding of physical fitness programs for the area's disadvantaged youth.

StreetFest 2005 . . .

. . . **Get into It!**

SportsFest 2005 was founded by D.E.F. Sports & Entertainment, a Mid-States Region corporation that specializes in the organization and management of sports tournaments and events for youth. D.E.F. Sports & Entertainment is also the producer of the Mid-States Region Invitational and the Grain City Wheat Festival.

II. Introduction

The appeal of SportsFest has grown steadily since its inaugural edition in 1998. Now in its eighth year, SportsFest will expand to more than 10 acres of the Old Fairgrounds, featuring full tournament competition in eight team and individual sports.

Our goal is to attract more than 52,000 participants in 2005, more than triple the number of attendees of the inaugural year. Attendance for the recently completed SportsFest 2004 is projected to reach 48,000.

Most recent market research indicates:

94% of attendees intended to return to SportsFest the next year.

87% rated their experience at SportsFest good to excellent.

74% reported visiting the Hometown Market Midway.

62% stated they expected to patronize sponsors of SportsFest.

95% attended with other family members or friends.

73% said they would return with more or the same number of family members or friends next year.

78% of families have school-age children involved in one or more organized sports activities.

45% of families have school-age children involved in two or more organized sports activities.

Of attendees surveyed . . .

71% are 18+ years of age.

58% are between 18 and 45 years of age.

68% have a household income of more than $50,000 per year.

84% have completed high school.

63% have completed college.

Source: Intercept surveys conducted during SportsFest 2003. Additional statistics and background are available upon request.

III. SportsFest 2005—Why Everyone Is "Getting into It"

SportsFest 2005 will combine proven favorites with attractions and programming that is totally new for 2005. There will be more to see, more to do, and more to enjoy than ever before. **Admission is free.** Tournament participation requires a registration fee to cover uniform T-shirts and other competition expenses.

This year's schedule includes eight sports tournaments for all age groups:

1. The Plainside Journal Baseball Classic
2. The Pyne Brothers Department Store Softball Tournament
3. The L&M Garden Center Field Hockey Championships[*]
4. Basketball[*]
5. Flag Football
6. P.B.F. Shoes Track & Field Meet
7. Shuffleboard[*]
8. *Archery (new for 2005)*[*]

[*]Includes paralympic competition.

Plus . . .

- All-Age Clinics for all eight featured sports
- An expanded 350-seat multivendor Food Pavilion, presented by FF Super-markets
- The Hometown Market Midway
- The KMMM-FM Radio Main Stage
- The Angel's Cola Entertainment Band Shell
- Three additional Entertainment Stages
- The Bob's Burgers Kid Zone
- The Mid-States Region Sports Hall of Fame Traveling Exhibit
- The SportsFest Country Store
- . . . and more!

Event Schedule

The 2005 edition of **SportsFest** will be held on the weekend of July 22–24. For our SportsFest partners and their guests, the fun will start right away.

Friday, July 22: 5:00 P.M.–10:00 P.M.

3:00 P.M.—Corporate Challenge (not open to the general public) Sports-Fest Sponsor companies may participate in our Corporate Challenge Ironman Tournament before the Grand Opening at no charge. Each company may register a team of up to 20 participants to vie for Mid-States Region dominance, competing in skills competitions in each of our eight featured sports areas. The event site is open exclusively to all sponsor company employees and their guests.

5:00 P.M.—Grand Opening The public is officially welcomed to the event site when our 2005 SportsFest Grand Marshal arrives in a procession of **MSCDA**-provided convertibles to cut the "starting line" ribbon. Guests enjoy entertainment throughout SportsFest as they explore our 10 acres of sports and activity areas.

6:00 P.M.—Mid-States Regional Media Challenge Newspapers, television stations, and radio stations compete for bragging rights in skills competitions within each of our eight featured sports areas, broadcasting live remotes and covering their stories from inside the dugouts and on the sidelines.

7:00 P.M.—Grand Opening BBQ Celebration, presented by Angel's Cola
The Mid-States Region's gastronomical event of the summer! Spread out the picnic blanket as you settle down to enjoy pit barbecue, ribs, chicken, roasted corn and local vegetables, fresh hearth-baked bread, ice cream, and apple pie with thousands of your potential customers, neighbors, friends, and family. While you eat, watch featured musical entertainment on the nearby KMMM-FM Radio Main Stage. Frisbees and beach balls optional!

Saturday, July 23: 8:00 A.M.–10:00 P.M.

8:00 A.M.—Let the Fun Begin! Mid-States Regional athletes of all ages begin competing in eight sports—baseball, softball, field hockey, basketball, flag football, track and field, shuffleboard, and archery.

Because competitors and their ardent supporters are always hungry, our Food Pavilion, presented by FF Supermarkets, opens with limited breakfast and coffee service at 7:00 A.M.

9:00 A.M.—All Entertainment and Activity Areas Open There is truly something for everyone at SportsFest 2005! Before and after checking out all the sports event action, guests will be free to explore the many products and services offered by our world-class sponsors at the **Hometown Market Midway.** The increasingly popular Midway is an outstanding opportunity for **MSCDA** and each of our participating companies to meet thousands of SportsFest participants and attendees firsthand, to demonstrate innovative new products, and to develop new customers.

Entertainment will abound at SportsFest 2005 with featured performers at the **KMMM-FM Radio Main Stage** and the **Angel's Cola Band Shell**, as well as **three additional entertainment stages** located throughout the event. Whether your interest is old-time rock and roll, country western, jazz, pop, blues, or blue grass, SportsFest 2005 has something for everyone and has become almost as much a showcase of local musical artists as it is of athletics. Don't be surprised to see your local high school band suddenly march across the Old Fairgrounds to the thundering cadence of drums and horns.

Kids from 5 to 12 are welcome to discover **Bob's Burgers Kid Zone**, a supervised activity center filled with safe play opportunities evocative of each of SportsFest 2005's eight featured sports. Parents can relax with a cup of Bob's famous coffee while their children enjoy either structured games or free play, inflatable bounces, and arts and crafts stations. Each young visitor receives a participant's gold medal courtesy of Bob's Burgers.

Every area athlete will want to visit the **Mid-States Region Sports Hall of Fame Traveling Exhibit**, an inspirational exploration of the rich sports heritage of our communities. Four generations of trophies, memorabilia, and photographs of great moments in Mid-States sports are sources of great local pride—as are the achievements and memorabilia on display of Mid-States alumni in college and professional athletics throughout the world.

A wide variety of delicious food will be available at our multivendor **Food Pavilion, presented by FF Supermarkets**. From burgers and wings to grilled sandwiches and healthful salads, the Pavilion will offer delights to suit the most discriminating palates. Although most SportsFest guests enjoy eating under the sun—or on the run—the dining area under the Pavilion tent has been expanded to accommodate those wishing to consume their meals in the shade and at a more leisurely pace.

Guests can shop for official SportsFest merchandise, local crafts, and take-home confections at the **SportsFest Country Store.** Concessionaires will also be on hand to offer sundries, including film, batteries, sunscreen, sunglasses, and other items to make the day at SportsFest that much more memorable and enjoyable.

11:00 A.M.—All-Age Clinics Begin   You're never too old and never too young to learn the rules of the game and get pointers from our region's accomplished athletes in all eight featured sports at the Sports Clinic attraction. Forty-minute sports clinics for a range of age groups are offered every hour on the hour until the start of the evening's events at 6:00 P.M.

1:00 P.M.—Picnic on the Green, Presented by Angel's Cola   Bring your blanket for a trip back to a simpler time. Enjoy a 5-cent glass of Angel's Cola as the Mid-States All-Star Brass Band plays a tribute to the music of the early twentieth century at the Angel's Cola Band Shell. Prizes will be awarded for the best circa 1905 costumes.

6:00 P.M.—Mid-States Region Pasta Cook-off, Benefiting Starlight Foundation   After a full weekend of watching or playing in athletic competition, replenish yourself at SportsFest's now famous pasta feast. Bring the whole family for heaping bowls of salad, spaghetti, meatballs and sauce, garlic bread, and other treats. Tickets are $10 for adults and $5 for kids, with proceeds benefiting the Mid-States Region chapter of the Starlight Foundation. Save room for dessert!

7:00 P.M.—Mid-States Region Fruit Pie Bake-off, Benefiting Youth Sports   Who bakes the best fruit pies in the Mid-States Region? You be the judge, and then destroy the evidence! Proceeds benefit our community's youth recreation programs.

8:00 P.M.—Headline Concert at KMMM-FM Radio Main Stage   A top-name musical artist (to be announced in late winter 2005) will round out a full day of fun. Past performers have included Cheryl Byrd, Second Ear, Cryptic Message, and Two for Holding.

Sunday, July 24: 9:00 A.M.–9:00 P.M.

9:00 A.M.—Let the Fun Continue!   Competition in all eight sports—baseball, softball, field hockey, basketball, flag football, track and field, shuffleboard, and archery—continues.

9:00 A.M.—All Entertainment and Activity Areas Open

11:00 A.M.—All-Age Clinics Begin   Forty-minute sports clinics for various age groups are offered every hour on the hour until 5:00 P.M., with "elite" clinics available for more seasoned athletes at 1:00 P.M. and 3:00 P.M.

7:00 P.M.—SportsFest 2005 Parade of Athletes and Medal Ceremonies   Cheer on all of your SportsFest 2005 neighbors, family, and friends. All registered tournament participants are welcome to march to the KMMM-FM Main Stage for a salute to the athletes and the presentation of medals. Everyone who participated in the eight featured competitive tournaments will be recognized.

8:00 P.M.—SportsFest 2005 Ice Cream Social, Benefiting the Mid-States Shelter   After the pomp and pageantry of the medal ceremonies, relax at the SportsFest Ice Cream Social, a place to greet your friends and meet new ones. The $3.00

sundae buffet, with do-it-yourself toppings, benefits the Mid-States Shelter. Take your sundae to your favorite location at SportsFest for the excitement at 9:00 P.M.

    9:00 P.M.—SportsFest 2005 Grand Finale Fireworks Spectacular   Tens of thousands of Mid-States Region citizens and guests will enjoy a spectacular fireworks extravaganza visible for miles around, set to a sports theme soundtrack broadcast on KMMM-FM Radio. When the show is over and the smoke clears, you will wonder just how you will be able to wait another full year to see what SportsFest 2006 will have to offer.

    Additional special events and entertainment will be scheduled throughout the weekend at times to be determined.

IV. How the MSCDA Can "Get into It!"

The **MSCDA** can "Get into It" in a big way as a title or presenting sponsor of Sports-Fest 2005, as a tournament sponsor, as an activity area sponsor, or as a nonexclusive event participant.

    SportsFest 2005 can provide members of the **MSCDA** with outstanding opportunities to feature their new models, offer test drives, raise awareness, promote special sales and financing incentives, and entertain important fleet customers.

    In addition, the **MSCDA** can reinforce its position as a major corporate citizen in our community, joining a proud family of sponsors that includes Angel's Cola, Bob's Burgers, FF Supermarkets, KMMM-FM Radio, L&M Garden Center, P.B.F. Shoes, Pyne Brothers Department Store, the *Plainside Journal,* Community Bank, Tomvel Ice Cream, Dell's Sports, and a host of official suppliers.

    The pages that follow describe just some of the ways the **MSCDA** can **Get into It!**

GOLD MEDAL—TITLE SPONSORSHIP

- SportsFest 2005 will be renamed **MSCDA SportsFest 2005.**
- The **MSCDA** will be integrated into the highly recognizable SportsFest logo and featured in all event site signage, banners, promotional point-of-purchase displays, newspaper advertising, television commercials, and event merchandise. All event press releases will include acknowledgment of **MSCDA** as the title sponsor of SportsFest 2005.
- All third-party sponsor promotions authorized by the event organizer will be required to include **MSCDA** identification in the event name.
- The **MSCDA** will be given the exclusive right to promote itself as the **"Official Car Dealership Association of SportsFest 2005."** All member dealers will be given the exclusive right to promote themselves as **"Members of the Official Car Dealership Association of SportsFest 2005."**

- The **MSCDA** and its member dealers will be granted exclusivity as sponsors of SportsFest 2005 in the automotive sales, service, and parts categories.
- The **MSCDA** will be granted the opportunity to conduct test drives, subject to safety restrictions, in a mutually agreeable area adjacent to the event site. The **MSCDA** will have the right to provide shuttle transportation from the main entrance of StreetFest to the test drive site.
- An **MSCDA** representative will be given the opportunity to participate as a featured speaker in the grand opening ceremonies, as well as during the closing addresses prior to the Fireworks Spectacular.
- An **MSCDA** representative will participate on-stage during the Medal Ceremonies on Sunday night.
- The **MSCDA** will be granted a 40′ × 40′ exhibit area in the Hometown Market Midway. Up to twelve (12) automobiles may be parked around the Midway as static displays, with signage promoting the test drives and dealer promotions.
- The **MSCDA** may, in addition, select one available tournament area for which it will be recognized as the presenting sponsor. Currently available tournaments include basketball, flag football, shuffleboard, and archery.
- The **MSCDA** may also select one available entertainment activity for which it will be recognized as the presenting sponsor. Currently available entertainment activities include the Fireworks Spectacular, Ice Cream Social, Pasta Cook-off, Fruit Pie Bake-off, and the Medal Ceremonies.
- The **MSCDA** will be granted the right to conduct an exclusive SportsFest 2005 sweepstakes promotion in the *Plainside Journal.*
- The **MSCDA** will receive two hundred (200) complimentary tickets to each of the Pasta Cook-off, the Fruit Pie Bake-off, and the Ice Cream Social.
- The **MSCDA** will receive one (1) complimentary team registration for the **MSCDA** SportsFest Corporate Challenge.
- The **MSCDA** will receive ten (10) complimentary athlete registrations for each of the tournament's eight featured sports.
- The **MSCDA** will have the exclusive use of a 40′ × 40′ VIP tent for private receptions and entertaining. (Furnishings, food, beverage, entertainment, signage, and decoration are at **MSCDA**'s cost.)
- The **MSCDA** will receive two hundred (200) complimentary daily passes to the SportsFest 2005 VIP Hospitality Tent.
- The **MSCDA** will receive twenty (20) backstage passes for the Headline Concert, including a meet-and-greet opportunity with the artist (subject to the artist's contract restrictions). Fifty percent (50%) of these backstage passes must be given away as part of a consumer promotion by the **MSCDA** and its member dealers.
- The **MSCDA** will receive fifty (50) VIP seating passes for the Headline Concert. Guests will be seated on a first-come, first-served basis.
- The **MSCDA** will receive one hundred (100) VIP SportsFest merchandise packs, each including a T-shirt, cap, pin, and commemorative poster. Fifty percent (50%) of these merchandise packs must be given away as part of a consumer promotion by the **MSCDA** and its member dealers.

MSCDA SPORTSFEST 2005
Gold Medal Title Sponsorship: $150,000

Silver Medal—Presenting Sponsorship:

- SportsFest 2005 will be renamed **SportsFest 2005, presented by MSCDA.**
- The **MSCDA** name will be associated with the SportsFest 2005 logo (e.g., Sports-Fest 2005, presented by **MSCDA**) and featured in all event site signage, banners, newspaper advertising, television commercials, and event merchandise. All event press releases will include acknowledgment of **MSCDA** as the presenting sponsor of SportsFest 2005.
- The **MSCDA** will be given the exclusive right to promote itself as the **"Official Car Dealership Association of SportsFest 2005."** All member dealers will be given the exclusive rights to promote themselves as **"Members of the Official Car Dealership Association of SportsFest 2005."**
- The **MSCDA** and its member dealers will be granted exclusivity as sponsors of SportsFest 2005 in the automotive sales, service, and parts categories.
- The **MSCDA** will be granted the opportunity to conduct test drives, subject to safety restrictions, in a mutually agreeable area adjacent to the event site.
- An **MSCDA** representative will be given the opportunity to participate as a featured speaker in the Grand Opening ceremonies, as well as during the closing addresses prior to the Fireworks Spectacular.
- An **MSCDA** representative will participate on-stage at the Medal Ceremonies on Sunday night.
- The **MSCDA** will be granted a 20' × 20' exhibit area in the Hometown Market Midway. Up to six (6) automobiles may be parked around the Midway as static displays, with signage promoting the test drives and dealer promotions.
- The **MSCDA** may, in addition, select one available tournament for which it will be recognized as the presenting sponsor. Currently available tournaments include basketball, flag football, shuffleboard, and archery.
- The **MSCDA** will be granted the right to conduct an exclusive SportsFest 2005 sweepstakes promotion in the *Plainside Journal*.
- The **MSCDA** will receive one hundred (100) complimentary tickets to each of the Pasta Cook-off, the Fruit Pie Bake-off, and the Ice Cream Social.
- The **MSCDA** will receive one (1) complimentary team registration for the Sports-Fest Corporate Challenge.
- The **MSCDA** will receive five (5) complimentary athlete registrations for each of the tournament's eight featured sports.
- The **MSCDA** will have the exclusive use of a 20' × 20' VIP tent for private receptions and entertaining. (Furnishings, food, beverage, entertainment, signage, and decoration are at **MSCDA**'s cost.)
- The **MSCDA** will receive one hundred (100) complimentary daily passes to the SportsFest 2005 VIP Hospitality Tent.
- The **MSCDA** will receive ten (10) backstage passes for the Headline Concert, including a meet-and-greet opportunity with the artist (subject to the artist's contract restrictions). Fifty percent (50%) of these backstage passes must be given away as part of a consumer promotion by the **MSCDA** and its member dealers.

- The **MSCDA** will receive twenty (20) VIP seating area passes for the Headline Concert. Guests will be seated on a first-come, first-served basis.
- The **MSCDA** will receive fifty (50) VIP SportsFest merchandise packs, each including a T-shirt, cap, pin, and commemorative poster. Fifty percent (50%) of these merchandise packs must be given away as part of a consumer promotion by the **MSCDA** and its member dealers.

SPORTSFEST 2005 PRESENTED BY MSCDA
Silver Medal Presenting Sponsorship: $100,000

Bronze Medal—Official Sponsorship

- The **MSCDA** name will be recognized on a rotational basis in banners, newspaper advertising, and television commercials. All event press releases will include recognition of **MSCDA** as an official sponsor of SportsFest 2005.
- The **MSCDA** will be given the exclusive right to promote itself as the **"Official Car Dealership Association of SportsFest 2005."** All member dealers will be given the exclusive rights to promote themselves as **"Members of the Official Car Dealership Association of SportsFest 2005."**
- The **MSCDA** and its member dealers will be granted exclusivity as sponsors of SportsFest 2005 in the automotive sales, service, and parts categories.
- The **MSCDA** will be granted a 10' ×' 10' exhibit area in the Hometown Market Midway.
- The **MSCDA** may select one available tournament for which it will be recognized as the presenting sponsor. Currently available tournaments include basketball, flag football, shuffleboard, and archery.
- The **MSCDA** will be granted the right to conduct an exclusive SportsFest 2005 sweepstakes promotion in print media of its choice at its own expense.
- The **MSCDA** will receive thirty (30) complimentary tickets to each of the Pasta Cook-off, the Fruit Pie Bake-off, and the Ice Cream Social.
- The **MSCDA** will receive one (1) complimentary team registration for the **MSCDA** SportsFest Corporate Challenge.
- The **MSCDA** will receive two (2) complimentary athlete registrations for each of the tournament's eight featured sports.
- The **MSCDA** will receive twenty (20) complimentary daily passes to the SportsFest 2005 VIP Hospitality Tent.
- The **MSCDA** will receive four (4) backstage passes for the Headline Concert, including a meet-and-greet opportunity with the artist (subject to the artist's contract restrictions).
- The **MSCDA** will receive eight (8) VIP seating area passes for the Headline Concert. Guests will be seated on a first-come, first-served basis.
- The **MSCDA** will receive twenty (20) VIP SportsFest merchandise packs, each including a T-shirt, cap, pin, and commemorative poster. Fifty percent (50%) of these merchandise packs must be given away as part of a consumer promotion by the **MSCDA** and its member dealers.

MSCDA:
The official automobile sales, service, and parts sponsor of
SportsFest 2005
$60,000

Achiever Medal—Official Supplier

- The **MSCDA** name will be recognized on a rotational basis in banners, newspaper advertising, and television commercials.
- The **MSCDA** will be given the right to promote itself as the **"Official Supplier to SportsFest 2005."**
- The **MSCDA** will receive ten (10) complimentary tickets to each of the Pasta Cook-off, the Fruit Pie Bake-off, and the Ice Cream Social.
- The **MSCDA** will receive one (1) complimentary team registration for the **MSCDA** SportsFest Corporate Challenge.
- The **MSCDA** will receive four (4) complimentary daily passes to the SportsFest 2005 VIP Hospitality Tent.
- The **MSCDA** will receive four (4) VIP seating area passes for the Headline Concert. Guests will be seated on a first-come, first-served basis.
- The **MSCDA** will receive eight (8) VIP SportsFest merchandise packs, each including a T-shirt, cap, pin, and commemorative poster.

MSCDA:
An official supplier to SportsFest 2005
$25,000

V. Next Steps

SportsFest 2005 and D.E.F. Sports & Entertainment are excited about the possibility of welcoming **MSCDA** to our prestigious family of sponsors.

Please note that only one title sponsorship, one presenting sponsorship, and a limited number of exclusive official sponsorships are available at this time. Additional official sponsors may be confirmed subsequent to the presentation of this proposal.

The sponsorship packages described in this proposal may also be customized to best fit the needs of **MSCDA**. We look forward to working with you to create a dynamic partnership that will help **MSCDA** meet its marketing objectives and exceed its expectations.

Please call:

Jack D'Andrea
Executive Director
SportsFest 2005
1836 Adams Street
Brownsville, MO 00000
Tel: 000-000-0000
Fax: 000-000-0000
Jdandrea@sportsfest.net

Sample Sponsorship Agreement

Note: This sample abbreviated sponsorship agreement is provided for illustrative purposes only. It should not be used as a legal document without the review and advice of competent legal counsel.

Date _____

Corporate Name of Sponsor
Attn: Contact Name
Address
Re: *Name of Event*

Dear _____:

This letter, when executed by the parties, shall set forth the agreement (the "Agreement") between _____ (the "Company") and _____ (the "Event Organizer"), relating to the Company's sponsorship of _____ (the "Event").

1. Definitions

As used herein, the following terms shall have the following meanings:

1.1. The "Event" shall consist of *(insert a full description of the event here, including dates, times, and location)* _____
_____.

1.2. The Company acknowledges and agrees that, subject to the Event Organizer's obligations to the Company as set forth herein, the Event Organizer shall have complete creative and operational control over every aspect of the Event.

1.3. "Marks" shall mean the following: (i) the name and logo of the Event, (ii) the name and logo of Event Organizer, (iii) any marks developed after the date of this Agreement that describe elements of the Event or contain the name of the Event.

1.4. "Term" shall mean the period beginning as of the date of this Agreement and ending on _____.

1.5. "Territory" shall mean *(specifically describe here the geographic boundaries defined by the sponsorship, i.e., the name of the community, state, or broader territory in which the sponsor will have marketing rights to the event)*

_____

_____

2. Marketing Rights

The Event Organizer hereby grants to the Company the following sponsorship rights in connection with the Event in the Territory and during the Term, subject to and in accordance with the terms and conditions set forth in this Agreement:

2.1. The Company shall have the right to use the Marks in connection with Event themed advertising and promotional programs in the Territory during the Term at its sole cost and expense. Each such advertising or promotional program shall be subject to the approval of the Event Organizer in its sole discretion.

2.2. The Company shall have the right to distribute product samples or premiums at its own expense using the Marks in the Territory during the Term. Each such product sample or premium prepared for distribution using the Marks must be approved by the Event Organizer in its sole discretion.

2.3. The Company shall be included in all print, radio, and television advertising promoting the Event, including but not limited to press releases concerning the Event, signage placed in various locations throughout the Event listing corporate sponsors of the Event, and acknowledgment in the Official Program.

2.4. The Company shall be entitled to five (5) public address announcements during the Event, each of no more than twenty (20) seconds duration. The timing and placement in the program of such public address announcements is at the sole discretion of the Event Organizer.

2.5. The Company shall be entitled to two (2) commercial spots of no more than thirty (30) seconds duration to be displayed during the Event on the scoreboard video screen and approved for use by the Event Organizer in its sole discretion. The timing and placement in the program of such commercial spots is at the sole discretion of the Event Organizer.

3. Other Benefits

(Note: Benefits outlined below are for a hypothetical sports event. Include all benefits other than Marketing Rights in this section.)
The Company shall receive, at no additional cost:

3.1. Number (#) tickets to the Event in the Premium Seating section of the Facility;

3.2. Number (#) tickets to the Event in other sections of the Facility on a best available basis;

3.3. Number (#) tickets to each of the pregame hospitality suite and the post-event party.

3.4. Number (#) invitations to the VIP athlete meet-and-greet opportunity on the evening prior to the Event.

4. Compensation

In full consideration for the rights granted and agreements made hereunder, the Company shall pay to the Event Organizer a fee equal to $_____.

5. Representations, Warranties and Covenants

The Company shall indemnify and hold harmless the Event Organizer from and against any claims, demands, causes of action, suits, proceedings, judgments, losses, liabilities, damages, injuries, costs, and expenses arising out of, resulting from, or which, if true, would arise out of or result from, any act or omission of the Company relating to this Agreement; or misrepresentation, breach of warranty, or other breach of any obligation or covenant made by the Company in this Agreement. Without limitation of the indemnification hereunder, the Company shall maintain both general liability and product liability insurance, in customary amounts and on reasonable terms, which policies shall include the Event Organizer as additional insureds.

6. Termination

The Event Organizer may terminate this Agreement by written notice to the Company should the Company fail to make any payment required hereunder when due, or observe or perform any of its other material obligations under this Agreement, in each case if such failure, if curable, is not cured within five (5) business days after receipt by Company of written notice thereof.

7. Miscellaneous

The Company shall not assign this Agreement to any person, corporation, or other entity without the prior written consent of the Event Organizer. The Event Organizer shall not assign this Agreement to any person, corporation, or other entity, other than to a parent, subsidiary, or other affiliate, without the prior written consent of the Company. Please indicate your agreement with the foregoing terms by signing and dating both of the enclosed copies of this Agreement and returning them to me. A fully executed Agreement will be returned to you promptly thereafter.

Sincerely,

Event Organizer

By: _____

ACCEPTED AND AGREED, this _____ day of _____, _____.

The Company

By: _____

Sports Event Participant Release

This sample participant waiver and release is provided for illustrative purposes only. It should not be used as a legal document without the review and advice of competent legal counsel.

Name ("Participant"): _____

Address: _____

_____

Telephone: _____

Release from Liability

By freely agreeing to participate in ____(name of event)____ (the "Event") as a volunteer, athlete, sports activity participant, or attendee, the "Participant," and if the Participant is younger than 18 years old, his/her parent or guardian, hereby voluntarily agrees to release ____(name of organizer)____ (the "Sports Event Organizer"), each owner, operator, and management agent of each event facility, each sponsor, agency, vendor, independent contractor, and person, partnership, or corporation engaged by the Sports Event Organizer, and each of their respective parent entities, subsidiaries, stockholders, affiliates and other related entities, and each officer, director, employee, volunteer, licensor, sponsor, partner, principal representative and agent of the Sports Event Organzier and each of the foregoing, and all of the foregoing's respective successors and assigns (collectively, the "Releasees"), from, and waive in respect of each

Releasee and covenant not to sue any Releasee for any and all liabilities, losses, damages, costs, expenses, causes of action, suits and claims of any nature whatsoever (collectively, the "Liabilities") arising from, based upon, or relating to personal injury or death to, or damage to or loss of property of, the Participant sustained in connection with the Participant's participation in any activity or event associated with the Event, or travel to or from any of the foregoing activities or events. Such release, discharge, waiver, and covenant not to sue shall include, but not be limited to, any and all such Liabilities caused in whole or in part by the negligence of any Releasee in connection with such Releasee's involvement with the Event.

Participant Assumes Risk

The Participant is aware of and understands the inherent risks and dangers of the Event in which he or she will be participating and the potential for injury that exists when participating in the Event, and agrees to assume all risk of and responsibility for personal injury or death to, or damage to or loss of property of, the Participant arising from, or relating to, the Participant's participation in the Event. Such assumption of risk includes, but is not limited to, any personal injury or death, or damage to or loss of property caused in whole or in part by the negligence of any Releasee. The Participant understands and agrees that, in the event of any injury to the Participant, none of the Releasees will be responsible for any decisions relating to medical treatment for the Participant or for such treatment itself.

Right of Publicity

Participation in the Event shall constitute permission to use the name, likeness, or any other identification of the Participant for advertising, publicity, or any other purposes in connection with the Event or the business of any of the Releasees, in any medium and at any time, in perpetuity, and without compensation to or right of prior review or approval by the Participant or his or her parent or legal guardian (except where prohibited by law). The Participant agrees, for itself and its personal representatives, executors, administrators, heirs, next of kin, successors, and assigns, to release and discharge each Releasee from, to waive in respect of each Releasee, and not to sue any Releasee for, any and all Liabilities arising from, based upon, or relating to any claim for invasion of privacy, violation of right of publicity, defamation, or appropriation in connection with any such use.

No Obligation of Releasees

None of the Releasees shall have, or be deemed to have, any obligation to the Participant hereunder or otherwise in connection with the Event unless set forth in writing signed by the Participant and the Releasee.

Miscellaneous

This Release shall be governed by and construed in accordance with the laws of __(state or province in which the organizer is incorporated)__. If any portion of this Release shall be held invalid or unenforceable, the remaining portion hereof shall not be affected thereby and shall remain in full force and effect.

Representations

The Participant and his or her parent or legal guardian states that he or she has had full opportunity to ask any questions regarding the Event that he or she may have, that he or she has read and understands this Release (or that his or her parent or legal guardian has read and understands this Release, and has explained it to the Participant), and that he or she has been given an opportunity to review this Release with anyone he or she chooses, including a lawyer, and has done so to the extent he or she wishes to do so. The Participant further states that he or she is in good physical condition, is physically fit to participate in the Event, and is not subject to any medical condition that poses or may pose any risk of harm or disability to others.

_____ Date: _____
(Signature of Participant)

I am over the age of 18 as of this date: _____ Yes _____ No

Name of Parent or Guardian (please print) if Participant is Under 18:

_____ Date: _____
(Signature of Parent or Guardian)

Emergency Contact Name: _____

Emergency Contact Telephone Number: _____

Sample Sports Event Rundown

MNO Sports, Inc.

FIVE COUNTY FOOTBALL TOURNAFEST
FINAL GAME RUNDOWN
(AS OF NOVEMBER 28)

#	Time	Segment	R/T	Description	Audio	Video/Scoreboard
1	7:00:00	**House Open**	0:30:00	Audience enters. Lights at preset levels. Gobos in corners. Stage managers to get players out of locker rooms at 7:25:00.	PA mike: Welcome and sponsor recognition (Pea Pond Mills, Pete's Pies, Faroff Airlines, Metro Daily News) over music CD #1	Event and sponsor logos in rotation; Welcome; sponsor logos during recognition (Pea Pond Mills, Pete's Pies, Faroff Airlines, Metro Daily News)
2	7:30:00	**Player Warm-Ups**	0:20:00	Players enter and warm up on field. Lights on full.	Music CD #2	Event and sponsor logos in rotation; Welcome
3	7:50:00	**Set Up Opening Ceremonies**	0:10:00	Players leave field. Dim lights to work level. Crew sets up opening ceremonies riser at 50-yard line Band, flag bearers, and kick line in position on sidelines at 7:57:00.	Music CD #3	Event and sponsor logos in rotation; Welcome; sponsor logos during recognition
4	8:00:00	**Five County High Schools All-Star Marching Band**	0:03:30	Lights on full. Massed Five County High Schools All-Star Marching Band, flag bearers, and kick line enter field from sidelines to drum cadence, then perform "Remember the Titans."	Fade CD music. Marching Band (Live)	"Please welcome the Five County High School's All-Star Marching Band!"
5	8:03:30	**Host Welcome**	0:01:00	Public address announcer welcomes J. J. Jayson. Jayson walks from sideline to opening ceremonies riser and welcomes audience. Jayson intros superintendent of schools.	PA mike for Host Introduction; the host mike	"WFMS host J. J. Jayson"

#	Time	Segment	Duration	Description	Audio	Script
6	8:04:30	**Superintendent of Schools**	0:02:00	Superintendent Anderson walks from sideline to opening ceremonies riser and speaks from host mike. Exits to sidelines when finished with remarks.	Host mike	"Superintendent of Schools Andrew Anderson"
7	8:06:30	**Introduction of the Players**	0:06:00	Jayson returns to mike. Band plays on cue as teams run from sidelines (without helmets!) to their respective 20-yard lines. Jayson introduces each player; players wave.	Host mike; Marching Band (live)	"The Five County High Schools All-Stars!"
8	8:12:30	**National Anthem**	0:02:00	Jayson introduces Betty Fumbles to sing National Anthem. Ms. Fumbles walks from sideline halfway to riser holding wired microphone. Players and singer face band's color guard. Fumbles sings.	Host mike; singer mike	"Our National Anthem"
9	8:14:30	**Ready to Go!**	0:02:30	Fumbles exits. Jayson thanks all, departs. Players to proper sidelines. Band, flag bearers, and kick line march off to "On Wisconsin!" Crew removes ceremony riser.	Host mike; Marching Band (live)	"Welcome to the Five County Football Tournafest!"
10	8:17:00	**Kick Off!**		Band continues playing until kickoff.	Marching Band (live) until kickoff	"It's Game Time!"

Glossary of Common Sports Event Management and Marketing Terms

Activation The promotional activities undertaken by a sponsor to promote its partnership with an event.

Amortization The technique of spreading the expense of physical assets over a series of years and events.

ATPB Audiotape playback.

Attrition penalty A financial penalty incurred when the number of guest rooms used by an event falls below an agreed-to percentage of the contracted number.

Blocking The process of identifying entrances, movement, and positions, as well as the exit of all participants, props, and staging in sequential order.

Build-outs Temporary seating areas added to existing inventory in an event facility.

B-roll Raw video footage taped in advance for editing into feature programming or live broadcast.

B-to-B Business to business. Describes companies whose primary customers are other businesses.

Click track Electronic metronome pulses that are broadcast to musicians, band directors, and choir directors over a headset.

Color changer A series of gels that can be manually or automatically changed on the same light.

Comps Complimentary tickets.

Conversion costs The expenses of preparing a facility for an event organizer and returning it back to its original condition.

CPM   Cost per thousand. A measurement used to compare the cost-effectiveness of exposure gained through advertising, promotions, and other sports marketing efforts.

Cue   A signal from the presentation director that a specific prescribed action by members of the production team is to be executed immediately.

CVB   Convention and visitors bureau. A city or regional agency whose mission is to attract events, conventions, and tourists to its area.

Demographics   Objective statistical characteristics of a particular audience.

Development costs   The expenses an organizer incurs in selling a sponsorship.

Diamondvision   Large projection screen manufactured by Mitsubishi. (See also *Jumbotron.*)

Economic impact   A measure of the dollars that will flow into or out of a region specifically because of the presence of a particular event.

File server   Digital storage device that can provide immediate access to a selection of programmed music, video, and graphics.

Follow spots   Manually operated spotlights that can be moved to follow action.

Fresnel   Type of stationary light that can provide various types of illumination, ranging from a focused spotlight to a more diffused floodlight.

Fulfillment costs   The expenses an organizer encounters in providing benefits to a sponsor.

Gel   A thin sheet of gelatin placed over a light source that changes the color of the beam.

General admission   Seating or viewing areas available to ticket holders entering the event venue on a first-come, first-served basis (also known as "festival seating").

Gobos   Glass or metal stencils that project logos and patterns in light.

Grassroots event   An amateur, not-for-profit community sports program.

Grid   The truss system on which lights and sound cabinets are mounted.

Gross potential   The total amount of money that can be generated by ticket sales if an event is sold out.

Guarantor   A sponsor company that agrees to cover an event's cash shortfalls with a grant or the guaranteed purchase of tickets.

Guerilla marketing   Efforts undertaken by a nonsponsor to give the appearance of being associated with an event.

I-Mag   Image magnification. The projection of coverage of an event on large video screens during a live event.

Insurance prize   A consumer promotion for a prize of extremely high value in which the slim probability of having to pay a winner is protected by an insurance policy.

Intelligent lighting   Computer-controlled lighting systems, including Cyberlights, Intellibeams, Varilights, and other brands.

Jumbotron   Large video screen manufactured by Sony. (See also *Diamondvision.*)

Kills   See *Seat kills.*

Lavalier ("lav")   Small microphone clipped to the clothing of the wearer, designed to be almost unnoticeable.

Leko   Type of stationary spotlight that can provide a sharp focus on a specific area.

Lessee   The event organizer renting a facility.

Lessor   The owner or management of the facility that is being rented to an event organizer.

Load-in   The process of receiving required event materials and equipment and setting up an event at the host facility.

Load-out The process of dismantling an event and removing all materials and equipment from the host facility.

Manifest A seat-by-seat listing of every ticket location in an event facility.

Marshaling area An area secured from public access that is used to hold sets, props, equipment, and people before they are needed.

Matrix board An electronic sign that can display scores, information, and logos.

Mike Microphone.

Mult box A box that cameras and recorders can be plugged into to receive a clear signal of sound from the public address system.

PA Public address. Can refer to the sound system used to make announcements, or to the announcement itself.

Pani projector A proprietary brand that projects very large still images.

Papering the house The distribution of complimentary tickets to generate a larger audience.

Par Type of stationary floodlight that provides a wide, diffused beam or "wash."

Pass-through rights The transference by a sponsor of some of its event benefits to its suppliers, distributors, retailers, advertisers, or other business partners.

Per diem A cash allowance paid at a per-day rate for meals and other personal expenses, such as laundry and non-business-related entertainment.

Pickup The percentage of hotel rooms actually used as compared with the total number originally reserved.

Pigi projector A proprietary brand that projects very large still and moving images.

Price breaks Divisions in event seating areas based on ticket prices.

PSA Public service announcement. An advertisement provided at no cost by a radio or television partner.

Psychographics The behavioral characteristics of a particular audience.

Pyrotechnics Fireworks.

Remotes Live periodic radio or television reports from the event site.

Reserved seating Event tickets that entitle the purchasers to exact seats.

Restrike time The amount of time required for lighting to be restored to its full intensity after it has been shut off.

RF Radio frequency. Refers to any wireless transmission of sound and/or video, such as RF microphones, walkie-talkies, RF cameras.

RFP Request for Proposal. A document prepared by event organizers for host cities, facilities, and vendors, that outlines business requirements for successful selection.

Rider An attachment to a performer's contract that lists all of the technical, travel, and hospitality requirements an organizer must provide.

Right-to-work state A state in which the organizer can hire any qualified laborer, whether or not a member of a union.

Riser Stage platform, usually built from prefabricated sections.

ROI Return on Investment. A measure used to evaluate the cost-effectiveness of a sponsorship.

Room block The total number of hotel rooms reserved for the event's needs over all nights required.

Room-night Occupancy of one hotel room for one night.

RP screens Rear projection screens, which display images projected from behind.

R/T Running time.

Seating manifest   A list of every individual seat in an event facility as defined by section, row, and seat number.

Seat kills   Seats removed from public sale because of obstructed views.

Sectional rehearsal   A rehearsal involving only a portion of the ceremonies' cast.

Server   See *File server.*

SOT   "Sound on tape." Tells the audio engineer that the sound on a video should be heard.

"Stand by"   A warning to be ready, that the next cue is imminent.

Step and repeat   A pattern of small logos printed on a banner or panel of drape.

Stickiness   How well a consumer remembers an advertisement or marketing program.

Strip   A package of tickets that includes admission to all events.

Strobe   A light that is capable of flashing brightly once briefly, or repeatedly at a rapid rate of speed.

Swag   (Colloquial) Complimentary apparel and merchandise used as gifts for volunteers, staff, and special guests.

Sync rights   Synchronization rights. The right to use a piece of music on the soundtrack of a video.

Tabling   The sponsor practice of staffing a kiosk or table at an event to demonstrate or sell its products.

Tweeter   A speaker cabinet used for high frequency (treble) tones.

Utility   Someone who accompanies a cameraperson, handling cables so they are neither tangled nor tripped on, or aiming the antenna that transmits images from a wireless camera to its receiver.

VIK   Value in kind. Products or services provided to an event instead of cash in exchange for a sponsor relationship or other promotional consideration.

VTPB   Videotape playback.

Walk-up sales   Admission tickets sold on the day of the event (as opposed to advance sales).

Wash   An evenly distributed level of light over a large area.

Woofer   A speaker cabinet used for low-frequency (bass) tones.

Index